IT'S NOT ALL ABOUT THE
OLD FIRM

IT'S NOT ALL ABOUT THE
OLD FIRM
Defying the Odds in Scottish Football

Scott Burns

Pitch Publishing Ltd
A2 Yeoman Gate
Yeoman Way
Durrington
BN13 3QZ

Email: info@pitchpublishing.co.uk
Web: www.pitchpublishing.co.uk

First published in the UK by Pitch Publishing, 2012
Updated and reprinted by Pitch Publishing, 2017

Text © 2012, 2017 Scott Burns

A CIP catalogue record for this book is available from the British Library.

Original edition ISBN: 9781908051493
Updated edition ISBN: 9781785313172

Cover design by Brilliant Orange Creative Services

Typesetting by Liz Short
Printed in Denmark by Nørhaven, Viborg

DEDICATION

TO DAD
(THOMAS GOURLAY BURNS 1948-2009)
like so many people in this book
an inspiration to everyone around him.

"THE Old Firm. Rangers and Celtic, as historical statistics point out, are Scottish football. Every now and again a short threat to their predominance will occur but these challenges are rarely maintained. As far as my thinking was concerned, to win anything you had to beat the Old Firm."

SIR ALEX FERGUSON

(*an extract from his book *A Light In The North – Seven Years At Aberdeen* by Alex Ferguson. Mainstream Publishing 1985)

INTRODUCTION

AS A sports journalist in Scotland I know only too well that when it comes to football that Celtic and Rangers dominate the majority of our sports pages and headlines. Every time you turn on a radio phone-in, a television programme or even click on a Scottish football website you know you are guaranteed 100 per cent saturated coverage of the Glasgow giants.

It is a constant sense of irritation to most fans who don't follow or have allegiances to Celtic or Rangers. There is a general feeling among other supporters that their clubs don't get a fair crack of the whip, knowing fine that an Old Firm injury story is likely to take precedence over a new signing at any other club. Sports editors and producers argue that they have to go with the Old Firm because they have the biggest fan bases and therefore are the main markets.

Yet, Scottish football is not all about two clubs. Some of the greatest achievements the game has seen have come from non-Old Firm teams.

I have been lucky enough to witness some of them and others I have watched from afar, from Aberdeen lifting the European Cup Winners' Cup and Dundee United winning the Scottish Premier Division title to Hearts and Hibs lifting the Scottish Cup.

I was throwing a few ideas around one night when I said to my wife, Amanda: "Do you think it would be a good idea to do a book of non-Old Firm success stories?" It was hardly a surprise that I got a positive response from my better half, who comes from a staunch Aberdeen-supporting family.

There have been hundreds of success stories but I knew it would be near impossible to cover them all.

The likes of Hibs, Hearts, Dunfermline and Dundee have all had their golden generations but it was, arguably, in the 1980s that, thanks to the

New Firm, Aberdeen and Dundee United, a brand new era in the Scottish game was spawned.

I still remember being subjected to the VHS recordings (video tapes for the benefit of the younger generation) of Aberdeen's various domestic and European successes when I headed to my Auntie Lorna's home for the summer holidays. I loved my football but I wasn't a Dons fan and at that time it felt like torture.

Now I look back on some of Aberdeen's achievements under Sir Alex Ferguson and they are right up there at the pinnacle of the Scottish game.

I, as a Motherwell fan, also stood on the Hampden terraces to watch my team lift the 1991 Scottish Cup. I have been back to a few other finals as a fan but I am still waiting to see my side lift another trophy.

To a lot of supporters it really is a once in a lifetime moment, to see your team win silverware.

The fans of Livingston and Raith Rovers will vouch for that while the likes of Hearts, St Mirren, Hibs and Kilmarnock have had more success than others.

Aberdeen and Dundee United fans have, maybe, been a bit spoiled for choice, along with St Johnstone and Highland rivals Inverness Caledonian Thistle and Ross County winning their first major trophies.

So I decided to charter every success from Sir Alex Ferguson's days at Pittodrie up to Hibernian finally ending their historic 114-year wait to get their hands on the Scottish Cup.

I know that many of these stories have been told before a million times or more and that was why I decided to try and do something different by writing this book through the words of the legends and heroes who helped make so many dreams become reality.

It was a privilege and a pleasure to speak to so many good people and for those I didn't interview I can only apologise. There were other players who proved more evasive than they were in the playing days – but I am glad the majority of people involved were more than happy to help.

I hope you enjoy the book and it brings back a few unforgettable memories and who knows, hopefully there will be a few more chapters that can be written over the coming years, like Aberdeen, St Mirren, St Johnstone, Ross County, Inverness and Hibernian have shown since this book was first published.

SCOTT BURNS
Sports writer with the *Scottish Daily Express*

ACKNOWLEDGEMENTS

The author would like to thank Alan Burrows, Malcolm Panton, Jeff Holmes, Ian Dawson, Greg McEwan, Paul Kiddie, Paul Smith, Charlie Duddy, Scott Fisher and Clive Hart for their help and assistance in making so many of these interviews possible.

I would also like to put on the record my appreciation to Stuart Darroch, Kevin Stirling, Shuggy Falconer, Graeme MacPherson, Graham Barnstaple, Mark Donaldson, David Hardie and Scott Davie for casting their expert eye over some of their favoured subjects.

Also on the photographic front I would like to thank Willie Vass and Eric McCowat for their top-quality pictures that more than tell the stories on their own. I also have to extend my gratitude to Ian Dawson at the *Daily Express* picture desk for all his assistance, as well as the use of the *Express's* cuttings library.

Also last and not least I would like to say a massive thank you to all the players, managers and coaches who made this book possible by sharing so many top and personal memories. Without you this book would never have happened.

CONTENTS

• ABERDEEN •
GOVAN'S FINEST HERALDS
A BRIGHT NEW DON

ABERDEEN chairman Dick Donald moved to replace Billy McNeill, who had returned to Celtic as manager, with the St Mirren boss Alex Ferguson in the summer of 1978. Ferguson, who had stepped on the managerial ladder at East Stirling, had done relatively well at Love Street but there were no obvious signs as to the greatness this young manager was about to go on and achieve in a glittering managerial career at Pittodrie and then Manchester United. In his first full season in the north-east the Dons finished fourth, reached the semi-final of the Scottish Cup and lost out in the League Cup final to Rangers – who had been Ferguson's local team and boyhood heroes. He also had a spell at Ibrox in a journeyman career that also saw him turn out for Queen's Park, St Johnstone, Dunfermline, Falkirk and Ayr United.

That first season showed that Ferguson had a side who could be more than competitive in the Scottish game although the start of the 1979-80 campaign didn't exactly go to plan. The manager felt it was time for change. Even if it meant upsetting the applecart and shaking some of Pittodrie's longest-serving stars out of their comfort zone. Veteran striker Joe Harper was one of those older heads. He believes Ferguson inherited the basis of a squad that could turn the Dons into a major force in Scottish football again.

Harper explained: "Going into that season I really felt we could do something. We had always been in and around the top four under Ally MacLeod and Billy McNeill and we felt we could kick on. We had also finished second a couple of seasons earlier so we knew if we found a bit more consistency we could maybe go one step further. Alex Ferguson had inherited a good core of experienced players and was also able to integrate top talents like Neil Simpson and Neale Cooper, who had come through the youth ranks. Everybody knew the team could be competitive but I don't think anyone realised just how good they would turn out to be. Ferguson was fortunate he walked into a job where everything was there for him to be a success."

Midfielder Gordon Strachan had arrived from Dundee a few years earlier and was viewed as one of Aberdeen's brightest and most creative talents. He thought the team's best hope of success would come via the cup competitions. Strachan admitted: "I can't say we went into that season thinking we would win the title. I knew we had a good team who were determined to do well but I certainly didn't have any thoughts of winning the league."

There seemed to be a good balance in Ferguson's squad between youth and experience. There were the likes of Harper, Bobby Clark, Willie Garner and Drew Jarvie, while they were supplemented by the up and coming talents of Strachan, Alex McLeish and Mark McGhee.

"That was my breakthrough season," central defender McLeish admitted, even though it was in a far different role from which he was to go on and make his name. "I was actually introduced to the team as a midfield destroyer. When I came into the first-team I couldn't actually get into the centre of the defence because of Willie Miller and Willie Garner. So I had to move forward and play in midfield. I was more than happy to play anywhere just to get a game."

Ferguson had a shrewd eye when it came to the transfer market and one of the gems he uncovered was McGhee. He persuaded the young striker to swap Newcastle United for the north-east of Scotland.

The striker recalled: "I looked at the fact that Aberdeen were among the top three or four teams in Scotland and what an opportunity it was to join a team like that. I was leaving Newcastle so it had to be something tasty to prise me away from St James' Park. The other thing that also went in Aberdeen's favour was that Alex Ferguson had tried to sign me when he was at St Mirren. I was still at Morton at that time. He told me that he had offered £25,000 and Morton had wanted £27,500 but the St Mirren board refused to pay the extra £2,500. Not long after that I went to Newcastle for £150,000. The Newcastle manager, Bill McGarry, told me I could stay and fight for my place but because Alex had been in for me before that was a big factor for me. He had tried to get me at Morton and still wanted me despite the fact I hadn't exactly set the heather alight in England. He was somebody who believed in me and that gave me great confidence."

Another tried and trusted path that Ferguson went down was back to Paisley and his former club St Mirren. One of the first players he brought in was midfielder Dougie Bell. Bell explained: "I had actually been freed by St Mirren when Ferguson took me to Aberdeen. Alex had been my manager at St Mirren and I had played a few games for him before he moved to Pittodrie so he didn't need to ask me twice."

The early signs didn't look too clever when Aberdeen lost their first league game of the season to Partick Thistle, but they recovered to register victories over Hibs and Dundee United before they slipped up again in a five-goal thriller at Morton. It was a period of highs and real lows for Ferguson and his team as they tried to find their feet. They managed to beat Rangers 3-1 at Pittodrie thanks to goals from John McMaster, Dougie Rougvie and Gordon Strachan but were brought crashing back down to earth as they lost to Celtic and crashed out of the Uefa Cup at the hands of Eintracht Frankfurt.

They knocked Rangers out of the League Cup and were given their chance to take revenge on Celtic in the quarter-final. They duly took it as they sunk Celtic 3-2 at Pittodrie thanks to a superb hat-trick from forward Steve Archibald. That was one of the big games of Alex McLeish's early Pittodrie career.

'Big Eck' recalled: "I remember the League Cup game against Celtic. The manager told me to go out and do a man-marking job. He told me I had to be like a scarf round the neck of the Celtic midfield. I went out and managed to do a job that night, along with the rest of the team as we progressed. That was when I knew I really could play at that level."

It wasn't such a joyous occasion for veteran Harper who suffered a serious knee injury that left his Pittodrie days numbered. Harper painfully recalled: "I felt good and had scored quite a few goals at the start of that season until disaster struck. I thought I had been hit by a sledgehammer because there was such a sharp pain in my knee. Alan Sneddon was the

Celtic player closest to me and I genuinely thought he had smashed me but it had actually turned out to be quite an innocuous challenge. The trainer came on, I got a bit of treatment and then I decided to play on. I got to the edge of their box and Danny McGrain then caught me with his knee. I collapsed again and as I went down I swung a punch at Danny because I thought he had also taken me out. I was later told he hadn't but it was just the pain of my knee giving way. I ended up being stretchered off and the Celtic fans were singing 'roll out the barrels, Harper's a barrel of s**t!' I responded by blowing them kisses."

Harper is in no doubt that injury turned out to be a blessing in disguise for Ferguson as he attempted to blood more of his own players into the team. He knew his own Pittodrie days were numbered. Harper said: "I was in doing my rehabilitation but I never really had much contact with the first-team. Alex never came in and asked how I was doing. It wasn't really surprising because we never really got on."

Harper's pain proved to be McGhee's gain as he finally got the run and chance he craved to show Ferguson he had what it took to take over Harper's mantle. The former Morton frontman didn't disappoint as he netted the winner in the League Cup second leg at Celtic Park, days after Archibald had hit the only goal in the league at Ibrox. Suddenly Parkhead and Ibrox were no longer places to fear.

"The start of the season it was primarily Joe Harper and Steve Archibald up front," McGhee admitted. "I got my break at Parkhead. I had struggled to establish myself after I had moved from Newcastle United but there was a game at Parkhead where Joe got injured and I went on and from there my Aberdeen career never really looked back."

Ferguson's Aberdeen showed on their day they were as good as anybody although there were still to be real disappointments along the way. It was to be the bitter taste of defeat in the League Cup final again, this time it was their New Firm rivals, Dundee United, who inflicted the damage in a 3-0 defeat after a replay.

The problem wasn't the big guns, it was the so-called lesser lights like Morton and Kilmarnock, where the Dons struggled. They lost at home to Killie at the end of February but from that point the rampant Reds never looked back, putting together an impressive unbeaten run in the league.

McGhee admitted: "There was so much determination about that team. The feeling got to a point where we felt we were invincible. We thought we were going to win every game. The manager was a big factor in that. He brought the team together. He didn't sign all the players but he did change us and make us better, individually and as a team. Gordon Strachan is probably the perfect example of that. He changed wee Gordon in terms of where he played on the field. He moved him forward and Gordon became a hugely more productive player.

"The manager also gave us a lot more structure and a plan to play to. Personally, I had been a player who had a lot of natural ability and liked to take players on and score goals. I played off the cuff but I had never been given a clear understanding of what I had to do for my team. Nobody had ever given me clear guidelines, but the manager sat me down and told me this is the minimum you need to try and achieve in every game. It was only when I came to Aberdeen, the manager stripped it all down for me.

"He told me I had to win that first header, hold the ball up and then start to beat people and score goals. I knew then even if I wasn't playing well I could still make a contribution. I suddenly had a purpose and that was true for so many of that team."

Midfielder Strachan recalled a big victory was their 1-0 win against Morton at the end of March. He said: "Drew Jarvie scored what turned out to be a really important goal against Morton. I remember that."

The wins kept coming and the newspapers and pundits were starting to realise Ferguson's Aberdeen were genuine title contenders.

McGhee explained: "I have no recollection of us being in that dressing room and thinking we could win the league. That was another one of the manager's psychological master strokes. Everything was played down and it was one game at a time. Therefore, there was never a great deal of anticipation within the squad that we were going to win the title.

"He would tell us the press were all based in the west of Scotland and they all hated to troop up here because we were stealing the limelight from their beloved Celtic and Rangers. He also raised the point that some of us were Celtic and Rangers supporters but here we were at Aberdeen because they didn't want us. We felt like rejects and that fired us up and so we always went out against the Old Firm with something to prove."

March closed with a 2-2 draw at Ibrox and that was in the middle of a really difficult spell for the long-serving Aberdeen goalkeeper Bobby Clark. He revealed: "My dad died on the Sunday and two weeks previously my wife's father had also passed away before we played Dundee United. It was a really emotional period and I hardly spent any time at Pittodrie because I was with my family down in Glasgow.

"After my dad died we were due to play Kilmarnock a couple of days later. I didn't want to play but both my mum and my mother-in-law told me I had to play because that is what my dad and father-in-law would have wanted. I played and thankfully managed to keep a clean sheet in a 4-0 win at Rugby Park. I could then concentrate on the off-the-field issues.

"Alex Ferguson also made the effort to come to my dad's funeral and I thought that was a great touch. I stayed down and trained with Clyde and then we played Celtic on the Saturday. That was the day I saved a penalty from Bobby Lennox and we went on to win 2-1. At the end of the game Bobby waited to catch me and said: 'I am sorry to hear about your dad.' Here we were both fighting to win the league and he showed his class to wait behind and pass on his condolences.

"There is no doubt the loss of my dad and father-in-law also gave me a personal drive to make sure Aberdeen ended up with the title."

April was going to decide whether or not Aberdeen were going to be able to go all the way, as they had to make two trips to Celtic Park with another against Dundee United thrown in for good measure. Trips to Ibrox and Celtic Park used to be filled with fear and dread but not for this Aberdeen team. It was filled with some big, big characters and winners into the bargain. Doug Rougvie, who used to warm up in front of The Jungle at Parkhead, admitted: "You had to show you weren't going to be intimidated by the opposition fans. We were hoping the opposition would be intimidated when they came to Pittodrie by our team but we were determined it wasn't going to be the case when we were on our travels. So warming up in front of the Celtic fans was one of the things I did. I took pelters from the Celtic fans but I was okay back then because I was a lot quicker than I am today. I don't think I would be as keen doing it today."

Goals from Jarvie and McGhee gave the Dons a win in their first of those two Parkhead visits. Bell, who came off the bench as a sub, admitted that match was a real season definer. Bell said: "We went on a good run and that got the confidence up. I think after we went to Celtic Park and beat them 2-1 we really believed we could win the title. The manager had certainly installed that belief into our play and I think Rangers and Celtic were probably more worried about playing us than we were about them."

The Dons looked almost invincible in the league but they came unstuck in the Scottish Cup as they lost 1-0 in the last four. That was a disappointment but they managed to pick themselves up and win 3-1 on their second visit to Celtic Park, thanks to strikes from McGhee, Strachan and Archibald. Strachan is in no doubt those wins helped Aberdeen get one hand on the championship trophy.

"Our whole world changed over those games," the fiery midfielder explained. "Beating Celtic in those two games shaped our dynasty for what was still to come. There is no doubt about that. The only way we were going to know if we could go and win in Glasgow was to go and do it and we did. It was then we believed we could be on the verge of something special."

Aberdeen defender Rougvie also reckons the fact that Billy McNeill had walked out on them for Celtic was another big motivation for everyone in red and white. Rougvie said: "We had put a late run together and managed to get some big results, like when we beat Celtic down at Parkhead. Our old manager, Billy McNeill, was in charge at Celtic so it was a big thing for us to beat them, especially in Glasgow. We just kept on winning and that was what happened. There was no doubt Fergie was still stamping his authority on the squad. He was on a learning curve like most of the boys. We were in uncharted water because the last time Aberdeen had won the league was 25 years before in 1954-55."

The last big obstacle Ferguson's team had to overcome was Dundee United. A Gordon Strachan goal managed to earn them a share of the spoils at Tannadice. Aberdeen knew if they beat rock-bottom Hibs at Easter Road the title would all but be in the bag.

By that point, the Aberdeen juggernaut was in full flow and it wasn't about to be stopped, as they crushed Hibs 5-0. Archibald, McGhee, local lad Andy Watson and a double from Ian Scanlon put Ferguson's side on easy street and over the championship finishing line.

Miller admitted he had tears in his eyes come the final whistle, knowing he had finally realised his dream of captaining Aberdeen to the title. He confirmed it was one of the only days in his career where his emotions got the better of him. "That was a really draining day," Miller said. "If ever there was a tear in my eye at any time during my playing career then it was probably that day. It had been a long-standing dream at the club – to see Aberdeen crowned as champions of Scotland again. It had been like that for the ten years I had been at the club and even before my time.

"We had finally done it, ending the Old Firm dominance. So that day at Easter Road was an emotional one because we had finally achieved what we had all set out to do. We had been in cup finals and won trophies but for every professional player the league is the big one. If you can win it then it always brings a really special moment. Winning the league was the catalyst that helped spur us on to have our future successes at home and in Europe."

For keeper Clark it was an afternoon he feared he would never see. The long-serving number one said: "It was special because twice previously we had lost the league on the final day of the season. We had been knocking at the door but Fergie was able to help us fulfil our dream. It was a very special moment."

Goal hero McGhee was still in a state of shock before the final whistle had even gone. He confessed: "It only dawned on me when the Celtic result came through, via our fans, that we had won the league. We certainly didn't expect Celtic to drop something in their match. I remember being overwhelmed with this sudden emotion of disbelief and excitement during the game at Easter Road. For the last ten minutes I felt like I was in a bubble and I wasn't hearing anybody else. It was such a new thing for most of us and we didn't really know how to react. Even when the whistle went it was still disbelief that we had actually done it."

For the rest of the young Dons they believed it was the start rather than the pinnacle of Aberdeen's achievements as they claimed their first title in 25 years and only the second in their history.

McLeish admitted: "I was quite blase about winning the league when I think about it now. I had been used to winning before I moved into the senior ranks and so I thought winning leagues was going to be a regular thing. It is not until you are older you realise what you have done and achieved. I remember Danny McGrain came up to me and congratulated us on winning the league and then said the hardest thing now will be to try and retain it. I found out the next season that he was absolutely spot on."

Local lad Andy Watson was the youngest player in the squad and one of only two natives in the team, with the other being Doug Considine. He recalled: "It was a great thrill winning the title with my home town team. It was massive to help Aberdeen win the title in my first season. I was only the third Aberdonian to pick up a winner's medal at the time so that was also a big thing for me and my family."

Rougvie is in no doubt that Ferguson got his team punching above their weight. The rugged defender said: "We knew we had won the league after we had beaten Hibs. Our goal difference was massive and we knew that Celtic were never going to turn that around. It was amazing to watch Fergie running up and down the park at the end of the Hibs game. He couldn't hide his joy and we felt exactly the same. We had been the also-rans for so long and to finally be crowned champions was just amazing. We were a provincial club who prior to that had massively under-achieved."

The celebrations started in earnest when the team got back to the Granite City. Ferguson was left unaware his car was being used to taxi his jubilant players around several of the Granite City's more popular nightspots. McGhee revealed: "I was due to play in a testimonial game on the Sunday at Greenock, but not long before that I had written off my car and didn't have any transport to get down the road. The manager told me to take his car. He had this big fancy Rover 2500 and all I remember was driving all the lads round the town in his car on the Saturday night. I was supposed to take it back on the Monday but I didn't end up getting back until the Tuesday. The gaffer was absolutely raging because he had been left driving about in Teddy Scott's white van for days."

Strachan revealed his celebrations were slightly different as his good fortune continued right into the night, as he went to play bingo with his parents. He explained: "It was great to get that medal. I remember after the game the manager let us stay down the road if we wanted. I went to the Edinburgh City bowling club to play bingo with my mum, dad and my wife. I won at that as well so it turned out to be a right good day!"

The title was officially clinched with a final day draw with Partick Thistle although it would have seen an almighty collapse in goal difference for the trophy to go anywhere else. Clark is in no doubt that it was Ferguson's magic that turned that squad into winners.

The keeper said: "Alex was a pretty special person. I worked with a lot of great people, like Eddie Turnbull, Billy McNeill and Ally MacLeod, at Aberdeen but Alex seemed to have that special Midas touch that made things happen. Alex just had this unbelievable drive about him. I also got to know him quite well because I was helping Lenny Taylor to run the youth programme, where the John Hewitts and Neale Coopers came from. Alex would always be in at the club first thing in the morning and would be back down to watch the kids at night. He would come down and watch the games to make sure he knew what was going on."

The title party went on for days in the Granite City with the highlight being the open-top bus from Bridge of Dee all the way to Pittodrie, as the Red Army piled on to the streets to salute their newly crowned champions. Rookie keeper Jim Leighton played a minor role but was still forced to join in. He said: "I was involved in the 1979-80 title-winning season. I played in one game, we got beat 2-1 against Kilmarnock, but Sir Alex still made me go round with the team on the bus. I wanted to sit downstairs because I didn't feel I had really contributed but he made me go up with the rest of the team.

"I stayed at the back and it was great seeing all the boys celebrating and taking bows in front of the fans. I was thinking to myself I would love to win something major in my career and hopefully I will get the chance to celebrate like this on an open-top bus further down the line."

That was the first major success for a lot of the Aberdeen team and for McGhee it was a totally new experience. He said: "The interesting thing for me was that as a kid I was brought up in Cumbernauld. I played for the school and we used to play teams in the Glasgow District, Eastercraigs and sides like that, and we used to get hammered. I would go home and tell my dad we had lost 18-1 but he would say 'well done, at least you got the goal'. I always played for teams who struggled so the first winner's medal I got in my career was that one with Aberdeen. It wasn't a bad one to start with."

Strachan, who was named as Scotland's player of the year and also earned his first international recognition that season, is in no doubt that things peaked at just the right time for the Dons that title-winning season. "It was a combination of things," Strachan insisted. "We had a lot of good, good players, we were all hungry and we all had a drive to do well. Factor all that in and you get the perfect storm and that was what happened with that Aberdeen team."

Clark left Pittodrie on a high to join up with the Scotland team that summer and picked up the injury that was to end his 17-year Aberdeen career. He painfully recalled: "After we won the league I went away with the Scottish squad to play Hungary and Poland. I had missed one game in our title success because of a bad back and when I came back from that Scotland trip I ended up needing surgery. By the time I was fully fit Jim Leighton was coming through and we also had Bryan Gunn, so I decided to call time because I knew Alex didn't need a 37-year-old at the end of the road."

The Scottish Premier Division trophy had barely been placed in the Pittodrie trophy cabinet when their perfection-seeking manager had started to plot bigger and better things. He was going to have to make changes for his first tilt at the European Cup as top striker Steve Archibald was sold to Tottenham Hotspur for £750,000.

Clark recalled: "I remember I went in to see Alex two weeks after we won the title. He was sitting in his office and I was still totally elated that we had won the league. For me, that was the pinnacle and my dream. We had won the other cups but the league was the real badge of being the best in the country. The manager, however, had already moved on and was looking towards the next season. I am sure he enjoyed the celebrations but even then he had bigger dreams for Aberdeen and that was doing well in Europe."

Dreams of making an immediate impact in the European Cup were crushed by Liverpool in the second round but it wouldn't be long before Aberdeen and Ferguson were to take their place among Europe's elite.

ABERDEEN'S 1979-80 TITLE-WINNING SQUAD
Bobby Clark, Jim Leighton, Steve Cowan, Stuart Kennedy, Doug Considine, Doug Rougvie, Alex McLeish, Andy Watson, Neil Cooper, Willie Garner, Willie Miller, Gordon Strachan, Mark McGhee, Ian Scanlon, Steve Archibald, Joe Harper, Derek Hamilton, Drew Jarvie, John McMaster, John Hewitt, Dom Sullivan, Doug Bell, Duncan Davidson.
Manager: Alex Ferguson.

2

• ABERDEEN •
LOCAL HEROES AND SCOTTISH CUP GLORY

ALEX FERGUSON had already awoken the sleeping giant that was Aberdeen when he had led them to the 1979-80 Scottish Premier Division title. He and the expectant north-east demanded more. Ferguson wanted his hands on more championships and he also desperately wanted to improve the club's rather disappointing cup record. The League Cup had been lifted in 1976-77 well before Ferguson had arrived in the Granite City and you had to go back to 1970 for the last time the Scottish Cup was decked out in the red and white ribbons of the Dandy Dons.

The 1981-82 season had started promisingly on the knockout stage as Aberdeen progressed to the last four of the League Cup before they eventually bowed out to New Firm rivals Dundee United. That gave Ferguson hope that if his team could hit top gear come May then they could be there or thereabouts when the Scottish Cup was being handed out.

The competition opened with a potentially tricky tie away to First Division title chasers Motherwell. However, the Dons were given the perfect start and never looked back as John Hewitt netted one of the quickest goals in the competition's history – inside ten seconds.

The record breaker said: "I scored in 9.6 seconds. It is still the quickest goal in the history of the Scottish Cup. The ball went wide to Stuart Kennedy. He took a touch and played a long diagonal ball. A defender let it bounce and I chased what looked like a lost cause and managed to get in behind him and fired it across the face of goal to beat Hugh Sproat at his far post."

That gave the Reds something to hold on to and they did precisely that, coming away from Fir Park as 1-0 victors. Midfielder Gordon Strachan admitted: "Everybody goes on about what a great side we had but Motherwell absolutely battered us that day. We got the early goal from John Hewitt and were then left to hold on for grim death."

Things didn't get any easier as Celtic made the trip to Pittodrie in the fourth round. Once again, it was Hewitt who was the hero as he hit the only goal of the game. Hewitt recalled: "Celtic were dominating and we were struggling but we managed to get the goal again. We got a corner from the left-hand side and I just turned to hook it over my head and into the net. That was really the start of the run we had. It was great."

Everybody knew that was a major hurdle out of the way. The last eight saw them drawn against another First Division side, Kilmarnock, who were also pushing for a return to the top flight. Killie travelled to Pittodrie and clearly weren't going there to make up the numbers. It proved to be a real Scottish Cup battle where Aberdeen had to battle all the way before they came out on top with a 4-2 win. Mark McGhee and Neil Simpson got on the scoresheet, along with Strachan who claimed a brace from the penalty spot.

Strachan recalled: "I scored a couple of penalties but what I remember from that game was the manager having a raging argument with their defender Ken Armstrong. He was going about scudding everyone. There was him and this other no-nonsense centre-half called Derek McDicken. What a pair they were."

Fellow scorer Neil Simpson also revealed how defender Doug Rougvie almost killed McDicken and Armstrong after the game. "They were the biggest team I had ever played against," Simmie admitted. "Their defenders Armstrong and McDicken were trying to do Gordon Strachan at every opportunity. I think they thought wee Gordon had fallen down a little too easily for one of the penalties. They were in the tea room after the game and Gordon's wife heard them saying 'if I get a hold of that Strachan I am going to rip him to bits'. That got back to us and big Doug (Rougvie) said: 'Leave it to me. I will go through to the tea room first' and he did. It is fair to say very little came out of the Kilmarnock camp after that."

That led to Aberdeen's second semi-final appearance of the season and this time they were desperate to go one step further than they had in the League Cup. It brought a clash against Ferguson's former club St Mirren. The first match at Celtic Park ended in a draw with a goal from future Don Frank McDougall being countered by another Strachan penalty. Neil Simpson admitted: "We were lucky to get a 1-1 draw because we didn't play well at all."

That meant both teams had to do it again in a replay that was moved to Dundee's Dens Park. It was another game that saw both sides fight to the death. In the end, goals from Mark McGhee, Neil Simpson and Peter Weir were enough to get the better of the Buddies, who had netted through Frank McAvennie and Doug Somner.

Simpson recalled his moment of magic that night. He said: "I received the ball just over the halfway line. I drove forward 20 yards and I just hit this 25-yarder. It just flew past Billy Thomson into the right-hand corner of the net. That was a good goal. I remember running to the Aberdeen fans. That was one of the few times where I really celebrated a goal. The game was won when Peter Weir and Mark McGhee also scored."

The Dons had booked their place at Hampden against Rangers, who had also taken a replay to see off plucky Second Division side Forfar Athletic.

Aberdeen pushed Celtic all the way in the championship chase, while Rangers were their nearest challengers but still some way behind the top two. That, however, didn't dent the confidence of the Ibrox side who clearly fancied their chances of coming out on top come 22nd May at the national stadium. Aberdeen eventually lost the title to Celtic and their final-day 4-0 victory over Rangers counted for very little. However, some misjudged comments from the Rangers camp were to disastrously misfire and make the Dons even more determined to put them in their place in the cup final.

Alex McLeish recalled: "We trooped off after the Rangers game. I remember one of their players walked off and said 'we will be OK in the cup final because Aberdeen never beat us when it matters'. That was stored and used before the cup final. Needless to say that particular Rangers player, who I won't name, was left slightly more than red-faced after the final whistle in the cup final."

Ferguson took his side off to Cruden Bay for their pre-match preparations. He went to great lengths to ensure there was to be no complacency within his squad after the thumping of the Light Blues the previous weekend.

Neil Simpson said: "It was a big occasion. It was a dream being an Aberdeen supporter and looking forward to playing in a cup final. The last time they had won the Scottish Cup was 1969-70. So to get to the final was a massive thing. I remember we all had to go out and buy our own cup final suits. We had certainly looked the part the week before. We beat Rangers 4-0. We gave them an absolute doing and so we were confident but Fergie kept saying 'this is the Old Firm and a cup final is different'."

That proved to be the case as Rangers made the perfect start when John MacDonald put them ahead. Aberdeen's equaliser had come from an unlikely source although Alex McLeish did give them a sneak preview of what was to come at their pre-match training camp. McLeish, who was more famed for his headed goals, said: "The manager took us up to Cruden Bay before the game. I managed to score a long range effort in training that week that flew into the bottom corner. I wasn't really renowned for scoring that many goals. I normally went into the box as more of a decoy. So when the ball came back out to me in the cup final I just decided to hit it and it curled in the top corner. It was probably one of my best goals, especially as it came in the cup final."

That was enough to take the game into extra-time. Mark McGhee then put the Dons in front and was never in doubt that the cup was going back to Pittodrie – even if he wasn't as confident in his own abilities. He said: "The thing about that Aberdeen team was that hardly any of us had experienced a cup final before. The razzmatazz was brilliant, for Alex as well. The whole build-up was different for us and I will never forget it. We were playing a Rangers team who were aging. They were on their last legs and we felt we had a real chance because we had the energy, youth and legs. It didn't prove to be as easy as that. It went to extra-time and we eventually came out on top but the experience and ability of Rangers ran us close.

"The extra-time makes it look as if it was easy but it wasn't. It was great to get a goal in a cup final. I was at the back post and I stooped to head it past the keeper. I maybe should have taken the ball down and I spent the next five minutes wondering what would have happened if I had missed because Alex wouldn't have let me live it down. Here I had scored in a cup final but I was still full of self-doubt."

He didn't have to wait long for Aberdeen to strengthen their grip on the trophy, when McGhee turned provider for his good friend Gordon

Strachan. Strachan admitted: "Alex Miller suffered a bad injury in the build-up. Mark McGhee squared it to me and I remember thinking the goal had gone from eight yards to eight inches. I was thinking I can't miss this. If I do it will go down as the worst miss in history. I just remember the elation I felt as I saw the ball hit the net. I knew then we were going to win the cup. Rangers were a really good team but it was probably our superior fitness that got us through in the end."

The final outcome was sealed in some style when home-grown Neale Cooper scored in the second-half of extra-time. It was a dream come true for the teenager. Cooper said: "It was amazing just to be playing in a cup final at 17. It really was great because I had been a ballboy at Pittodrie and here I was, a local boy, playing for Aberdeen in a cup final. The fact we won it was even more amazing and then to score the final goal was just beyond my wildest dreams.

"It was quite bizarre. The keeper had come out and the ball just hit me on the shoulder. I didn't know where the ball was and then I turned around and saw I had an open goal. My biggest challenge was deciding how to finish but I just decided to smash the ball into the net. My mum and sister were at Hampden and to know they were there when I lifted the cup meant everything to me."

Even for some of the older players it was also their first experience of Hampden glory. Dougie Bell, who had come off the bench, said: "It was great to be at Hampden and to savour my first cup winner's medal. I also felt I played my part because I set up Neale's goal, so I, at least, felt I had made a contribution on the day."

The celebrations went on long into the night and got into full swing when the team headed to Gleneagles for their post-match winners' party. Ferguson might have had 13 heroes out on the pitch but his stars were about to meet another one that night. Neale Cooper revealed: "It was a great night and we were joined by Hollywood actor Burt Lancaster who was up filming *Local Hero*. Quite a few of the boys had their pictures taken with the great man."

It was the first medal of what was to be a distinguished career for Jim Leighton. He admitted it left him with a special feeling that will live with him forever. "That was my first medal and whenever you win something for the first time it is always the best," admitted Leighton. "Every time you win something it is great but the first time I won any of the domestic trophies in Scotland was special. The 1982 Scottish Cup win was great, especially the way we did it, taking the match into extra-time and then scoring three goals.

"Whenever I won something you always saw me acting like an idiot with a silly hat or the daftest scarf. My dad, my wife and a lot of my friends were at the game, which was good. The joy of the moment is special and allows you to do things that are out of character. That is the good thing about these occasions because the people close to you are there for you during the low points and so it is good to give them something back on days like this. We went on to have a great night back at Gleneagles before we returned for the open-top bus."

That was to be the start of a long love affair with the Scottish Cup for Ferguson, his players and the Granite City.

ABERDEEN'S SCOTTISH CUP RUN 1981-82
* Third round (23rd January 1982 at Fir Park)
    Motherwell 0 Aberdeen 1 (Hewitt)
* Fourth round (13th February 1982 at Pittodrie)
    Aberdeen 1 (Hewitt) Celtic 0
* Quarter-final (6th March 1982 at Pittodrie)
    Aberdeen 4 (McGhee, Simpson, Strachan 2 PENS)
    Kilmarnock 2 (McGivern, Gallagher)
* Semi-final (3rd April 1982 at Celtic Park)
    Aberdeen 1 (Strachan PEN) St Mirren 1 (McDougall)
* Semi-final replay (7th April 1982 at Dens Park)
    St Mirren 2 (McAvennie, Somner) Aberdeen 3 (McGhee, Simpson, Weir)
* Final (22nd May 1982 at Hampden)
    Aberdeen 4 (McLeish, McGhee, Strachan, Cooper) Rangers 1 (McDonald) (AET)

ABERDEEN'S SCOTTISH CUP-WINNING TEAM:
Jim Leighton, Stuart Kennedy, Alex McLeish, Willie Miller, Doug Rougvie, Gordon Strachan, Neale Cooper, Neil Simpson, John McMaster (Dougie Bell), John Hewitt (Eric Black), Mark McGhee.
Manager: Alex Ferguson.

3

• DUNDEE UNITED •
CHAMPIONS AND THEN CHEATED OF
EURO SUCCESS

THE seeds of expectation were sown by Jim McLean when his Dundee United team lifted back-to-back League Cups. The 1979-80 success was where it all started, as United beat Aberdeen in a replay to lift the first major trophy of their 70-year history. The following season McLean's Terrors followed things up with a successful defence of their trophy as they beat local rivals Dundee in the final.

Winger Eammon Bannon admitted: "When you win things it does give you more confidence. We had won a couple of League Cups and we had also come close to winning the league a couple of seasons earlier. We also knew every other team inside out. We knew that on our day we could beat Aberdeen, Hearts or Celtic, although if our rivals were on form then they were also more than capable of beating us. We also knew how to win, even away from home.

"The only nut we really failed to crack was Rangers at Ibrox, although they were never really big title rivals in the early-80s. Playing in front of big crowds at Ibrox and Celtic Park was definitely a challenge. I think if our Dundee United team had been in blue or green and white hooped shirts then I think we would have won the league a lot more than on the one occasion we did."

Those early years saw United burst on to the Scottish scene as part of the New Firm, along with Alex Ferguson's Aberdeen. Those triumphs and another Scottish Cup final appearance proved that United were a team who were very much an emerging force in the Scottish game. The challenge to Glasgow's big two from the north-east was driven by McLean and his Aberdeen counterpart, Ferguson.

McLean said: "Alex Ferguson is a very good friend of mine from way back, when I went down to do my second SFA coaching badge at Largs. I was unfortunate enough to be picked to room with Alex. I don't think anybody else wanted to room with him. From then on we became very good friends apart from when we played each other. I remember one day I was in a restaurant and Alex was also there. He came over, battered me on the head and said 'I need you and you need me'. I said: 'What the hell do I need you for?' Fergie replied: 'You need me to beat Rangers and Celtic and I need you to beat Rangers and Celtic.' He was spot on."

The core of McLean's team was made up of graduates from the Tannadice youth set-up, like Richard Gough, Maurice Malpas, Paul Sturrock and Ralph Milne, along with a good blend of experienced campaigners like David Narey, Paul Hegarty, Hamish McAlpine and John Holt.

"I was fortunate because we had a real, good quality of player at that time," McLean conceded. "Far too often we had to sell players to balance the books but we always seemed to have a good crop of youngsters. To be fair everybody at the club put in a lot of hard work trying to find good young players. I remember in my early years at Dundee United I hardly went to church on a Sunday because I was too busy out and about taking in local matches, looking at young players."

Young Malpas was one of the youngest members of the first-team squad and he spent his early years juggling his football around his studies. He admitted: "I was still part-time that season. It was great for me because I would go away to college to study for my (honours) degree in electrical engineering. It allowed me to get away from the pressure and spotlight of the press, especially later in the season when we were right in the title race. I was in my fourth year and I still had another year to go.

"The closer we got to the end of the season and people realised we were contenders then the more journalists and television cameras started to appear. I was lucky I could stay out the way. I used to train at night and I went under the radar. It was great for me, as a young player, because I was able to concentrate on my football. It was a good time being up at the top of the table."

United started the season on fire. In all competitions they went 17 games unbeaten, that included league, Uefa Cup and League Cup fixtures. The first defeat came in the League Cup as they lost 2-0 at Celtic Park. They did win the Tannadice return but went out 3-2 on aggregate. A highlight of that run was a big 4-2 win over Rangers that showed a bit of what was to come. Ralph Milne was one of the stars of the show with two goals, as Davie Dodds and Richard Gough also netted.

Milne recalled: "One of my early memories from that season was when we beat Rangers 4-2 in the November. I managed to score a couple of goals but my last one was quite incredible for me. Paul Sturrock played me through and one-on-one with the goalkeeper and I just hit it with the outside of my right foot and it just flew into the top corner. That was a big result for us."

The team were always likely to score goals with the attacking talents of David Dodds, Paul Sturrock and Milne. At the other end, they had one of the best defences around. Malpas was certainly helped by the older heads around him. "I felt comfortable among the lads," the left-back confirmed. "I played all that season but the Paul Hegartys, Hamish McAlpines and David Nareys dragged me through that year. They kept me right, so it was pretty easy for me to turn up and play. That is not to say that if I did have a poor game that I wouldn't cop it from the manager. The good thing about that team was that we all got it from Wee Jim at some point, but the others would stand up and take their share of responsibility. We won and lost together."

There were also the underrated heroes that might not have stolen the headlines but more than grabbed the attention of the opposition. Paul Sturrock said: "We had a great team from back to front. We had so many top players. A lot of players won international caps and others didn't, when they should have. For example, Ralph Milne is one of the most underrated players I have ever seen. It was a sin that he never won a Scottish cap. We also had a lot of unsung heroes like Derek Stark, John Holt and Billy Kirkwood. They were like dogs of war for us. They put their foot in and gave the team some real steel. Gordon Strachan called them the men with no faces because whenever he was tackled he would get up and all he would see was the back of their heads. We had a good balance in that team."

Enforcer Billy Kirkwood admitted that he and John Holt would take it in turns to take the opposition's danger men out of the game. He said: "I used to take great delight in kicking Gordon then running off. Myself and John used to take turns at kicking him because we knew he would start moaning and it would put him off his game. But it is fair to say Aberdeen also had a few kickers of their own in Neil Simpson, Neale Cooper and Doug Rougvie. Most teams had players like that in their ranks."

McLean also drilled into his team the morals of giving their all for the Tannadice faithful. "As the manager you are mostly responsible for satisfying your supporters," McLean claimed. "It isn't a case of satisfying the players because they get paid for doing their job. Yes, we rely on them to get the results for the supporters but the supporters are still the most important people because they hand over their hard-earned money to watch and support the team."

A big disappointment in that season was the thumping defeat away to Aberdeen that November. It left McLean to wonder about his defence and to tinker with his tactics. Gough said: "I scored a few goals up at Aberdeen that season. I remember I got one in a match and we ended up getting beat 5-1. I then recall getting moved into centre defence because Wee Jim wanted to push David Narey into midfield. That is how we went into the run-in."

The tactical awareness of both McLean and his young assistant Walter Smith was second to none and was a big thing in United's armoury. They were more than able to adapt, as Sturrock admitted: "Wee Jim actually pioneered the 4-5-1 system that a lot of teams are adopting now, although it quickly turned into a 4-3-3 with Ralph and Davie Dodds down either side and myself through the middle. We would always press the ball from the front and that proved successful in Scotland and also in Europe. Wee Jim's tactics were spot on that night we beat Celtic, even when we were down to ten men. I was meant to be on the left against Danny McGrain but as soon as Jim saw that Murdo McLeod was at right back he switched me out to the opposite side. It worked and that just showed you what a top tactician Jim McLean was. He had a knack of exploiting the weaknesses in the opposition."

The start of 1983 produced a 2-0 derby win over Dundee, but then United, temporarily, went off the rails. They lost to Aberdeen and Rangers and drew with Hibs. Another big disappointment was their Uefa Cup exit to Bohemians. It ended a gutsy run which had seen them knock out

PSV Eindhoven, Viking of Norway and Werder Bremen.

Paul Hegarty recalled: "We were really disappointed to go out to Bohemians, although it probably turned out to be a blessing in disguise. If we had gone through then who is to say we would have still won the league. I am sure if we all knew we were going to win the league then we would have taken it but losing to Bohemians was a blow because that was in the quarter-final of the Uefa Cup."

There was no time for self-pity as it was straight into a New Firm clash where they bounced back at Pittodrie. Ralph Milne was the hero and the villain in the 2-1 win. Milne recalled: "After we went out of Europe, Paul Sturrock got injured. Our next game was against Aberdeen and Wee Jim asked me if I would play at centre-forward and go up against Alex McLeish and Willie Miller. I agreed but at the back of my mind I was saying to myself I don't fancy this at all.

"It wasn't until I took to the pitch and I said to myself just give it a go. I ended up scoring two goals and got sent off as we won the game. I ended up losing my bonus and a week's wages for getting sent off. I didn't even argue my case because I just didn't think it was worth it."

The Dons were also heading for European Cup Winners' Cup glory and that eventually took its toll on them as they failed to keep pace with a rampant United side and Celtic.

Dundee United were never outside of the top four and it was then that the penny really dropped that they were genuine title contenders. McLean admitted: "Every game, for me, was vital. No matter what your last result was you had to focus on winning your next game. I was also lucky because we managed to develop youngsters and to sign so many good players. I have to say I didn't always think we could win the title. We just took it one game at a time and when we got to the second-half of the season that was when reality dawned that we might have a chance."

Going into the final run-in two of the biggest challenges they faced were trips to Parkhead. The outcomes of those game against Celtic would go a long way to shaping Dundee United's title ambitions. United beat Rangers at home 3-1 before they made their first trip to the East End of Glasgow. It didn't go well as Frank McGarvey and Charlie Nicholas gunned down United. It was a hard one to take but they could still make up for it. They beat St Mirren and returned to Parkhead in a very different mindset to the team who had previously left with their tail between their legs.

United managed to come from behind to record a famous 3-2 win with only ten men. Sinning Gough explained: "I had already been booked when Davie Provan fell into me on the edge of the box. He tried to head butt me on the ground and I threw him off and we both ended up getting yellow cards, of course that was my second and I was sent off. I ended up back in the dressing room and I just heard a big roar and I genuinely though Celtic had scored again. It wasn't until the boys came back into the dressing room and were jumping up and down that I realised we had won."

Paul Hegarty had put United ahead and then it was game of penalties with Nicholas and Eammon Bannon converting. Tommy Burns then levelled for Celtic again. It was left to Ralph Milne to become the hero.

Milne recalled: "We played really well against Celtic and my only regret was my goal wasn't shown on television because that was one of the best goals I have scored. Eammon Bannon hit the byline and cut back on to his right foot and I managed to get in front of my marker and volley it high over Pat Bonner in the Celtic goal. Parkhead just fell silent because there was only a few minutes left. I ran away absolutely delighted with myself and ended up straining my hamstring in the celebrations."

Bannon reckons that win installed the belief among the players that the impossible dream really could happen. He said: "We were never really in the driving seat, we were always either in second or third spot. Then things just snowballed. We had put a couple of wins together and then Celtic lost a couple. We ended up playing Celtic at Parkhead in a night game. We beat them and that result really made everybody sit up and take notice."

The Parkhead red card not only left Gough out of the team but also out of pocket – leading to an angry exchange with McLean. Gough, who made his Scotland debut earlier that season, said: "I was suspended for the next couple of games after the Celtic match and we won, so that same month I checked my wage slip and I was furious because Wee Jim had decided not to pay me any win bonuses for the games I missed. I was raging and so I went to see Walter Smith.

"I argued that it wasn't fair because I only got sent off against Celtic because I thought Provan was going to score. Will I just let him go next time and then we don't end up winning the championship? I then went to see Jim and he started screaming and shouting at me. It was worth it because in the end I think I got half the win bonuses that I was due."

The good thing was United's destiny was in their own hands. Midfielder Billy Kirkwood admitted: "The good thing going into those final few games was that we knew if we won the matches then we would be champions. Morton, Motherwell, Kilmarnock and Dundee and we certainly saw all four of them as winnable matches."

They put four past Kilmarnock and Morton, although at Cappielow it was at the other end where United had the biggest problem. Hegarty explained: "Hamish McAlpine got an injury at half-time. I can assure you it was a nerve-wracking experience. It was a worry because Hamish was a big player for us and back then you never had a substitute keeper on the bench. I had a laugh and joke in training and so I ended up with the gloves. I was just lucky the boys in front of me were different class. I hardly had anything to do because the defenders played so well in front of me. I think I had one save and we ended up winning the match quite convincingly."

The Taysiders also beat Motherwell 4-0 with Eammon Bannon pulling the strings and stretching the patience of his manager to breaking point. Hamish McAlpine revealed: "Eammon had been our corner taker and I remember he went through a spell where he struggled to find a tangerine jersey. He came in at half-time one day and Jim said 'you'd better not take another corner again!' Then minutes into the second-half and Eammon was right across to take it. I looked at the dugout and Jim McLean was going berserk. Eammon swung in a corner and we scored. I turned to Wee Jim again and he was standing there shaking his head in disbelief."

The bizarre thing was that although McLean was a perfectionist he eased off going into those final games. "Jim was probably a different person in those games," Sturrock claimed. "He realised the importance and he kept away from the team for a lot of it. It was Walter who took most of the training and took the team talks. I think Jim appreciated the pressure he sometimes put on people."

The title came down to the final day and United could be crowned champions for the first time at Dens Park, the home of their city rivals.

Left-back Maurice Malpas recalls their laid-back pre-match journey up the street that today wouldn't have been allowed by the police. The Dunfermline-born star said: "We walked up from Tannadice to Dens Park. Could you imagine that happening today? The streets were packed but I remember walking up the road without a care in the world. I was just looking forward to the game. I just went in auto-pilot and the game just flew past."

The nerves were certainly calmed by a brilliantly-worked goal in the fourth minute that was built from the back. Goalscorer Ralph Milne proudly recalled: "I told my dad before the game that I was going to score and thankfully I did. When the game started David Narey played it up to Paul Sturrock and he tried to play me in and was about ten yards out with his pass. I turned and said 'I am not on a motorbike'. The next time he got the ball he slipped as he passed it and I managed to read it and get inside. I saw the goalkeeper coming out and I thought I have got him here and I managed to stick it away. It is probably the goal I will remember the most from my career and I am sure it will be the same for a lot of Dundee United fans."

United double their advantage when David Narey was tripped inside the box. Dundee keeper Colin Kelly so nearly broke their hearts with a brilliant penalty save but he was finally beaten at the second time of asking.

A simply relieved Eammon Bannon said: "I scored from a rebound after I had seen my penalty saved. Penalties are always pressure but if you are confident then you are not really that nervous. It didn't bother me. OK, my penalty was saved but at least I hit the target and got a second chance. I missed my first one at Hearts when I was 18. I blasted it over the bar. I learned that was the golden rule, always make the goalkeeper work."

The title race looked to be done and dusted but there was still time for the Dark Blues to breathe some life into proceedings. Iain Ferguson pulled a goal back for Dundee and left United midfielder Billy Kirkwood firmly in the sights of his furious manager. Kirkwood revealed: "It was my headed clearance that set-up Iain Ferguson's goal and it made it a very tense finale for us. I don't know if Jim was shouting at me at that time. I was used to it, it was like water off a duck's back. Thankfully, we managed to hold on and all was forgotten by the final whistle."

Long-serving keeper Hamish McAlpine admitted the final minutes were nail-biting to say the least. "When Iain Ferguson scored for Dundee there were a few nerves but we were still 2-1 up and looking fairly comfortable," McAlpine claimed. "But, we couldn't become complacent because we knew Dundee would be trying their hardest not to let their city rivals win the league on their own patch. I remember the game, especially the final ten minutes. I kept shouting to the dugout to ask how long to go.

They couldn't hear me and clearly their attentions were elsewhere.

"I just looked up at the clock at Dens Park and it showed there were three minutes to go. It was the longest time of my life. The clock looked like it had stopped. We were also aware that Celtic were beating Rangers, we heard that from the crowd. I was just so relieved when the final whistle went and I knew we were champions."

Also the final countdown left striker Paul Sturrock in agony, in more ways than one.

Sturrock recalled: "My hamstring went in that final game of the season at Dens Park. It went in the last ten minutes of the game and it was a nightmare. I was injured but I kicked every ball and what made it even worse was that I was also sitting next to Jim McLean and Walter Smith, which was an experience in itself. That probably left me in as much pain as my hamstring! The injury ended up keeping me out for four or five months at the start of the following season. It meant I had to miss the early rounds of our European Cup campaign."

Winger Ralph Milne had set United on their way and was also well-positioned come the final whistle to avoid the massive black and tangerine pitch invasion. He explained: "I went over to the other side of the pitch at the end of the game because I knew the field was away to get invaded. So when the whistle went I think I was the first one up the tunnel and into the away dressing room. Then after everything was calmed down the police allowed us to go out for a lap of honour. That was amazing."

Delighted manager Jim McLean achieved so much in his long spell at Tannadice but he is in no doubt that day was his and the club's crowning glory. It was also ironic that the league was won at the ground where he started his coaching career. McLean said: "You only have to look at how many other teams outside Celtic and Rangers have actually won the league. It hasn't happened very often at all. There is no doubt that was the greatest achievement for me personally and for all the players we had at the time. All the success we had was down to them.

"How good you were can be gauged by whether or not you won the league. The league was always vital to me. I also have to say I don't know how we managed to win the title with as few players as we did. I suppose we were lucky with injuries and we had a wee bit of good fortunate along the way."

It may have been the highlight for McLean and most of the others but not everybody in that title-winning squad was happy with how the championship was clinched. "It was a pretty rubbish game," Eammon Bannon simply stated. "If I am being honest I didn't enjoy the game or the celebrations as much as I should have because we hadn't won the title with the same flair and attacking play we had shown over the rest of the season. I had envisaged us beating Dundee 3 or 4-0, that is how stupid I was. It was nothing like it. It was a pretty nervy and dour affair. The most important thing was that we won and if I could turn back the clock to that day then now I would celebrate like mad. You also think will it happen again? But of course it didn't. I am not sure you will ever see another non-Old Firm team winning the league again."

The feelings in the Tannadice ranks that day were a mixture of joy, jubilation, disbelief and of sheer relief. Paul Hegarty, who like Hamish McAlpine and David Narey had played in every league game that season, joked: "Looking back could you have imagined if we had lost the league to our local rivals, Dundee? That would have been virtually unforgivable. We got there although it was quite nervy. Some of the results might have looked quite comfortable but I think we started to feel the pressure. We got ourselves in the driving seat and it was just relief when we ended up getting there."

The celebrations back at Dens Park were also a bit flat as manager Jim McLean had refused to jinx things by allowing any celebratory drinks into the away dressing room before the game.

Paul Hegarty explained: "Jim McLean was superstitious. There was no champagne in the dressing room because he didn't want us to be left with egg on our faces. So when we got back in we had nothing to drink and we had to send somebody up to the Hilton hotel to get some bottles of champagne. I could understand why Jim did what he did. You would rather win the league and not have champagne than look stupid, have it on ice and then you fail to win the league.

"We ended up going back to Frank Kopel's house to celebrate because there was nothing organised by the club, although we did have a few wee drinks in the Tannadice boardroom after we walked down the road from Dens Park."

Hamish McAlpine admitted that even a lot of the Dundee fans joined their United counterparts to cheer the new champions of Scotland back down the road to Tannadice. "I don't even think Jim McLean slagged any of the team after the game," McAlpine laughed. "That showed he must have been happy. It was probably due to the fact that nobody would have listened. We all got it from Wee Jim at some point but he always did it to get a reaction or to make you a better player. We had won the league and it didn't matter how much he ranted and raved, but in all seriousness he was delighted, like every single one of us. When we walked from Dens to Tannadice the street was just mobbed. There were even a few Dundee fans who clapped us. That was a nice touch."

The initial celebrations may have been a sober affair but the drinks started to flow even though the club had pencilled them in for a testimonial at Forfar Athletic the next day. Ralph Milne revealed his far from ideal preparations. He said: "I ended up leaving a house party at 5am and had to be at Forfar for that testimonial. I was as match-fit as you can be under those circumstances."

Eammon Bannon had also planned a road trip to Edinburgh for an old pal – although he knows he would be crazy to make such a journey in that condition today. The former Chelsea and Hearts star admitted: "Our celebrations were pretty low-key. Also the next day I missed the celebrations in Dundee because I had agreed to go down and play in Jim McArthur's testimonial. I ended up going down to Edinburgh with a raging hangover."

The other amazing feat was the fact that the championship had been clinched using just 20 players, although it was mainly a core of 15 or 16 that McLean really called upon. Paul Sturrock admitted: "We gelled very quickly and we had a very good season. We didn't use a lot of players either, I think it was something like 15 or 16, which was quite incredible. We were lucky with injuries and we also had strong characters who were able to play through a lot of their injuries. I struggled with a hamstring injury in the final four or five weeks of the season. It meant I could hardly train if I wanted to be fit for the Saturday and I had to take pain-killing injections just to get me through."

For a certain Richard Gough it was to be the first of ten Scottish League titles, although the other nine were to be achieved in the light blue of Rangers. The former Scottish international said: "It was my first championship and although I won quite a few in my time it was a very special championship. We had a great squad and that back four was one of the strongest I played with in my career. The defence was the springboard for the team, that allowed the flair players to kick on."

For many other top-quality players that was to be the one and only title medal of their careers. Looking back the common consensus is that it is unlikely the title flag will ever be seen flying above Tannadice again.

"It is only as the years have passed that people have realised what an enormous achievement it was," Paul Hegarty claimed. "Looking back Sir Alex Ferguson's Aberdeen team have won the league but outside the New Firm nobody else has come close. If I am being truthful I don't know if we will see Dundee United win the league again. I hope I am wrong but it would take a real monumental effort."

Youngster Maurice Malpas was delighted to get a taste of the high life so early in his career and hoped it would be the first title of many. That was something that never quite materialised.

He explained: "It was a great feeling but I remember thinking we will be doing this again next year and the year after. I didn't really appreciate what a great achievement it was. I didn't realise until much later what a lucky boy I had been. We had another couple of chances to win the league again but we never got over the line. What we achieved, looking back that season, was phenomenal."

Sturrock, who ended up top scorer with 24 goals, admitted his league title medal is the pride of his medal and cap haul. The Ellon-born striker fought off tough competition from Milne and Davie Dodds. He said: "I finished top scorer but we never had a competition. I never saw myself as a goalscorer. I saw myself more as a playmaker. Looking back it was pleasing to finish top scorer but the real achievement was winning the league. There have only been three teams who have won the Premier League outside of the Old Firm. So it makes my medal a very unique one and something I feel really proud of."

Bannon believes the New Firm made the most of a talented young crop of players and the Old Firm's lack of financial muscle to produce such a golden era in the Scottish game. "There were probably three reasons why the New Firm emerged," Bannon stated. "The Old Firm weren't spending big, big money like happened when Graeme Souness arrived at Rangers. The second thing was that it also came at a time when Aberdeen, Hearts and Dundee United produced a good crop of players. It was a boom time for Scottish players coming through the ranks.

"The final reason was that it was during the old contract system and players couldn't just walk out when their existing deals came to a close. Now it has gone full circle, the players now have the power come the end of their deals. They can go to the club that gives them the most money or that suits them best. Back in our day if the club wanted to keep your registration then you couldn't move to another club."

The 1983-84 season also brought even more to look forward to at the bottom end of Sandeman Street. The Terrors were about to get their first crack at the European Cup. The champions of Scotland could now test themselves against the best in Europe. The team had already done themselves proud in previous seasons in the Uefa Cup but now they were deservedly going shoulder to shoulder with the best.

Maltese side Flamrun Spartans were thrashed in the qualifying round then Standard Liege were sent packing before a tighter affair in the quarter-final saw United squeeze past Rapid Vienna on away goals. That amazing run put McLean's men into the last four where they were drawn against the might of Italian giants AS Roma. They started well and goals from Davie Dodds and Derek Stark in the home leg gave them a more then credible 2-0 win to take over to the Stadio Olimpico for the return. United lost 3-0 in the Italian capital amid some rather ugly and dubious circumstances.

"The referee from the second leg against Roma was bribed as we all know," Sturrock disappointingly stated. "Roma have recently admitted that was the case. I find it a disgrace that Uefa have not overturned that original decision especially after Roma's admission. It was quite obvious because the referee was laughing and joking with the Roma players and gave them everything. It wouldn't have mattered what the score was in the first leg because they would have got whatever result they needed in the second leg because of the referee.

"That was a big disappointment for me because I have no doubt we were a better team than Roma. It still annoys me we didn't win and I feel so upset about the way we were cheated and so much so that I am still thinking about writing a letter to Sepp Blatter to tell him how I feel. Roma's runners-up medals should be taken off them and given to our Dundee United team."

The final whistle saw some ugly scenes and saw some United players and officials get involved in some ugly scuffles with the Italians. Milne, who is still United's all-time European top scorer, reckons that sort of underhand approach was rife within the game. "It was disappointing but wasn't the only time it happened," Milne insisted. "I am certain that it happened in quite a few of our European games over the years. It seemed to be a common occurrence especially when you went to some of the eastern European countries."

For Billy Kirkwood it was a nightmare for a game that should have been such a showcase to end. Kirkwood admitted: "It just showed that even back then that the authorities always wanted the so-called bigger teams in the finals. It was hard to take but it is a long time ago now. I still have some good memories from that semi-final, especially from the first game against Roma at Tannadice. Playing against top stars like Falcao was something you dream about."

Since then former Roma director Riccardo Viola confirmed that his side paid French referee Michel Vautrot £50,000 ahead of the second leg.

It was no surprise to Jim McLean as he had already been told that his team had been cheated and Europe's governing body had tried to cover it up. McLean revealed: "I was at a game in Perth and I got out of the car and the late Ernie Walker shouted on me. He said I have to apologise for what happened against Roma. He told me we had been cheated by Roma and he had no doubts at all. He told me he had been on the Uefa committee and had tried to do all he could for justice but the football authorities had just brushed it under the carpet. It has since been confirmed that Roma did attempt to bribe the officials.

"It does leave an open wound. It annoys me because sport should be kept clean and there is no doubt it wasn't around that time. The medals should have been taken off the Roma players for even attempting to bribe the referee. What I can say is that I still don't think we played well enough in the second game to win the match. We had the players to do it but we didn't perform over the two legs."

Malpas revealed the locals had been up to their dirty tricks from the moment United touched down in Italy. He explained: "We were evacuated from our hotel the night before the game, there was aggro in the tunnel and the team coach also got stoned coming into the ground. It was disappointing the way it all ended. I think to get to the last four of the European Cup is right up there with winning the league. It was unbelievable for a team and a squad of our size."

The Scotland defender also admitted it made it even harder to watch Roma take their place in the European Cup final, although justice was done when Liverpool beat them to lift the trophy. The one silver lining from that season was the young defender was given his international break.

Malpas admitted: "It was disappointing to watch that European Cup final between Liverpool and Roma, knowing it could have been us. The good thing for me was that I got capped after we lost to Roma. Jock Stein was in our travelling party and he pulled me in at the airport and told me I would be getting capped for Scotland. I made my debut later that year and that made up for a lot of the disappointment."

Manager Jim McLean was a major factor in United's success although his disciplined, no-nonsense approach wasn't always popular with his players and others within the game.

Richard Gough is in no doubt that had it not been for McLean then they would never have achieved what they did. Gough admitted: "Every time I am back up in Dundee I try to pop in and see Wee Jim. For me, I have huge respect for him. My dad was a soldier when I was growing up so I was used to the discipline. His bawling and shouting never bothered me. It probably inspired me more than anything. He was very good for me and I have always held him in high regard. He is crazy but in a good way. He had a real talent for spotting good young players or something in other guys who clubs disregarded. He also would never accept second best."

That is one of the main reasons why McLean, who also led his team to the 1987 Uefa Cup final, will be assured of his place in Scotland's footballing hall of fame. "Jim McLean has to go down as one of the legends of the Scottish game," Sturrock insisted. "He led a provincial club like Dundee United to the one and only Premier League title in their history and also into the semi-final of the European Cup. When was the last time that happened? He might have upset his players at times but he will still be remembered as a giant of the Scottish game."

The last word however must be left to McLean. When asked about the day he led Dundee United to the title, he said: "Contrary to popular belief I do smile from time to time and believe me my players gave me something to smile about and be proud of the day we won the league."

DUNDEE UNITED'S TITLE-WINNING SQUAD:
Hamish McAlpine, Maurice Malpas, Derek Stark, Richard Gough, Paul Hegarty, David Narey, Ian Britton, Ralph Milne, Billy Kirkwood, Paul Sturrock, David Dodds, Eammon Bannon, Graeme Payne, Iain Phillip, John Holt, Alex Taylor, John Reilly, John Clark, John McNeil and Derek Murray.
Manager: Jim McLean.

4

• ABERDEEN •
THE GOTHENBURG GREATS

ABERDEEN already had a couple of seasons of European experience under their belt. Alex Ferguson and his team were beginning to find their feet after being left short against Liverpool in the 1980-81 European Cup and then by German giants Hamburg in the Uefa Cup the following campaign. The 1982-83 season they entered the European Cup Winners' Cup after they had beaten Rangers to lift the Scottish Cup.

Striker Mark McGhee admitted: "Winning the league and Scottish Cup changed the mindset at Aberdeen. People were now asking can we win more? There was a different expectation from outwith the club than within it. That season there wasn't a priority. It was a case of flat to the floor in every game and every competition. We didn't save anything for anyone. We hardly trained because the games came so thick and fast."

The draw was certainly kind to the Dons as they were paired with Swiss minnows Sion in the preliminary round. The tie was finished after a clinical 90 minutes at Pittodrie. Sion were cruelly put to the sword as they were hit by seven without reply. Eric Black, Gordon Strachan, John Hewitt, Mark McGhee, Stewart Kennedy, Neil Simpson and an own goal put Aberdeen on easy street.

Simpson recalled: "I scored a chip from the edge of the box. That Sion team weren't that bad but we were at the top of our game. Everything we hit that night ended up in the net. It was an unbelievable performance."

McGhee also got in on the act in the 4-1 second leg win in Sion. He netted a double, while captain Willie Miller and young John Hewitt also netted to give Aberdeen an impressive aggregate win.

McGhee admitted: "I scored a scrambled goal in the first game. I think I had six attempts at it although I have to say I was never a clinical finisher. That win was a huge confidence booster to us all. It was all new to most of the boys and we didn't really know what to expect. We were still relative euro novices. I then scored a couple out in Switzerland and it was just a game we wanted to push aside so we could look forward to the next round."

The first round proper also left Aberdeen a million miles away from the glamour and big names as they clashed with Albanian side Dinamo Tirana. The first leg, once again, was at Pittodrie and after a stuffy display the visitors were finally broken by a solitary strike from Hewitt. The second leg was even tighter as Aberdeen held out for a goalless draw to squeeze through.

For Gordon Strachan that trip was an eye-opener – on and off the field. "I remember going to Tirana and normally when you visited countries like these then 99 per cent of the people were poor and then the other one per cent had everything," Strachan claimed. "In Albania they had absolutely nothing. Everyone was in the same boat. They had absolutely nothing! I thought if that is communism you can keep it! We went to the hotel and there was absolutely nothing, not even a television."

Aberdeen continued to make solid progress and were handed another favourable draw when they landed Lech Poznan in the second round. Another clean sheet and goals from Mark McGhee and Peter Weir gave the Dons a decent lead to take out to Poland.

"Poznan had one of the biggest central defenders I have ever seen," McGhee joked. "I think he was 6ft 7in, at least. It was a tight affair and I got our opener but it was hard and we were glad to get Peter Weir's goal to give us a bit of a cushion."

Everybody at Pittodrie knew they would be pushed to the maximum in the second leg but once again the Dons managed to shut up shop and make it back-to-back wins with a Dougie Bell goal. He revealed how the famous Fergie hairdryer helped him blow the Poles away.

"McGhee put a header across the face of the goal and I was there to head it in," Bell admitted. "I was just delighted to get the goal because it not only killed the tie but also got the manager off my back. He had spent the entire half-time interval slaughtering me and Peter Weir and had even said he was going to take us both off."

Scotland and Aberdeen defender Alex McLeish is in no doubt those early European ties provided vital experience and know-how for everyone at Pittodrie. He explained: "Sion, Tirana and Lech Poznan were all hard games and matches that were all potential banana skins. But we showed our character, mental strength along with our ability to play got us through those early rounds. Games like the ones against Tirana were really tight and we had to stay focused and concentrated to get through. They were arguably tougher than some of the bigger names we faced in the tournament that season."

Aberdeen had a lot to look forward to going into 1983 as they pushed for the title, the Scottish Cup and success in the European Cup Winners' Cup. The glamour and glitz that the north-east public craved eventually came at the quarter-final stage when Fergie's men were matched with the German superpower of Bayern Munich.

This time there was no home game to help them find their feet. They went straight into the cauldron of Munich's Olympic Stadium, the football home of world superstars like Karl-Heinz Rummenigge, Klaus Augenthaler, Paul Breitner and Uli Hoeness. Goalkeeper Jim Leighton revealed how the Aberdeen players had been fired up by disrespectful comments from Bayern's Hungarian coach Pal Csernai after he had travelled to watch them beat Dundee. Csernai was made to re-evaluate his opinion after a superb rearguard action handed the Dons a morale-boosting goalless draw.

Leighton said: "That was the first time we had made European football beyond Christmas. We drew Bayern and the omens also weren't good because we had never beaten a German team. Bundesliga teams were the yardstick at that time but we had always just come up short against them, going out by the odd goal or even on away goals. Their manager had also written us off because he had come over and watched us on the Saturday and claimed there was no way Aberdeen would beat Bayern because the average age of our team was only 22-and-a-half. Fergie had always been telling us we were good enough to win that tournament and the performance we put on in Munich that night also made us believe we could. We could easily have won that match by a couple of goals. That result and display gave us the confidence that we could take them back to Aberdeen and beat them."

Young Neale Cooper, who had come through the ranks, rates that evening in Munich as the pinnacle of his playing days. He said: "The game out in Munich goes down as my all-time favourite game. We were up against a team of superstars and we went out with a game plan that completely nullified them. They had top players like Karl-Heinz Rummenigge and Paul Breitner. I was up directly against Breitner and it was amazing just being on the field with somebody like that. But the manager made sure that reputations counted for nothing. When it came to the games we believed we could hold our own against the best."

Captain Miller helped to make sure there were no gaps in the Aberdeen defence that evening but that was more than could be said about his mouth. He painfully recalled: "I got my front tooth kicked out. Rummenigge was pretty famous for his overhead kicks back then, that was his trademark. They had a corner and he attempted an overhead kick at the near post. The ball was there to be won. I went and won it with my head and Rummenigge caught my front tooth and it just cracked and pinged out.

"In those days there wasn't as much advanced technology as there is now and I had to come back in the plane with a bit of chewing gum stuck into the root and that with a couple of pain-killers helped to numb the pain. Believe it or not my tooth has caused me unbelievable pain and discomfort ever since. The pain and torture though was certainly worth it as it helped us to progress in the European Cup Winners' Cup."

Ferguson gave Dougie Bell the man of the match award, just ahead of Peter Weir, out in the Olympic Stadium and then rewarded him with the axe as they returned to play Kilmarnock in the league.

Bell proudly admitted: "The manager gave me the man of the match award after that game. It was one of those games where I was able to run at the Bayern defence and that was probably my forte. I knew that if I had gone on a run in the domestic games then I would have got dog's abuse and sooner rather than later the board was going to go up with my number on it. I felt I had done really well and I came back on a real high. We then played Kilmarnock in the game after we came back and after praising me to the high heavens I didn't even make the substitutes' bench. That was the way the manager was and you just had to get on with it."

The scene was set for a rocking European night at Pittodrie with the winner-takes-all second leg. This time Ferguson was more interested in knocking out the Germans than containing them.

"The manager sent us out with a game plan to cancel them out in Munich," McLeish revealed. "We defended really well and really snuffed them out. We came back to Pittodrie and the manager told us to go out and win it. He told us you only need to score one more than them – which was easier said than done!"

A 24,000 crowded crammed into Pittodrie hoping to witness one of Scottish football's greatest ever European nights. That hope quickly turned to despair when Klaus Augenthaler cracked home the opener and gave Bayern a vital away goal, although Neil Simpson levelled to give the home faithful some hope. Simmie admitted: "I'm probably the goalscorer that nobody remembers. Everybody knows the guys who scored our final two goals but everyone forgets mine.

"Alex McLeish played it to Mark McGhee. He crossed it to the far post and Eric Black managed to get it back. Klaus Augenthaler was on the line to stop it. Normally he would clear his lines but he obviously thought I am a great player and I will have time to take it down. As Augenthaler took a touch I took him and the ball and it ended up in the back of the net. It was a great feeling."

The Dons looked to be down and out when Hans Pflugler put the Germans back ahead. Going into the final 15 minutes Fergie and his side needed a miracle – and they more than produced one. The brilliantly crafted dummy free kick routine of John McMaster and Gordon Strachan, before the latter curled the ball on to the head of McLeish for the equaliser, will be forever guaranteed a place in Pittodrie folklore. The stunned Bayern players weren't even given time to regroup when Aberdeen famously turned the tie on its head when super-sub John Hewitt netted the winner.

He recalled: "John McMaster had set up a chance for Eric Black that the goalkeeper saved. I think the goalkeeper was taken a bit by surprise because he didn't catch the ball or push it over the bar. He just palmed it into my path. The manager always told us to follow up in case the goalkeeper spilled. I did that but I actually got there a fraction too early and if you watch the goal back my standing leg, my right, goes away from me, but I still managed to hook my left foot round the ball and direct it towards goal and it went through the goalkeeper's legs and into the net.

"I got a bit of luck but people say you make your own luck. For atmosphere that night at Pittodrie was right up there. I have never seen or heard anything like it in terms of atmosphere. I don't know if we will ever see another night like it in Aberdeen's history."

Aberdeen managed to see that famous win out and Leighton believes that was his team's top performance of that trophy-encrusted campaign. The keeper admitted: "Pittodrie was some place to play on a European night. We had a great record at Pittodrie and they were special occasions out there in front of the lights. I would say that night beating Bayern was bigger than even beating Real Madrid in the final."

That evening will go down as one of Aberdeen's greatest European nights but it wasn't one that satisfied all the fans. Strachan joked: "Everyone knows I don't listen to radio phone-ins and maybe that night is the reason why. All the boys decided to go out for a drink after the Bayern game but I just decided to go home and gather my thoughts and take it all in myself. So as I was driving home an Aberdeen fan came on the radio on one of those phone-ins. He said: 'The whole Aberdeen team were brilliant, apart from that Gordon Strachan. He was nowhere near it tonight!' I couldn't believe it! We had just produced one of the greatest Europe results in Scottish football history and I was still getting stick."

The rigours of battling for success on three fronts also took its toll on Ferguson's limited squad and after the high of beating Bayern they plunged to the low of losing at home in the league to title rivals Dundee United. That Pittodrie defeat allowed their New Firm rivals to go on and claim their one and only title.

McLeish admitted: "It was after that game that I think the manager realised he needed to rotate his squad more. We had just beaten Bayern Munich and we played Dundee United that weekend. They were the better team and deserved to beat us. They went on to win the league and they deserved to win the title although for us it was probably a step too far."

All efforts were being directed into their European campaign and they were given hope when they avoided Real Madrid in the semi-finals. The Spaniards landed Austria Vienna while Ferguson's finest went head-to-head with Belgian outfit Waterschei.

It was a match where Aberdeen went in full of confidence and it wasn't to be misplaced as they tore Waterschei apart in one of the most one-sided European semi-finals of all time in the Pittodrie first leg. The Dons, who were watched by Sir Alf Ramsey and Jock Stein, were inspired by a midfield masterclass from Dougie Bell in the 5-1 win. Bell joked: "That is the game all the Aberdeen fans talk about when I see them. I played over 200 games for the club but it seems like Waterschei was the only one they really remember."

Eric Black sent the Dons on their way. He said: "I scored the first goal. It was hardly a classic because it came off my shin but to score in the semi-final of a European tournament was great."

The second came from a fine solo effort from Simpson. "That was probably one of my best goals for tenacity and a little bit of skill as well," Simmie beamed. "I took the ball off somebody, sidestepped another and I opened up with a decent strike that beat the keeper. It was some feeling to score in a European semi-final. We had beaten Waterschei 5-1 and we could start thinking about the final. I remember going to training. There was an old guy who used to come and watch us. We came out and he was shaking his head and he said to us that away goal against Waterschei could be costly!"

The icing was put on the cake as a Peter Weir goal and a Mark McGhee double made it a glory night despite Lars Gudmundsson's late consolation. McGhee admitted: "We thought it was a good draw but we never anticipated the first leg demolition. The whole night was rocking and rolling. Dougie Bell was exceptional, that was his big night. Dougie crossed the ball for me and I managed to nick it past the keeper at the front post. My second came when Strachan crossed. I had three or four attempts blocked before I netted to make it 5-1. It was unbelievable and we just wanted to see the second leg out and look forward to the final. I am sure Waterschei were a better team than they showed at Pittodrie."

Before the return Aberdeen also had a last-four clash with Celtic in the Scottish Cup. They won that match, thanks to a Peter Weir goal. That game also cruelly ended the Europe dream of one particular Don.

Bell recalled: "I broke my ankle in the Scottish Cup semi-final against Celtic. I played on because Eric Black and Neale Cooper had already gone off with knocks. It wasn't until I got on the bus that my ankle really began to swell up. I went to the hospital the next day and it was put in plaster for a fortnight although I still thought I could be ready for Gothenburg. Everything went to plan until we had a bounce game and my ankle went again."

The second game with Waterschei was nothing more than a formality. The Belgians did salvage some pride with a 1-0 win but the real damage to Aberdeen was done to defender Stuart Kennedy. Gordon Strachan admitted: "What I remember from that night was Stuart Kennedy suffered that horrific knee injury. It was such a shame because he struggled to play after that and never got back to the level we had seen when he was at his peak with Aberdeen. He was a good player and a great professional."

The game, however, did give Ian Angus a rare taste of the European arena. The midfielder said: "I picked up a Cup Winners' Cup medal but it doesn't really mean a lot to me because I only played 40 minutes in the entire run. I played in the second leg of the semi-final against Waterschei but apart from that I was on the bench for the rest of the games."

Real Madrid, not surprisingly, brushed aside the Austrians in the other semi-final so Ferguson and his team would provide the final obstacle in Gothenburg's Ullevi Stadium. Ferguson, a master of the footballer's mind, went to great lengths to put the emphasis on his team rather than the legendary Spaniards.

McGhee said: "None of us were allowed to think that it was Real Madrid we were going to be playing. Alex protected us from Real Madrid and who they were. There was no talk of them. I didn't go into that game in awe of Real Madrid. He had everybody in Pittodrie briefed that he didn't want people to talk Real Madrid up, even the press."

The Aberdeen manager and his loyal assistant, Archie Knox, had their preparations set out to a tee, from the players to the travel arrangements of their wives. Doug Rougvie revealed: "Fergie got all the wives in and even gave them their itinerary for the trip to Gothenburg, which looking back now was quite funny. They had to take certain items of hardware, like sleeping bags, towels and soaps and all that. They basically had to take all this stuff because they were being put up in dormitories. That gave the boys a bit of a laugh."

Euro fever gripped the Red Army as thousands of fans made the trip to Sweden, by ferry, fishing boat, car and plane. Ferguson also decided to add some additional experience to his backroom staff when he invited Scotland and European Cup-winning Celtic boss Jock Stein to travel with his Aberdeen team.

Every one of the players went out not hoping but believing that they would lift the European Cup Winners' Cup. Jim Leighton said: "None of the players had one negative thought in our heads, we believed we would be heading back to Aberdeen with the trophy. We were going to play the might of Real Madrid but every one of us had 100 per cent belief we would beat them. There were no doubts whatever. We trained the night before on the pitch and then came off and Real Madrid went on after us. Fergie wouldn't even let us stay and watch them in case anybody became overawed or any seeds of doubt were put into our heads."

Captain Willie Miller echoed those sentiments. "Confidence was the over-riding feeling," he admitted. "When you go into big games you have to have confidence, determination and self-belief if you are going to achieve anything. Confidence was always an important factor and we had that after we knocked out Bayern Munich. The Germans were always one of the top teams and if you could beat them then you always felt you had a great chance of winning the tournament."

Neil Simpson is in no doubt that confidence came from the manager. "We almost felt invincible and that was down to Fergie," Simpson acknowledged. "Tactically we were spot on and we had determined players with a lot of skill and flair. It was good and things really took off and we even made the seven-inch Europe single. I felt as confident going into that game as I did going into a normal league game."

For local boys John Hewitt and Neale Cooper the pre-match build-up was when they realised what they were on the verge of. Cooper said: "I was rooming with John Hewitt and we went to our beds in the afternoon for a sleep. We were just lying there speaking about the game. We couldn't believe that two local boys from Aberdeen were about to play in a European final."

Hewitt was just delighted to be involved because the majority of his season had been curtailed by injury. He said: "I knew I would be on the bench. I was just grateful to be involved, knowing I might get the chance to play some part."

Strachan also decided he had time for a late haircut in the final build-up. He revealed: "I remember we were sitting on the bus on the way to the game. I had the personal cassette player on and I was listening to a bit of Meatloaf. It was just the wettest day. I remember going out for my warm-up and it was so wet that I actually went and got a pair of scissors off Teddy Scott and cut my hair so I could actually see. I went into that game quietly confident.

"I didn't see Real Madrid as a problem. That wasn't arrogance but we had played a lot of the top English sides, like Ipswich, Southampton and West Ham in friendlies and beaten them, so I knew we had a good team. I just remember it was a hard, hard game and the conditions were just a nightmare."

Ferguson was never one to show a great deal of sentiment but that evening he did when he named Stuart Kennedy on the bench even though he wasn't 100 per cent fit. Rougvie admitted: "Stuart was on the bench but was nowhere near fit. It was a night where Fergie showed a very rare moment of leniency. I had to play left-back as Stuart was injured."

The heavens opened and there had been fears that the game might not go ahead – as Ferguson built his players up to believe they were as good, if not better, than the likes of the greats like Johnny Metgod, Uli Stielike, Santillana and Jose Camacho.

McGhee joked: "It was the wettest night in Swedish history. It was like Noah's flood. My mum, brother and friends were there although my dad was working abroad and missed it. We believed Real were looking down their noses at us. They seemed pretty dismissive and that suited us that they had as good as lifted the cup. Even the international press had Real Madrid down as winners and were giving us a pat on the back for just getting to the final. We just blanked everything out and it was 11 versus 11 and that was how we focused on it. It was a huge shock to a lot of people that it didn't turn out like that."

Cooper revealed how those early exchanges showed that reputations counted for nothing. "I was up against Uli Stielike and I managed to make my mark with a couple of hefty challenges on him," the midfielder admitted. "The heavy conditions and sodden pitch also probably helped us."

The Real Madrid stars might have been taken aback but they were left staggered when Aberdeen went ahead after a well-worked move. Goal hero Black explained: "We had a corner, which wee Gordon took. We had discussed things before with Alex McLeish coming in late at the back post. Gordon then flighted the ball in, Alex has got a good contact on it, forcing the goalkeeper to make a save and the ball spiralled and then spun into the mud. The pitch, probably, has helped me because the ball stuck a bit and it gave me time to react to get a toe on it to beat the keeper and send the ball into the far corner. It was a great feeling although it didn't last that long because Real Madrid got a quick equaliser."

The leveller was down to a rare error from a Dons stalwart rather than any individual brilliance from Real. A red-faced McLeish admitted: "I had been involved in Eric Black's opener and then I had a hand in Real Madrid's equaliser, 99.9 per cent of the time I would have played a ball back to Jim Leighton but this time it got caught up on the heavy surface. Santillana got there before Jim and won the penalty that saw Juanito get their equaliser. It was a real sore one but I knew I had to recover and show my mental toughness. I was even more determined to help us win the game."

It was a blow to be pegged back but Mark McGhee was always confident that Aberdeen would rise again – even if they had to put up with some rough-house tactics from Real. He said: "The pitch was heavy but I still felt fresh. I also felt we were physically stronger than the Real Madrid players. I had a great battle with the legendary Spanish defender Jose Camacho. I felt I battered him and eventually he got taken off. I remember his replacement, San Jose, came on and the first chance he got he punched me in the face. I couldn't believe it. It probably took my jaw about a year to get over it."

McGhee managed to pick himself up and help Aberdeen land the knockout punch on the European heavyweights. McGhee recalled: "I found myself out on the left in Weir's position. He played me in and I just focused on trying to get the ball off the ground. It was on my left foot and I knew I had to get the ball away. I barely got it in the air because John had to stoop for it. I knew people were running into the box. I didn't pick John out, I just put it into an area where I hoped we would get a chance."

Hewitt had already had a premonition on the bench that he would come on to score the winner. He said: "If you ask any front player then you always have a feeling you will score. It was hard coming on to get up to speed and to adapt to the conditions. I was just hoping for a chance and it eventually came. John McMaster played it to Peter Weir who beat a couple of men and gave the ball to Mark McGhee.

"I was just watching Mark because I didn't know what he was going to do. Sometimes he would cross or on other occasions he would beat his man and then cut back and beat him again. I was bearing in on goal, unmarked, and when he did cross it, the keeper came out and I knew he wasn't getting it. It was just a case of me directing my header into the empty goal. I was ecstatic.

"The importance of my goal didn't sink in for me until the following day when we returned to Aberdeen and saw fans everywhere. That win has been the highlight of the club's history and probably will be for evermore."

Aberdeen might have been in total control but there was still time for a few nervy moments as the Scots tried to see the game out. Leighton admitted: "We knew it was pretty close to the end when they got that free kick. I remember I had lined up the wall and Peter Weir, who is not religious in any way, was shouting at the top of his voice 'please God, please God, don't let them score. They don't deserve to score'.

"They put the free kick straight into my arms but the referee made them take it again. I went full out for the second ball and I just dived at it. I can't tell you how wide of the post it went. I couldn't tell you if it was going one inch inside or outside of the post. I was just hoping I was going to hear the ball splash into a puddle than hit the back of the net. Thankfully, it went wide."

The final whistle went and the celebrations, quite literally, left Ferguson floored. Black revealed: "I had been substituted so I was on the bench when the final whistle went. I just remember Bryan Gunn knocking over the gaffer and leaving a big size ten on his back. There was a sort of chuckle and a euphoria combined. We just couldn't believe we had done it as we charged onto the pitch. Even then we couldn't believe we had just won the European Cup Winners' Cup against one of the biggest clubs in the world."

Captain Miller, who become only the third Scottish skipper to lift a European trophy, went up to pick up the cup. He believes the achievement of that night has grown with every passing year.

Miller recalled: "I felt joy and enormous pride when that whistle went. At the time I was also pretty ecstatic and there was a real feeling of achievement. I had a lot of different emotions and it is a night that will live with me forever when I went up and I lifted the trophy. It was a special feeling going up there as captain of such a great team. I don't think any of us realised how big that trophy was going to be."

McLeish was delighted and acknowledged he owed a huge debt to super-sub Hewitt. McLeish admitted: "When the final whistle went I was delighted but I also felt as if John Hewitt had got me right off the hook. Winning that trophy was amazing. At the time I probably didn't realise what we had done. But looking back now it must go down as one of the greatest ever achievements in British never mind Scottish football. This team of nobodies, made up only of Scottish players, could go and win a European tournament, knocking out Bayern Munich and Real Madrid along the way. I don't think we will see anything like it again."

McGhee reckons it is a game that will live with him forever. He said: "It was a very individual feeling at the end of the game. It was such a big moment for us and Scottish football but also for our family and friends. I loved every medal I picked up in my career but scoring for Scotland against England and winning the Cup Winners' Cup were two massive things for me."

Leighton also rates that night in the Ullevi as the greatest of his much decorated domestic career. The number one said: "The pinnacle for me was playing for Scotland in the World Cup opener against Brazil at France 98. Domestically, the highlight was lifting the European Cup Winners' Cup. No other Scottish team has won a European competition since. I don't know if we will see another Scottish club win a European trophy, especially in my lifetime.

"I was just delighted we won it outright. Even if we had won it on penalty kicks it wouldn't have been the same as beating Real Madrid in a match. We put on an incredible performance and if we had beat them 3-1 or 4-1 then they couldn't have complained. We just ran over the top of them in extra-time."

Neale Cooper was delighted his family had been there to enjoy the occasion with him. "I was so excited when the final whistle went," the midfielder admitted. "I just couldn't believe it. Then my mind went to my mum and my sister in the stands and then to my dad. I lost him when I was five and I just felt sad that he hadn't been there to perhaps see my crowning moment."

Strachan was also pleased that he was able to give his family something back after they had supported him through all the ups and downs. He said: "I was just delighted for my family. They had always come and supported me and I was happier more for them than myself. What we achieved that night was unbelievable. I don't think it dawned on me until several years later, just what we had done that night in Sweden. It wasn't just a great thing for Aberdeen but the whole of Scotland. It was amazing and I don't know if we will see anything like it again."

Almost the whole of Aberdeen turned out to welcome their Euro kings back. Neale Cooper recalled: "We flew back into Aberdeen and we couldn't believe how many people were there waiting for us. We went on the open-top bus the next day and the town was absolutely amazing. There were Aberdeen fans everywhere and what a feeling. It was a fantastic achievement and it clearly meant so much to so many people. Probably one of the greatest results in Scottish football history and one I don't think that will ever be repeated."

Neil Simpson confirmed it was an amazing reception. "They reckoned there was over 100,000 people on Union Street that day," he claimed. "It made the hairs on the back of my neck stand up. I will never forget those scenes."

Black has been left with similar feelings. The striker said: "The reception we got when we arrived back in Aberdeen was breathtaking. There were 200,000 people out on the streets. It was something we never could have imagined. The response from the north-east public was fantastic. We won a lot of trophies during that time but that day was just unforgettable. I can still relive it now, with the open-top bus going down Union Street. It is something I will never forget."

There was even room for a bust-up between McGhee and Ferguson before the Pittodrie lap of honour. It is still unclear as to what happened but it is believed McGhee took exception to something his manager said. Ferguson, for once, took the blame before they patched up their differences and they both headed down to the harbour with the European Cup Winners' Cup to welcome the St Clair ferry back to port on the Friday.

Aberdeen ended the season by going on to lift the Scottish Cup as well but McGhee is in no doubt that European run cost them the league, which was eventually won by their New Firm rivals, Jim McLean's Dundee United.

McGhee said: "I definitely think Europe and the Scottish Cup left us short in the league. We were going into the league games with injuries and the Cup Winners' Cup became a distraction. It definitely cost us a few points and we only lost the league by one point. I think we should have won the SPL that season. We were all disappointed to the point where it did affect our feeling about the other two wins. Ridiculous as it seems it was an opportunity of a lifetime to claim a unique treble."

That Aberdeen team also picked up another trophy as they were named as Europe's elite. "Adidas also voted us the best team in Europe," Simpson revealed. "There was Barcelona, Inter, Real Madrid, Bayern Munich, Waterschei and Paris St Germain and we ended up winning it. It was some achievement."

There is a firm belief that fantastic achievement will never be repeated by another Scottish club. Rougvie admitted: "That team was a one-off. For a provincial club like Aberdeen to win a European trophy was truly amazing. Before that people thought that the Old Firm were the only teams in Scotland who had that sort of capability. So for us it was beyond belief."

The European Cup Winners' Cup is no more but Aberdeen have assured they have their place in the competition's history archives. Jim

Leighton explained: "I went to the last European Cup Winners' Cup final at Villa Park in 1999. Lazio beat Real Mallorca and Uefa wanted every club who had won the competition to send down a couple of representatives to the game.

"I went down with Ian Donald (the chairman and son of Dick Donald) and we went on the pitch in the years the teams won the competition. It probably wasn't until that point I realised the enormity of our achievement because in 1982 I had Allan Simonsen of Barcelona on my left and Antonio Cabrini of Juventus on my right."

ABERDEEN'S EUROPEAN CUP WINNERS' CUP RUN 1982-83

* Preliminary round first leg (18th August 1982 at Pittodrie)
    Aberdeen 7 (Black, Strachan, Hewitt, Simpson, McGhee, Kennedy, Balet OG) Sion 0
* Preliminary round second leg (1st September 1982 in Switzerland)
    Sion 1 (Bregy) Aberdeen 4 (Hewitt, Miller, McGhee 2)
* First round first leg (19th September 1982 at Pittodrie)
    Aberdeen 1 (Hewitt) Dinamo Tirana 0
* First round second leg (29th September 1982 in Albania)
    Dinamo Tirana 0 Aberdeen 0
* Second round first leg (20th October 1982 at Pittodrie)
    Aberdeen 2 (McGhee, Weir) Lech Poznan 0
* Second round second leg (3rd November 1982 in Poland)
    Lech Poznan 0 Aberdeen 1 (Bell)
* Quarter-final first leg (2nd March 1983 in Germany)
    Bayern Munich 0 Aberdeen 0
* Quarter-final second leg (16th March 1983 at Pittodrie)
    Aberdeen 3 (Simpson, McLeish, Hewitt) Bayern Munich 2 (Augenthaler, Pflugler)
* Semi-final first leg (6th April 1983 at Pittodrie)
    Aberdeen 5 (Black, Simpson, Weir, McGhee 2) Waterschei 1 (Gudmundsson)
* European Cup Winners' Cup final (11th May 1983 in the Ullevi Stadium, Gothenburg) Aberdeen 2 (Black, Hewitt) Real Madrid 1 (Juanito PEN)

ABERDEEN'S EUROPEAN CUP WINNERS' CUP-WINNING SQUAD

Jim Leighton, Doug Rougvie, John McMaster, Neale Cooper, Alex McLeish, Willie Miller, Gordon Strachan, Neil Simpson, Mark McGhee, Eric Black (John Hewitt), Peter Weir.
Unused subs: Bryan Gunn, Stuart Kennedy, Ian Angus and Andy Watson.
Manager: Alex Ferguson.

• ABERDEEN •
FERGIE'S FURY AT HIS
HAMPDEN HEROES

ABERDEEN may have been Scottish Cup holders but it would have been fair to say the competition wasn't at the top of their list of priorities going into the 1982-83 season. There is no doubt the European Cup Winners' Cup and the Scottish Premier Division were the two main targets. That is not to say Alex Ferguson and his team were going to give up their Scottish Cup without a fight.

The first match in their defence saw them travel to Easter Road in the third round. It turned out to be a relatively straightforward 4-1 win. Peter Weir, Andy Watson, Mark McGhee and Neil Simpson all scored, Gordon Rae responding with Hibs' goal.

Simpson recalled: "It was a really windy day. There was a big crowd at Easter Road and they were very vociferous that day. They were right on top of us. The ball came into the box and I just hit it. The keeper saved it and I just followed it up and put it away. I also set up Andy Watson's goal but it was a good team performance that day. It was a very good victory because it was a potential banana skin."

The fourth round brought about a north-east derby with Dundee. It proved to be a closely-fought encounter with another Simpson strike enough to push the Dons through. Simmie said: "I scored the goal. Peter

Weir crossed it and I fired in a shot that came off the turf and went in. It wasn't a great strike but it was in keeping with the game. I had also played for the Scotland Under-21s and I was voted man of the match against East Germany. I scored and Gordon Strachan was also in the full squad and had also been voted man of the match in that game. It was built up with us both being top international players but we both had shockers against Dundee."

The quarter-final brought a trip to Partick Thistle. It proved to be anything but Firhill for thrills. It was another nervy performance. Neale Cooper and Peter Weir got the goals in the 2-1 win. It still proved to be a sore one for winning goalscorer Cooper. He admitted: "I didn't score many goals but I was pleased with my effort against Partick Thistle which set up a semi-final against Celtic. I got caught by Tommy Burns's elbow in the Scottish Cup semi-final. I came back on and got whacked in the face again and had to go off. It ended up ruling me out of the starting 11 for the semi-final of the Cup Winners' Cup."

Aberdeen also had the last four of the Scottish Cup to look forward to where they were drawn against Celtic, while Rangers met St Mirren in the other game. Aberdeen managed to sneak through thanks to a solitary goal from Peter Weir, but Rangers and St Mirren had to go to a replay before Sandy Clark booked a place in the final for the Light Blues.

The Dons, certainly, fancied their chances and rightly so although Ferguson knew it was going to take an almighty effort, especially as his side were due to play in the European Cup Winners' Cup final against Real Madrid just ten days before. Ferguson and his team did themselves and Scotland proud by sinking the Spanish giants and lifting the first European trophy in their history. It had taken 120 minutes and there was no doubt it had drained Aberdeen's stars physically and mentally. Would they have enough to return to Hampden and see off Rangers?

The first-half certainly looked as if there was a hangover. The Dons struggled to get going and it led to Ferguson losing the plot with one of his side's star performers after a goalless first 90 minutes. Jim Leighton revealed: "In all the cup finals I played for Aberdeen I hardly had anything to do, even the European Cup Winners' Cup final. This cup final was probably where I was at my busiest. I had a couple of saves to make in that final but in the rest of the finals I was hardly called into action at all. Ironically, that was the final where Fergie and I ended up at each other's throats at the end of normal time. We came off the pitch and I was the first one he went for. He screamed at me 'you're their effin best player'. I felt I hadn't done anything wrong and he was out of order and we ended up nose to nose. Willie Miller ended up pulling me away and kept me away from him for the rest of the day."

Aberdeen's players kept going to the death and managed to claim the glory thanks to a goal from Eric Black. Black recalled: "I scored the only goal and it was a dreadful game. The energy had been zapped from us after Gothenburg. The manager wasn't slow it letting us know we had let our standards slip with the television interview he gave on the pitch at the final whistle. We had let him down a bit but to win both trophies within a fortnight was still pretty special."

Alex Ferguson let rip in front of the television cameras as the team started their lap of honour. He said: "We were the luckiest team in the world. It was a disgrace of a performance. Miller and McLeish won the cup for Aberdeen. Miller and McLeish played Rangers themselves. It was a disgrace of a performance. I don't care about winning cups, it doesn't matter, we set standards a long time ago and I am not going to accept that from any Aberdeen team."

Ferguson's comments did nothing to endear himself to his squad. He also seemed to have forgotten that those same players had also lifted the European Cup Winners' Cup. McGhee admitted: "It was one of those games where we never got to the levels we hoped. It was a dull affair although I was delighted to win. I maybe wasn't surprised by Alex's outburst because nothing with Alex surprised me because he always set the standard. It did, however, shock us and disappoint us because we had just won the cup. By the next morning, to be fair, Alex apologised to us all. I think Dick Donald (the chairman) had maybe got a hold of him and talked some sense into him. But Alex is also human and to be fair he does see both sides."

Midfielder Neale Cooper admitted that even the Aberdeen players hadn't realised what Gothenburg had taken out of them until they stepped on to the Hampden pitch. He explained: "The manager blasted us in the dressing room with the Scottish Cup sitting there in the dressing room. It was like we had lost the final! He had been upset because we had set a standard but we hadn't hit those heights. I know I hadn't played well but I have to say looking back I was totally drained. I had played so many games domestically and in Europe that my tank was empty. I was just delighted to end the season with the cup."

Leighton is in no doubt that Ferguson's outburst was a major blunder. The keeper said: "The manager's comments on the field after the game turned the celebrations into a bit of a damp squib. It is one thing making the comments he did in private but it is different when you do it on television. His comments were definitely damaging to the players. The chairman, Dick Donald, came into the dressing room after the game and he was delighted because it was just days after we had just won the European Cup Winners' Cup. The manager might have been critical about our performance but, as players, we didn't realise what Gothenburg had taken out of us until we took to Hampden that day."

Gordon Strachan also claimed that the Dons were so spent that it was a case of them falling over the Scottish Cup winning line. Strachan explained: "I had just walked into the dressing room and I didn't know what was happening. I was just emotionally drained. I just slumped on to the bench. I was just absolutely knackered. I had played something like 50-odd games that season, along with Willie and Alex, and in that final I had nothing left. I was just running on true grit just to get through that game. The good thing is that Sir Alex's rant has kept every single one of that Aberdeen team going on the after-dinner speaking circuit."

The only two players that avoided a tongue-lashing were central defenders Willie Miller and Alex McLeish. Ferguson has praised them but he didn't miss their team-mates. McLeish admitted: "The manager had just set such high standards. We had just lifted the European Cup Winners' Cup and he expected us to go out and win the trophy in style. He was disappointed but he was a big enough man to apologise to us all after it."

Neil Simpson revealed that McLeish and Miller came in for some ribbing from the Pittodrie dressing room for being Ferguson's golden boys on the bus trip back up the A90.

Simpson explained: "We were coming back up the road and we were getting the open-top bus at a layby outside of Aberdeen. We had all got it in the neck for our performance apart from Willie Miller and Alex McLeish. We were all shouting just drop Alex and Willie off because they were the ones who had won Aberdeen the cup. We said there was a tandem waiting for them. We were all p****d off but to be fair to the manager he later apologised although I think he was maybe told to."

It wasn't to be the worst of seasons for Aberdeen as they walked away with the European Cup Winners' Cup and the Scottish Cup, although there is no doubt that their European adventures cost them another trophy.

"The Cup Winners' Cup cost us the league that year," Leighton claimed. "We were still going on adrenalin and alcohol into our final league game against Hibs before we went to Hampden. We went in against Rangers running on empty and it took a great and resolute performance that helped us dig out a result. I would be the first one to say that Rangers were the better team that day but it took a fair bit to beat our Aberdeen team. We defended really well and we still managed to win extra-time and it showed our fitness levels and will to win."

ABERDEEN'S SCOTTISH CUP RUN 1982-83
* Third round (29th January 1983 at Easter Road)
    Hibs 1 (Rae) Aberdeen 4 (Weir, Simpson, Watson, McGhee)
* Fourth round (19th February 1983 at Pittodrie)
    Aberdeen 1 (Simpson) Dundee 0
* Quarter-final (12th March 1983 at Firhill)
    Partick Thistle 1 (McDonald) Aberdeen 2 (Cooper, Weir)
* Semi-final (16th April 1983 at Hampden)
    Aberdeen 1 (Weir) Celtic 0
* Scottish Cup final (21st May 1983 at Hampden)
    Aberdeen 1 (Black) Rangers 0 (AET)

ABERDEEN'S SCOTTISH CUP-WINNING SQUAD
Jim Leighton, Doug Rougvie (Andy Watson), John McMaster, Neale Cooper, Alex McLeish, Willie Miller, Gordon Strachan, Neil Simpson, Mark McGhee, Eric Black, Peter Weir (John Hewitt). Manager: Alex Ferguson.

```
   _____
  /     6     \
 |            |
 |            |
  _____/
```

• ABERDEEN •
THE SUPER TREBLE

ABERDEEN entered the 1983-84 campaign full of confidence. They may have lifted the European Cup Winners' Cup and the Scottish Cup but there was still a strong feeling of unfinished business among the Pittodrie playing squad. They might have produced one of the greatest seasons in their history but it came at a cost – the Scottish Premier Division title as Dundee United pipped them at the post.

Striker Eric Black said: "It seemed that we were going from one cup final to another during that period. We lost the league the season we won the European Cup Winners' Cup and that definitely impacted on our domestic campaign. We didn't have the size of squad that teams have now, so the demands were quite high on all the boys."

There was a real rivalry between United boss Jim McLean and Aberdeen's Alex Ferguson, although at times they joined together to take on the Old Firm. The legendary management pair made sure that Ibrox and Parkhead were no longer the fortresses they once were.

Keeper Jim Leighton said: "Fergie took the fear away from going to Glasgow. It meant other teams started to have the same belief and would go to Glasgow confident they could win at Ibrox or Parkhead. During that spell Rangers and Celtic ended up halfway down the league. That remained the case until Graeme Souness arrived at Glasgow and started spending big money on players like Chris Woods and Terry Butcher. After that teams became more negative again and the fear factor returned to the Old Firm."

Ferguson wasn't prepared to rest on his laurels and he went out and added to his squad. His old team, St Mirren, once again, proved a happy hunting ground. New boy Billy Stark recalled: "I signed a couple of weeks after Aberdeen had won the European Cup Winners' Cup. I was really excited to be joining a top team although I knew with midfield players like Peter Weir, Neil Simpson, Neale Cooper and Gordon Strachan that I faced a real fight to get into the Aberdeen midfield."

The talent along with the existing core of players and a manager seeking perfection meant that standards were never going to be allowed to drop – on or off the pitch. Neale Cooper admitted: "The manager was a hard taskmaster but that was only because he demanded the best. You had to be strong because he could be hard on you. If you couldn't take it then you weren't going to last long at Pittodrie. I always used it as a motivation and a kick up the backside. He was as hard off the park as he was on it. I used to have quite light hair and after I came back from holidays it would be bright white. He didn't like it so he would send me round to the local hairdresser to get a brown rinse through it. That just showed how meticulous he was."

Cooper admitted Ferguson was tough taskmaster. He was never scared of crossing the line and that also spurred the team on. The midfielder added: "Alex had such a mentality that anything less than a win was disappointing. It was a tough attitude to have but I think it helped the team push the boundaries. There was also a real togetherness and determination and that came from the manager."

The link between Ferguson and Archie Knox and their team was captain Willie Miller. The experienced central defender had been skipper before he arrived and his career went from strength to strength under Fergie. Miller explained: "I had a good relationship with Sir Alex. It was built on trust. He trusted me to lead the team on to the park and to be his voice on there. We had a mutual respect for each other and we didn't have too many confrontations. We had the odd argument and set-to but that was normally, I felt, for the benefit of the team. In that type of circumstance even if you thought you were right there could only be one winner and that had to be the manager. He would still listen to our views even if he didn't necessarily always take them on board. In general I felt we had a good, solid relationship."

The basis of that Aberdeen team centred around the rock-solid defensive trio of keeper Leighton and the central defensive partnership of Miller and Alex McLeish. The team knew that with all three of them on form then they had a great chance of success.

Dougie Bell admitted: "Our success was built on a really solid defence. We had Jim Leighton, Willie Miller and Alex McLeish who were top defenders but in front of them we also had a lot of players who were really good on the ball. We knew we could go out and trouble any team, in Scotland or in Europe."

The other thing, as Ferguson has proved throughout his management career, is that he has no fears about throwing kids into the first-team fold. The likes of Leighton, Cooper, John Hewitt and Eric Black had all been blooded by the Aberdeen boss in previous seasons.

Leighton admitted: "I went straight from Deveronvale into the Aberdeen first-team. I played a lot of games, domestic and European games. It was a great experience and Fergie was never scared to throw any of the young boys in. He probably never believed that we would all have kicked on the way we did, collectively. He then added the odd player every year to fill in the jigsaw through the years."

The likes of Dundee United and Aberdeen had now passed the Old Firm but everyone inside of Pittodrie knew it would still be madness to write Rangers or Celtic off.

The team opened up with a five-goal thrashing of St Johnstone and beat Rangers but dropped points at Motherwell and a home defeat to Dundee United kept the feet firmly on the ground. October was far better with four wins and just one league defeat against Hibs. A 3-1 Pittodrie win over Celtic, thanks to John Hewitt, Alex McLeish and a Gordon Strachan penalty, proved to be a real confidence booster.

Black said: "The crux of winning any title was beating Rangers and Celtic and we did that both at Pittodrie and away. That team just wanted to win everything. The expectation levels also went up after we lifted the European Cup Winners' Cup. We had a strong bond between the players combined with a great worth ethic and ability."

The Dons were a team on a roll and had no problems taking care of Rangers or Celtic but it was against the so-called lesser lights they struggled. Leighton admitted: "I wouldn't say there were any games or saves that stood out in that season. I never looked at games and said I did this or that. As a team we were really strong. We could go to Tannadice and Glasgow and get results. Where we used to struggle more was going to places like Morton, St Mirren and Partick Thistle.

"If we had been a Rangers or a Celtic, with their support, then our team would have won everything every year. I am not being critical of the Aberdeen support because they are up there with the best but we always played our best football when the stadiums were full. Sometimes we would be a wee bit flat going to these venues, which weren't full, after we had played in full houses against some of the biggest teams in Europe."

There was also room for one more European success when the Dons took on European Cup winners Hamburg in the European Super Cup final. Aberdeen's players, at least, had the confidence of beating Bayern Munich en-route to the European Cup Winners' Cup.

Ferguson's men also owed Hamburg one after they had previously knocked Ferguson's team out in one of their early European adventures – in somewhat dubious circumstances.

Midfielder Neil Simpson said: "I still had a bad taste in my mouth playing Hamburg a few years before that. One of their players went down and won a penalty when I wasn't anywhere near him. The guy dived. That put us out and we really should have given them a doing at Pittodrie. We definitely felt we owed them one." Aberdeen had to ride out waves of German attacks although Mark McGhee and John McMaster both had chances in that first match that ended goalless.

It all came down to the Pittodrie return and a superb second-half performance from the Dons saw off their visitors. Simpson made sure he took his revenge on the Germans with the opening goal. He recalled: "Peter Weir had a cross and John Hewitt mis-hit a shot. It came off one of their players and through my legs. Mark McGhee stood on a defender on the line and I swerved and managed to hit the ball into the corner. That was the springboard for us to go and win the cup."

Within a minute, Aberdeen had doubled their lead and effectively claimed their second, consecutive European title. McGhee was the man who put Hamburg to the sword. McGhee said: "Peter Weir took a corner and I think Willie Miller headed it back for me to knock it in from close range."

Weir had been inspirational on the night and he was given something else to celebrate at the final whistle. Keeper Jim Leighton admitted: "We wiped the floor with Hamburg. It was a good celebration because we won the trophy but also because Peter Weir's wee boy was born just before the match, although, his wife Mary, never told him until after the game. It turned into a real night of joy."

Club secretary Ian Taggart had decided to keep the news from Peter on the advice of his manager. It had the desired effect.

The Reds were more than happy to take a bow with the Super Cup but it clearly wasn't in the same league as their European Cup Winners' Cup triumph. "It has become more important now than it was at that time," McGhee stated. "We saw it as a bonus, win or lose, there wasn't to be a lot lost or gained by winning. Since then it has gained greater importance."

That seemed to be a common view among that Pittodrie squad. Strachan claimed: "I didn't really give the Super Cup a second thought back then. I treated it more like a pre-season friendly, more like the Charity Shield, but looking back it was a fabulous achievement to beat the European champions. The Super Cup has taken on more significance now and when you look at the top managers, like Sir Alex Ferguson and Jose Mourinho, they always include the Super Cups among their list of achievements. So that shows how big our win was."

The team certainly had a thirst for further success and put together a 27-match unbeaten domestic and European run that left them ahead of the chasing Scottish pack, in particular. That charge was eventually ended by Ujpest Dozsa although the Dons still managed to knock them out in the quarter-final.

The team were going well in the league while also trying to defend their European Cup Winners' Cup crown. They gave it a good go by disposing of Akranes, Beveren and Ujpest Dozsa before their hopes were ended at the semi-final stage to Porto. Yet Aberdeen thought they had struck gold in avoiding Juventus and Manchester United in the last four.

Leighton said: "We wanted to win the league and do well in Europe but it didn't happen because we lost to Porto in the semi-final. Nobody had really heard of them. We were pleased with the draw because the other semi-final was between Juventus and Manchester United. We thought who are we going to play in the final. I am in no doubt if it hadn't been for the European Cup Winners' Cup the previous we would have won the league. Dundee United might dispute that but I am in no doubt we would have won it at a canter had it not been for Europe."

The first leg ended in a 1-0 away defeat in Portugal. It was a night that Dougie Bell will never forget. "I didn't play well against Porto and the manager absolutely slaughtered me," he revealed. "I probably shouldn't have played because I had a hamstring problem but I did and it was fair to say I didn't do myself justice. We came back and the next day the manager asked where I was going because I was to play for the reserves against Rangers. What could I say?"

The Dons still had a chance to salvage things in the Pittodrie return but this time there was to be no happy ending as once again they lost 1-0. Mark McGhee recalled: "That Porto game was strange. Normally when I stepped out at Pittodrie in a European game I would have an extra spring in my step but that didn't happen. We normally felt we could beat anybody but that night I never got going and neither did the team. We were poor and we never gave ourselves a chance that night. I have since spoken to Willie Miller about that night and even he felt the same as me. Maybe the team had gone as far as it could and had blown a gasket."

That was the start of the Porto revival as they stepped out of the shadows of Benfica and Sporting Lisbon. Gordon Strachan said: "It was seen as a big disappointment when we lost to Porto because Benfica were always seen as the big Portuguese side. But that side who beat us a couple of years later went on to lift the European Cup. That shows just how good they were, although maybe we didn't realise it at that time.

"We didn't play as well as we had hoped and maybe it was just a case of so many games over three or four seasons catching up on us. If we were fit we played and we didn't miss many games through injury, probably because the manager always told us he would tell us when we were or weren't fit. We just got on with playing the games."

That left Ferguson's men with no distractions on the home front. They returned after the Porto exit to beat Dundee away and St Johnstone at home. Suddenly the Dons were on the verge of winning their first title in four years. They travelled to Tynecastle where a solitary goal from Stewart McKimmie was enough to return the Scottish Premier Division trophy back up the A90.

Neale Cooper admitted: "We had done well in the cups and so the objective was to go one better and to win the league. If you win the league over a season you prove you are the best team and that is what Alex Ferguson and the players wanted us to do. So when we won the league that season I think we proved to everyone that we were the best team in Scotland."

Captain Miller was the man charged with raising the trophy again and he believed they had kicked on from 1979-80.

Miller said: "I am not taking anything away from any of Aberdeen's title wins but I definitely believed the 1979-80 title was the biggest because it finally broke that long drought. That first title gave us a lot of confidence and from there we felt Aberdeen could dominate the game in Scotland. For a wee period of time in the game we did that. I have heard people say that we would go to Celtic Park and Ibrox and the opposition would be more frightened of us than we were of them because Sir Alex Ferguson's teams had an aura, confidence and self-belief that we could go down there and beat Rangers and Celtic.

"It is not an easy thing to do, certainly not on a regular basis. Yet that season we went down to Parkhead and beat Celtic there twice in the closing weeks. I remember those wins shocked a lot of people because they didn't think it was possible for an non-Old Firm team to go to Glasgow and play without fear and beat them when the pressure was on. To us it was just another challenge. Those two wins over Celtic definitely sit high up there, for me, in that season's run-in."

Alex McLeish had learned his lesson from the previous title success and wasn't about to let this occasion slip away in the same way. Big Eck admitted: "Winning that league was one I did appreciate a lot more. I knew what it meant to win the league and that time I was really able to savour it. We had missed out the previous season but this time we were determined to go all the way and we did precisely that."

Striker John Hewitt admitted that bonding off the park made the team even stronger on it. Hewitt said: "It didn't matter how we played, we knew the rest of our team-mates would give everything for us. We played for one another and stuck by one another. We had a great team spirit and you just can't buy what that Aberdeen team had. We were together all the time with the football but we also used to meet up one Sunday a month to have a few beers and to watch the football. To be fair to the manager he encouraged us to go out because he knew it would make the group even stronger."

Dougie Bell knew that Aberdeen team were now the team the Old Firm were chasing. Bell admitted: "That was my second league winner's medal and it probably meant the most to me," the midfielder revealed. "I had been a first-team player for the campaign and I felt I had played my part. It was just great to bring the league trophy back to Pittodrie. We were no longer in the shadows of Rangers and Celtic."

Mark McGhee finished that campaign as top scorer although he was more than backed up by Gordon Strachan who pitched in with 19 from the midfield. Strachan admitted: "We had a right good side and I managed to score a right few goals in the league that I was really proud about."

There was also a certain trip to Hampden to look forward to as Ferguson looked to help them claim a league and Scottish Cup double for the first time in their history.

The Scottish Cup campaign had started with a sticky tie against Kilmarnock. It took a replay after a 1-1 draw at Pittodrie for the Dons to progress. Goals from Strachan, Miller and Peter Weir got them through. Next up came Clyde where Neale Cooper and Ian Angus netted in a 2-0 win. Cooper recalled: "I scored with a good drive down at Clyde and it helped us on our way. It was a good win but one that was hard fought."

That then brought a New Firm stalemate at Pittodrie before United were beaten 1-0 at Tannadice by a Mark McGhee effort. Next up it was their city rivals, Dundee, who were dispatched in the semi-final by strikes from Strachan and Ian Porteous.

Celtic stood between the Dons and an unprecedented double, but before then Ferguson had a number of issues. Strachan had decided enough was enough and he wanted a fresh challenge at the end of the season. Doug Rougvie and Mark McGhee were also ready to fly the nest as well.

Strachan admitted: "I was hardly speaking to the manager in my final few months at Aberdeen. There was a lot going on with Mark, Doug Rougvie and myself all possibly leaving. There were a lot of politics at the time and that maybe took away from the football. I didn't even know where I was going."

Top scorer McGhee's defiant stand almost cost him his cup final place. "I remember before the cup final Alex Ferguson told us that any of us who were thinking about leaving could forget about playing in the cup final," McGhee revealed. "I went to see him because I had the option to go to Hamburg or to a couple of teams in Italy, including Bari. So I went to see him and told him my situation and he told me that I wouldn't be playing in the cup final. I just had to accept it although I knew I wasn't the only player in that position."

Rougvie revealed he didn't want to leave but had very little option when Aberdeen refused to give him a significant wage rise. Rougvie said: "Gordon had told Fergie he was leaving quite early on and then Mark jumped on the bandwagon after that. I had no intention of going. All I was after was a decent wage. Aberdeen were notoriously bad payers and Fergie would break up his team just for a few pennies. But to be fair he was still on a learning curve back then. I think he has learned his lesson since then. That is why he has managed to last so long at Manchester United."

Ferguson eventually relented with McGhee and all three of his contract rebels were included in his starting 11 at Hampden. That left some of his squad, including young Steven Cowan, disappointed. The striker recalled: "Fergie named Billy Stark as one on the subs and it was between Dougie Bell, Tommy McIntyre and I for the final slot. He left it until the Saturday and told us Dougie was going on the bench and the rest of us could go and do what we wanted to do."

It was a competition the Dons and Ferguson were keen to keep a hold of. Neale Cooper admitted: "That was our third consecutive final and by that stage we were pretty confident we would win the cup. We didn't take anything for granted and we knew we had to earn the right but we definitely believed we were good enough."

Eric Black gave the Dons the perfect start with the opening goal. He said: "I remember a lot of people were complaining about my goal because they thought I had almost taken Pat Bonner's head off. One or two people thought the goal should have been disallowed. The ball was up in the air and I went for it and decided I couldn't wait any longer. I disagree I definitely made contact long before I made contact with Pat."

A late Paul McStay goal took the game into extra-time before McGhee popped up to vindicate Ferguson's decision to play him with the winner. McGhee recalled the events in and around that cup final. "A couple of weeks later Alex called me in and told me he had a change of heart and he was going to play me in the final," he said.

"I think he knew he could trust me to go out and give everything. I think I showed that when I got our cup final winner. Gordon Strachan floated in the perfect cross and I volleyed it home at the back post. That proved I was committed right to the end. I had to think long and hard about leaving because we had a great team but some of our top players, like Strachan, were about to leave and there was also the financial element. We might have won European trophies but I actually earned more from my Adidas boot deal at Hamburg, outwith my basic wage, than I did at Aberdeen. I was just pleased to bow out on a high."

Stark had recovered from a hip problem to make the cup final bench. He insisted: "It was a fantastic period for the club and a lot of that was down to the determination and dedication of Sir Alex Ferguson. We had a good team and we were also fortunate that the Old Firm didn't have the same financial muscle as they have had in recent seasons. Just thinking back then I really did take medals and cups for granted. I picked up that Scottish Cup and I knew I would win more medals at Aberdeen because we had such a good bunch of players."

Cup final hero McGhee believes the three Scottish Cup wins were up there with the European Cup Winners' Cup. He said: "Everybody talks about Gothenburg but the three cup finals in a row were massive for me. I loved the Scottish Cup, Hampden and everything that goes with cup finals. They were some of my best memories and the finals were also around my birthday which made them even more special."

Jim Leighton admitted one of his biggest regrets was the fact that team wasn't kept together and given a tilt at the European Cup. "Winning the league was great," the keeper claimed. "We had finally got there and that helped to wipe out some of the disappointment of the previous season. The one disappointment was that championship-winning team was broken up at the end of that campaign, so we never got a chance to make a real push in the European Cup.

"I am not saying we would have won the European Cup. None of us would say that but it would have been nice to see how far we could have gone and if we could have won it. It would have been nice to have a crack at it with that team. We had beaten Hamburg, Real Madrid and Bayern Munich – some of the best teams in Europe - so we had nothing to fear."

Strachan eventually quit for Manchester United, where he was to be later joined by Ferguson and Leighton. The midfielder admitted: "I didn't know where I was going although I knew I would be leaving. I just kept playing and trying to do my best. The fact we were so successful right up to the end showed that all the boys were committed and determined to do as well as they could. I was pleased to have signed off on a high knowing the finger could not be pointed at me in any way. It looked like I was going abroad to the German side Cologne but then at the last minute Manchester United came in for me and I dropped everything for that."

McGhee ended up packing his bags for Hamburg while Doug Rougvie went to Chelsea. Rougvie was able to bow out as a winner. He admitted: "We had just come off our most successful season ever. We had won the league, the Scottish Cup and European Super Cup. The club have never achieved a treble like that before. Aberdeen went on to win the league the following season and I think it was the momentum that kept things going."

Gordon Strachan has since had a rocky relationship with Ferguson but he is in no doubt he is the best football boss the game has ever seen. "I didn't always see eye to eye with Sir Alex Ferguson but there is no question he is the best manager ever. What he has achieved in the game speaks for itself."

Strachan also believes that team may have been broken but the bond between all that Aberdeen squad will always be there. He said: "Looking back, what we achieved at Aberdeen was absolutely phenomenal. I look back on my time at Aberdeen with a lot of pride and enjoyment. Probably with more enjoyment than pride. In my house you wouldn't know I had played for Aberdeen, Leeds United or Manchester United, but you would see lots of pictures of me and my friends, a lot of them I made when I was up at Pittodrie."

EUROPEAN SUPER CUP 1983-84
* Final first leg (22nd November 1983 in Germany)
    Hamburg 0 Aberdeen 0

ABERDEEN: Jim Leighton, Neale Cooper, Doug Rougvie, Neil Simpson, Alex McLeish, Willie Miller, Gordon Strachan, John Hewitt, Mark McGhee, Dougie Bell, Peter Weir.

* Final second leg (20th December 1983 at Pittodrie)
    Aberdeen 2 (Simpson, McGhee) Hamburg 0

ABERDEEN: Jim Leighton, Stewart McKimmie, John McMaster, Neil Simpson, Alex McLeish, Willie Miller, Gordon Strachan, John Hewitt (Eric Black), Mark McGhee, Dougie Bell, Peter Weir.

ABERDEEN'S 1983-84 TITLE WINNING SQUAD
Jim Leighton, Willie Miller, Alex McLeish, Doug Rougvie, Mark McGhee, Neale Cooper, Gordon Strachan, Peter Weir, Neil Simpson, John Hewitt, Dougie Bell, Eric Black, Stewart McKimmie, John McMaster, Ian Angus, Billy Stark, Brian Mitchell, Tommy McIntyre, Ian Porteous, Willie Falconer, Stevie Cowan, Ian Robertson, Paul Wright.

SCOTTISH CUP 1983-84

* Third round (13th February 1984 at Pittodrie)
    Aberdeen 1 (Weir) Kilmarnock 1 (Gallacher)
* Third round replay (15th February 1984 at Rugby Park)
    Kilmarnock 1 (McKinna) Aberdeen 3 (Strachan, Miller, Weir)
* Fourth round (18th February 1984 at Shawfield)
    Clyde 0 Aberdeen 2 (Angus, Cooper)
* Quarter-final (17th March 1984 at Pittodrie)
    Aberdeen 0 Dundee United 0
* Quarter-final replay (28th March 1984 at Tannadice)
    Dundee United 0 Aberdeen 1 (McGhee)
* Semi-final (14th April 1984 at Tynecastle)
    Aberdeen 2 (Porteous, Strachan) Dundee 0
* Scottish Cup final (19th May 1984 at Hampden)
    Aberdeen 2 (Black, McGhee) Celtic 1 (McStay) (AET)

ABERDEEN'S SCOTTISH CUP-WINNING TEAM

Jim Leighton, Stewart McKimmie, Doug Rougvie (Billy Stark), Neale Cooper, Alex McLeish, Willie Miller, Gordon Strachan, Neil Simpson, Mark McGhee, Eric Black, Peter Weir (Dougie Bell). Manager: Alex Ferguson.

• ABERDEEN •
THE NEW-LOOK CHAMPIONS

ABERDEEN may have started the campaign as the Scottish Premier Division champions but Alex Ferguson's squad was very different from the one that had clinched the 1983-84 title. Ferguson was forced to do some major surgery after some of his biggest stars were attracted by the riches of clubs down south and across Europe. Gordon Strachan left for Manchester United, while Doug Rougvie headed for Chelsea and top scorer Mark McGhee dug out his passport and set off for a new challenge with Hamburg.

The three weren't the only big players who felt it was time for a change although over the piece Ferguson managed to persuade the majority of his stars to stay put. Goalkeeper Jim Leighton explained: "We were always hoping we could defend our title. We had a lot of good players but we also had a lot of boys who were starting to get itchy feet and wanted to try something different. I was in that position myself a couple of years later. I wanted to leave after the World Cup in Mexico in 1986.

"I felt I had done everything at Aberdeen and I wanted to try somewhere new, but I still had two years left on my contract and the club wouldn't let me go. I didn't complain because I had signed a four-year contract in good faith, so it would have been wrong for me to kick up a fuss. I just accepted things and got on with it. There was interest in a few of us through the years but I would estimate we only found out about 20 per cent of the interest. Fergie kept the rest to himself."

The question was how would Ferguson be able to replace that sort of quality even if his budget had been increased significantly? The critics and so-called experts knew Aberdeen still had a core of real quality but doubted whether the goal threat and attacking flair of McGhee and Strachan, respectively, could ever be replaced.

Ferguson had already started to build his team up again, with the likes of Billy Stark and Stewart McKimmie arriving the previous season. The high-profile summer departures allowed them their chance to stake a first-team claim. The biggest issue however was who was going to be competing with Eric Black and John Hewitt at the top of the scoring charts.

He brought defender Tommy McQueen in from Clyde and decided that his old St Mirren striker Frank McDougall was the man to replace McGhee. Former St Mirren man Billy Stark said: "We had a good bunch of players and the manager also added some very good signings in Frank McDougall and Tommy McQueen. They came in and really added something to the squad. We lost mainstays like Gordon Strachan and Mark McGhee, who had lifted the European Cup Winners' Cup, but Frank and Tommy came in and really hit the ground running. Tommy was a solid full-back while Frank was a real goal-getter and was arguably more potent than McGhee. His scoring record speaks for itself."

McDougall insisted he was always confident he could make an impact in the Granite City. He admitted: "There was no pressure. We had a good team and playing with guys like Willie Miller and Alex McLeish made it so easy. I genuinely believed I could win the league when I joined Aberdeen. They had just won the European Cup Winners' Cup and were the dominant force in Scotland at that time."

Captain Willie Miller also knew that very few people could doubt their legendary Aberdeen manager when it came to unearthing a gem in the transfer market. Miller said: "Sir Alex could change players and lose top stars but he had a special talent when it came to finding replacements and putting out winning teams. He has continued that even at Manchester United. The players he brought in did well, especially that season. Frank McDougall was a goalscoring phenomenon for us, he really was. His ability in front of goal was up there with the very best."

Aberdeen started well in the league but crashed out of the League Cup to Airdrie and disappointingly exited the European Cup at the first stage to Dynamo Berlin. The Dons were suddenly being written off in some quarters, but that only helped Ferguson to motivate his players and get them to batten down the hatches and adopt the bunker mentality. Neil Simpson said: "With Alex Ferguson he was a great man-manager. He had the press against us and the whole of Glasgow, basically he had us feeling like everybody was against us. It was a siege mentality, let's all stick together and get through this. It definitely worked."

There was a reaction to the European exit as they then lost to Celtic. Stark said: "We lost that first game against Celtic. I missed a penalty in the game and I took absolute pelters from Sir Alex Ferguson. It topped off a miserable day because we didn't have the greatest of games. It was definitely a setback but one that allowed us to bounce back and show we had the mental strength to see things through."

Ferguson, eventually, got his players regrouped, as they set off on an impressive eight-match winning sequence. Included in that run was another Ibrox victory. "We won 2-1 at Ibrox thanks to goals from myself and Frank McDougall," Stark recalled. "It was a really wet day and I managed to score with a diving header at the traditional Celtic end before Frank got our winner. That was at a time when Rangers had top players like Davie Cooper and Jim Bett, so that was a big goal for me that season."

Aberdeen were still at the forefront of the championship race although it wasn't such a Merry Christmas and Happy New Year. Draws with Dundee and St Mirren and two defeats to Dundee United set the alarm bells ringing.

The Dons then responded in some style, getting back on the goals trail as they scored 12 against Hibs, Morton and Rangers. The 3-0 win over Rangers at Pittodrie more than wrecked Jock Wallace's second coming as Ibrox manager. "I would say that was my best season," Neil Simpson claimed. "I felt I played really well and there was an extra bit of responsibility because Neale Cooper also got injured at the start of that campaign. It was my most enjoyable season. We had a game where we beat Rangers, who welcomed Jock Wallace back as their manager. We had just come back from Spain and I scored a goal. Everybody was saying Rangers were back and we just killed them."

That Rangers win was also a big one for hat-trick hero McDougall. He joked: "I got a hat-trick against Rangers so it was always good being a Celtic fan."

Ferguson refused to let standards slip. He kept demanding more and more. Stevie Cowan admitted: "Fergie just kept pushing us on and on. There was no respite. We also had some big characters who were determined to win. All the boys had to play to a decent level to get in that team. I never felt under any extra pressure. I don't want to sound big-headed but I was always confident that Aberdeen team would win. My pressure only came from trying to please the manager. I had to make sure I did the best for myself and the team."

Even with all the changes that had been made at Pittodrie, the Aberdeen players still believed they were as good if not better than the rest of the competition in Scotland. Neil Simpson said: "A lot of the boys who had made us successful had left but we were still a decent team. We maybe weren't the European force we once were but we were still a good team in the Scottish Premier League."

The thing with Ferguson was that you knew you were never safe – even if you and the team played well. Cowan, who worked with Fergie for nine years during his career, admitted: "I had him at St Mirren before I joined him at Aberdeen. I could give you hundreds of incidents when he lashed into me. We had just beaten Dundee United 4-2. He came into the dressing room and I thought the team had done well and I had also done pretty well. He came in and ripped me to shreds, screaming at me: 'You think you are a f*****g player?' That was his way of keeping us all in place. He knew we had done well but he was never going to let us get carried away with our success because there were still other games to be won."

Another big performance from Cowan came in Aberdeen's 2-1 win at Ibrox where he netted and then watched Eric Black grab the winner. Cowan said: "The games that always stand out are the ones against the Old Firm. I remember a game where we won 2-1 at Ibrox in April 1985. I scored our opening goal. That really set us on our way going into the final straight."

That win boosted confidence ahead of the Scottish Cup semi-final but the Dons finally lost their grip on that competition when Jim McLean's Dundee United knocked them out. Stark painfully recalled: "Dundee United put us out of the Scottish Cup after a replay and that was a big disappointment because it was a really tight affair and we were unlucky to go out. Also it cost us the chance of claiming a second consecutive double which was pretty much unheard of outwith the Old Firm."

A thumping home win against Dumbarton saw Aberdeen move to within touching distance of the title and they knew if results went their way they could reclaim their crown when Celtic came to Pittodrie.

Scotland midfielder Roy Aitken silenced the home crowd when he put Celtic ahead through a first-half penalty. It was then left to Captain Courageous to level and get Aberdeen the point they needed to win the league. Willie Miller joked: "I scored with a bullet header into the top corner. I didn't have too many opportunities in my career to score a goal as telling as that in my career. I was never knowing for my goalscoring abilities. It was nice and really pleasurable to celebrate winning the title in that manner. From a personal point of view, it was a fantastic game and day.

"But I, as well as everybody, else knew the title was won over the entire campaign and not just on that day. We all pulled together as a team to put ourselves in the position and I was just lucky enough on that day to grab a bit of personal glory."

Top scorer Frank McDougall was taken off just before Miller's equaliser although he more than played his part with an impressive 28 goals. He was also delighted to win the title for the first time. McDougall recalled: "I got taken off just before the goal. I had a decent game but Fergie still took me off, like he did. But Sir Alex is a genius and nobody can argue with him when it comes to football – his record speaks for itself. It was just a fantastic afternoon. It was great to finally be winning things because I had come so close many times with St Mirren and always fallen short."

Stark also made sure that Strachan had been long since forgotten about as he also broke the 20-goal barrier from midfield. He believes that the Dons showed that during that period they and not the Old Firm were the dominant force.

Stark said: "It was ironic that we clinched the title with a 1-1 draw with Celtic. We lost only four league games all season. I also scored 20 goals so I was delighted with my contribution. The main threat that season came from Celtic who had top players like Frank McGarvey, George McCluskey, Roy Aitken, Tommy Burns and Pat Bonner. It was good because it was also a time where Rangers struggled prior to the Graeme Souness revolution."

Even Aberdeen great Jim Leighton didn't believe he would win the title with Aberdeen once never mind in consecutive seasons. Leighton admitted: "We were an arrogant team without arrogant players, as a team we believed we could beat anybody but we never had any big-time Charlies or people who thought they were superstars. We had arrogance because we knew we were a good team. I think I maybe showed some of that arrogance but I am by no means an arrogant person and neither were any of the other lads. We just had a confidence in ourselves and each other. I grew up in the west of Scotland with Rangers and Celtic winning the league every other season. Not for a minute did I think I would win it twice with Aberdeen."

Ironically, that 1984-85 season is the last time a team outside of the Old Firm has been crowned champions of Scotland.

John Hewitt is in no doubt a lot of the success that Aberdeen had in that period was down to the best manager the British game has ever seen – Alex Ferguson. The striker said: "We all had our exchanges with the gaffer through the years but he was always and still is an exceptional person. He is just a born winner. He doesn't accept defeat. As a player if you didn't share that view then you were quickly moved on.

"His record speaks for itself. As far as I am concerned he is the greatest manager ever. There hasn't been another manager like him and probably never will be. People speak about Sir Matt Busby and Jock Stein but for me Fergie is the man. He has done it in Scotland and now with one of the biggest clubs in the world. To do it continually the way he has is some achievement."

ABERDEEN'S TITLE-WINNING SQUAD

Jim Leighton, Willie Miller, Neil Simpson, Stewart McKimmie, Tommy McQueen, Billy Stark, Alex McLeish, Eric Black, Frank McDougall, Ian Angus, Neale Cooper, Dougie Bell, Peter Weir, John Hewitt, Willie Falconer, Stevie Cowan, Ian Porteous, Brian Mitchell, Bryan Gunn, Brian Grant, John McMaster, Paul Wright, Joe Miller.
Manager: Alex Ferguson.

• ABERDEEN •
FERGIE SIGNS OFF WITH A CUP DOUBLE

ABERDEEN and Alex Ferguson had conquered Europe, won the SPL title and lifted the Scottish Cup but the one domestic trophy that had continually eluded him was the League Cup. The Scottish Cup had practically been on permanent display in the Pittodrie boardroom during the early-80s but the nation's other cup competition had proved to be far more elusive. The closest they had come was in the title-winning season of 1979-80 where they made it to the League Cup final but lost to Dundee United after a replay.

The 1985-86 campaign certainly saw the Dons open up their campaign in some style with a convincing 5-0 home win over Ayr United in the second round of the League Cup. Doubles from Frank McDougall, Billy Stark and a Tommy McQueen penalty eased Aberdeen through against the First Division outfit. The next round saw them make the trip to St Johnstone. The Second Division side put up a lot more resistance before goals from John Hewitt and McDougall, again, sealed the 2-0 win at Muirton Park.

The quarter-finals set up an all-Scottish Premier Division clash when the Dons hosted Alex MacDonald's Hearts. It was a typically hard-fought encounter that saw Aberdeen come out on top thanks to a solitary goal from Eric Black.

Then in the last four they found themselves having to face up to the challenge of another fellow title-chaser in the shape of New Firm rivals Dundee United. Eric Black took first blood as he netted the only goal of a tight Tannadice clash. The Dons had the edge and with home advantage going into the second leg thoughts already started to stray towards Hampden. Aberdeen managed to make that dream a reality as a Frank McDougall goal at Pittodrie gave them a 2-0 aggregate win over their north-east contemporaries.

Hibs, managed by John Blackley, lay in wait in the final, after the Leith outfit beat Celtic in the quarter-final and then Rangers in the last four.

Ferguson had a few selection issues of his own ahead of the final. Jim Bett had been ruled out and midfielder Ian Angus had also been too hasty in writing himself off. Angus explained: "I was meant to be on the bench but in the training I didn't think there was any chance of me making the game so I told the manager. I still travelled down and by the time of the final training session I felt great. I said to the manager that I felt OK but he said it was too late and Stevie Gray was taking my place on the bench."

Bett's disappointment, however, was at least silver-lined. He admitted: "I missed the Hibs final because I was injured. I still got a medal because I had played in previous rounds which was good."

On their day the team from the capital could be a difficult opponent but Aberdeen knew that if they played to their capabilities then there was only one place the trophy was going to be heading – the long overdue location of Pittodrie. That was evident before a ball was even kicked. The match was all but over in the tunnel before the players had even taken to the field.

Jim Leighton explained: "I remember Tommy Craig, the Hibs assistant manager, spoke to me after the game. He said his team had lost it in the tunnel. Willie was at the front, I was next and big Alex was behind me. We were all really focused and just staring ahead. There he knew Hibs had lost the final before they had even kicked a ball."

The view that Hibs' bottle had gone at the national stadium was also backed up by Hibs midfielder Paul Kane.

Defender Alex McLeish revealed: "We played really well that day and I remember Paul Kane, who I later played with at Aberdeen, told me that we had pretty much won that final in the tunnel. He admitted he and the rest of their team were looking at our players and had felt intimidated standing next to us. We certainly went out, played well and deserved our win."

Aberdeen didn't have to wait long to go in front. Neil Simpson recalled: "I set up Eric's goal. Frank McDougall played a great ball inside. I swung in a cross-cum-shot and Eric slid in and stuck it away."

Most of the Dons camp knew even at that stage Hibs were dead and buried. Leighton said: "We went ahead quite early in that game and when we did that it was very rarely that we were pulled back. We won that final fairly comfortably."

Billy Stark then doubled Aberdeen's lead. He said: "John Hewitt set my goal up. He swung in a cross and I managed to glance it past Alan Rough."

Black claims that Stark stole that goal from him and ended up costing him a Hampden hat-trick as he sealed the win with Aberdeen's third. Black recalled: "I remember Billy's goal because I was away to put it in and he came flying across me and put the ball into the net. I still managed to score a couple of goals but I always joke Billy denied me my hat-trick. My goals came from a header and a three-yard tap-in. It was another trophy to add to the scrapbook because that was my only League Cup winner's medal."

Frank McDougall was delighted to finally pick up his first cup winner's medal and to finally help Aberdeen and Ferguson get his hands on the League Cup. The striker said: "I had played in a few semi-finals at St Mirren and I had scored but we lost on every occasion. I was quite nervous going into the game. It was my first cup final, it was live on television and the nation was watching. Even when the final whistle went I was a bit overawed that I had finally won a cup winner's medal. I was delighted for Sir Alex because that also ended his League Cup jinx and finally let him get his hands on the trophy for that first time. He had never won it and it was something he was desperate to achieve."

Final goalscorer Stark reckons Hibs deserved a lot of credit for getting to Hampden and the 3-0 scoreline probably flattered Aberdeen a little. "It looked quite comfortable but it was far from it," the midfielder claimed. I think the manager took great delight from it because it was his first League Cup final win."

The trophy also saw goalkeepers Bryan Gunn and Jim Leighton create a bit of history of their own. The pair, between them, helped Aberdeen to go through the entire competition without losing a goal. Leighton revealed that was always an aim they set themselves ahead of every tournament.

The Scotland keeper said: "I missed the first two games. Bryan Gunn played in them and I came back for the remainder of the competition. We never lost a goal in that competition between us, which was great. We had been trying to go an entire competition without losing a goal. We had gone through a Scottish Cup campaign losing just one goal so we had always tried to go one better and not concede a goal. We never went public on things but internally we would always try and set up wee challenges for ourselves here and there."

The Dons finally had the League Cup in the bag and continued to fight for a domestic treble although IFK Gothenburg killed off their European ambitions in the quarter-final of the European Cup.

Aberdeen continued to fight it out with Dundee United, Celtic and Hearts in the title race while they also made good progress in the Scottish Cup. It proved to be an all-Angus affair in the opening two games. Billy Stark, Willie Miller, Frank McDougall and Alex McLeish all netted in the 4-1 Pittodrie win over Montrose. They then had to travel to Gayfield in the next round and it took a Joe Miller winner to see off the Red Lichties. A John Hewitt double wasn't enough to see off Dundee at Dens Park and the two teams had to do it again after a 2-2 draw.

Eric Black scored for the Dons while Ray Stephen netted for Dundee before Peter Weir managed to hit the winner in extra-time.

The last four draw saw Aberdeen paired with Hibs while Hearts were to play Dundee United in the other game. Like the League Cup final the match ended up in an easy 3-0 win for the Dons, Billy Stark, Eric Black and Joe Miller getting the goals.

Stark recalled: "I stooped to score a header. 3-0 flattered us but that happened quite a lot. We were so strong defensively and then we always looked likely to score."

Title rivals Hearts also saw off United to book the other slot in the final.

The Pittodrie outfit were still in the mix for the league but slip-ups against some of their rivals proved their undoing.

Stark admitted: "We lost games to Celtic and dropped points against Hearts which pretty much put us out of the title race. We struggled because it was a heavy winter. Hearts managed to get quite a few of their games on and that allowed them to push ahead and in the end the backlog tripped us up."

Hearts and Celtic slugged it out on that famous final day shoot-out.

Hearts went in knowing a point at Dundee would be enough but they lost and the Hoops thrashed St Mirren to seal one of the most dramatic final days that has ever been witnessed. The damage that defeat did to the Tynecastle side was catastrophic and the Dons knew it only aided their own cup final cause.

Leighton recalled: "I was injured and there were a few of us sitting in the stand watching the final league game of the season against Clydebank. We were all in the stands when we heard that Dundee had beaten Hearts. It was a horrible thing that happened to them but we were delighted because we knew we were playing them the following week. As soon as we heard what had happened at Dens Park we were rubbing our hands knowing we had a real chance of lifting the Scottish Cup.

"When you lose big games and aren't used to it then psychologically it can be so damaging. We knew that ourselves. If we hadn't lost to Liverpool and Hamburg then we would never have bounced back to win the European Cup Winners' Cup. Hearts hadn't had that experience and we knew they would be vulnerable."

There were still some major in-house issues that also left things far from perfect behind the scenes at Pittodrie. Eric Black told Ferguson he wanted to leave and was immediately bombed out of the Scottish Cup final squad. This time, unlike Mark McGhee, previously, there was to be no u-turn and Black missed out.

Black recalled: "I watched the game in the house. It was slightly different from being out on the pitch. There was no relenting in my position and that was why the status quo was maintained. I can understand the manager's position, now that I have also been in management. I can respect his decision even though I will probably never agree with it."

Leighton is in no doubt that their manager could have dealt with Black a lot better than he did. He said: "I was in that day and when Eric came back out he was chalk white. He explained what had happened and then it was a case of I'll see you later. We, as players, didn't think the manager had handled that situation in the right manner."

Ferguson was also up to his old tricks and mind games with the press and Hearts in the build-up to the final. Neil Simpson revealed: "I wasn't fit and the week before the cup final I scored a hat-trick in a reserve win over St Mirren. With 20 minutes to go I tweaked my groin and Archie Knox told me I should have had more sense and came off. Fergie told me I had to play in the final league game before the cup final. I didn't make it, although the manager told me to go out and train in the build-up to make it look like I was going to play."

There was no doubt that the disappointment of blowing the league was something that the Aberdeen players felt they could use to their advantage. "It was a huge blow to them losing the league the week before," Bett sympathised. "You could sense they were down but you also had to be aware of any possible backlash. In the end we were just too strong for them. The game plan was to start well and get an early goal."

Midfielder Neale Cooper reckons the pain and hurt of Dens Park was still written all over the faces of the Hearts players as they took to the Hampden pitch. Cooper said: "We played Hearts the week after they lost the league and I knew as soon as we stepped into the tunnel that we were going to lift the cup. I could see in the faces of the Hearts players how damaging that final game against Dundee was.

"The players just looked absolutely shell-shocked and they looked like they wanted to be anywhere but Hampden. I think every one of the Aberdeen players sensed they had gone and it proved to be the case."

John Hewitt shattered the brittle confidence of the Hearts players with the opener. Hewitt recalled: "Hearts had been flying that season but we still knew getting them on a big pitch like Hampden would suit us. We had players who could keep a hold of the ball and pass it better than they could. That was how it worked out. I managed to pick the ball up inside their half and I just kept going forward. I then touched the ball to the side of Craig Levein and fired in a shot that flew in at the keeper's near post from 25 yards. We knew after we had gone ahead we would be hard to beat. I then scored my second just before half-time and after that I knew we were on our way to winning the cup."

Aberdeen then netted a third through Billy Stark. "I was just delighted to play some part of the cup final because I injured my calf a few weeks before the final," Stark revealed. "I was really worried I wasn't going to make it but I managed to make the bench and I also got on and managed to score. Peter Weir played a cross in from the left and I ran from the back post. A couple of players went for it and missed it. That allowed me to get on the end of it and send a diving header past the keeper. It was a great feeling although I should have had a couple of goals that day but I had another goal chopped off even though there was nothing wrong with it."

The game was clinched as John Hewitt netted his second to cap another memorable Hampden day for the Dons.

Stark was delighted to have scored in two cup finals. He said: "To score in both cup finals in the one season is something I am very proud of because there aren't many players who are able to say that. The manager also demanded that we win two trophies every season. Thankfully we managed to achieve it although we were disappointed the league wasn't one of those trophies.

"The open-top bus journeys were amazing. Sir Alex Ferguson was like a kid with the trophies on the bus. He just loved to win although the next day it was all forgotten about and he was concentrating on the next trophy."

Jim Bett was delighted to finally leave Hampden as a winner. "I had lost a few finals and so it was good to win one," he beamed.

It was a season of glory with two trophies lifted but there was still a tinge of disappointment come the end of the 1985-86 campaign. McLeish admitted: "To win two trophies in a season was no mean feat although we were still a bit disappointed that we didn't get a bit closer in the league."

Frank McDougall also revealed he had played through the pain barrier for his manager. The injury kept him out of the final league run-in and McDougall believes that cost Aberdeen the title. McDougall said: "I was struggling with a back problem. I was toiling badly but Fergie asked me to play in the cup final, so I filled myself with pain-killers and went out and played for him. I had to get through it for him and Aberdeen. Hearts had lost the league and I felt we were absolute certainties to win the cup and I was proved right. We had top players and we knew we had a top team.

"I had missed a lot of games in the run-in to the league. We weren't that far away but I know Sir Alex Ferguson wrote in his own book that if I had been fit then he reckons Aberdeen would have gone on to pip Celtic to the title that season. I am not saying that was the case but it was certainly good to hear and it showed what Sir Alex thought of me as a player. Also that season we managed to beat Celtic 4-1 and I scored all four goals. That was a big highlight for me – especially being a Celtic fan. That was probably my greatest performance in an Aberdeen shirt."

That proved to be the end of an era for many of that Aberdeen squad. Eric Black eventually did controversially depart to join French side Metz. He may not have left on the best of terms but loved his time at Pittodrie.

Black said: "My time at Aberdeen was sensational. I only have good memories of the players and teams I played in. It is only now I realise how successful we actually were. We were just in a run where we believed we could win everything. It was just nice to be part of something so special."

It also proved to be Jim Leighton's final winner's medal – despite going on to play for another 14 years. Leighton admitted: "I won all my medals in a period of four years. I finished in 2000 and I never won another medal. I played in other cup finals with Aberdeen, Hibs and Manchester United but I never managed to get my hands on another winner's medal. So that is why I look back on that period with Aberdeen with such great pride."

Frank McDougall also had to call time on his career because of his back problem. That news came on the same day that the biggest loss of all came to Aberdeen. It was announced that Ferguson was leaving Pittodrie to become the new manager of Manchester United.

McDougall said: "It was just wear and tear of the bones and there was nothing I could do but hang up the boots. I actually went to see a specialist and I was told I had to retire the same day as Sir Alex was going to Manchester United. When I came back to Pittodrie and told him he was absolutely gobsmacked. It was hard to take but the positive thing was that I was bowing out on a high. I won every domestic trophy with Aberdeen and the golden boot, so it wasn't a bad way to say cheerio. It was still hard calling it a day at 28 when I should still have been in my prime."

For a lot of people, including McDougall, that really was the end of an era.

ABERDEEN'S SKOL CUP RUN 1985-86
* Second round (21st August 1985 at Pittodrie)
      Aberdeen 5 (Stark 2, McQueen PEN, McDougall 2)
      Ayr United 0
* Third round (28th August 1985 at Muirton Park)
      St Johnstone 0 Aberdeen 2 (Hewitt, McDougall)
* Quarter-final (4th September 1985 at Pittodrie)
      Aberdeen 1 (Black) Hearts 0
* Semi-final first leg (25th September 1985 at Tannadice)
      Dundee United 0 Aberdeen 1 (Black)
* Semi-final second leg (9th October 1985 at Pittodrie)
      Aberdeen 1 (McDougall) Dundee United 0
      (Aberdeen won 2-0 on aggregate)

* Skol Cup final
    Aberdeen 3 (Black 2, Stark) Hibs 0

ABERDEEN'S SKOL CUP-WINNING TEAM
Jim Leighton, Stewart McKimmie, Brian Mitchell, Billy Stark, Alex McLeish, Willie Miller, Eric Black (Stevie Gray), Neil Simpson, Frank McDougall, Neale Cooper, John Hewitt.

ABERDEEN'S SCOTTISH CUP RUN 1985-86
* Third round (5th February 1986 at Pittodrie)
    Aberdeen 4 (Stark, Miller, McDougall, McLeish) Montrose 1 (Brown PEN)
* Fourth round (15th February 1986 at Gayfield)
    Arbroath 0 Aberdeen 1 (Miller)
* Quarter-final (8th March 1986 at Dens Park)
    Dundee 2 (Harvey, Brown) Aberdeen 2 (Hewitt 2)
* Quarter-final replay (12th March 1986 at Pittodrie)
    Aberdeen 2 (Black, Weir) Dundee 1 (Stephen) (AET)
* Semi-final (5th April 1986 at Dens Park)
    Aberdeen 3 (Stark, Black, Miller) Hibs 0
* Scottish Cup final (10th May 1986 at Hampden)
    Aberdeen 3 (Hewitt 2, Stark) Hearts 0

ABERDEEN'S SCOTTISH CUP-WINNING TEAM
Jim Leighton, Stewart McKimmie, Tommy McQueen, John McMaster (Billy Stark), Alex McLeish, Willie Miller, John Hewitt, Joe Miller, Neale Cooper, Frank McDougall, Jim Bett, Peter Weir.
Manager: Alex Ferguson.

• ST MIRREN •
THE SAINTS GO MARCHING IN

THE date Saturday 31st January 1987 will be forever etched in Scottish Cup folklore. It was a day when a posse of reporters headed to Love Street expecting to see a major cup shock when Highland League side Inverness Caley came to town.

Alex Smith's St Mirren had other ideas as one of the biggest upsets of all time happened some 13 miles up the road at Ibrox where the now infamous Adrian Sprott netted the only goal of the game to give Hamilton Accies a famous win against Graeme Souness's big-spending Rangers.

Manager Smith, who had arrived the month earlier to replace Hibs-bound Alex Miller, said: "If I am being honest Inverness Caley probably could have beaten us. They missed a couple of great chances at 0-0 before we went on to clinch the game quite convincingly. In the end we got through and the shock came at Ibrox as Adrian Sprott scored the only goal of the game for Hamilton."

The Buddies saw off the brave Highlanders thanks to goals from Kenny McDowall, Ian Ferguson and Frank McGarvey. McDowall recalled: "I scored the opener that day. What I can remember was the pitch was absolutely frozen solid. It was that bad we all had to play with

Astroturf trainers. The match would never have been played in those conditions today. We were just fortunate that we did enough to get through. We just took it one game at a time and thoughts of Hampden at that stage were beyond our wildest dreams."

The door opened further for Saints when Aberdeen crashed out of the competition to Celtic in a third round replay. Smith explained: "I had just arrived and I knew we couldn't qualify for Europe through the league and so the cup was our best option. So I drummed it into the players that we could be five games away from Europe."

The Paisley outfit had to negotiate their way past a local derby with rivals Morton in the next round. That was easier said than done. They had to fight back from being 2-1 down to win 3-2 thanks to a Paul Chalmers double and a Ferguson strike.

Ferguson recalled: "I actually missed my penalty but I managed to score the rebound. My one abiding memory from that incident was the Morton ball boy behind the goal who started giving me stick for missing my initial spot kick. He was obviously a passionate Morton fan although I did have the last laugh when I stuck in the rebound."

For teenager Paul Lambert the derby was a real eye-opener. He explained: "It was my first full season as a full-time professional. I was only 17 and suddenly I was playing the game I loved for real. I still saw it as a hobby. It still felt like I was playing with my pals at school or in the local park. It really didn't feel any different. The Morton game was a prime example. It was a derby and there was a great atmosphere but I didn't really feel under any pressure although we saw what winning that game meant to the fans."

Youth was a theme that ran through that St Mirren side, as David Winnie, Ferguson, Ian Cameron and Lambert all made their mark. Young Brian Hamilton admitted: "I had just turned 19. We had quite a young side but we also had a good blend of youth and experience. It was probably one of the best dressing rooms I was ever in. Some of the boys were a bit off the wall with their antics but when it came to professionalism and wanting to win we were top class. It was a fantastic learning curve for me."

Momentum continued to build as they saw off Raith Rovers 2-0 in the last eight thanks to goals from Chalmers and Peter Godfrey. Suddenly the Buddies were set for Hampden and the added bonus was that the Old Firm were nowhere in sight, as Hearts knocked out Celtic in the fourth round. Now everybody left in the competition believed it could be their year. Dundee were paired with city rivals Dundee United while St Mirren headed to the national stadium to take on Hearts – who were still hurting from blowing an SPL and Scottish Cup double the previous season.

Smith admitted: "Hearts were on a really good run under Alex MacDonald and they went into the game as big favourites but it was also massive for us as we were only 90 minutes away from a Hampden final. Tony Fitzpatrick was injured for that game and I ended up playing four youngsters in Brian Hamilton, Ian Cameron, David Winnie and Ferguson, along with 17-year-old Lambert."

Hampden veteran McGarvey stoked up the war of words before the game. He joked: "I said after we had beaten Raith that our name could be on the cup. We got Hearts in the semi-final and I noised them up before the game by telling the papers that Hearts never won anything, after they had thrown the double away the previous season. I wasn't trying to be disrespectful. I was just trying to put seeds of doubt into the minds of the Hearts players. They also had a few players missing so I fancied our chances going into the semi-final."

Ferguson, thanks to his lucky pre-match sweets, Sports Mixtures, kept up his goal-a-game record with the opener and it looked like it might be enough until Gary Mackay levelled for Hearts. McDowall said: "We knew what a place in the final meant to everyone. I know my heart certainly sunk when I looked back and I saw Gary Mackay's equaliser go in off the post."

The match looked like it was destined for a replay – where Hearts would have had all their top stars fit again – until a moment of McGarvey magic at the death.

McGarvey fondly recalled: "The cross came in and Kenny McDowall went for it and the bell flew up into the air. I just turned and swivelled in one movement to volley the ball into the net. I knew as soon as I connected it was going in and then I heard the big roar from our fans. It was massive because I knew if it had gone to a replay Hearts would probably have beaten us."

The former Celtic and Liverpool star didn't always see eye to eye with all his team-mates but everyone had to admire McGarvey's brilliance that night. "Billy Abercrombie was the captain and I don't think it is too strong to say we hated each other," McGarvey candidly admitted. "He said to me after that Hearts game that he couldn't stand the sight of me but he liked to have me in his team. I had to take that as a compliment as it came from such an unlikely source."

Campbell Money believed, touch wood, St Mirren's name was on the cup. The Scotland squad keeper admitted: "Looking back all the goals I lost on that cup run actually went in off the post. The two goals we lost to Morton and Mackay's shot all came off the post. So it was all quite bizarre how things shaped up in that run."

Dundee United edged out their city rivals to book their final place, although it is fair to say Jim McLean's men had their eyes on a far bigger prize – the Uefa Cup. Sandwiched between their two-legged final against IFK Gothenburg they had the small matter of a Scottish Cup final.

The St Mirren camp could at least just focus on Hampden. Boss Smith took young Lambert out of the firing line to rest him ahead of the final, as the Saints finished seventh in the Scottish Premier Division. Lambert said: "I honestly have to say that I didn't really worry too much about playing at Hampden. I wasn't concerned about it. Alex Smith told me the week before the final I was playing. I pretty much played without fear. The fear came when I got older.

"I didn't feel under any pressure. I knew as a 17-year-old that I wasn't really going to get too much stick. I just decided to go out and enjoy it. We were also only 90 minutes away from really achieving something massive."

Smith took his players away to Seamill to swot up on Dundee United but his young midfielder Ian Cameron was studying for another type of final examination. "What I remember more than anything was that the cup final was bang in the middle of my university exams," Cameron recalled. "I was studying accounts and my lecturers had to bring my exam forward to the Saturday morning so I could play at Hampden. I basically sat the exam at 8am, finished at 11.30am and headed to the team hotel for noon.

"I even missed the team talk but fortunately the manager had named me on the bench. I really appreciated that because I couldn't even stay down at the team hotel before the game because of my studies. I think I went down on the Thursday night to train, had my dinner and went back home on the train."

One of the cup final squad had already started to hog the front page headlines in the run-up to the final. 'Bad Boy Billy' had been splashed across the tabloids as captain Abercrombie's personal life became big news. "I had problems in my personal life and I had just left my wife," the Saints star revealed. "I had actually left a few weeks earlier but I think my wife had just waited to maximise the exposure by leaking it out to the press in the week of the cup final.

"I walked downstairs for breakfast at Seamill and I saw the majority of the boys sitting with their papers with my face plastered across the front of them. I have to say I was totally focused on the cup final and even those headlines couldn't put me off. I had been involved in nine semi-final defeats and this time I was determined to make this one count."

McGarvey was also fired up to produce some more Hampden heroics against a club who had tried to sign him a couple of years earlier. He explained: "Dundee United actually tried to get me when I was at Celtic but it didn't come off. I wish I had joined them because they were a top team and I knew I would have had a chance of doing something in Europe under Jim McLean, one of Scotland's top managers. I wanted to go to United but McLean insisted all his players had to live within a close radius of Dundee and I was unwilling to uproot my family because my kids were settled at school. So maybe if things had worked out I could have been playing in the cup final against St Mirren."

There wasn't such good news for Godfrey, Gardner Speirs and Chalmers, while veteran Tony Fitzpatrick made the bench. Fitzpatrick was shocked to be handed a jersey after missing the bulk of the season with a knee injury and a broken jaw. "I really didn't expect to be involved because I had only played part of the final league game against Rangers. I hadn't been involved in any of the other Scottish Cup games and so when Alex told me I was going to be named among the substitutes I was delighted and really surprised. I also have to say I felt for the other boys who weren't even named in the 13."

Manager Smith inspired his team with his pre-match team talk. "My team talk was quite simple," the St Mirren boss confirmed. "I told my players that they could be one match away from becoming St Mirren legends. I played the same team who had won the semi-final. Fitzpatrick was also fit and I decided to put him on the bench, knowing he could come on and calm the team down if it was needed."

The game was labelled the family final but both sides, by their own admission, were far from their best. Dundee United looked leg-weary after their 1-0 first leg defeat in Gothenburg. Saints also got a big slice of luck when United's Iain Ferguson had a strike chalked off.

Keeper Money explained: "The one save that stands out was the one where Dundee United had their goal disallowed. Ian Redford cut the ball back and I managed to get a touch to push it away from Kevin Gallacher. He ran on and Iain Ferguson put the ball into the net but it was ruled out because Gallacher had strayed into an offside position. If I hadn't got a touch and Gallacher had scored then it could have been all so different if United had gone 1-0 ahead. Fortunately, it happened back then because if it had happened today with the change of the offside rule that goal would have stood."

It was left for St Mirren's Ferguson to write himself into the history books with his extra-time winner. "It came from a long ball over the top from Brian Hamilton," the midfielder explained. "I got in front of John Clark and managed to get my head on the ball. I just ran clear and smashed the ball in with my left foot. I remember seeing the ball hit the net and the feeling I had as I ran towards the St Mirren fans.

"It was great. This young guy from the east end of Glasgow who had gone to finals to watch Rangers and here I was scoring a cup winner for St Mirren. It was good to get the goal because I have to say before that I had been pretty poor. It was one of my worst performances for St Mirren but that is all forgotten about now because of the importance of that goal."

The Saints defence, including Tommy Wilson, David Winnie, Neil Cooper and Derek Hamilton, did the rest as they shut up shop to seal the famous win. Central defender Cooper picked up the man of the match award. He said: "I might have been man of the match but it could just have easily been any of my team-mates who took to the field that day. We did well. It wasn't a great game but we did our jobs and we won the cup. We had beaten some good teams along the way and I don't think anybody can argue that we deserved to win the cup.

"As a defender, I was just delighted to have kept a clean sheet and to have contributed to the team. It was also my first medal and that made it even more special. I know there were far better players than me who have never won a medal, so I know how lucky I was to win that cup with St Mirren."

Skipper Abercrombie famously lifted the cup in what turned out to be one of his proudest moments. The midfielder said: "It was just a really brilliant moment to walk up those stairs and to lift the cup as captain of St Mirren. Ever since I was eight I had wanted to be a professional footballer and to lift a cup at Hampden. That day my dream and that of thousands of St Mirren fans came true."

Club captain Fitzpatrick was also hugely moved by Abercrombie's offer to ask him to lift the cup with him – although he declined. Fitzpatrick explained: "It was just a tremendous feeling when that final whistle went. I turned around and it was just a mass of black and white all around the ground. Going up to lift that cup was something special. Billy actually tried to get me to go up and lift the cup with him but I refused. It was a tremendous gesture but I had hardly played and didn't feel it was right.

"I was more than happy to let Billy go up and lift the cup as St Mirren captain. It was great. I had been at St Mirren for years and to see the delight on people's faces was amazing. Winning that game put a huge smile on the entire Paisley community."

McGarvey admitted the feeling was nothing like when he lifted the cup as a Celtic player. "Winning a trophy at Celtic was completely different to winning something at St Mirren," he insisted. "My over-riding feeling was of joy and achievement. At Celtic the pressure was only off you until the next tournament started. It was a great day for me and proved I had made the right decision in joining St Mirren. It was great going back to Paisley and seeing what that cup meant to them. It was right up there with my Scottish Cup winner for Celtic."

Smith was also overjoyed that he and his assistant Jimmy Bone, who had been born within three miles of him, had managed to guide the Buddies to glory. Smith admitted: "I remember I was being interviewed on the pitch by Chick Young and my ranting almost turned into a party political approach to promote Paisley. I kept telling Chick what this would do for Paisley and listening back these days it still leaves me quite embarrassed.

"I also had to laugh because my interview went on forever. I remember John Greig was in the old Hampden press box and he opened the window and shouted down 'give it a rest, the groundsman wants to go home tonight'."

McDowall knows things might have turned out slightly different had their opponents not also been battling it out in Europe. "Dundee United were a great side and it is only now I have been involved with Rangers that you realise how much a European campaign can take out of you," the Buddies favourite explained. "What Dundee United achieved that season was unbelievable, for a Scottish club to get to a European final. The fact the Scottish Cup final was sandwiched between the two legs of the Uefa Cup final makes it even more remarkable. I think if they had beaten us at Hampden then they would have gone on to win the Uefa Cup as well."

Cameron, who ironically also passed his accountancy exam, said: "It was great to get on, be involved and to lift a cup. It wasn't the greatest of games but try telling that to any of the thousands of St Mirren fans who will never forget that day. It was just brilliant and to top things off I also managed to pass my exam so it fair to say it will be a day I will never forget."

Fellow youngster Hamilton added: "I didn't feel I had the greatest of games. I was involved in the build-up to the goal but other than that I felt the game passed me by. I also could have scored in normal time but I missed but that summed up my career, when it came to big games. It was strange because I wasn't really that nervous before the game.

"Certainly, looking back at my performance I certainly wasn't nervous enough. It was strange because I thought I would be playing in cup finals every season but I remember looking at boys like Tony Fitzpatrick and Billy Abercrombie and they were shaking with nerves because they knew what the game meant to them. I certainly felt completely drained when the final whistle went. It turned out to be a fantastic experience, seeing what it meant to everybody in Paisley. It is probably only now I realise what it meant to everybody connected with the club."

Lambert was another who had just swapped school for the pro game and he didn't realise what that St Mirren team had achieved until several years later. Lambert explained: "I was delighted to have won a medal and I thought it was going to be the norm. How wrong I was. I remember my dad said to me 'you don't realise what you have achieved'. I just looked at him and said 'yeah, OK'. He was actually happier for me than I was for myself.

"It wasn't until a good few years later that what I achieved at St Mirren actually sunk in. In fact I had to wait another ten years before I won another trophy and that was with Borussia Dortmund. I still look back on that cup win with enormous pride. It was amazing to lift a cup at just 17. Only now do I realise how lucky I was playing in such a great team. I also picked up a big cup win bonus. Alex Smith said he would give me enough for a new sports car. I think it got me a new suit while he turned up with his new top of the range Mercedes. Enough said."

Manager Smith also knew what the win meant to everyone connected with Paisley and the surrounding areas. The cup-winning boss admitted: "It has left me with fantastic memories. That team played with their hearts on their sleeves. They were all good, honest and hard-working guys. They were great to manage and they did Paisley and the club proud. There was no doubt getting to Hampden gave everybody in the area a massive lift but winning the cup took it to another level altogether.

"It was just a great, great day for every St Mirren fan. There were families of two and three generations going to the game together. It was just a brilliant time for everybody connected with St Mirren."

Not surprisingly, Paisley was brought to a standstill as the cup-winning squad returned home for a heroes' welcome. McDowall recalled: "It is amazing that our team has now gone down in St Mirren history. Going back to Paisley and seeing what it meant to all the fans was amazing. My family and in-laws were all in the crowds. There were bodies everywhere even on the top of lamp posts, anywhere they could get a glimpse of the cup. Even when you go to the new St Mirren Park it is great to see all the old pictures because it always brings back some unbelievable memories."

Hero Ferguson also knew his goal had achieved a once-in-a-lifetime feat. "It had been back in the late 50s when St Mirren had last won the Scottish Cup and our team did it in the 80s," Ferguson admitted. "Scottish Cup wins only happen once in a blue moon for teams like St Mirren and so when they do happen they are really special."

The clocks were also turned back as the pubs and clubs dropped the price of drink back to the 1950s, when the Buddies had last taken the famous old trophy home. The class of 1987 had their own open-top bus parade before they flew off to play in an end of season tournament in Singapore, where they beat Southampton along the way to lifting the Epson Cup.

Smith joked: "It was a great night although some of them were still complaining about the prices. We went back to the Excelsior Hotel at the airport and we had a great night although we were due to fly to Singapore the next day. I actually put Paul Lambert home at 11pm with his parents because he was only 17. He also wasn't going to Singapore because I felt it was too far for him to go."

The Hampden win handed Saints a return to Europe in the European Cup Winners' Cup. Smith got off his mark quickly to get one over on Celtic when they nicked their Seamill base for their preparations ahead of their clash with Tromso. The Buddies beat the Norwegians 1-0 at home, thanks to McDowall's goal – although things were far from ideal behind the scenes, as Bone clashed with McGarvey.

Striker McGarvey said: "Jimmy had been out of order the night before the game and then during the match Lambert and myself were our two best players. We were playing out of our skins but the manager decided to take us off. I asked Jimmy Bone why and he said it was tactical. I said 'tactical' and just laughed. I went into the dressing room and next thing I knew Jimmy came in and went for me. Lambert tried to break it up and got thrown against the wall. There wasn't a punch thrown. It was more of a wrestling match and was split up when the rest of the team came in.

"I ended up writing out a transfer request and giving it to our directors right after the game. It only needed Alex Smith to get us to shake hands but it didn't happen. Jimmy went on to tell everyone he gave me a kicking. I have faced up to him over it since but even he knows that was complete nonsense."

St Mirren sneaked through after a goalless draw in Norway before their brave European run came to an end as Belgian side Mechelen, who went on to lift the Cup Winners' Cup, knocked them out.

There was also to be a silver-lining for cup hero Ferguson, as he got his dream move to Rangers after the Euro exit. Ferguson admitted: "People say I only got my move to Rangers on the back of the cup final, but that is rubbish. There is no doubt my cup final goal helped but Rangers look at players over a period of time rather than over two or three games. But what I have to say is if it hadn't been for St Mirren and playing alongside some very good team-mates I would never have got that move."

ST MIRREN'S SCOTTISH CUP RUN 1986-87
* Third round (31st January 1987 at Love Street)
  St Mirren 3 (McDougall, McGarvey, Ferguson)
  Inverness Caledonian 0
* Fourth round (21st February 1987 at Cappielow)
  Morton 2 (Alexander, McNeil) St Mirren 3
  (Chalmers 2, Ferguson)
* Quarter-final (14th March 1987 at Starks Park)
  Raith Rovers 0 St Mirren 2 (Godfrey, Chalmers)
* Semi-final (11th April 1987 at Hampden)
  Hearts 1 (Mackay) St Mirren 2 (Ferguson, McGarvey)
* Scottish Cup final (16th May 1987)
  Dundee United 0 St Mirren 1 (Ferguson)

ST MIRREN'S CUP-WINNING TEAM
Campbell Money, Tommy Wilson, Derek Hamilton, Neil Cooper, David Winnie, Ian Ferguson, Paul Lambert (Tony Fitzpatrick), Billy Abercrombie, Brian Hamilton, Kenny McDowall (Ian Cameron), Frank McGarvey.
Manager: Alex Smith.

10

• ABERDEEN •
THE DANDY DONS CLAIM AN OLD FIRM CUP DOUBLE TO REMEMBER

FOLLOWING in the footsteps of Alex Ferguson was always going to be a big ask. The late Ian Porterfield tried before he passed the gauntlet on to the experienced management duo of Alex Smith and Jocky Scott.

Smith, who led St Mirren to Scottish Cup glory in 1987, said: "I didn't feel pressure trying to revive the glory days of Sir Alex Ferguson. I thought it was fantastic what he achieved and the way he went about things in his time at Pittodrie. I watched what he did closely and rather than use it as a weight around my neck I always tried to use what he did as an inspiration to what could be achieved."

Smith and Scott's Aberdeen ran Rangers all the way in their first full campaign and there was a real hope and belief they could get the Dons back on the silverware trail. Scott explained: "Before we started we agreed the boundaries that Alex would manage and be the public face of the club while I got on with the training and coaching of the players. It worked well and we had a good team with top professionals and internationalists to call upon."

Graeme Souness's multi-million pound Rangers squad were always going to be favourites to win the league but the Dons felt they had more than a fighting chance, in all competitions. They had also pushed Rangers all the way in the previous two Skol Cup finals. Smith and Scott, along with the Red Army, hoped it would be third time lucky, especially after they crashed out of Europe at the cynical hands of Rapid Vienna.

The chance to collect medals and trophies at Aberdeen was a big factor in Scotland star Charlie Nicholas's decision to swap the bright lights of Arsenal for the northern lights. Nicholas said: "When I moved to Aberdeen I have to be honest and say it wasn't the move I anticipated. I was close to joining the French team Nice because at that time I was having problems with George Graham. Aberdeen were in the mix and it wasn't until I sat down and looked at things closely that it really became an option. They had been a successful side and still had the basis of a top squad. I knew they had good players, who could still win trophies and those were the things that convinced me to move to Pittodrie."

The Skol Cup campaign kicked off with a convincing 2-0 victory over Albion Rovers thanks to strikes from David Robertson and Willem van der Ark. The Dons eased into the next round with a crushing 4-0 win over Airdrie, through goals from Paul Mason, Ian Cameron and a Jim Bett double.

Next up were Smith's former club, St Mirren, who stood between the Dons and a place in the semi-finals. Goals from Mason, Bett and an own goal were enough to seal an efficient 3-1 win and sent the Dons back to Hampden to take on Celtic. It was a tense affair in the last four before Cameron came off the bench to grab the only goal.

Cameron explained: "I saw Pat Bonner off his line when the ball broke to me and I just decided to go for it. I managed to get a good connection and it flew over his head. It was great to see the ball hit the net but I am certain that Bonner would have saved it if he had stayed on his line. I was delighted to score the only goal. My family were still down in Glasgow and it was great that they were there to see it. That was a big result. I suddenly had thoughts of another visit to Hampden but that was short-lived because I ended up suffering concussion in a league game and ended up being ruled out of the final."

That result, however, did soothe a major headache for Smith, proving his players could still go to Glasgow and win against all odds.

Smith admitted: "That was massive going to Hampden and beating Celtic. But you knew by their characters that this squad could go into the lion's den and overcome the Old Firm. Most of the players had done it in the past and knew they could do it again. They were all international players who had played at the top level and that win just rubber-stamped their belief."

Rangers were still ahead in the league although Aberdeen remained on their coat-tails. The Ibrox giants also crushed Dunfermline 5-0 in the other semi-final to ensure that the top two went head to head in the Skol Cup final.

Aberdeen still had all the old heads like Willie Miller, Alex McLeish, Stewart McKimmie, Bett and Robert Connor but Smith and Scott decided to mix it up by throwing one of the club's rising stars into their Hampden starting 11. Smith explained: "I remember the morning of the game we stopped off at Abbotsinch and I pulled Eoin Jess, who was only 17 at the time, to one side and told him he would be starting, but he wasn't to tell a soul, apart from his parents."

Jess admitted the news left him in a state of shock. He said: "I was just delighted to be part of the squad. I was still changing in the away dressing room with the rest of the young boys and getting hammered if I ever wandered into the first-team dressing room. I thought I might have got on the bench if I was lucky, so to be told I was starting was really something. I have to say I was really excited. I knew I was going up against guys like Terry Butcher but I can't really say I felt any fear."

Scouse midfielder Mason had also started to make his mark on the team, after a slow start to life at Pittodrie. The fired-up star said: "We knew everything was against us. Rangers and Celtic had more fans, nine out of ten officials would be against us and there was also the media but that just spurred us on. We had strong characters and more importantly good players who felt they could go to Glasgow and win. I had also failed to make the team the previous Skol Cup final and that whetted my appetite, personally, not to miss this one."

Scottish international Connor had lost the previous two League Cup finals and was adamant Rangers weren't going to make it an unwanted hat-trick. Connor said: "Those disappointments made us determined we were going to beat Rangers. The boys who had also played under Sir Alex Ferguson had been used to winning and you saw the hurt in them when we lost those finals. They had been used to winning."

That determination helped the Dons hit the front through Mason. The Englishman recalled: "I was really nervous before the final. I could hardly sleep because I was that wound up, but when the action started I was fine and I really settled down after my first goal. Connor lobbed a high ball back into the box. I saw Chris Woods off his line and I managed to time my jump perfectly to head the ball over him and into the net."

Rangers, however, were a tough nut to crack although their equaliser, a Mark Walters penalty, fell into the highly controversial category. A frustrated Willie Miller said: "Ally just backed into me and then just fell. I remonstrated with the referee George Smith and then I went and told Ally just what I was thought of his antics.

"Ally told me I should watch the tackle back again on television. I did watch it and I have watched it another 40 times since and it wasn't and it will never be a penalty. I still remind Mr McCoist of that incident to this day."

The teams were level after 90 minutes before Mason put Aberdeen ahead again after an extra-time rocket from co-manager Scott. The Englishman said: "Before I scored I got a bollocking from Jocky because I hadn't made a run forward to support Charlie and Jocky wasn't slow in telling me. So the next time Robertson threw the ball up the line and van der Ark flicked it on for Charlie I was waiting for his cut-back.

"I hit it and it went through a cluster of players and ended up in the back of the net. I never said anything to Jocky but it proved I listened to him. After all, it ended up getting me a cup final winner that I will never forget."

The Skol Cup was to be the last trophy the legendary Dons skipper Willie Miller was to hold above his head, while for some of his less experienced team-mates it was their first taste of glory. Miller said: "When we won that cup all I felt was enormous relief. I had lost the previous two finals to Rangers and I don't know how I would have coped if they had made it three. I was used to winning things so to go two or three seasons without a trophy was really hard.

"I had a knee problem at that time but I never ever thought that would be my last trophy. I still thought I could play on for another couple of years although that later turned out that it wasn't going to be the case."

Boyhood Aberdeen fan Brian Irvine, who had appeared as a second-half substitute, said: "I was delighted because I had missed a few cup finals and this time I had played my part. It was a dream come true because I was an Aberdeen fan and to lift a trophy at Hampden as an Aberdeen player was unbelievable."

Smith also believed his side fired a warning shot across the bow of Rangers with that win. The experienced boss said: "I felt we deserved to lift the trophy because we had been the better team. It was a real achievement because Souness and Walter Smith really had Rangers going at that point. It was Aberdeen's first trophy in a few years and it sent down a message that my players and team were going to be strong contenders for everything in Scottish football, including the SPL title. McLeish, Miller and Bett were the rocks on which our Aberdeen team was built."

Cup hero Mason admitted it took him a while for his Hampden heroics to sink in. Mason joked: "After the final whistle went I think I was on cloud nine for two or three days after it. You always dream of playing in a cup final but to score twice in one was just amazing. What a feeling. Looking back at the DVDs I was only 27 and at the peak of my playing days."

Aberdeen were rocked as Miller continued to struggle with his knee injury, while Theo Snelders also had to go under the knife. Snelders explained: "My knee had been causing me problems. I played in the League Cup final by taking pain-killers but I couldn't go on and needed an operation. Initially I was told I might not play again that season but I went back to see my surgeon in Holland and he insisted I would be OK and he was right."

Despite those serious setbacks the team continued to fight for glory on three fronts. They were further boosted when Dutch international and European Cup winner Hans Gillhaus arrived from PSV Eindhoven. He immediately showed an eye for goal.

However, it was another Dutch striker in van der Ark who stole the glory and the match ball in their Scottish Cup opener at Partick Thistle. "The day I scored three goals at Partick Thistle was probably my best game for Aberdeen," van der Ark admitted. "It was a real hard battle but we played really well. "I got the match ball and a little trophy for being one of the first foreign players to score a hat-trick in the Scottish Cup."

The ever-impressive Brian Grant, Mason and an own goal completed Aberdeen's impressive 6-2 rout at Firhill. It was a big one for striker Nicholas. He explained: "Gerry Collins really got me up for that game. I always like going to Firhill because it was my old stomping ground and I had a lot of friends at the games, although they mostly supported the Jags. Anyway big Gerry had been in the papers mouthing off that the likes of Bett and myself wouldn't fancy it and they would beat us at Firhill. Alex and Jocky put the article up in the dressing room and after that they didn't have to do too much of a team talk."

Nicholas then pitched in with Gillhaus to give Aberdeen a 2-1 win over Morton, with former Everton keeper Bobby Mimms between the sticks. The Dons continued to fire on all cylinders as Hearts talked the talk but failed to walk the walk. They were thumped by goals from Bett, Gillhaus, Irvine and Nicholas.

Irvine admitted: "Hearts was a big one because they were in good form at that time. John Robertson and Scott Crabbe were also scoring lots of goals and they told the papers they were going to knock us out of the cup. That was also put up on the notice board and gave us all the motivation we needed to set them straight."

There was another tricky tie to follow against New Firm rivals Dundee United in the semi-final. Aberdeen proved deadly although United also gave them a helping hand at Tynecastle. Big Irvine netted and had a big part in their second. The defender said: "Charlie Nicholas knocked the ball back across the face and I was there to knock it past Alan Main. I then challenged Mixu Paatelainen at a corner and the ball came off him and went flying into the net. So we made a decent start."

It was then left to Gillhaus to kill United off. "I scored again and in that game we just destroyed Dundee United," the Dutchman recalled. "We played really well and they just couldn't cope with us. It was great for us but I also felt for my friend Freddy van der Hoorn. He scored an own goal to make it 4-0 and wrap up a disastrous day for United. I didn't want to rub it in at the final whistle but I have reminded him of it since."

Boss Smith was also delighted with the performance and decided that same team was going to be his cup final side to play Celtic, who had seen off Clydebank in the other semi, meaning heartbreak for veteran Miller. Smith recalled: "Willie had been out since the October but he was really pushing and trying to get back for the final. He managed to get a couple of reserve games and also played in our final day win over Celtic, which meant Celtic had to beat us in the final to get into Europe. But I told Willie the day before the final that he wasn't going to be involved. I also decided not to put him on the bench because I wanted cover for two or three positions. He wasn't happy but he accepted it professionally."

Aberdeen's young guns, like Scott Booth and Jess, also caused Smith a selection headache when they took their chance after Smith had rested some of his top stars ahead of the final. The young pretenders thrashed their cup final opponents 3-1 and left Celtic needing to win at Hampden to qualify for Europe.

"Dundee United needed us to beat Celtic in the final game to qualify for Europe," Snelders recalled. "The manager rested quite a few of the experienced boys and put out a lot of the youngsters although I played because I still needed games. I remember standing there thinking that Jim McLean will be writing a letter of complaint when he saw our team but it would have turned to a letter of congratulations come the final whistle."

There was also some unwanted transfer speculation in the build-up with Nicholas set to rejoin their Hampden rivals Celtic after the cup final. Nicholas revealed: "It was a straight choice between Celtic and the French side Toulon. By the time of the final it looked like I was going to Celtic and there were endless rumours that I was going back there although nothing had been agreed at that point. I just wanted to go out and win the Scottish Cup because it was the only domestic medal in Scotland I hadn't won."

The final was a nervy affair and the conspiracy theories began to kick in when Nicholas missed a great chance to put Celtic to the sword. The former Scotland star admitted: "I had a great opportunity. I went in with Paul Elliott and the ball broke to me quickly. I didn't get a chance to react and I just had to swing at it but Elliott managed to scramble it off the line. Alex McLeish had a right go at me at half-time, telling me I should have buried it, but he didn't need to tell me because I knew myself I should have buried it."

Neither side was able to make the breakthrough after 90 minutes and extra-time and it went to the dreaded shoot-out – the first Scottish Cup final to be decided in such a way. Darius Wdowczyk missed the first for Celtic to give Aberdeen the advantage although Grant blazed over to let him off the hook. A gutted Grant painfully recalled: "I felt quite confident when I was walking up but in my run-up I changed my mind and blasted the ball over. Walking back I wanted the ground to open up and swallow me, the embarrassment of missing a penalty and fearing what the possible consequences could be left a real horrible feeling inside."

That miss heaped the pressure on Nicholas to score and take things into sudden death – against his future employers. Nicholas recalled those frantic moments. He said: "I took my time as I walked down towards the old Rangers end and suddenly the Celtic fans started to clap me. I don't know if they knew I was going to rejoin them or were just hoping, as a Celtic fan, I would miss. I also knew that if I missed there would be all these conspiracy theories.

"I just tried to stay focused and when I put the ball down I was suddenly facing my good friend Pat Bonner, who I had faced many times in training. I just kept my focus and went for the top corner and fortunately that was where it ended up. I was relieved but I didn't really celebrate but I never did when I scored against Celtic."

Both sides kept their cool until Anton Rogan stepped up to take Celtic's tenth penalty. Dons keeper Snelders recalled: "The funny thing was that we never practised for a penalty shoot-out. Everybody was scoring and I remember walking past Pat Bonner and joked it is going to come down to us to take penalties. The Celtic players were also trying to wind up the crowd before Graeme Watson's penalty. So when it came to Anton Rogan's penalty I did the same and tried to get the Aberdeen fans going.

"The referee came over and warned me. That left Rogan standing over the penalty even longer. I then started moving my body from side to side again. I also knew as a left-footer he was likely to open up and hit the ball across his body, so I just dived left and fortunately I managed to make the save. I just turned to the Aberdeen fans and shouted 'yes' and what a feeling."

That left Irvine to become the unlikely hero – although there was one major fly in the ointment as he had never taken a competitive penalty before. Irvine explained: "Theo had just saved Anton's penalty and that took the pressure off me. I knew if I missed then it would be back to sudden death so I wasn't as concerned if the pressure had been on me to score to keep us in the match. It wasn't as if I took penalties either because that was the only one I took in my professional career.

"I had watched a lot of the penalties and they had gone into the top right-hand corner, as I was facing. So I decided that was where I was putting it. There were no guarantees but I went for it and the ball ended up in the back of the net. When I saw the ball go in it was a pretty unique experience. It was just such a feeling of joy watching 20,000 Aberdeen fans celebrate and then I just grabbed and embraced big Theo. It was comic book stuff for me – being able to score a cup final winner for my boyhood idols Aberdeen."

A relieved Grant admitted: "It was great to win the cup although there was still a bit of disappointment that I had missed a penalty. I also had a great deal of sympathy for Wdowczyk and Rogan because their penalty misses were costly. It is fair to say I got a fair bit of stick from my team-mates, like Stewart McKimmie, for missing my penalty that night."

McLeish stepped up, in Miller's absence, to pick up the old trophy. McLeish said: "It was a great day because not only had we won our second trophy of the season but it was also the first trophy I had picked up as Aberdeen captain. It was probably even bigger for me than lifting the Cup Winners' Cup. So it was a great honour although I also felt for Willie because he had missed the final through injury. I remember Peter Grant came up to me after the game and told us we deserved our win. That meant a lot to me."

Co-boss Scott was also delighted with their season's work. He said: "It was one of my best seasons in management, if not the best in terms of silverware. I loved my time in Aberdeen because it was a great, well-run club with top people behind the scenes."

For Nicholas it was also the perfect way for him to show his dedication to the death and to sign off in style. "I was delighted and it proved by winning two cup medals that I made the right choice in joining Aberdeen," Nicholas insisted. "I knew I was leaving them but I was pleased I had helped put Aberdeen back on the map again. I was also delighted because I had finally managed to get my hands on a Scottish Cup winner's medal. I had the full set and I was able to put it in a wee display and give it to my dad, like I did with all my medals. I could see what it meant to him and that made that season at Aberdeen even more special for me."

Local boy Jess was also delighted to finish his first full season with two winner's medals even though he never got off the bench in the Scottish Cup final. He said: "It was some experience. I used to look up to guys like Miller and McLeish and now suddenly here I was standing beside them with two of the biggest cups in Scottish football – this local lad from Portsoy. It was just so surreal and I didn't really take it in until a few years later."

The team returned to their hotel in Anstruther although Nicholas and Bett had to play catch-up after the team bus left them and their wives to make it back to Fife after their drug tests. That was followed the next day by an open-top bus parade round the Granite City.

Manager Smith explained: "Once again the streets of Aberdeen were packed. We took both cups with us and I remember coming off the bus. I was greeted by a local Aberdonian guy who said 'the double is great but next season we are expecting the treble'. I was just trying to enjoy what we had achieved but that is the pressure that comes with success."

Gillhaus played a major part in the Scottish Cup win but he wasn't able to take his north-east bow as he had to jet off and join the preliminary Dutch squad for the World Cup in Italy. The talented striker said: "I basically flew from Glasgow to Holland, so I didn't really get to celebrate with the rest of my team-mates. It wasn't until I came back for pre-season and all my team-mates were talking about the scenes in Aberdeen that I realised what I had missed out on. The good thing was that I made the Dutch World Cup squad so that was at least some consolation."

There were also some personal trophies to arrive at Pittodrie with McLeish named football writers' player of the year and Bett given the players' player award.

That team just about picked up everything but midfielder Connor is adamant they never claimed the big prize their abilities deserved. Connor said: "To win two cups in the one season was a tremendous achievement. No side outside of the Old Firm has done it since. So that in itself gives me a real satisfaction looking back on that season. It was no shock because we had a great team and although I had a great time at Aberdeen, the one thing is that we never won the league during that period. We definitely had a team that was good enough but it just wasn't to be."

ABERDEEN'S SKOL CUP RUN 1989-90
* Second round (16th August 1989 at Cliftonhill)
    Albion Rovers 0 Aberdeen 2 (Robertson, van der Ark)
* Third round (23rd August 1989 at Pittodrie)
    Aberdeen 4 (Mason, Cameron, Bett 2) Airdrie 0
* Quarter-final (30th August 1989 at Pittodrie)
    Aberdeen 3 (Mason, Bett, OG) St Mirren 1 (Shaw)
* Semi-final (30th September 1989 at Hampden)
    Celtic 0 Aberdeen 1 (Cameron)
* Skol Cup final (22nd October 1989 at Hampden)
    Rangers 1 (Walters PEN) Aberdeen 2 (Mason 2) (AET)

ABERDEEN'S SKOL CUP-WINNING TEAM
Theo Snelders, Stewart McKimmie, David Robertson, Brian Grant (Brian Irvine), Alex McLeish, Willie Miller, Charlie Nicholas, Jim Bett, Paul Mason, Robert Connor, Eoin Jess (Willem van der Ark).

ABERDEEN'S SCOTTISH CUP RUN 1989-90
* Third round (20th January 1990 at Firhill)
    Partick Thistle 2 (Campbell, Charnley PEN) Aberdeen 6

(van der Ark 3, Grant, OG, Mason)
* Fourth round (24th February 1990 at Pittodrie)
  Aberdeen 2 (Gillhaus, Nicholas) Morton 1 (Turner)
* Quarter-final (17th March 1990 at Pittodrie)
  Aberdeen 4 (Bett, Gillhaus, Irvine, Nicholas) Hearts 1
  (Colquhoun)
* Semi-final (14th April 1990 at Tynecastle)
  Aberdeen 4 (Irvine, OG, Gillhaus, OG) Dundee United 0
* Scottish Cup final (12th May 1990 at Hampden)
  Aberdeen 0 Celtic 0 (0-0 AET, Aberdeen won 9-8 on
  penalties)

ABERDEEN'S SCOTTISH CUP-WINNING TEAM
Theo Snelders, Stewart McKimmie, Alex McLeish, Brian Irvine,
David Robertson, Paul Mason (Graham Watson), Brian Grant,
Jim Bett, Robert Connor, Charlie Nicholas, Hans Gillhaus.
Manager: Alex Smith.

• MOTHERWELL •
THE STEELMEN LAND SOME PRECIOUS METAL

THOUGHTS of Hampden were a million miles away when Motherwell were drawn away to holders Aberdeen in the third round of the 1991 Scottish Cup. Well had traditionally struggled at Pittodrie so it wasn't a tie that had Tommy McLean and his men jumping for joy, as the Dons had been major players in Scotland and had continually pushed Rangers all the way in those early nine-in-a-row years.

Ian Angus, who headed back to his former club, admitted: "Aberdeen were a team who were still challenging for the title and were Scottish Cup holders into the bargain. It was definitely one of those games, along with the Old Firm, that we were keen to avoid."

The Steelmen under McLean were renowned for their defensive approach, especially at venues like Ibrox, Parkhead and Pittodrie. That was how that opening cup tie panned out until super-sub Stevie Kirk stepped off the bench. Kirk explained: "I was sitting on the bench when we got the free kick and I said to Tommy: 'This is it, I can score from here'. Tommy spoke to Tom Forsyth (his assistant manager) and then put me on. He told me to get Davie Cooper to put the ball into the back post so I could attack it.

"I went on and Davie just looked at me and said: 'Do you not want to shoot?' I thought it was a bit far out but I decided to give it a bash. He rolled the ball to me and I fired in a shot. I thought Theo Snelders had it covered but he let it go again. I couldn't believe it when the ball hit the net."

Craig Paterson helped to keep Aberdeen out in the 1-0 win and revealed how that forced the club to open the purse strings. The experienced defender said: "We had beaten Aberdeen in the first game and that brought a decent first bonus for the players. The club then had to keep pushing it up the further we went in the Scottish Cup. That season we felt we could really do something. We had a decent team but the signing of Davie Cooper helped take us to another level. I played him with at Rangers and he was a genius. He was that good he could turn draws into wins and defeats into a point."

The reward in the next round was a home tie with promotion-chasing Falkirk. The Bairns were top of the First Division and headed to Fir Park determined to show their top-flight credentials. Motherwell took the lead through cult hero Nick Cusack although that was cancelled out by Sam McGivern. Winger Joe McLeod produced his most famous moment in claret and amber when he scored to put Well ahead but his hopes of glory were denied when Alex Taylor squared things again, but Motherwell weren't to be denied. Englishman Cusack scored again before the hero of the previous round struck again. Kirk said: "The ball came across and I just toe poked it past Gordon Marshall for the fourth."

The manager reckoned the belief started to spread through his squad from then on. "With every win the confidence grew," McLean admitted. "I actually felt we had a similar spirit to the one we had at Rangers when we won the European Cup Winners' Cup."

The Motherwell fans started to think along similar lines when they were handed a home clash against Allan McGraw's Greenock Morton, who boasted rising stars like Alan Mahood and Brian Reid. The first match proved to be an anti-climax for all concerned as both teams cancelled each other out in a rather drab, goalless draw.

Paterson admitted complacency sneaked into Motherwell's play that day. "When we got Morton at home we fancied our chances after beating Aberdeen and Falkirk," he candidly said. "Maybe we were over-confident and thought we would stroll past them but we didn't play well at all. Morton also had a couple of ex-Motherwell players in John Gahagan and Davie McCabe and they were determined to do something against their old team. A draw was probably a fair result and Tommy McLean didn't miss us after the game."

Well were still strong favourites going to Cappielow. The nerves were calmed when skipper Tom Boyd put his team in front thanks to a rather fortuitous strike. "I broke forward from my own half," the captain revealed. "I played it to Davie Cooper. He hit the goal line and pulled the ball back for me. Brian Reid came in and tried to blast it clear and I blocked it with my head and managed to guide it into the net. It left me in a state of shock because I never really scored that many goals."

It was still to prove a worrying night and visiting nerves were shredded when former Fir Park favourite Gahagan levelled for Morton. McLean joked: "I had tried to get Gahagan to score goals at Motherwell for years and then he suddenly came back and scored against us."

It was a setback and although both sides huffed and puffed neither could find an extra-time winner. That led to a penalty shoot-out. Davie Cooper, Iain Ferguson, Stevie Kirk and Bobby Russell all netted to give Well a 4-3 lead. Morton's Mark Pickering then fired over, allowing Colin "Psycho" O'Neill to step forward and slam the ball past David Wylie to book Motherwell's semi-final place.

McLean said: "The tie was that close that it probably had to go down to penalties. When it gets to that stage it is pretty much a lottery. The good thing is that we had strong characters in that squad who showed when it came to the pressure of penalties we could handle it and that proved to be the case."

Well joined St Johnstone, Dundee United and Celtic in making up the semi-finals. The Steelmen were hoping for a bit of luck in the draw – although they didn't get it. Angus admitted: "If I was being honest I would have wanted anybody but Celtic, but that was the tie we got. To be fair the boys were still pretty confident because Motherwell had always had a decent record against Celtic that season."

Captain Boyd turned down the chance to swap the Scottish Cup for the last four of the FA Cup. "Six weeks before the final I was given permission to talk to the Nottingham Forest manager Brian Clough," the talented left-back explained. "He wanted to sign me so I could play in their FA Cup semi-final with West Ham. But it just didn't feel right and I decided to stay with Motherwell. I think history will show I made the right decision."

Manager McLean was able to breathe a huge sigh of relief. He had managed to keep one of his top stars and was able to head for Hampden with his strongest side. Motherwell had a few close things, as they managed to keep Celtic out, while Well striker Iain Ferguson almost won it at the death with a long-range thunderbolt that beat Pat Bonner but smashed back off the woodwork. "It was basically the last kick of the ball," Ferguson recalled. "I just got a really good connection and I thought it was going in until it moved at the last minute and came back off the woodwork. I just turned and said, 'maybe that is our chance gone'."

Dundee United saw off rivals St Johnstone 2-1 in the other semi-final and Celtic were expected to join them in the final. Dutch star Luc Nijholt, who had battled back from a broken leg at Parkhead, said: "We had already beaten Celtic twice in the league so we believed we could still win. There was definitely confidence within our team even though everybody else was expecting Celtic to go through."

The pressure was definitely on Celtic although one Motherwell player was feeling it more than any other. "I used to be sick before every game and Tommy McLean told me on one occasion he was going to stop buying me a pre-match meal because it was just going to waste, claimed Northern Irish cap O'Neill. "Anyway, I had my head down the toilet when there was a thump at the door and then the referee asked to have a look at my boots. I was that bad that I had to take them off and throw them under the door."

Celtic went ahead thanks to Paul Elliott but Well levelled through Dougie Arnott before Anton Rogan put the Hoops ahead. The Parkhead club tried to turn the screw but former Pollock junior star Arnott kept their dream alive again. Arnott joked: "Nobody remembers my two goals. I honestly thought our chance had gone after Fergie cracked the woodwork at the end of the first game. Then we came out and Celtic gave us a real battering.

"They took the lead and I thought here we go, but we got our heads down and dug in. Then Ian Angus had a shot which deflected into my path and I was able to put it away with my left foot. That side wasn't my strongest but I knew the manager would have slaughtered me if I hadn't taken it on. Celtic scored again but we still believed we could come back and we did when Nijholt swung in a great cross and I managed to get my head on it. I was named as the man of the match and I have to say it was probably the greatest night of my playing career."

Motherwell's dream then looked like it could become reality when O'Neill fired his Hampden wonder goal high past Pat Bonner. O'Neill recalled: "My close friend Anton Rogan tried to wind me up and said 'you've blown it' after we had drawn the first game. Then he scored one of Celtic's goals to put them ahead. So when I had the chance to get on the scoresheet I went for it. I was 35 yards out and I just decided to have a go. I hit it perfectly and I knew as soon as it left my boot that it was going in. I then went absolutely mental when I scored and of course I purposely bumped into Anton on the way back."

The final became reality when Well sealed their famous win through Kirk. He said: "I flicked the ball forward to Phil O'Donnell. He battled to get the ball and then laid it back to me. I knew we had bodies in the box so I instinctively chipped the ball up to the back post. I was just sticking it up there hoping somebody would put their head on it and stick it away.

"I knew the wind would also take the ball and at one point I thought it was going to fly over the bar and then it changed direction and drifted in. The ball hit the stanchion, post and the bar. The ball had gone in but I think the only other person who saw it cross the line was the linesman."

Suddenly the final brought on extra significance for McLean. Not only had he led his team to Hampden but he was also going head to head against his older brother Jim McLean, the Dundee United manager. McLean junior, however, knew the importance that Scottish Cup run had in lifting the whole of Lanarkshire.

He said: "I said to the players that they were playing for Motherwell and the surrounding areas. There was a lot of doom and gloom with Ravenscraig closing down. I felt this was a chance for the team to give something back and to give the people something they could be proud of again."

The league campaign saw Motherwell finish safely in sixth place but in those final weeks the attentions had turned to Hampden. The increased exposure also allowed Motherwell to pick up a few unexpected perks. "I never had a decent pair of boots during all my time at Motherwell," Paterson joked. "Then a couple of weeks before the final we were flooded with top of the range Puma gear. There were boots, training kit, tracksuits and trainers, etc. I then found out the club had a deal with Puma over the previous three years.

"Eight of the starting cup final team had to wear Puma boots, so there were boys who were pulling off the strips of their own boots and painting on Puma signs. It was all very amusing."

The McLean brothers thought they had fine tuned their preparations but then they were rocked by personal heartbreak days before the final when their dad passed away. Tommy admitted: "It was a real blow to both Jim and I, but we knew the show had to go on for all the players and the supporters. It was their big day and we also knew our dad wouldn't have wanted things any other way either."

McLean took his men to Irvine for their cup final get-away but it was more like a casualty ward. Tom Boyd was troubled with an ankle ligament problem, Angus was toiling with a hamstring strain while O'Neill's knee was causing major concern. Boyd admitted: "It was touch and go because I didn't play in a competitive game between the semi-final and the final."

Angus's injury had to be given even longer. The experienced midfielder explained: "I had been struggling with a hamstring problem and I didn't train in the build-up to the final. I ended up spending half my time on a rubber ring to try and help ease the problem. The manager was keen for me to play and left his team until the last minute. There was a pitch and putt in front of the hotel and the physio had me out there doing a fitness test on the morning of the game."

McLean decided to play both and put O'Neill on the bench. That meant there was to be Hampden heartache for John Philliben and Cusack. McLean said: "I had two big decisions to make. Did I start with Iain Ferguson or Stevie Kirk and was I going to play John Philliben or Craig Paterson? I felt for John because he had played in every game but I went for Craig because I was worried about Darren Jackson's pace. I also picked Iain because I knew Kirkie could make an impact from the bench.

"O'Neill also passed a fitness test on the Friday and I thought he deserved his place after his penalty winner against Morton and his goal against Celtic. I believed he was fit. I later heard stories he had to keep icing his knee up but I don't know if they were true or not. If they were then I would be very disappointed."

Ferguson was delighted to be starting against his former side alongside Arnott. "I was standing in the tunnel and some of my best friends were across from me in the Dundee United team," Ferguson bizarrely admitted. "Guys like David Narey, John Clark and Davie Bowman were all there. It was strange because I had lost two Scottish Cup finals during my own time at Dundee United and now I wanted to leave the same guys heartbroken.

"I remember there was a bit of shouting and banter in the tunnel and I piped up: 'Don't worry lads these guys don't know how to play at

Hampden'. Needless to say I got some right dirty looks and expletives fired back in my direction."

United's Freddy van der Hoorn caused some concern when he struck the woodwork early on but it was Motherwell who took first blood. Ferguson explained: "I started the move and played it to Jim Griffin down the line. He went forward and then I continued my run and he picked me out with a great cross which I managed to head in.

"I had spoken to Tommy McLean the night before and he had been swithering whether to start me and bring on Kirkie or vice versa. I had scored and I felt I was playing well but it still wasn't enough and the manager substituted me at 2-1. The manager knew I wasn't happy and I don't think our relationship was ever the same again after that."

McLean admitted he made the decision because he thought he would later have to put Kirk in goal after keeper Ally Maxwell cracked his ribs in a bruising mid-air challenge with United powerhouse Clark.

The Well boss said: "We decided to put Kirkie on early because we were looking for him to make an impact and we also thought with Maxwell's injury we might need to later put him in the goals. Ally was really struggling but he did brilliantly to play on. I don't think any of us realised the extent of his injury until after the final whistle."

The heroic keeper was clearly distressed although he could do very little as Davie Bowman fired in United's leveller but Well bounced back. Cooper chipped in a free kick, Paterson challenged Clark and the ball fell to O'Donnell.

Paterson said: "Young Phil was as brave as a lion as he dived in to head in the second goal. He took a kick in the ribs but he was prepared to go in where it hurt for the sake of the team. It was a great way for him to score his first goal for Motherwell."

The Lanarkshire side then extended their lead. Goal hero Angus said: "Fergie played the ball up to Kirkie and he took a bad touch, although he claims he meant to lay it off. The ball sat up nicely and I managed to hit it sweetly from 20 yards and it flew past Alan Main."

John O'Neil pulled a goal back for United before Darren Jackson levelled in the final minute to break Well hearts. Arnott, who held his hands up for that goal, recalled: "Phil O'Donnell started up on one of those trademark runs of his. I saw him and I really should have just run the ball into the corner but I tried to thread it through to Phil and I over-hit it. It went through to Alan Main. He picked it up and within one kick and bounce Darren Jackson had put the ball into the net. I just thought oh no what have I done? I expected a bollocking from Tommy but he just told us 'you have won it once you can win it again'."

That hammer blow and a half-fit keeper meant United were odds-on favourites but Motherwell's super-sub had other ideas – just four minutes into extra-time.

"The cross came in from Coop and I was surprised to have been left unmarked just eight yards from goal," Kirk revealed. "Main went for it but didn't get anywhere near it. He claimed he had been fouled by Chris McCart but that was nothing compared to John Clark's challenge on Ally Maxwell that left our goalkeeper up against it. The ball came to me out of the crowd and the hardest thing was trying to get it past Maurice Malpas and Jim McInally, who were standing on the line. I managed to squeeze the ball in. Maxwell made a great late save from Malpas and then what a feeling when the final whistle went."

McCart also dismissed Jim McLean's after-match comments that he had fouled the United keeper. He said: "I just went up for the ball and as I jumped my hand got entangled with Alan's and he couldn't get a full hand on the ball and it spilled. I made a genuine attempt to play the ball and Alan came into me. I didn't barge into him."

Boyd was able to go up and lift the famous old trophy as the first Motherwell captain since 1952. "I was just so proud to go up as captain to lift the cup," the skipper admitted. "Also it was one of the best finals of recent times. I later left for Chelsea and so that was a nice way for me to say goodbye."

McLean was delighted but admitted it was an emotional day. He said: "Both Jim and I had agreed before the game that if we won the cup we wouldn't be seen jumping around on the pitch. In the circumstances we knew it just wouldn't have been right. So when the final whistle went all I felt was relief because there had been such a build-up of things over the week, with everything that happened. I went back to the dressing room and I don't want to give too much away but it is fair to say I shed a few tears. I also felt for Jim because I also knew what he was going through."

After the Hampden lap of honour it was back to Fir Park for even more celebrations – although they were missing two of their Hampden heroes. Angus explained: "I missed most of the celebrations at Fir Park because I was picked for the drugs test but I just couldn't urinate. I was there for hours and once I eventually got away I went to see Ally up at the

Victoria Hospital. He was still in a lot of pain but I think he was more annoyed because he was going to miss the celebrations. By the time I got to Fir Park things were beginning to die down."

It was special a night for Ferguson although he had a lot of sympathy for his former team-mates who had suffered even more Hampden heartache. Ferguson said: "I was a local boy from Newarthill. I had gone to Braidhurst High so I knew what it meant for everybody in Motherwell to win the cup. It was great although I also felt for my old Dundee United team-mates. I knew what they were going through and even after the game I bumped into Davie Bowman's wife and she was just in a flood of tears. That showed the differing emotions on both sides."

Arnott was also delighted he had got off the hook. He said: "It was just amazing. I had lost the junior and amateur Scottish Cup finals so to win the main tournament at the third attempt was just amazing. It is a day I will never forget."

The next day the team took to the streets on their open-top bus parade. Kirk admitted: "It was great showing off the cup at Fir Park and the open-top bus celebrations the next day were unbelievable. I didn't know there was that many people in Lanarkshire because the streets in and around Motherwell and Wishaw were absolutely mobbed. The scenes were amazing."

Defender McCart added: "That night back in Motherwell and the next day will live with me forever. I even spoke to Davie Cooper and he had won everything at Rangers but he admitted it was unbelievable to be up there with the Scottish Cup because there was never any chance of an open-top bus parade in Glasgow, with either half of the Old Firm."

Nijholt also admitted it was a dream weekend. He said: "I won the Scottish Cup there and had a great time at Motherwell. The club will always have a very special place in my heart."

That was to be the end of an era for many of the team as Boyd was sold to Chelsea for £1m while Maxwell and Paterson were frozen out after they refused to sign new deals.

McLean had to regroup as Well got ready for their first venture into Europe, via the Cup Winners' Cup, where they were drawn against Polish side Katowice. Their nightmare first leg saw them crash 2-0 before two goals from Kirk and another from Cusack levelled the tie at Fir Park but they crashed out on away goals. Kirk admitted: "It was a big disappointment because we should have gone through."

That famous cup-winning team and European entrants have written their names into the history books of Motherwell FC. The big tragedy of it all is that O'Donnell, Cooper, Jamie Dolan and Paul McGrillen are no longer with us.

McCart admitted: "There aren't many days that go by when you don't think about the guys we have lost. They played a major part in Motherwell's success over that period and they will never be forgotten by the fans or their team-mates."

MOTHERWELL'S SCOTTISH CUP RUN 1990-91

* Third round (26th January 1991 at Pittodrie)
  Aberdeen 0 Motherwell 1 (Kirk)
* Fourth round (23rd February 1991 at Fir Park)
  Motherwell 4 (Cusack 2, McLeod, Kirk) Falkirk 2
  (McGivern, Taylor)
* Quarter-final (16th March 1991 at Fir Park)
  Motherwell 0 Morton 0
* Quarter-final replay (19th March 1991 at Cappielow)
  Morton 1 (Gahagan) Motherwell 1 (Boyd) (AET,
  Motherwell won 5-4 on penalties)
* Semi-final (3rd April 1991 at Hampden Park)
  Celtic 0 Motherwell 0
* Semi-final replay (9th April 1991 at Hampden Park)
  Motherwell 4 (Arnott 2, O'Neill, Kirk) Celtic 2 (Elliott,
  Rogan)
* Scottish Cup final (18th May 1991 at Hampden Park)
  Motherwell 4 (Ferguson, O'Donnell, Angus, Kirk) Dundee
  United 3 (Bowman, J O'Neil, Jackson) (AET)

MOTHERWELL'S SCOTTISH CUP-WINNING TEAM

Ally Maxwell, Luc Nijholt, Tom Boyd, Jim Griffin, Craig Paterson, Chris McCart, Dougie Arnott, Ian Angus, Iain Ferguson (Stevie Kirk), Phil O'Donnell, Davie Cooper (Colin O'Neill).
Manager: Tommy McLean.

12

• HIBERNIAN •
HANDS OFF HIBS TO HAMPDEN GLORY

THE 1991-92 season was always going to be a campaign that every Hibs fan will look back on with great fondness – even if they hadn't lifted the Skol Cup. The fact there was still a Hibernian FC was a major achievement in itself after Wallace Mercer, the chairman of bitter rivals Hearts, had launched his controversial takeover bid, in an attempt to merge the two capital teams.

The bid, not surprisingly, was met by outrage and anger by the Easter Road support, who launched the now infamous Hands Off Hibs campaign that, in the end, managed to save the club, along with the help and financial backing of Kwik Fit founder Sir Tom Farmer.

It meant manager Alex Miller was able to continue his job of trying to turn the club's ailing fortunes around on the pitch. Money was limited but he was able to generate funds by selling and bringing in his top target Keith Wright from Dundee.

Miller explained: "It was the year after we had come out of receivership under Sir Tom Farmer. He signed for the liability and we were able to wipe out our debt, which was a massive weight off everybody's shoulders. It also meant that I could sell Paul Wright to St Johnstone and that allowed me to bring in Keith Wright, who was my only signing I paid money for that summer. If I had sold a player before that the money would have gone straight to the banks so it was good to at least freshen up the squad with some quality. I think the signing of Keith was definitely the catalyst for our success."

For Wright it was an easy decision, despite all the club's previous problems, being a lifelong Hibee. Wright admitted: "The Dundee chairman Angus Cook told me that he had accepted offers from Hibs and Aberdeen. He didn't care where I went as long as I went because Dundee needed the money after they had failed to win promotion to the Premier Division.

"I met with Jocky Scott at Aberdeen but Hibs blew me away. I was also a big Hibs fans but they went out of their way to get me to Easter Road. Alex Miller met me in a hotel in Perth, along with a couple of directors and the chairman Douglas Cromb. That showed how much they wanted me so I decided to join Hibs, especially after I had been given assurances their financial problems were behind them."

Miller also knew his side needed a bit more experience and leadership and they pulled off a major coup when they persuaded Scotland and former Celtic midfielder Murdo MacLeod to swap the Bundesliga giants Borussia Dortmund for Leith.

"I felt it was time to come back from Germany," MacLeod explained. "The main reason for me coming back was my kids and for their schooling and education. The kids were going into secondary school and I just thought going home would be better for them. So word was put out that I wanted to come back and Hibs and Alex Miller expressed an interest in me right away.

"Dunfermline also wanted to sign me. I met with both clubs but I ended up picking Hibs. Traditionally, Hibs are the bigger club and I felt we could go places even though I knew they had come close to going under the previous season. I had been aware of the Hands Off Hibs campaign because I had got the *Daily Record* sent out to me every day when I was out in Germany.

"I knew what was going on in Scottish football and I saw the lengths the Hibs fans had gone to save their club. That showed how much passion the supporters had for their club and I knew that would grow tenfold if we could win something. As for the finances I was never too worried about that side of things. Also when you had such a successful businessman like Sir Tom Farmer involved then that also gave the club a lot of stability."

Another big character, in experienced English keeper John Burridge, was recruited to take over the void left by Andy Goram's sale to Rangers. Burridge had a wealth of top level experience with the likes of Wolves and Crystal Palace but admitted his early days at Easter Road were something of a culture shock.

Burridge said: "I didn't know anything about the Hands Off Hibs campaign when Alex Miller rang me and asked me to go up. When I arrived at the club and heard what had happened it came as a bit of a shock to me. Thank goodness for Sir Tom Farmer. The morale within the dressing room was terrible. It was at rock-bottom. I had to help try and lift the place.

"I had umpteen fights with Alex Miller because he tried to put a dampener on things, telling the players they weren't good enough. It was an uphill struggle but we had some good players and we got them picked up and believing in themselves. I was good at lifting spirits and trying to improve the mood in the dressing room. I also had to take on Alex Miller because at times I thought he would pick on the players. I stood up to him and I think that helped to lift the dressing room. The boys went on to prove what good players they were that season."

The new-look Hibees made a positive start to their league campaign and the confidence continued to grow with every victory. The Skol Cup started with a straightforward 3-0 victory against Stirling Albion. Tommy McIntyre, Gareth Evans and Keith Wright got the goals. Central defender McIntyre admitted that game also split his family. He said: "The game was played at St Johnstone because Stirling still had their artificial surface and couldn't play their games at home. It was funny because my cousin, Tom O'Neill, was a coach with Stirling Albion at the time. They were doing well at Stirling Albion but we also went into the match in good form and that showed. I managed to score in the game. A corner came in and I ended up scoring with a toe-poke. It wasn't a glorious strike but a goal is a goal."

The next game saw Hibs squeeze past Kilmarnock in the next round in a five-goal thriller. Skipper MacLeod, midfielder Pat McGinlay and Wright got the goals. Defender Graham Mitchell said: "We played every game away from home. We did well and the only game where we lost goals was against Kilmarnock. Defensively, we were really solid in that campaign. It certainly provided the team with a great platform. We did really well and the confidence grew with every game that we won."

That win over Killie set up another trip to Ayrshire – this time to take on Ayr United.

Winger Mickey Weir admitted Hibs struggled against the Honest Men and he copped it in the neck from manager Miller for his first-half performance. He recalled: "We started the season really well and by the time the cup kicked off the games couldn't come quickly enough. The draw also helped us and allowed us to build up a bit of momentum, although it is fair to say we struggled against Ayr.

"We were poor especially in the first-half and I also struggled. The manager slaughtered me at half-time because he didn't think I was working hard enough. He certainly got me angry with his verbal volley and to be fair it worked because I played a lot better in the second-half."

In the end, Hibs managed to squeeze through thanks to goals from McGinlay and Wright. Striker Wright said: "The Ayr United manager George Burley was out on the pitch before the game getting presented with his manager of the month award. That normally proves to be a bad omen and I hoped that would be the case that night. That is exactly how things turned out for George and Ayr. I also managed to get a goal when I got in front of my marker to glance a header into the net."

Suddenly, the green side of Edinburgh were looking forward to a semi-final – although it is fair to say they didn't get what they were looking for in the draw. Captain MacLeod said: "I went through to Glasgow for the semi-final draw. There were Dunfermline, Airdrie, Rangers and ourselves. We just walked into the press room as the draw was being made and it came out Rangers versus Hibs.

"I said: 'No, wait a minute, surely Rangers have to get somebody else'. We then had the photographs taken and I started doing the press interviews. I then said if you are going to beat either side of the Old Firm then it is easier in a semi-final because nine times out of ten Rangers and Celtic win when they get to the final."

The task may have caused Hibs teams of previous seasons to buckle but this team had a belief and a real inner mettle. Weir said: "I was rooming with Gordon Hunter before the semi-final. I told Gordon we were going to win. I just felt we had a good team, we were playing well and I just thought we would beat them. I felt it in my bones we could do it. I knew if we played the way we could then we could beat Rangers.

"For us this game was more like the final. It was a big one for me because it was my first appearance at Hampden. If was the same for a lot of us but as soon as I arrived at Hampden I was determined to do well. If you can't play there you can't play anywhere."

Hibs were also boosted by the news that Rangers would be missing their influential defender Richard Gough for the game. Manager Miller admitted: "The semi-final win was a big one and we got lucky that night when we found out that Richard Gough was to miss the game. He was a big player for Rangers and it allowed us to work on a game plan which could exploit his absence. I was also confident that if I could get my strongest 11 out and we could play the way I knew we could then I believed we could win the game."

Madcap keeper Burridge also showed that when it comes to football that reputations count for nothing as both teams got ready to take to the Hampden pitch. He joked: "I noised Mark Hateley in the tunnel before we went out. We were all lined up. I shouted 'oi, Hateley, if you come into my box I am going to break your back. Your dad might have been a good player but you aren't a patch on him'. I also knew Ally McCoist from his time at Sunderland. I then said: 'McCoist you were down at Sunderland and you were rubbish' or words to that effect. Hateley came up to me and I told him to get lost and I reckon that helped to give a lot of our team the belief they needed before they went on the park."

It was no surprise to Miller, who had almost ended up in the divorce courts because of Burridge's full-on approach. The boss admitted: "Budgie was just mad. He used to phone the house at 6.30am and tell me he was on the train and what training he expected that day. My wife told me I had to sell him because she couldn't put up with any more of his early morning alarm calls."

Team-mate Weir also admitted that their number one brought a whole different approach to training and football at Easter Road. Weir laughed: "He used to take his moped up with him on the train from Newcastle. He was a real character. I remember one of the first days he arrived he had the youth team taking all these chairs and tables out on to the training pitch. The next thing we knew he had the youngsters firing balls off the tables and chairs so he could dive and test his reflexes.

"There was also a time after one game when he was just sitting there with nothing but his boots and his gloves on. Also he was one of the first players to use all these motivational books and talks. He would walk about with his personal cassette recorder and the tape would tell him how good a goalkeeper he was. He thought he was the best keeper in the world. I also listened to a couple of his tapes and to be fair they really did motivate you."

Certainly when it came to the semi-final, Burridge was a man inspired and his performance allowed Wright to grab the glory with his early goal. Wright recalled: "Mark McGraw and Andy Goram went for a ball. Goram punched it and it landed at the feet of Mickey Weir. He flighted a decent ball into the box and instead of challenging me the two Rangers defenders split and allowed me to head it straight into the middle of the goal. I expected to get clattered.

"It gave us a great early start. I know that a lot of the Hibs fans missed my goal because there was an accident on the motorway and a lot of them got held up. I often hear their stories how they had to listen to my goal on the radio because they were still stuck outside the ground."

Dunfermline saw off Airdrie in the other semi-final and suddenly Miller's men knew who stood between them and Skol Cup glory. Hibs were odds-on favourites and that was something new to them. Skipper MacLeod said: "We were suddenly in the final against Dunfermline and now we were the favourites. That added a bit more pressure on us because a lot of the boys hadn't played in a final or won a lot of trophies before. We knew we couldn't just think that we just have to turn up if we wanted to win the final."

Expectation was heightened as Hibs beat Dunfermline in the league in the run-up to Hampden. Midfielder Brian Hamilton recalled: "We played Dunfermline in the league just before the final and beat them fairly convincingly so that gave us a lot of belief and confidence going into the final. Everybody made us big favourites to win that game. Everybody tipped us to win and it was by no means a certainty when you look at the players Dunfermline had in their team at that time, players like Davie Moyes, Billy Davies, Istvan Kozma, Scott Leitch and George O'Boyle. They had some really good players but we were still strong favourites."

Hibs knew they were hitting form at just the right time although the timing of defender Gordon Hunter on the morning of the final was far from ideal. Weir explained: "The cup final was the day the clocks went back. Gordon Hunter hadn't put his clocks back and he had arrived at Easter Road an hour too early. He thought he was late and ended up starting to drive through to Glasgow himself. Eventually one of the lads got a hold of him and told him we were just arriving at Easter Road so he was able to turn back and come through with the rest of the team on the bus."

Boss Miller turned to another famous Hibs fan for motivation and to get his players into the swing of things ahead of the big game.

Wright said: "I remember the golfer Bernard Gallacher came into our hotel with Sir Tom Farmer when we were getting our pre-match meal. He was a big Hibs fans and he came in and gave us a big motivational talk and then told us how proud he was of us being a Hibs fan. It was a nice touch."

Hibs were now potentially 90 minutes away from lifting their first trophy since 1972, the glory days of the famous Turnbull Tornadoes. Lifelong Hibee Weir knew what the final meant. He said: "It was a lifetime ambition of mine to walk out at Hampden in a cup final with Hibs. I grew up supporting Hibs and the first time I stepped into Easter Road I was determined to win something as a Hibs player.

"I had seen some great players play in the green and white and they had never won anything. I was determined I was going to win something. I also knew I was carrying the hopes of all my friends and family, who were also massive Hibs fans. That in itself put a bit of extra pressure on my shoulders. But it was a pressure I was more than happy to take if it meant bringing silverware back to Easter Road."

The pressure seemed to be a weight on the shoulders of many of the Hibs team, who had failed to play anywhere near their potential in a goalless first-half. It was left to Miller to fire his team up with an inspired half-time team talk.

The manager said: "The first-half of the final we really didn't do ourselves justice. The players all seemed to be nervous and we just didn't play well at all. I just told them at half-time to make sure that when they left this stadium they did it without any regrets because this was a day where they could become cup winners. Thankfully they went out and by the final whistle there were no regrets."

MacLeod admitted his team needed to hear a few home truths. He conceded: "I don't think we played that well in the first-half. We were a bit nervy and too many of us looked as if we thought we were going to win the game regardless. We spoke about things at half-time and we told the boys: 'If you want to win this then you need to go out and prove you want to win it'. Credit to the boys they did precisely that in the second period. We showed more desire, looked more determined and we looked a lot sharper. We put them under a lot of pressure and in the end got our rewards."

Hibs finally got their big break through a disputed penalty when Weir went down under a challenge from Dunfermline defender Ray Sharp. Weir insisted: "It wasn't a dive. I ran into the box and I simply lost control of the ball and my balance at the same time. Sharp fell into me and knocked me over. I fell to the ground and I wasn't expecting the penalty to be awarded. But when I got up and the referee awarded the penalty I wasn't going to turn it down. Keith gave me pelters and still does but I can honestly say I didn't dive. I didn't go down looking for the penalty."

That left McIntyre with the chance to put Hibs ahead from 12 yards. McIntyre, who coolly slotted home, recalled: "There is always a bit of pressure. I was always confident I would score. I knew where I was putting my kick and I had already done my homework and watched some videos of the Dunfermline goalkeeper, Andy Rhodes, as to which way I thought he would go. Thankfully, it worked out well as I placed the ball past him. When I saw the ball hit the net I had a mixture of emotions, from elation and joy down to relief, for myself and the team to get our noses in front."

That settled the nerves before Wright latched on to a Weir pass to slot home the second and to ensure the Skol Cup was heading to the capital. Wright said: "I felt a lot of pressure going into the game because I didn't want to let the Hibs fans down. Then to get the second goal, that finished it, was amazing. Mickey and Gareth Evans pressured the Dunfermline defence. The ball fell to Mickey and he just played a ball that split their central defenders and I just ran on to it.

"I didn't know if I was offside or not although the television replays showed I wasn't. I was suddenly one on one with Andy Rhodes. Ironically I had scored a similar goal against him in the league, so I went the same way. I scooped it past his right-hand side. He went the right way but I managed to put it away. It was amazing when the final whistle went and I had achieved my boyhood dream of winning something with Hibs."

The final whistle led to wild celebrations for the Hibs support and the players. Weir proudly recalled: "The final whistle was just amazing. Winning the cup with Hibs meant I had achieved everything I had set out to do in the game. It was also great for the club and supporters after everything they had gone through in previous years. The one disappointment was that I never got to lift the cup. It wasn't passed along the line. It didn't disappoint at the time but looking back now it is a big regret."

Captain MacLeod admitted it was a real fairytale to go up and lift the cup after everything the club had gone through. MacLeod said: "When you look and everything flashes by from the previous year, what happened at the club and how close they came to going out of business. Then suddenly I was at Hampden holding up a cup. It was probably one of the proudest moments of my life.

"I achieved so much at Celtic, which was expected, but to go to Hibs, a club who were on their backside, and help them lift a major trophy at Hampden was special. It was great for the club and showed the team spirit we had."

Goal hero Wright was also pleased to have got his hands on a winner's medal for him and his mum, in particular. He joked: "It was great for my mum and dad to see me win a trophy with the Hibs. It was even sweeter for my mum because she had been the bar steward at the Craigmillar Hearts club for more than 25 years. She had taken a lot of stick because I was a Hibee so it was good to give her some ammunition to fire back at the Hearts fans."

It was also a moment of vindication for boss Miller who had come under some fierce criticism in previous seasons from his own supporters. He admitted: "I had taken a bit of stick from the fans but they didn't really know the whole story of what had been going on at the club behind the scenes. The previous board had always told the fans we had the money to buy whoever we wanted but the truth was we didn't have a penny. But the board kept pushing this out because it deflected the pressure away from them and that suited them down to the ground.

"I was delighted to win the Skol Cup but my immediate thoughts went to my family. They are the ones who have to take the stick when things aren't going so well, so it was good to see them get some enjoyment back from that cup win. I had won the League Cup five times as a player so it was great also to win it as a manager and to have six winners' medals. That is a record I am very proud of. It was also my first major win in management. I had won Renfrewshire Cups and the Tennents Sixes but this was my first major trophy as a manager."

Keeper Burridge also believes lifting that Skol Cup was the biggest achievement of his playing days. He said: "I won the League Cup with Aston Villa and won promotions with Wolves and Crystal Palace. They were all good times although winning the cup with Hibs probably topped the lot. Winning the cup that season was a miracle, especially as to how close the team had come to going out of business. It was probably the big highlight because those other clubs were expected to win. Nobody in Scotland expected Hibs to win anything that season."

McIntyre admitted that day was not also for the players but their families and the fans as well. He said: "It was great to make a wee bit of history. It is a nice memory to have from that day, knowing I helped Hibs to win a trophy. It was also great because all my family were there. My mum never really went to games but she was there with my dad and my close family. It was good to share the occasion with them."

The glory wasn't to end there for Wright as he finished as the competition's top scorer and won a watch for netting the last goal in the final. Wright explained: "One of the sponsors came up to me after the game and handed me a box for scoring the last goal in the tournament. I opened it up and there was a Rolex watch inside. Brian Hamilton was raging and tried to claim it because he had hit the post with an effort in the final minutes.

"I was delighted to score in the final because it also meant I had scored in every round. I ended up finishing as the competition's joint top scorer with Mo Johnston and we ended up sharing holiday vouchers. Brian Hamilton was adamant I should have given him some of them but my wife was desperate for a holiday so he had no chance."

Hamilton reckons his free kick just about summed up his football career. He said: "I was always one of these guys who would hit the post or the defender on the line. I never seemed to be the luckiest of players and that proved to be the case that day. I had a free kick and I curled it over the wall and beat Andy Rhodes but it came back off the post. It bounced back out and Keith ended getting the Rolex for scoring the last goal in the competition."

Weir delayed the celebrations and the return to Edinburgh because he couldn't supply a post-match urine test. He admitted it was still worth the wait. Weir said: "I have never seen so many Hibs fans in all my life and I had been to some big Hibs games through the years. There were fans who had come from as far afield as Ireland and Aberdeen to see us parade the trophy. As we got to the Maybury there just seemed to be more and more fans. That for me just shows the power of football. How many other occasions would bring out so many fans from so many places?"

Ex-Celtic man MacLeod acknowledged it was a new experience for him being able to go on an open-top bus parade in Scotland. He said: "Apart from Dortmund, where we won the cup, and the whole town came out, I think there was 250,000 people out in Dortmund that day. But to go back through Edinburgh on an open-top bus was just absolutely incredible. Normally if you win with the Old Firm you go back to the hotel and you are locked in a back room somewhere out of the way.

"For me, that day with Hibs was really special because all my family were also on the bus. We then went back to Leith and I thought there won't be many people here because all the Hibs fans were in the city centre but all around Easter Road the streets and pavements were just full."

The Hibs fans packed out Easter Road as they waited for their heroes to return but Miller decided to give some of the club's unsung heroes their day in the sun. Miller said: "It was the first time we had won a cup in nearly 20 years. So I knew what it meant to everybody at the club, who had worked hard behind the scenes to make Hibs a success. That is why when we got back to Easter Road I got the late Jackie Auld, Davie Brown and the groundsman Pat Frost to take the cup out to the fans because I felt they deserved it for all the years of hard work and devotion they gave to Hibs, along with my coaching staff as well."

The cup win also brought the successful squad another major financial windfall – even if it came from illegal means. Captain MacLeod explained: "We put a bet on right at the start of the season. I was behind it and I can't really explain why we decided to do it. I just felt we should have a target for the season.

"So I went round the boys and they all put money on us ranging from £5 to £20, nothing silly, at 40-1. I said we have a chance of winning this so why not bet ourselves. I didn't realise at the time you are not allowed to put bets on in games you are involved in. I know it is wrong but I don't see the problem in backing your own team to win a game or a competition.

"It was a talking point and gave us even more motivation to be even more successful. I collected the money and got somebody to put the bet on and then to collect our winnings. It proved to be a good added bonus for the boys because a lot of them weren't on big wages."

HIBS ' SKOL CUP RUN 1991-92

* Second round (20th August 1991 at McDiarmid Park)
    Stirling 0 Hibs 3 (McIntyre, Evans, Wright)
* Third round (27th August 1991 at Rugby Park)
    Kilmarnock 2 (Campbell, McSkimming) Hibs 3 (MacLeod,
    McGinlay, Wright)
* Quarter-final (3rd September 1991 at Somerset Park)
    Ayr 0 Hibs 2 (McGinlay, Wright)
* Semi-final (25th September 1991 at Hampden)
    Hibs 1 (Wright) Rangers 0
* Skol Cup final (27th October 1991 at Hampden)
    Hibs 2 (McIntyre PEN, Wright) Dunfermline 0

HIBS' SKOL CUP-WINNING TEAM

John Burridge, Willie Miller, Graham Mitchell, Gordon Hunter,
Tommy McIntyre, Murdo MacLeod, Mickey Weir, Brian
Hamilton, Keith Wright, Gareth Evans, Pat McGinlay.
Substitutes: Neil Orr, David Beaumont.
Manager: Alex Miller.

13

• DUNDEE UNITED •
A SPECIAL BREW HELPS TO END AN 85-YEAR WAIT FOR THE SCOTTISH CUP

THE legendary Jim McLean led Dundee United through the most successful period in their history but the one trophy that continually eluded him and the club was the Scottish Cup. He had guided his unfashionable side to SPL and League Cup glory, as well as a Uefa Cup final appearance, but he was never able to burst United's Scottish Cup hoodoo as they were always the bridesmaid, coming out second best in all six of his Scottish Cup final visits. It was hard for a born winner to swallow because he had been desperate to become the first United manager to get his hands on the famous, old trophy.

It wasn't to be and after moving upstairs to become United chairman one of his first tasks was to find his own replacement. The appointment was made in July 1993 and it came right out of the blue when Yugoslav Ivan Golac was unveiled as Dundee United manager. Golac had made his name as a solid right-back at English side Southampton.

His managerial credentials weren't quite so impressive when he was given the keys to the manager's office at Tannadice. He, however, had been in charge of Partizan Belgrade when they famously knocked Celtic out of the European Cup Winners' Cup back in the 1989-90 season. He also came within a whisker of landing the Celtic job before Liam Brady was appointed. Golac had also been in charge of English minnows Torquay before McLean and United came calling.

United captain Maurice Malpas recalled: "There had been noises in Jim McLean's final few months that the club were looking to go down the Liverpool 'Boot Room' route and appoint from within. The likes of Paul Hegarty and Paul Sturrock were thought to have been in the running to replace Wee Jim. I remember I was on holiday in Florida when I bumped into Jim. I asked him if the club were any closer to appointing a manager but he said no. I phoned my dad a couple of days later and he told me Ivan had got the job. It came as a bit of a surprise. Ivan had a decent pedigree as a player but he didn't really have much of a name as a manager. I think the fact he had come so close to getting the Celtic job had been the big thing in turning the heads of the Dundee United directors."

Golac faced a massive job as he attempted to follow in McLean's footsteps. He was also the polar opposite of his new chairman. Golac was so laid-back he was almost vertical, while McLean had been intense and in your face. The former Yugoslavian international was more off the cuff, having claimed to have learned basic English from listening to Rolling Stones records.

He, at least, inherited a decent mix of youth and experience although one of his first tasks was to replace Duncan Ferguson, who was sold to Rangers for £4m, then a British club record deal. Golac immediately used some of that money to recruit his former Partizan Belgrade star Gordan Petric. The classy central defender came in for a bargain £500,000.

Petric recalled: "There had been a bit of interest for me in Germany and a couple of other countries but I knew I wanted to move to Scotland when Ivan Golac made the call. He had been my coach at Partizan Belgrade. I knew him well and he believed in me and I thought at that stage joining Dundee United was also the best move for my career. Also with all the troubles around Serbia and Croatia at that time it was very difficult to move clubs back home so you found most top players moving abroad if they got the chance."

Golac cast his net far and wide and also brought in little-known Trinidad and Tobago striker Jerren Nixon from ECM Motown. The outspoken United boss then piled the pressure on him by hailing him as a future £10m player. He later re-assessed that prediction and in typical Golac style raised Nixon's future value nearer the £15m mark. Unfortunately, Nixon and United blew hot and cold as the Tannadice players took time to adapt to Golac's outlandish ways.

United midfielder David "Psycho" Bowman admitted: "Ivan just seemed to be on a different planet at times. He was so different to Jim McLean. I needed somebody like Jim who was on my back all the time. That got the best out of me. Ivan was the complete opposite. He let the players get away with too much and the words holiday camp come to mind when I think back. Even in training we would work on free kicks and Ivan would end up taking them all himself.

"He would say 'I'm the best' and would continue to curl them in until we had to push him out of the way to let the team get some practice in. Then he took us for a walk in the middle of spring and told us all to smell the flowers. We thought Ivan had lost the plot when he came out with all that smell the flowers stuff."

Player-coach and skipper Maurice Malpas admitted it came down to the senior players like Bowman, Jim McInally and himself to maintain the discipline in the dressing room.

Malpas recalled: "It was bizarre because Jim would fine us for anything, whether it be a t-shirt left lying on the floor or dirty boots but Ivan didn't really bother about anything like that. Ivan was just so laid-back.

"On match days he would disappear for a couple of hours before kick-off so he could pick up his family and take them to the game. He would then pop his head round the dressing room door at 2.50pm and wish us all the best. Even in training there were times when he would take us for a walk down to Camperdown Park. We would go to the restaurant down there and he would order us all coffee and bacon rolls, but he would never have any money to pay the bill. It was usually left to one of the players to come back down and square up the bill later on. It was sheer madness."

The new more-laid-back approach might have been a culture shock for some of McLean's old guard but for others it was a breath of fresh air. Defender Brian Welsh said: "Ivan gave me a lot of confidence as a player. Obviously, when he came in he took to me as a player and my confidence just grew from there, knowing my manager had total belief in me.

"I was also lucky that season because I played in the majority of the games and another big factor was that I managed to remain injury-free. I was a little unlucky under Jim McLean with injury. I couldn't get a real run and found myself in and out. Under Ivan, I knew if I was fit and playing well then I would stay in the team. That was a big thing for me."

United finished sixth in the Premier Division in Golac's first season but it was in the Scottish Cup where his side really shone. Yet their first step in the competition was hardly a convincing one as they narrowly saw off Arbroath in a five-goal thriller at Gayfield. Goals from Scott Crabbe, Craig Brewster and a Billy McKinlay penalty were enough to sink their nearby Angus rivals.

The competition was stepped up when United were handed a home draw against top-flight rivals Motherwell. They fell behind to a Stevie Kirk goal before a quickfire Craig Brewster double put United back in the driving seat. They thought they had done enough before they were stunned by John Philliben's late leveller.

"I scored a couple of goals that night and that was the highlight of the early cup run for me although it was a bit of a body blow to be forced into a replay," Brewster recalled. "Motherwell were really fancied but we went down to Fir Park and got the win thanks to a great goal from Brian Welsh. We played really well and the only disappointment was the fact Scott Crabbe broke his leg that night."

Goal hero Welsh admitted his goal had been a gamble that more than paid off. "I just remember that I broke out for the back," the big defender explained: "I used to get the occasional rush of blood to the head in a game and I would go and charge forward. On this occasion I just decided to go for it because we needed a goal. I just kept running forward. Eventually we swung a ball into the box that was headed back out by a Motherwell defender. It fell to me and I just managed to stick it in the corner.

"I just ran off in front of the Dundee United supporters. It was great because we had a really big support that night and a lot of people had written us off after Motherwell had battled back in the first game at Tannadice. That win certainly gave the players a lot of belief."

Another trip to Lanarkshire beckoned in the quarter-final. Airdrie were next up and Alex MacDonald's 'Beastie Boys' were never going to be a pushover. United were held 0-0 at Broomfield. Golac's side faced another replay and an Airdrie side who made the trip to Tannadice on the back of a ten-match unbeaten run. Their confidence, however, was to prove unfounded as United eased past them thanks to goals from youngster Andy McLaren and Billy McKinlay.

That set up a New Firm clash with Aberdeen in the semi-final. The

Dons had been pre-match favourites in a game that would have topped the bill a decade earlier. Aberdeen went ahead through Duncan Shearer before Welsh popped up again to keep United's cup dream alive.

"It would have been an injustice if we hadn't equalised," Welsh insisted. "We absolutely battered Aberdeen. We had so many chances but John Burridge was a man possessed for them in goals that night. Aberdeen went ahead pretty much against the run of play and we just kept trying to push for the equaliser.

"I ended up playing the last ten minutes before I scored, more as a centre-forward than a centre-half because we were just so desperate to score. We eventually got the goal. A cross came into the box and I managed to get my head on it and direct it past Burridge. I was delighted to get the goal but I knew after the ball had hit the net that there was no way we were going to lose this game."

Things certainly seemed to be pointing that way as Jim McInally netted the only goal of the Hampden replay to sink the Dons just three days later.

Welsh said: "Jim McInally got the goal and if I am being honest we probably didn't play as well as we did in the first game but we got the result and that was the most important thing. I think that result was important because it helped us believe we could end all talk of United and Hampden hoodoos."

It meant another cup final appearance but too many bookings meant Scottish international midfielder Billy McKinlay missed the final through suspension.

Fellow midfielder McInally recalled: "I remember Billy was close to tears and we couldn't blame him for feeling like that. We all really felt for him. It must have been the worst feeling in the world and it would have been a real blow for him to miss a cup final. Scott Crabbe broke his leg before the cup final so we went out at Hampden not only to win the cup for ourselves but also for Scott and Billy."

The following night Rangers ensured they would be United's cup final opponents after a Mark Hateley double saw off Kilmarnock 2-1. Walter Smith's side were red-hot favourites as they went into the game looking to clinch back-to-back trebles. Most people expected Rangers to wrap up that heroic feat in some style but showman Golac had other ideas.

Bowman explained: "The one thing about Ivan Golac was that he protected all his players or his boys, as he liked to call us. In the build-up to the final he took the spotlight right off us. Ivan did all the interviews and took centre stage and that was great because we could get on with our preparations for the game. The build-up was bizarre because he took us to a hotel in East Kilbride and we were allowed to go golfing and even go to the horse racing at Hamilton just days before the game. Ivan just kept telling us not to worry because we were going to win the cup. It worked a treat because when we walked out at Hampden I think we actually started to believe him."

Things went well when Golac's side took to the field, as they stifled the threat of Ally McCoist, Hateley and Gordon Durie with considerable ease. There was also a real confidence within the United team as they took to the field. Welsh explained: "I just always felt we were going to win the cup that day. We deserved to be there and I knew another 90 minutes and we could get our hands on the cup.

"I was up against Mark Hateley, who is one of the best strikers that Scotland has ever seen, but I always enjoyed playing against him. I managed to get the better of him that day while Maurice Malpas marked Ally McCoist out of the game, then behind us there was Gordan Petric, who never looked flustered, in a cup final or in any other game for that matter."

The United boss Golac and loyal first-team coach Gordon Wallace had also noticed a real weakness in Rangers' play which they felt their players could exploit. They did precisely that just two minutes after the break when Christian Dailly charged down Ally Maxwell's kick-out. He skipped past the keeper and rattled the ball off the post before Craig Brewster netted his now legendary strike.

Dailly, the then-Scotland Under-21 skipper, explained: "At half-time I was told to close Ally Maxwell down at every opportunity. He hadn't looked too comfortable with his kicking and we thought it was something we could use to our advantage. So when I saw Dave McPherson get the ball and pass it back to Maxwell I took a chance and sprinted towards him. Luckily he didn't kick the ball too cleanly and it came off me. I managed to take the ball round the keeper and although the angle was tight I was confident I was going to score. I fired in the shot but to my shock and horror it came back off the post."

It was left to Brewster to grab the glory as he followed up to knock the rebound into the empty net. Life-long Arab Brewster admitted that goal changed his life forever as he became a Hampden hero and a United legend.

"I was so close that it was almost impossible to miss," Brewster joked. "I had just followed up Christian's shot and I was just praying it would come back off the back post. I just remember what a great feeling it was as I saw the ball hit the net. I then ran off to celebrate because being a United fan I knew how big a goal it potentially could have been."

Rangers did rally but their treble dream was left in tatters when United's Dutch keeper Guido van de Kamp made a great save to deny their talismanic substitute Alexei Mikhailichenko. Van de Kamp said: "It was a good stop but that was what I was in the team to do."

It sparked wide celebrations in Dundee and in the tangerine and black sections of Hampden. Malpas was the man who made history as the first United captain to lift the Scottish Cup – ending 85 years of hurt and frustration in the process.

Malpas recalled: "It was more a relief than anything else when I finally lifted the Scottish Cup with Dundee United. I had been to six or seven previous Scottish Cup finals and had never managed to get my hands on a winner's medal up to that point. I was 32 and I thought it might be my last chance to finally get my hands on the trophy. When we beat Rangers I just remember the sheer relief when the final whistle went. The fact I was captain and one of the more experienced players made it even better."

Golac was delighted to have succeeded where his illustrious predecessor McLean had failed. The Yugoslav said: "Winning the Scottish Cup with such a young team was a magnificent achievement, especially when you looked at the differing finances. My boys were on around £300 a week compared to the Rangers boys who were on ten times that. But we proved that we can not only compete with them but beat them."

Chairman McLean was also delighted United had finally put their Scottish Cup final hoodoo to bed – although he wasn't the man who delivered. McLean admitted: "It was a magnificent day for Dundee United. It was about the club and not Jim McLean. It was about our manager, the players and the fans. It was for them to enjoy. It was just great to get the monkey off the club's back."

It was a day that young David Hannah will never forget – because he was given a very public dressing down during the on-field celebrations. Hannah got slaughtered for wearing a Rangers top he had swapped with Ian Ferguson, after the game. Hannah joked: "Maurice started giving me some light-hearted stick, pointing at my shirt and telling me to get it off. He carried it on into the dressing room and everyone jumped on the bandwagon. I took absolute pelters from everybody."

Golac's two main signings, Petric and Nixon, were also delighted their debut season in Scotland had been silver-lined. Petric said: "It was a very young team and to win a trophy in my first season in Scotland was great, especially with Ivan as my manager. That Scottish Cup win was down to Ivan and the atmosphere and environment he created for his players at Tannadice.

"Even as a foreign player I knew the importance of lifting that cup, as Dundee United had lost so many finals under the legendary Jim McLean. I had won leagues and cups back home with Partizan Belgrade but that day with Dundee United was definitely up there. Also I went on to play another six or seven years in Scotland and that was all down to my initial love affair with Dundee United. I actually played more club football in Scotland than I did in Serbia, so I now class myself as half-Scottish."

Nixon, who came off bench for the final few minutes, admitted: "It was the greatest day of my life. At one point I thought I might not get on the pitch because Andy McLaren had been playing so well. Fortunately I got my chance and to get a cup winner's medal so soon after joining United was amazing."

That match was also to be van de Kamp's farewell as he failed to agree a new deal with United and returned to Holland. Van de Kamp said: "It was the first winner's medal of my career and I'll always treasure it. It was a fabulous feeling when we won the cup."

United returned to the City of Discovery to toast their victory and it was almost as much of a challenge as it had been facing Walter Smith's side hours earlier.

"It was great to finally get a winner's medal and I really owe Ivan for helping me to achieve that," Bowman acknowledged. "It was such a great day and that night back in Dundee was unbelievable. We had agreed to take the cup to a supporters' club in Dundee so Maurice, Jim (McInally) and I took it up there and I don't know how we didn't lose the cup because we weren't exactly in a fit state to look after it. We went back to the Earl Grey Hotel for our official party but things got so silly with the drinks that Jim McLean actually stopped the free bar."

Captain Malpas admitted it took a few days to sober up as more than 20,000 fans took to the streets to celebrate United's success as they took a well-deserved open-top bus parade.

Malpas said: "I don't remember much about the game or the

celebrations. But the one thing that does stand out for me was when I went to Tesco on the Monday. An old man came up to me and said: 'I am going to die a very happy man!' That, for me, sums up what it means to people to see a club like Dundee United lift the cup."

Brewster always knows he will be eternally linked with that famous day and no matter what he does his goal will live on. The big striker later returned for a short and unsuccessful spell as United manager but failed to hit the same heights he did as a player.

Brewster explained: "Players don't realise at the time the significance of winning, or scoring a particular goal. We stopped Rangers winning a second successive treble with that win – a great Rangers team including McCoist, Durie, Hateley and Richard Gough – and it was a special day for us. But I still didn't take it in. I think when a win like that happens once, you presume it will happen to you again. Which it does if you play for Rangers or Celtic but not for the rest of us.

"Jim McLean had umpteen attempts and couldn't win the cup and then Ivan Golac came in, a larger than life figure, told us we were going to win the Scottish Cup and we did. I had stood on the Hampden terraces watching United lose finals. To suddenly be on the pitch, part of the winning team, scoring the winning goal, was the stuff that dreams are made of. My dad said it was one of the greatest days of his life and that pretty much sums it up for me. My dad still has my medal and jersey up in his house."

Defender Welsh admitted that the celebrations probably went on too long and ended up seeing United start the following season with a cup hangover. Welsh said: "The party went on for days. Even after the official events there were quite a few get-togethers. I remember we had a barbecue at my house on the Tuesday before we were due to fly to Trinidad and Tobago for an end-of-season tour. When we came back I would probably admit that our pre-season wasn't as tough as it should have been. We ended up going to Hibs on the first game of the season and we got hammered 5-0. The manager and the board weren't happy that day and we all ended up getting fined. That quickly put our Scottish Cup success out of our thoughts."

The following season Golac vowed to retain the Scottish Cup but it was never likely to happen. He fell out with the board and McLean when they refused his request for £1.5m to bring in the players he felt would take United to the next level. There were also contract rows with Billy McKinlay, Gary Bollan and Jim McInally, which failed to help dressing room morale. Golac was eventually sacked as United went from Scottish Cup winners to the embarrassment of being relegated from the SPL in less than 12 months.

Golac said: "If you look at it logically, I should have been able to stay as long as I wanted to. Any manager winning the Scottish Cup with a club in those circumstances should choose the time when he leaves. But I felt it was going to happen. They had a lovely song, Love Is In The Air, after the final, but I could sense something else. They needed someone they could handle easily. I'm too hard to handle.

"Jim McLean and I shook hands. I'm too nice and too polite, not nasty. A lot of things happened which I never said to the press. It was bad for United. United were the losers, the supporters were the losers. Not me. That's how I felt then and I still feel that way. If I had stayed, many more trophies would have been on the way. But I'm too positive to be bitter."

DUNDEE UNITED'S SCOTTISH CUP RUN 1993-94
* Third round (29th January 1994 at Gayfield)
Arbroath 2 (Sorbie, McKinnon) Dundee United 3 (Crabbe, Brewster, McKinlay PEN)
* Fourth round (19th February 1994 at Tannadice)
Dundee United 2 (Brewster 2) Motherwell 2 (Kirk, Philliben)
* Fourth round replay (1st March 1994 at Fir Park)
Motherwell 0 Dundee United 1 (Welsh)
* Quarter-final (12th March 1994 at Broomfield)
Airdrie 0 Dundee United 0
* Quarter-final replay (15th March 1994 at Tannadice)
Dundee United 2 (McLaren, McKinlay) Airdrie 0
* Semi-final (9th April 1994 at Hampden)
Aberdeen 1 (Shearer) Dundee United 1 (Welsh)
* Semi-final replay (12th April 1994 at Hampden)
Dundee United 1 (McInally) Aberdeen 0
* Scottish Cup final (21st May 1994 at Hampden)
Dundee United 1 (Brewster) Rangers 0

DUNDEE UNITED'S SCOTTISH CUP-WINNING TEAM
Guido van de Kamp, Maurice Malpas, Gordan Petric, Brian Welsh, Jim McInally, Dave Bowman, David Hannah, Alec Cleland, Christian Dailly, Craig Brewster, Andy McLaren (Jerren Nixon).
Manager: Ivan Golac.

• RAITH ROVERS •
DANCING ON THE STREETS OF RAITH

AFTER relegation from the Scottish Premier League the 1994-95 season looked like it could be another long hard campaign for Raith Rovers. The hangover and disappointment left a black cloud hanging over the Starks Park club and there seemed to be very little for manager Jimmy Nicholl or the Rovers fans to get excited about.

The colourful Ulsterman explained: "I decided to stick by the same players despite our relegation but even in the First Division we were absolutely hopeless in those early months. We were all on a bit of a downer. I was beginning to have doubts over a few of my players. We certainly didn't look like a team who were capable of pushing for promotion."

The one glimmer of hope, however, was Raith's Coca-Cola Cup form. They kicked off with a convincing 5-0 thrashing of Ross County. Colin Cameron and Gordon Dalziel grabbed goals while Ally Graham grabbed centre stage with a stunning hat-trick. Striker Graham recalled: "I managed to get a hat-trick, including a couple of headers from Danny Lennon's crosses."

That set the Fifers for a crack at SPL side Kilmarnock and they were slain by another Raith hat-trick hero. "I still remember my goals," a free--scoring Cameron admitted. "My first was a side-foot volley from eight yards. My next was an overhead kick from Ally Graham's knockdown and

I sealed things when I ran through and lifted the ball over the keeper. It was a good win and beating an SPL side certainly gave us belief we could put a decent run together."

Stevie Crawford revealed the real secret behind Cameron's goal success. He said: "It wasn't until a few weeks after that Colin told us that he had gone to McDonalds for his pre-match. If Jimmy Nic had found out he would have killed him but after his hat-trick he would have probably tried to get him a loyalty card."

In the First Division the only place they looked like going was down as they slumped into the bottom half.

A trip to Perth to take on St Johnstone was up next in the cup. Shaun Dennis netted a rare goal while the impressive 3-1 win was sealed by Lennon and Graham. Lennon said: "St Johnstone had tried to play offside but Colin Cameron put me through and I was able to run half the length of the pitch before I slotted it under the keeper."

Suddenly Raith Rovers were looking at a last-four showdown and Lady Luck shone again when they were drawn against Airdrie, while Celtic and Aberdeen met in the other semi-final. Not that Raith's players could take anything for granted as they were left haunted by their B & Q Cup exit to the Diamonds, which, ironically had come after a penalty shoot-out. That wasn't the only thing that was to spook Nicholl and his men, after he had taken them to the infamous Nivingston House hotel in the Cleish Hills, for their pre-match preparations.

"I remember I sat up in bed in my hotel room and one of the two glasses on top of the television just tipped over," Nicholl insisted. "Then I turned and looked at the clock and the hands were going all over the place, left and right. I phoned my assistant, Martin Harvey, and he didn't believe me so he came down and saw the madness for himself.

"I then went down to see the porter and he told me I'd better sign the visitor's book and sure enough there were dozens of other supernatural sightings and bizarre happenings that had occurred within the hotel noted in the book. The porter asked: 'Has the ghost got into bed with you yet?' I said 'what?' then I read on and there was an old women ghost who sneaked into people's beds and left a cold presence next to you."

Striker Dalziel claimed Nicholl cooked up his own special tactics to keep the ghost at bay. He said: "The gaffer seemingly slept with his case beside him the rest of the night – just to make sure there was no chance of anybody getting in beside him."

Dalziel also knew it was no laughing matter. The club captain admitted: "It was that bad that I roomed with Ally Graham and we both had the light on although Davie Kirkwood slept right through everything. I woke up in the middle of the night and I was certain I could see somebody standing at the end of my bed. I shouted on Ally but he thought I was on the wind-up. I went downstairs later and the porter told me the room was haunted.

"The former owner used to shoot rabbits out of our bedroom window. He was then diagnosed with cancer and ended up shooting himself. A lot of the boys thought it was a good laugh and were hiding behind curtains and doors and then jumping out on people. Big David Sinclair was a big, tough centre defender and there was one incident when some of the boys jumped out on him and he ran off as fast as anybody I have ever seen. Like him I couldn't wait to leave."

That wasn't to be the end of the Nivingston House affair because the team were halfway to McDiarmid Park for the semi-final when Nicholl realised he had left veteran defender David Narey behind. Nicholl explained: "I was a stickler for time and I didn't realise David had missed the bus. We were already well on the way and didn't have enough time to turn back. In the end, I had to phone the hotel and get the chef to drive him up to the game."

The former Scotland defender certainly wasn't hampered by his late dash as he had a hand in Graham's opener. The big striker joked: "I think big Narey had a nosebleed when he burst forward. He squared it to Dalziel who toe-poked it into my path and I managed to stick it in the corner."

Raith looked to be in total command until a questionable decision from referee Bill Crombie. He adjudged Raith keeper Thomson had handled outside the box and sent him off. Thomson's take was slightly different. He insisted: "I grabbed the ball and I felt quite confident that I was inside my area but the referee said I had come outside. The television replays have since shown I did gather the ball inside the box and to be fair to Bill the next time he officiated one of our games he came up and said he shouldn't have sent me off. That was decent because he didn't need to say anything."

Thomson's heartbreak allowed 17-year-old reserve keeper Brian Potter to become an overnight star. The teenager was beaten by Stevie Cooper's screamer but then went on to make a string of top saves as he had to stand up to a real aerial bombardment from the Diamonds. His heroics helped to take the tie to extra-time and then the lottery of penalties.

Dennis, Steven McAnespie, Cameron, Crawford and Lennon all netted from 12 yards to leave young Potter to take the glory as he dived to his right to save Alan Lawrence's penalty and book Raith's place in the final. Not that the youngster got to enjoy his hero status for long as he was too young to hit the legendary Kirkcaldy night club Jackie O's with his team-mates and was sent home in a taxi. The hangover for the rest of the squad took a while to kick in and was a reason why they lost the following weekend's derby 5-2 at home to Dunfermline.

Cup final fever started to kick in when Celtic saw Aberdeen off. Suddenly all eyes were on Ibrox but there was to be heartache for one of Nicholl's main men. "I got injured about ten days before the final," captain Lennon recalled with more than a hint of disappointment.

"We were training and one of the youngsters Mark Quinn, who I used to pick up on the way through to the ground, mistimed a challenge and caught me. I tried to play on but something cracked. I went for an x-ray and had it confirmed I had broken my metatarsal. There were a few tears but I knew I just had to get on with it. At least I can say it was me and not David Beckham who made the metatarsal injury fashionable."

The shock cup run gave Raith a new focus and they started to climb the league table, as their players battled for cup final places. Youngsters Crawford, Dair, Steve McAnespie and Cameron were all pulled by Nicholl the night before and given the dream news that they were going to start against Celtic at Ibrox. The advanced warning seemed to do the trick.

Dalziel revealed: "The dressing room before the game was pretty bizarre because the young guys were really cool and confident. The experienced boys like David Narey, Ian Redford and myself were more nervous than the likes of Craw, Mickey and Jason. They treated it like it was a stroll in the park rather than a cup final."

Keeper Thomson also reckons hosts Rangers played their part in ensuring that Raith didn't slip up. "I remember a lot of the Celtic boys struggling with the pitch but we went into the dressing room before the match and there was a box of long studs waiting for us," Thomson revealed. "I don't know if the Rangers backroom staff had left them or not?"

The team talk from Nicholl was simple and to the point. The Fifers, backed by more than 11,000 fans, weren't going out just to make up the numbers. "I knew over 90 or 120 minutes we could compete with the Old Firm," Nicholl insisted. "I had belief in my players and I knew if they went out there and were brave and got on the ball then they could win the cup."

Rovers couldn't have asked for a better start when Crawford took centre stage to score a stunning opener. Crawford recalled: "I remember the corner from the left, I took a touch, did a wee side step and then fired a shot into the corner, which skidded off the surface and past Gordon Marshall. I couldn't believe I had scored in a cup final and what a feeling running up the stand in front of the Raith Rovers fans. I did my Klinsmann celebration and was quickly joined by my team-mates. I then thought to myself you need to get a grip because there is still so long to go."

Celtic were no strangers to the big stage and levelled through Andy Walker and then just six minutes from time Charlie Nicholas netted their second with a header. Graham, who was playing against his boyhood heroes, said: "When Nicholas scored I thought that was it. The story actually goes that some of the wives saw officials taking the cup down with green and white ribbons on it." That turned out to be somewhat presumptuous and premature as Raith's brave players picked themselves off the canvas.

Young Dair, who battled bravely on despite a knee injury, provided the inspiration. He said: "I continued on with the game and had a part in our equaliser. I fired in a shot which Gordon Marshall saved and it came back out."

There waiting to pounce was the legendary poacher Dalziel. He recalled: "I saw Jason cut inside and I knew he was going to shoot. I just thought it was a case of nothing ventured nothing gained and that is why I followed in. Fortunately, the ball bounced up off the keeper and presented me with a tap-in from five yards. I turned and all I could see were Celtic supporters everywhere but what a feeling.

"I definitely think that was the turning point for us. I remember going back for the restart and the look on the faces of Tony Mowbray and Mark McNally said it all. They were absolutely sick. It was then I knew we would win the cup."

The match went into extra-time. Raith had the better of the play but they couldn't dig out an equaliser and it went to penalties and to sudden death, with Dennis, McAnespie, Cameron, Dair, Jason Rowbotham and Crawford all scoring. Crawford said: "I remember my penalty and Jason Dair's weren't the greatest of efforts, looking back Gordon Marshall could probably have saved both of them but they sneaked under him. What a relief for both of us."

Goal hero Dalziel, who had been substituted, couldn't even watch the shoot-out – even though he was the club's regular penalty taker. He said:

"I ended up in the tunnel beside the BBC reporter Chick Young. All I could see was the Raith Rovers supporters and I knew by their reaction if we had scored or Celtic had missed."

Suddenly keeper Thomson, who had been the semi-final villain, was one save away from becoming a Starks Park legend. He proudly recalled: "Brian (Potter) had a wee superstition of throwing the ball up in the air before the taker could get it. I didn't save any of the early penalties, so I decided to throw it up in the air to Paul McStay. I had also made up my mind the way I was going because I had come close to stopping Mike Galloway's kick.

"Right-footers normally put it to the right so I just dived full length to my right and saved it. Even then there was a delay because the referee, Jim McCluskey, pointed at me but I thought he was signalling for a retake and then I realised he only wanted the ball back. I just ran to the centre circle and I just can't describe the feeling of helping Raith Rovers to win the cup."

Dalziel admitted the proudest moment of his career was stepping up to lift the Coca-Cola Cup. The captain said: "It was a big, big honour and a day I will never forget. When I was a youngster I thought the ultimate was scoring in an Old Firm game, which I did, but now looking back to help Raith Rovers to win a major competition against Celtic is without doubt the highlight." His fellow hitman Graham echoed those sentiments. He added: "Without question it was the best feeling I've ever had in my life."

That kicked off the party but it wasn't until the team, including Davie Sinclair and Julian Broddle , took the trophy back home that the celebrations really got into full swing. Midfielder Cameron admitted: "We went back to Kirkcaldy and the place just came to a complete standstill. I have never seen so many people in the streets. We went back to the Dean Park Hotel for a private function and then headed off down the High Street, although the directors didn't trust us with the cup. We ended up in Jackie O's and what a night."

Dair had soldiered bravely on in the final and even a pair of crutches weren't going to stop him. The winger admitted it wasn't the wisest of moves. Dair recalled: "I didn't end up going to the hospital until the Monday and when I did I was told I would be out for six or seven weeks."

Manager Nicholl had to be dragged out of his bed for a sponsor's press conference the following day. "I was half-cut for three or four days after the final," he joked. "I went back to my local pub and I stopped drinking about 7.30am. I decided enough was enough and went to my bed only to be awoken by the phone at 10.30am. I was told I needed to be at Starks Park for a press conference. I was still steaming and I remember I went there and I was an absolute mess both physically and mentally. I looked a right state but I couldn't have been happier."

It would have been quite easy to put away the tools and dine out on that success but Rovers still had unfinished business to attend to in the First Division. Cameron admitted: "The cup is normally seen as a distraction but for us it had the opposite effect. Our season just snowballed. We went on an unbelievable run and we were only training Tuesday, Thursday and Friday. The manager was happy because we were winning games and we were also pretty fresh."

A superb 14-game unbeaten run culminated in the title being clinched with a nail-biting, final day draw at Hamilton. Cameron explained: "We knew a draw would be enough and we had a few chances although we never took them. Then the nerves set in and for the final 30 minutes we spent the match watching the clock tick down. In the end it was just a massive relief to clinch the league. It was just such a great achievement for Raith to win the Coca-Cola Cup and the First Division in the one season."

Nicholl reckons his squad deserved enormous credit for the way they turned their stuttering season around. "The players could quite easily have lived off the cup success and finished mid-table in the First Division but they really pushed themselves and deserved to win the title," their proud manager beamed. "It just topped off the perfect season and the fact we had so much to look forward to."

Dair still remembers the on-board madness as the double winners tried to make their way back to Kirkcaldy on the team bus. "To win the league, cup and qualify for Europe was just amazing for a First Division club," Dair insisted. "I thought it was going to be the norm every season but I have never experienced anything like it since."

Getting his hands on the First Division trophy was the ideal way for Dalziel to say his farewells to Starks Park – as he checked out and left his former team-mates to go boldly where no other Raith Rovers team had gone before. "Winning the title was just the perfect end to the season," Dalziel acknowledged. "After winning the cup and sealing a return to the SPL it was perfect and a fitting reward to all the players and staff who had put everything into the season to make it such a successful one."

The reward for winning the cup was their first venture into European football. The preliminary round saw them up against Faroese minnows Itrottarfelag. A big crowd packed into Starks Park to see a convincing 4-0 victory thanks to goals from Dair, Tony Rougier, McAnespie and Cameron. Dair said: "It was great to play in Europe but to score the first goal was amazing and is something great to have on your CV." The tie was all but over although the return leg was more of a challenge – in more ways than one!

"The trip to the Faroes was a real *Planes, Trains and Automobiles* affair," midfielder Barry Wilson revealed. "Everyone who has been to the Faroes will know how short the runway there is and it is a nightmare when you are trying to land. We were told on our flight that there were only three or four pilots who could make the landing and I am certain our pilot wasn't one of them.

"The whole plane was being battered all over the place. Guys had their heads in their hands and were reaching for sick bags but big Ally Graham was the worst. He was really panicking and was shouting 'we are going to die!'"

Even when they finally got to their hotel the team had to make their own entertainment. Dair admitted: "All I remember about the Faroes was the team hotel. It was that boring that one night the entire team held a hide and seek competition. We were in the middle of nowhere and it was that bad we had sheep grazing on our hotel roof."

The game itself was a slightly livelier affair. It ended 2-2 and set up a clash with Icelandic side Akranes. They provided a far stiffer test, as they were able to call on the Gunnlaugsson twins, Arnar and Bjarki, but Raith managed to freeze them out at Starks Park.

Midfielder Lennon set the Fifers on their way with a double. He recalled: "Colin Cameron rolled the ball back to me and I hit a shot which took a deflection off one of their defenders and wrong-footed their goalkeeper. My second came from a decent move which led to me anticipating an Ally Graham knockdown to drill the ball into the bottom corner."

Midfielder Wilson got the other goal as the Fifers claimed a 3-1 first leg win. Wilson said: "That was my European debut and it was a great night at Starks Park. I managed to pop up to make it 3-1 with a wee dink over the keeper."

Defence became Raith's only form of attack in the Icelandic return.

Boss Nicholl came up with a madcap plan which included a four-man defence with two sweepers behind that. They lost 1-0 but in the end the ultra-cautious tactics paid off – thanks to the heroics of Thomson between the sticks and decent performances from Julian Broddle and the late Ronnie Coyle.

Nicholl, looking back now, said: "I don't know what came over me. I just thought I had to do something because the Gunnlaugsson twins looked like they could cause us problems and I wanted to cut out the space between the full-backs and central defenders. We got battered and I remember thinking after the game how did we escape from that? Needless to say I have never used that tactic again."

Colin Cameron admitted their penalty box was like the Alamo as Thomson's goal led a charmed life. "It was real backs to the wall stuff after they scored but credit to the defence because the likes of Davie Sinclair and Shaun Dennis threw themselves at everything."

Thomson, who made a wonder stop to keep out Siggi Jonson's net-bound free kick at the death, revealed: "It was a big win because we knew we could get a big team in the next round. We just didn't know how big."

That result not only had the Rovers fans celebrating but also their bank manager. Steve McAnespie was sold for a club record £900,000 to English side Bolton Wanderers then they hit the Uefa Cup jackpot. It was three-times European champions Bayern Munich who came out the hat in the second round of the Uefa Cup. They boasted the likes of Jurgen Klinsmann, Jean-Pierre Papin, Christian Ziege, Oliver Khan, Markus Babbel and Lothar Matthaus.

The tie was that big that Raith had to switch the home leg from Starks Park to Easter Road. Bayern even tried to change the match ball. Lennon revealed: "Bayern's officials offered us something like £1,000 to change the match ball from the Mitre Delta to an Adidas Tango. We refused and I believe we tried to get them to swap the ball in the second leg but they refused our offer of two Argentina chews and a Mojo bar."

In the end, Rovers' fortunes still took a dive through a Klinsmann double. Graham admitted: "We did well but the second goal really killed us. We were really disappointed with that. The only good thing was that I picked up the man of the match award although in the grand scheme of things it meant very little."

Raith looked down but try telling that to the 5,000 Rovers fans who made the trip to Munich. Lennon admitted they had to be dragged off the Olympic Stadium the night before the game. The Raith star joked: "It was just amazing and I think that was the only time we trained that season where there wasn't somebody on Poop Scoop duty, like when we trained up at Beveridge Park'."

Davie Sinclair had the honour of leading Raith out against Bayern. Things didn't look good when the German giants were awarded a first-half penalty but the usually lethal Frenchman Papin skied it. Suddenly fear was replaced by hope when Lennon won a free kick just outside of the Bayern box. He picked himself up and took the kick. Lennon said: "I shaped as if I was going to whip the ball in for the defenders to attack. I then gave Khan the eyes and went for the shot. I got a wee bit of luck when it deflected off the wall and flew into the net. I didn't realise exactly what I had done at the time. That came after. The only thing that was in my thoughts was rescuing the tie."

Suddenly Nicholl's upstarts were walking off at half-time on the verge of something massive. Dair said: "We got the goal from Danny Lennon and I still remember walking in and the big scoreboard reading FC Bayern 0 Raith Rovers 1. That was an amazing feeling and it must have been unbelievable for the fans."

Raith star Cameron admitted even their colourful boss, for once, was lost for words. "Jimmy came into the dressing room and we were all expecting his team talk and he just started laughing," Cameron revealed. "We just looked at him and he said: 'I am not going to say anything. Just go outside and look at the scoreboard. That says it all'."

Nicholl knew the European giants were creaking when two world legends were waiting to give the Bayern players what for. "I was walking down to our dressing room when I saw Franz Beckenbauer and Uli Hoeness waiting outside the Bayern area," Nicholl admitted. "The boys came in and I started my team talk but all we could hear was Hoeness and Beckenbauer going right through the Bayern players. They were screaming in German and suddenly they would throw one of our player's names in. I just started laughing and told the players to get up to the wall to see if they could hear their own names. Even the players starting laughing and I think that relaxed them."

The Raith miracle may have come off when Rougier had a great chance but he slammed the ball into the side-netting.

Graham revealed how Bayern's players had totally underestimated the fighting Scots. Graham said: "There was a point where Bayern were attacking and I turned to my marker Thomas Helmer and said: 'Why aren't there a lot of Bayern fans here?' He replied: 'There will be a lot more at the weekend when we have a big game against Borussia Monchengladbach'. I just thought you big German, arrogant so and so."

Unfortunately Helmer had the last laugh as Klinsmann and Babbel struck to finally end Raith's brave European run. Bayern went on to lift the Uefa Cup but no team gave them as much of a fright as Nicholl's merry men. Crawford said: "When you speak about that period in Raith Rovers' history it puts a smile on people's faces. Looking back with the success and dressing room we had I would say that was the greatest spell of my playing career."

RAITH ROVERS' COCA-COLA CUP RUN 1994-95
* Second round (17th August 1994 at Victoria Park)
    Ross County 0 Raith Rovers 5 (Cameron, Graham 3, Dalziel)
* Third round (31st August 1994 at Starks Park)
    Raith Rovers 3 (Cameron 3) Kilmarnock 2 (Montgomerie, Williamson)
* Quarter-final (20th September 1994 at McDiarmid Park)
    St Johnstone 1 (O'Neil) Raith Rovers 3 (Dennis, Lennon, Graham)
* Semi-final (25th October 1994 at McDiarmid Park)
    Raith Rovers 1 (Graham) Airdrie 1 (Cooper) (AET, Raith Rovers won 5-4 on penalties)
* Coca-Cola Cup final (27th November 1994 at Ibrox)
    Raith Rovers 2 (Crawford, Dalziel) Celtic 2 (Walker, Nicholas) (AET, Raith Rovers won 6-5 on penalties)

RAITH ROVERS' Coca-Cola CUP-WINNING TEAM
Scott Thomson, Davie Sinclair, Shaun Dennis, David Narey, Steve McAnespie, Colin Cameron, Jason Dair, Stevie Crawford, Julian Broddle (Ian Redford), Gordon Dalziel (Jason Rowbotham), Ally Graham.
Manager: Jimmy Nicholl.

15

• ABERDEEN •
THE COCA-COLA CUP PUTS THE FIZZ
BACK INTO ABERDEEN

THE 1995-96 season was hardly a campaign that suggested success was going to be in the offing at Pittodrie. Aberdeen had been embarrassingly knocked out of the Scottish Cup by lowly Stenhousemuir and only maintained their Premier Division status after coming through a nervy, two-legged play-off against Dunfermline Athletic. It was hardly the introduction that the former Scotland captain, Roy Aitken, had hoped for after he had taken the step up from assistant boss to replace the Pittodrie legend Willie Miller.

The late end-of-season rally at least showed that although the Dons had struggled they had something about them. "We were absolutely flying at the end of the previous season," top scorer Billy Dodds admitted. "The confidence was high and we were really playing well. In the end that is what kept us up, as we ended up winning the play-off against Dunfermline. That run gave us such belief and we were confident we could kick on the following season."

The Coca-Cola Cup saw Aberdeen make their competitive bow in the 1995-96 campaign, after a mixed bag of results in their pre-season fixtures against English opposition. It was their first cup tie since the embarrassing Ochilview debacle and the Dons players were keen to avoid further embarrassment as St Mirren made the long trip to the Granite City.

Striker Scott Booth put on a man of the match performance, netting twice along with Dodds, to help them see off the Buddies 3-1. A relieved Booth said: "The St Mirren tie was a big one because it was our first game since the Stenhousemuir defeat. That day was a disaster. I was in the stands and you could see things unravelling in front of your eyes. So there was a bit of a fear factor when it came to cup ties. But we had kicked on since then and we played well against St Mirren, where I scored a pair of goals. My first goal was a strike from inside the box and my second was a sclaffed shot, which I managed to put into the net from a couple of yards."

The game was a big night for young hopeful Craig Ireland who made his Dons debut, along with Dutch trialist Ettiene Verveer who came on as substitute but was never seen in red again.

Aberdeen then opened up their league campaign with a 3-2 win over Falkirk and then immediately had to return to Brockville to take on the Bairns in the third round of the Coca-Cola Cup. The second coming was more convincing as strikes from Booth, Joe Miller, Colin Woodthorpe and an own goal helped the Dons to a convincing 4-1 victory. Delighted goal hero Woodthorpe said: "I had missed the end of the previous season through injury so I was determined to make up for lost time. I started the season really well and I had something like two goals in ten games which wasn't too bad from left-back."

His fiery team-mate Dodds was almost on the end of another kind of knockout after a half-time tunnel scuffle with Falkirk heavyweights John Clark and Joe McLaughlin. The former Scottish international recalled: "We played really well and what I remember in that game getting booted all over the place and then big John Clark took me right out. He just clothes-lined me. Then Mo Johnston ran 50 yards to start calling me a diving b****** when he hadn't even seen the incident. Big John should have been sent off but the referee didn't see it and he walked away laughing, knowing he had got away with it.

"Then just as I was heading to the dressing room Joe McLaughlin clobbered me on the back of the head and I turned round and hooked him. Then suddenly it all kicked off. Big Joe, John Hughes and Mo were all there and suddenly I knew I was going to be a dead man. Then my team-mate Peter Hetherston, who was as hard as they come, came from nowhere, stood there and said 'come on then, who's first?' They all backed off and at the end of the day Silky saved my skin."

English full-back Woodthorpe admitted it was nothing out of the ordinary to see Dodds going head to head with somebody, including his own team-mates. "We had a lot of fiery characters in that dressing room," the defender admitted. "It just showed the determination we had to do well. I mean Dodds and Gary Smith were the worst. They were always fighting. There was one day where the manager had to drive them back from training from Balgownie in his car.

"When they got back to the ground Gary was nursing a black eye and Billy had his hand all bandaged. It was comical and that wasn't the only occasion. They once almost game to blows on the golf course, as they argued over a preferred lie."

The fighting spirit started to spread through the team and that was shown when the Dons came through a potentially tricky quarter-final clash against top-flight rivals Motherwell at Fir Park. They were pushed all the way and into extra-time after John Inglis and Dougie Arnott's goals had cancelled each other out. Inglis said: "I remember the night being cold and wet and the goal I scored went through a body of players in the six yard box."

It was left to striker Dodds to take centre stage and to once again become the darling of the Red Army. Dodds admitted: "My winner that night remains one of my favourite goals. An angled cross came over. The ball fell behind me but I managed to stick out a leg and volley the ball back across the goal, beyond the keeper and into the net. I ran behind the goal and got booked for celebrating in front of our big, travelling support. It was worth it because it was a big goal and proved to be the winner at a tough venue."

For backup keeper Michael Watt it turned out to be a real turning point in his Pittodrie career. The youngster had come through the ranks but had played second fiddle to the ever-consistent Theo Snelders. However, an injury to the Dutchman opened the door for Watt that night. Watt recalled: "I came in for Theo and although we won and I thought I did okay I had fully expected to be back on the bench again for the league game on the Saturday. That was the norm round that time but fortunately the gaffer decided to stick by me. It gave me great confidence and I went on a run and kept my place in the team for most of the season. It was just an amazing confidence booster to get the nod in front of somebody of the calibre of Snelders."

Suddenly the Dons could look forward to a semi-final showdown, with Dundee, Dundee United and all-conquering Rangers in the draw. A clash with one of their north-east rivals was the preferred option although their cup hopes were dashed when they were drawn against the Ibrox giants, who boasted top stars like Paul Gascoigne, Ally McCoist and Gordon Durie. It at the very least guaranteed another trip to Hampden.

Dodds said: "We were all delighted to have made the semi-finals although I think all our hearts sunk when we were drawn against Rangers. They were a formidable force with the likes of Paul Gascoigne and were clearly the best team in the country at that time."

Aberdeen were dealt a blow in the run-up to that game as left-back Woodthorpe broke his foot in a league game with Motherwell. He frustratingly recalled: "I went for a challenge with Paul Lambert and ended up breaking my foot about three weeks before the semi-final. I was still hopeful I could make the final but it didn't happen and I ended up missing pretty much the rest of that season."

It didn't derail Aberdeen too much and they came out all fired up against Rangers, who were caught cold by a deadly performance from two-goal Dodds. "We just went out that night, played well and passed the ball about for fun," Dodds admitted. "Everything just clicked and we went in front. I went after a ball with Andy Goram. I thought just go, just go. You can get there in front of him and I did. I managed to get to the ball and stick it through his legs for the opener.

"Even then we continued to play well and I got my second when Stephen Glass swung in a cross and I was left completely unmarked at the back post and managed to head the ball in. I thought it is 2-0 surely we have done it now but then Oleg Salenko got a goal back although we continued to play well."

Local hero Eoin Jess then played to the galleries with a bit of showboating, playing keepie-uppie to play out time out on the wing, much to the delight of the big travelling Aberdeen support. Jess admitted: "It wasn't something I planned. I just saw the ball come to me and I thought why not, I am on the same stage as Paul Gascoigne. Why not do it? I did it and it almost backfired because Rangers got their goal back and pushed to try and get their equaliser.

"Fortunately we played well enough and deserved to win the game but Roy Aitken gave me a right going over after the game for my party trick. To be fair the Aberdeen fans still talk about it today so at least it was something they appreciated."

Dodds reckons Jess showed guts and when it came to natural ability he was as good as any of Rangers' top stars, including Gazza. "Eoin was absolutely brilliant that night," Dodds acknowledged. "He was up against Gascoigne and players like that but he just ran the show. He was magnificent with surging runs and his little twists and turns. The Rangers players just couldn't get near him. Then at the end he started showboating by playing keepie-uppie. It was the nearest thing I have seen to Jim Baxter's moment of magic against England at Wembley. It infuriated Rangers but their players couldn't get close enough to kick him. Even when they did Eoin would just laugh and it would infuriate them even more."

Inglis reckons beating Rangers was the real high point of the cup run. He said: "For me the final was beating Rangers in the semi-final." Fellow central defender Smith echoed those same thoughts. Smith admitted: "It was the Rangers nine-in-a-row side so to beat them was some achievement. But to be fair we had a decent record against the Old Firm."

Aitken and his men booked their cup final place and then found out they would be playing First Division side Dundee, who had shocked their city rivals in the other semi-final. It put one of Aberdeen's top stars under serious pressure to make sure the cup headed to Pittodrie.

Dundonian Stephen Glass admitted: "I wanted to win the trophy first and foremost for Aberdeen because I was an Aberdeen player but then there was also an added incentive because my family, including my brother, are big Dundee United fans. So they told me in no uncertain terms could I let Dundee come back with the trophy. I think I would have been banned from Dundee if that had happened and some of my family might even have disowned me."

An injury to Watt left manager Aitken in a cold sweat. "Three or four weeks before the final I ended up getting stretchered off against Celtic," Watt revealed. "Andy Walker caught my kneecap with his studs and it started to swell up like a balloon. I then found myself out of the team and I didn't think I was going to play in the final until the manager decided to recall me for the Raith Rovers game just before it and then I went on to keep my place."

While there was good news for Watt there was heartbreak for Booth just before the big day. Booth painfully recalled: "It was two or three days before the final and we were out training on the Pittodrie pitch. Roy Aitken was throwing up a few balls at the end of the session to practise our volleying. I just stretched to volley the ball and I felt something in my thigh go. I knew it was serious and I just couldn't believe it.

"It was the first cup run where I had really contributed and now I knew I was going to miss the final. The manager gave me right to the last minute but even when I went out for my fitness test I knew myself I wasn't going to make it and that proved to be the case. I was absolutely gutted."

Smith had sampled the bitter taste of cup final defeat with the Dons and knew the pressure was on as his side were odds on to see of the Dark Blues, who were keen to replicate the Coca-Cola Cup exploits of First Division Raith Rovers. He said: "It was against the so-called lesser teams where we seemed to struggle. That was the thing looking forward to the final. There was suddenly a role reversal and we were the favourites to beat Dundee, knowing we would have taken all the stick if we had lost. It was also a big thing for me because I had lost in a previous cup final and it had also been a few years since Aberdeen won a trophy, so the pressure, probably, was on us."

Dundee also had rising star Neil McCann who was tipped to terrorise the Aberdeen back line and makeshift right-back Brian Grant. Grant recalled: "Colin Woodthorpe missed the game so Roy Aitken decided to move Stewart McKimmie to left-back and told me the day before I was playing right-back. I had filled in there a few times and I was just glad to be starting in the cup final. I knew I was up against McCann and all the talk from the Dundee camp was that he was going to tear us apart. He ended up being subbed and had a quiet game. He claimed he was injured but even when I see him now I always joke with him and say: 'Do you want out of my pocket yet?'"

Goal-a-game Dodds continued to be Aberdeen's lucky omen as he settled the nerves with the Hampden opener. "We all felt we had a great chance although we knew we couldn't be too complacent because Dundee were still a good side," the chirpy striker admitted. "We had a good feeling and it got even better when we got to Hampden and we were greeted by thousands of Aberdeen fans, who were desperate to see their side back to winning trophies. We got on top and eventually got our goal. The cross came in and I missed it at the front post but then the ball eventually fell back into my path and I was there to sweep the ball away. It was a good start."

Dundee never really played to their potential and Shearer killed off their hopes just after the restart, with decent shifts also put in by £1m man Paul Bernard and Joe Miller.

Shearer said: "Glass picked the ball up on the left and whipped a cross into the box. I managed to get in between two Dundee defenders to head the ball high into the net. Both Dundee defenders were down getting treatment after the goal and it took them so long to return that the Aberdeen fans continued to chant 'it's a goal Duncan Shearer' over and over again. Wee Billy, who had scored the first, was standing next to me and he joked: 'Are you the only f*****g player in this team?' It was a great moment for me having scored a goal in a cup final and listening to the fans chanting your name."

Defender Inglis helped keep the door shut at the other end to ensure skipper Stewart McKimmie could step forward and lift the cup. "The game against Dundee was almost an anticlimax as Dundee weren't the best of sides at that time," Inglis candidly admitted. "It meant the game was a little bit of a tense occasion as we were clear favourites but still knowing anything can happen in 90 minutes of football! Wee Doddsie and Duncan Shearer got the goals needed and we were intent at the back to be as disciplined as possible."

They saw the result out 2-0 and star man Glass was at least able to return home with his head held up high. "I had just come down from collecting my medal when I was given a Coca-Cola-branded bike from the sponsors because I had been named man of the match," the youngster revealed. "It was great and to be named man of the match was great but for me it had been a real team effort. Jess was actually trying to get me to ride the bike round on our lap of honour. Fortunately, I thought better of it and we ended up throwing it in with the hampers and kit and took it back up the road with us. My father-in-law still has it, so it has gone to good use."

Portsoy-born Jess picked up another winner's medal but reckons that Coca-Cola Cup win was the big one for him. Jess said: "I don't think anyone could argue that we deserved to win the cup. We beat Motherwell away from home and Rangers at Hampden so nobody could argue that we got an easy run. It had been a difficult season the year before so to come away with a cup was brilliant for everybody connected with Aberdeen.

"It was the first time we had won a trophy in a few years and it really gave everybody at Aberdeen a big lift. I would also say looking back winning that Coca-Cola Cup was probably a bigger thing than my Skol or Scottish Cup winner's medal. I was older and more experienced and I probably appreciated it a lot more second time around."

Smith was pleased to have ended his Hampden hoodoo. He admitted: "I was delighted to have finally picked up a cup winner's medal, as the only other medal I had picked up was when I won the First Division at Falkirk. It was good to walk up the steps knowing you were a winner although in a strange sort of way it wasn't as good as maybe I had thought it was going to be. Maybe it was a bit lower key but when we got back to Aberdeen and eventually had the open-top bus parade you could see what it meant to the fans and the city. I had quite a few ups and downs at Aberdeen and I was just delighted to give the fans a trophy, especially after the ups and downs of the previous season."

Captain McKimmie and Inglis were forced to put their celebrations on hold. Inglis admitted: "The team bus left for Aberdeen without McKimmie and myself. I couldn't urinate for an hour after the match, as a result when we arrived back the celebrations had already started."

The team returned to the Granite City to celebrate at the New Marcliffe Hotel at Pitfodels. It was a bittersweet night for Woodthorpe, who said: "That was probably the biggest disappointment of my career missing that game. It was the one and only time one of my teams had got to a final and I missed it through injury. I was delighted for the team but personally it was a nightmare.

"My dad was ill with cancer and I really wanted to be out there to lift a cup for him but it didn't happen. I remember we went back to the Marcliffe Hotel and it was a great night. I think I wrapped things up at 5am in the morning but throughout the night I just wouldn't get my picture taken with the trophy because I just didn't feel part of it."

The players and Aitken had to wait another week before they were able to take their open-top bus round Aberdeen. Booth said: "I didn't play in the final but the open-top bus parade and celebrations were absolutely brilliant. Every Aberdeen side is compared to the great Pittodrie sides of the 1980s. You heard all about their legendary tales and as an Aberdeen fan I also watched them, so I knew how much I wanted to try and emulate them. So to be part of a squad who brought a trophy back to Pittodrie was brilliant. Seeing the delight on the fans' faces, knowing you had been part of a squad that had made its own bit of history."

Cup final goal hero Shearer added: "I had played at Wembley in play-off games with Swindon and Blackburn but this was my first real cup final winner's medal. It really was special for me because I honestly thought the chance had passed me by. Then to be going round Aberdeen on the open-top bus was absolutely amazing. The streets were jam-packed with Aberdeen fans. It had been a few years since they had last won a trophy so they really did turn out in force that day. That and the cup final are two days I will never forget."

Watt was living the dream as a lifelong Dons fan. The keeper admitted: "For me it is the season that really stands out for me because I was the first-choice keeper for most of the campaign. We managed to win the cup and also finish third in the league which was a great achievement after what had gone on in the previous campaign. It was a dream come true because I was an Aberdeen fan born and bred and here I was helping the team to win a cup and being cheered on by fans and friends in the street."

Long-serving defender Brian Irvine had missed the cup run as he battled against multiple sclerosis. Irvine said: "I had been diagnosed with MS in the summer and I was pushing to get back for the final but it just came too soon. I was still delighted, as an Aberdeen fan and team-mate, to see the team go out and lift the cup."

That cup gave the Dons the belief they could get back challenging and they did that in the league by finishing a creditable third, behind Rangers and Celtic. The team also started to break up when Smith decided to make full use of the Bosman ruling to join French club Rennes.

"It was strange because I told Roy that I wanted to keep my options open," Smith revealed. "I hadn't signed anything or had any other offers but I just wanted to wait and see what my options were. Roy demanded I go and tell the media I was leaving. McKimmie told me I shouldn't have done it but I stupidly agreed. If I had been a bit more experienced I would have said no.

"So I went in front of the press and then suddenly the fans started booing me and getting on my back. I knew then I had to move although it wasn't until I left Aberdeen that I agreed to sign for Rennes. If I am being honest if the Aberdeen deal was still on the table I would have probably signed it. At least I left on a high with a cup winner's medal although I was fortunate enough to return to Aberdeen a year later."

Since then the Dons have struggled to hit those dizzy heights again.

ABERDEEN'S Coca-Cola CUP RUN 1995-96
* Second round (19th August 1995 at Pittodrie)
    Aberdeen 3 (Dodds, Booth 2) St Mirren 1 (McLaughlin)
* Third round (30th August 1995 at Brockville)
    Falkirk 1 (Johnston PEN) Aberdeen 4 (Booth OG,

Woodthorpe, Miller)
* Quarter-final (20th September 1995 at Fir Park)
    Motherwell 1 (Arnott) Aberdeen 2 (Dodds, Inglis) (AET)
* Semi-final (24th October 1995 at Hampden)
    Aberdeen 2 (Dodds 2) Rangers 1 (Salenko)
* Coca-Cola Cup final (26th November 1995 at Hampden)
    Aberdeen 2 (Dodds, Shearer) Dundee 0

ABERDEEN'S Coca-Cola CUP-WINNING TEAM
Michael Watt, Stewart McKimmie, Stephen Glass, Brian Grant, John Inglis, Gary Smith, Joe Miller (Hugh Robertson), Duncan Shearer, Paul Bernard, Billy Dodds, Eoin Jess (Peter Hetherston). Manager: Roy Aitken.

• KILMARNOCK •
THE WRIGHT ROAD TO
SCOTTISH CUP SUCCESS

The 1996-97 campaign didn't exactly kick off in a blaze of glory for Kilmarnock. They found themselves struggling badly at the bottom of the Scottish Premier Division and in the end manager Alex Totten paid the price with his job. Kilmarnock decided to wait to name his successor and gave reserve team coach and former striker Bobby Williamson the job in a caretaker capacity.

Williamson recalled: "Alex had actually asked me to go to Falkirk with him as assistant manager but I decided to stay and give it a crack at Kilmarnock. In my first game we lost heavily to Dundee United and I actually had doubts whether or not I could turn it around. The players seemed to have lost all confidence and were feeling sorry for themselves. I went in and tried to install some belief in them.

"I knew I could have been sacked at any time but I wanted the players to do it for themselves and the club. I also said it was up to them whether they wanted to play football in the First Division or in the Scottish Premier Division. I also introduced some younger boys who brought a bit of freshness and then slowly we started to see a steady improvement."

Williamson had nurtured youngsters like David Bagan, Jim Lauchlan, Mark Roberts and Alex Burke and decided nothing would be lost by fast-tracking them into a first-team that maybe didn't lack ability but was short of confidence.

Burke said: "I made my debut when we were at the bottom of the league but Bobby was great. He just told us to go and do what we were good at. He was great at taking the pressure off us and as a 19-year-old I probably didn't feel the same fear or strain as maybe some of the more experienced boys."

Results picked up in the league but the dog-eat-dog nature of Scotland's top flight meant they struggled to move away from the drop zone. Speculation continued over the vacant Rugby Park hotseat and it looked like Williamson would be making way sooner rather than later.

"I wasn't really thinking about myself because I knew I could be out the door at any time," Williamson admitted. "There was a lot of speculation during the season about new managers coming in. Guys like Alex MacDonald were linked with the post while I think Mark Hateley was actually offered it and turned it down. So I wasn't exactly looking too far down the line. I was more interested in trying to keep the pressure away from the players."

The Scottish Cup campaign also looked unlikely to be a source of inspiration. The Ayrshire men eventually saw off plucky East Stirlingshire 2-0 thanks to goals from Kevin McGowne and Tom Brown.

McGowne said: "Mark Roberts wanted to take the free kick but I ended up shoving him out of the way. I went for power and managed to stick it past their keeper. It was an important goal because East Stirling caused us a few problems and it wasn't until wee Tam scored the second that we could actually relax a wee bit."

Killie's campaign wasn't helped by the loss of Ally Mitchell through a freak training injury. The experienced midfielder admitted: "I missed most of the season with a blood clot in my left calf. I actually crushed a vein in my calf using one of the weight machines in the gym. The doctor was actually quite worried and he was going to send me to see a specialist but fortunately the blood-thinning tablets started to work although I spent most of the campaign on the sidelines."

The cup gave them a trip to Clyde where they managed to come through thanks to a dubious Paul Wright penalty. The Killie striker admitted: "The thing I remember before the game was the comments of the Clyde striker Eddie Annand, who told the papers they were about to knock us out. That was pinned up in our dressing room and added a bit more edge to our game.

"I have to be honest, it wasn't the greatest of games and was decided by my penalty. All I remember was their defender pulling me and it was enough to knock me off balance. I got up and the referee pointed to the spot and fortunately I managed to put it away. You need a wee bit of luck in the cup and we definitely got some that day."

Next up was Morton who were dispatched by a five-star Killie performance. John Henry netted a hat-trick while Wright and McIntyre finished the Greenock side off. MacPherson said: "The Morton game was the match where we really clicked. We played some good stuff and we were also clinical in front of goal. That win gave us a lot of belief."

Killie were still fighting for their lives in the league while they continued to battle for cup glory. The Rugby Park board however had seen enough in Williamson and gave him the job, along with his assistants Gerry McCabe and Jim Clark, on a permanent basis as they went into their Scottish Cup semi-final. Dundee United and Killie were evenly matched after a goalless first game. They did it all again in an Easter Road replay, where McIntyre ended up being the late hero.

"The two semi-finals were the worst games ever," McIntyre candidly admitted. "Fortunately I managed to get the goal four minutes from time. I just saw this great ball coming into the box and I just raced through a mass of bodies to get to the front post, where I got a foot on it and managed to stick it away. It was such a great feeling to see the ball hit the net. It was also late on so there was next to no time for Dundee United to fight back. It was a great feeling to be looking forward to a cup final. I had been involved in one at Airdrie but this was my first as a top team regular."

Captain Ray Montgomerie admitted the moment the final whistle went was one that stands out for him – especially when it emerged they would be playing First Division side Falkirk, who had stunned Celtic in the other semi-final. The long-serving defender said: "It really hit home at the end of that game for me, the fact we were suddenly in a Scottish Cup final. It, for me, probably brought a better feeling than lifting the cup. I know when I say that it surprises a lot of people. I just remember back to the 1994 semi-final we lost to Rangers when our then-manager Tommy Burns told us to look around these surroundings because it wouldn't be long before we were back here."

With a cup final place in the bag they were then able to focus on safeguarding their top-flight status and they really kicked on. Manager

Williamson admitted: "We actually did well to dig ourselves out of trouble because we picked up some good wins over both Rangers and Celtic along the way. We were actually in a good run of form but the problem was that the other teams round about us were also still picking up points, so it went right to the wire. Thankfully, we did enough and the players deserve a lot of credit for that because they put a real shift in and played some good football."

Their cause wasn't helped when top striker Wright missed the league run-in and was touch and go for the Ibrox final. Wright explained: "I was a doubt for the cup final because I ended up needing 13 stitches in a thigh wound after a tussle with Dunfermline's Andy Tod. I wasn't able to do anything for three weeks and I lost a lot of fitness. I did a lot of work with Hugh Allan and fortunately a few days before the final he said I was able to play. I wasn't 100 per cent fit but Bobby decided to go with me."

In the league it came down to a final day nail-biter, where a Gary Holt goal saw Killie pick up the point they needed against Aberdeen to keep themselves up. A relieved MacPherson said: "The cup was a release because we had spent most of that season fighting to stay in the Premier Division. We only achieved survival in the final few weeks of the season after we drew with Aberdeen. That result was massive because it took a lot of pressure off our shoulders although going into the cup final as favourites brought a slightly different pressure. Falkirk had beaten Celtic but we were the top-flight side and everybody expected us to beat them."

It turned into a bit of a hairy ending for Holt and defender Dylan Kerr as they turned their attentions to the cup final. "I actually put a bet on with Gary," Kerr revealed. "I bet him I wouldn't get a haircut if he kept his goatee beard. He won because I started to look like a gypsy and there was no way I was going into a cup final looking like that. I wish I hadn't because my cup final haircut wasn't the best although I didn't look as bad as Gary who put on his best cat weasel impression."

Williamson took his team away to Seamill where he decided to stir things up as Killie got ready to go up against a Falkirk side managed by their ex-boss Totten. The Rugby Park chief had a cunning plan to fire his own players up ahead of the big showcase.

Midfielder Mark Reilly recalled: "I remember in the build-up to the cup final Bobby Williamson had us all together for a team meeting. He said 'I have heard that your old gaffer Alex Totten doesn't think much of you'. He said he had heard that Alex thought Paul Wright was the only real top player we had. I don't know if Bobby had heard that or he was just playing mind games to get us fired up for the final. I know quite a few of us were determined to go out and prove Alex wrong though."

The Kilmarnock manager decided to give his players the option of staying at the team hotel or at home the night before the cup final. Two of Williamson's youngest stars decided to go for an unconventional build-up to the biggest game of their lives. "I remember the night before the game I travelled through and stayed at Bagan's flat and looking back I have to laugh at our pre-match preparations," Alex Burke revealed. "We ended up going round to one of his friends and on the way home we ended up dropping into McDonald's. We had already had our tea but here we were stuffing our faces with Big Mac meals.

"I then realised I had forgotten to take casual shoes for our night out after the game so the morning of the cup final David and I had to make for the shops so I could buy shoes. Looking back now it was funny but we really were young and daft. We were walking up the street eating ice cream and there were Kilmarnock fans everywhere getting ready to go to the final. Fans kept coming up to us. I don't think they could believe two of their players were out shopping hours before the final."

Skipper Montgomerie admitted the bus journey to Ibrox was where the pressure finally disappeared. "I was the local boy from down the road in Saltcoats and every day everybody was talking about the cup final," Montgomerie explained. "I also had the pub with my brother and we ended up running seven buses from there. There was something like 250 fans so I had to help sort out tickets and transport, etc. So when I was on the bus and saw all the fans as we made it to Ibrox I just remember feeling a weight coming off my shoulders. Suddenly the only thing I had to worry about was the game and nothing else."

He also had to play a captain's role in the tunnel before they stepped out on to the Ibrox pitch. "We were all standing in the tunnel and all our boys were really quiet," Montgomerie admitted. "The Falkirk players were coming out and shouting and screaming and banging the walls. I just turned to the boys and said: 'Remember, the game is won out there and not in the tunnel'."

Manager Williamson also sensed there were a few nerves as Kilmarnock and Falkirk went head to head. He admitted: "I remember turning to the fans and trying to encourage them because things were a bit flat. I spoke to a few of them after the game and they insisted they had been shouting and screaming but I don't know if it was maybe a bit of nervousness and apprehension from them and the players because we were going into a cup final against a team from the First Division."

It seemed to have the desired effect as Wright struck to put Killie ahead. The striker recalled: "Alex Burke swung in a cross and Kevin McGowne flicked it on. As he did I peeled off from the goalkeeper to the back post and fortunately my gamble paid off as I managed to find the time and space to get my shot away. I sclaffed my shot but fortunately Falkirk didn't have anyone at the back post and it went in. Then for five or ten seconds I just lost myself and just ran away celebrating before I quickly realised I had ran to the Falkirk end. Before I got time to turn around I was swamped by my delighted team-mates."

Kilmarnock then had a great chance to wrap things up when McIntyre was sent clear but Falkirk veteran Andy Gray got back to make a vital saving challenge. At the other end, a brilliant save from Dragoje Lekovic denied big Kevin James.

Falkirk thought they had got themselves level when James flicked on Gray's long throw and Neil Oliver swept the ball home at the back stick. However, their joy was short-lived when referee Hugh Dallas ruled it out for offside and manager Williamson admitted it was a play his team had worked on.

Williamson said: "It was tight but the television replays showed he was marginally offside. I am thankful for that because if the decision hadn't been given then history would have changed. But to be fair it was something we used to work on. I encouraged my defenders to clear the six yard box, the penalty spot and then the box, to try and play the offside trap. Fortunately, we got a bit of luck and it came off in the final."

The Bairns kept knocking at the door but couldn't find the equaliser and Killie held out for their famous win. A relieved Reilly admitted: "The first-half we did OK but after the break we didn't play at all and we ended up holding on. When the final whistle went it was just a mix of relief and elation."

Manager Williamson immediately made for the opposition dugout when the final whistle went. "I was delighted to win the cup but my immediate feelings were for Alex Totten," the cup-winning boss admitted. "He had been in charge of the two teams who had made the final and had still walked away a loser. I have a lot of respect for Alex and I did feel for him because he was a very proud guy. He had the faith to give me my first coaching job and had tried to take me to Falkirk as well, so Alex is always a guy I will be forever grateful to.

"The one thing that did annoy me was that as I went to shake Alex's hand Jim McIntyre and Paul Wright decided to shower me in juice and I was left soaking from head to toe. I was absolutely furious with both of them."

Montgomerie did the honours as he picked up Kilmarnock's first Scottish Cup for 68 years. The proud skipper said: "I had seen so many great players and legends of the game lift the cup and suddenly I was leading Kilmarnock up there. It was just so surreal, going up there knowing your family and friends were in the stands watching."

For striker McIntyre picking up a Scottish Cup winner's medal was the perfect birthday present. "Holding on made it a great day for me," McIntyre beamed. "It was also my 25th birthday so to walk away with a Scottish Cup winner's medal made it even more of a special day. It was just the best feeling in the world when that final whistle went."

Mitchell reckons that day was the best of his career although he felt the team did let the supporters down. The straight-talking midfielder said: "The one thing that I now look back on with a bit of regret was the JJB Sports t-shirt fiasco. They had agreed to throw £2,000 or £3,000 into the kitty if we walked up and lifted the cup with their branded t-shirts on. We agreed to do it but looking back I don't think it was right. We should have picked up the cup wearing Kilmarnock strips. That is the one thing I look back on with a lot of disappointment."

Experienced defender MacPherson was delighted and tried to get some of the younger boys to take their big day in. "I was one of the more experienced players and I know what it meant to me," the full-back explained. "I tried to tell the younger boys like Burke and Bagan to make the most of it because it might only happen once in their careers. It was great because all that team now have a medal and something to look back at and show from our careers."

Kerr admitted it was some achievement although he caused a few dressing-room flutters when he sneaked out with the cup. "It was great," Kerr admitted. "Here we were, a group of players who had been released and discarded by this club and that club and suddenly we had come together to show what a good team we were. We then went on to do really well in the following seasons so it definitely wasn't a flash in the pan. After the game I caused a bit of a stir. Everybody thought the cup had been stolen but I was out the front of Ibrox with it showing it off to the fans."

The party was also just beginning and Kilmarnock's stars headed home to take their open-top bus parade – as thousands turned out to pay their own tributes to their newly-crowned heroes.

Williamson said: "Looking back and remembering all the people out in the streets in Kilmarnock that day still gives me goosebumps. It was a marvellous occasion and hopefully we did the club and the people of Kilmarnock proud. I am sure we did."

Mitchell admitted it was chaos as everybody scrambled for a bird's eye view of the cup. "I know a lot of players win a lot of cups but that Scottish Cup winner's medal is absolutely priceless to guys like me," the Killie midfielder insisted. "It is not every day a provincial club like Kilmarnock win a cup so when we do it means even more. It was great to go round with the cup and credit to the Falkirk fans, they also stayed to show their appreciation as well. Then the scenes when we got to Kilmarnock were just madness. There were thousands of people. They were up lamp posts, hanging out of windows or even sitting on shop roofs."

For former Rangers star MacPherson it was also a new experience. He said: "If you are an Old Firm player you will never see scenes like we did when we went back to Kilmarnock with the cup. It started off with two or three hundred people and then in the end there were thousands. The open-top bus parade was meant to get back to Rugby Park at 6pm but we didn't get back until 8pm because there were so many fans out in the streets. It really was a special occasion."

Kerr also got it in the neck as he never told his family and friends about the bus parade. "I didn't even know there was going to be an open-top bus celebration round Kilmarnock," the defender admitted. "I had something like 125 family and friends who had come up to the final and they all missed the celebrations because they were down in Troon getting drunk. I was far from popular when they found out they had missed another party."

Two of Kilmarnock's stars also have a constant reminder of that day. "I was still half-cut from the cup celebrations," Kerr revealed. "I then headed to Dublin for a bender for a few days with my friends. I was still out of it when I came back. I'd just got back to Scotland and Holt phoned me to say he was away to get a Kilmarnock tattoo on his leg. I stupidly went to the tattoo parlour and I fell asleep and when I woke up I had a new Kilmarnock tattoo on my leg. It, at least, gives me a reminder of my time at Kilmarnock and of course our Scottish Cup win."

Every single one of those players are still treated like heroes when they return to Rugby Park and Reilly reckons that sums up what that team achieved. "The medal is great and nobody can take that away from you but for me the most important things are the memories," Reilly insisted.

"The memories of the final and then the open-top bus parade round Kilmarnock. It probably took a few years to sink in but looking back it was a very special for me to say I was part of Kilmarnock's Scottish Cup winning squad. It is always great going back to the club because you always get a fabulous welcome for what we achieved for Kilmarnock."

Defender McGowne is in no doubt the cup win kicked off a golden era and a return to Europe for the pride of Ayrshire. McGowne admitted: "There is no doubt the cup win was the catalyst for Kilmarnock to kick on and do well over the next six or seven years. After we won the cup and stayed in the Premier Division we just went from strength to strength, regularly getting to cup finals and finishing in the top half. We had some great times and the good thing was that it was the same nucleus of players and coaching staff who helped Kilmarnock to lift the cup."

Captain Montgomerie was also left sweating when his medal was stolen from his parents' home – but a quick appeal to the Ayrshire public saw him quickly re-united with his pride and joy. Making it a happy ending for everyone connected with the blue and white of Killie, apart from maybe those who had to listen to Chick Young and him singing the Rugby Park anthem, Paper Roses, live on television. "It wasn't one of my proudest moments," Montgomerie admitted.

KILMARNOCK'S SCOTTISH CUP RUN 1996-97
* Third round (25th January 1997 at Rugby Park)
Kilmarnock 2 (McGowne, Brown) East Stirling 0
* Fourth round (15th February 1997 at Broadwood Stadium)
Clyde 0 Kilmarnock 1 (Wright PEN)
* Quarter-final (8th March 1997 at Cappielow)
Morton 2 (Mahood 2) Kilmarnock 5 (Henry 3, Wright, McIntyre)
* Semi-final (14th April 1997 at Easter Road)
Kilmarnock 0 Dundee United 0
* Semi-final replay (22nd April 1997 at Easter Road)
Kilmarnock 1 (McIntyre) Dundee United 0

* Scottish Cup final (24th May 1997 at Ibrox)
Kilmarnock 1 (Wright) Falkirk 0

KILMARNOCK'S SCOTTISH CUP-WINNING TEAM

Dragoje Lekovic, Dylan Kerr, Kevin McGowne, Gus
MacPherson, Ray Montgomerie, Mark Reilly, Gary Holt, Alex
Burke, David Bagan (Ally Mitchell), Jim McIntyre (Tom Brown),
Paul Wright (John Henry).
Manager: Bobby Williamson.

• HEARTS •
SCOTTISH CUP GLORY FOR THE BOYS IN MAROON

IT HAD been 36 long and frustrating years since Hearts had lifted a major piece of silverware and their long-suffering fans had to go back a further six years for the last time they had seen the Scottish Cup back at Tynecastle. There had been a few close things but the return of former player Jim Jefferies, as manager, gave everyone in and around Tynecastle hope that they were finally on the verge of something big. Jefferies, slowly but surely, fused together a team of experienced professionals, mixed with some fine home-grown talent that had come through the Tynecastle ranks.

There is no doubt, looking back, that the pinnacle for his side was the 1997-98 season. That Hearts squad pushed the Old Firm all the way in the Scottish Premier Division title race before they eventually ran out of steam in the final run-in and had to sit back and watch Celtic prevent Rangers sealing ten in a row. Many believed that the Jambos, with a bit more luck, could have gone all the way and won the championship. They had a good team and were determined that they weren't going to be left empty-handed in that campaign.

Their Scottish Cup campaign opened up with a relatively easy third round clash at home to the now-defunct Clydebank, who have since re-emerged in the junior ranks. Australian midfielder Thomas Flogel and David

Weir got the goals in a straightforward win.

It was more of the same in the next round when lowly Albion Rovers were swept away thanks to a double from the eccentric Angolan winger Jose Quitongo and a penalty from Colin Cameron.

The boys in maroon were handed another home tie, this time against Ayr United, in the quarter-final. The Honest Men were also seen off with minimum fuss. Paul Ritchie and Flogel scored before Ian Ferguson pulled one back for the visitors, but further strikes from Stevie Fulton and Jim Hamilton completed the rout.

Captain Gary Locke still recalls Hamilton's goal, which had more than a touch of good fortune attached to it. He explained: "I hit a shot and it was that bad I didn't even wait to see where it had landed. I started to run back to the halfway line but when I turned back around I saw Jim Hamilton running away celebrating. My shot had taken a bad bounce and their keeper had done everything but catch the ball before it fell to Hammy to stick away. I later saw the highlights and I joked that it was because my shot had so much spin on it that the keeper couldn't cope with it. I still don't know how he didn't hold it."

Even Hamilton laughs when he recalls his goal. He reckons his team's performance in that game made everyone sit up and take notice. Hamilton said: "The ball came in and their goalkeeper dropped it, leaving me the simplest of tap-ins. It was a pretty convincing win. We played well and Ayr United really struggled to cope with us."

That put the Jambos into the semi-final draw, along with the Old Firm and First Division side Falkirk. The end result was one that had every Hearts player and fan jumping for joy as they were paired with the Bairns and the Old Firm were left to go head to head.

Assistant manager Billy Brown admitted: "I think we got the best of the draw. We got a bit of luck all the way through in that run. The longer we went on the more I got the feeling it was going to be our year. We had been pretty consistent all season. We had come close to winning the league and if a couple of results hadn't gone against us at the end then we could well have won the title that season as well."

Hampden was being rebuilt so instead of a trip to the national stadium Falkirk and Hearts headed to Ibrox for their last four clash. The capital side were certainly full of confidence and got the perfect start when French striker Stephane Adam, who had arrived from Metz, netted within five minutes against the Bairns.

Adam recalled: "A free kick from the left was crossed in and Jim

Hamilton played the ball back to me to fire in at the back post. I hoped that goal was going to settle the nerves and we would go on and win the match quite convincingly but it never really happened like that."

Hearts went in at the interval 1-0 ahead but Falkirk had put them under the cosh and were unlucky not to draw level. Manager Jefferies knew his team had underachieved and wasn't prepared to let such a massive opportunity slip from their grasp. He wasted no time in stripping the paint off the Ibrox dressing room walls and laid into his players, with the main target of his anger being the lackadaisical Flogel.

The Austrian recalled: "That was my first season and I had been in and out of the team but I saw that cup run as a way of establishing myself in the first-team. I remember at half-time in the Falkirk game I came in and the gaffer and Billy Brown went absolutely mental at us. Falkirk had been all over us and had dominated our midfield. I came in and the manager, quite rightly, starting having a go at me personally because I had also been poor.

"I had a bottle of water in my hand and he just grabbed it and threw it at me. It smashed off the wall and the water soaked quite a few of my team-mates, who had been sitting beside me. I ended up getting substituted 15 minutes into the second-half for Lee Makel but that it is fair to say that was the wake-up call for my Hearts career. I think after that rocket I actually started to find my feet at Hearts and in that match, thankfully, so did the team."

Skipper Locke admitted it was par for the course for Jefferies and Brown to lose the plot in the dressing room because they had such a massive desire for their teams, in particular Hearts, to do well.

"It was nothing new for the manager or Billy to go off on one," Locke joked. "I remember after we had beaten St Johnstone. The game had been on Sky but they (Jefferies and Brown) weren't happy with our performance. They still had us locked in the dressing room at 10.30pm. Eventually Stevie Fulton said: 'Can we go and see our kids before they head off to school?' I think the wee groundsman thought he was going to be there for the night but such is Billy and Jim's passion for their football and for Hearts."

However, even the full wrath of the Hearts management team wasn't enough to wake their side out of their slumber. Falkirk got a more than deserved equaliser four minutes from time through ex-Hibs star Kevin McAllister and it was only then Hearts came to life.

Talented winger Neil McCann scored again for Hearts in the final minute and then laid on Adam for his second of the game – to gloss over what had been a far from convincing 3-1 win. The Frenchman admitted: "My second was very much a counter-attack as Falkirk pushed for a goal. I ran forward, took a reverse pass from Neil McCann and stuck the ball away. I felt then we were heading to the final."

Assistant Brown was honest enough to admit Hearts had got through by the skin of their teeth. "We were lucky to beat them because Kevin McAllister had the game of his life that day," Brown acknowledged. "It wasn't until Falkirk equalised that we really showed our full potential and in the end we got the late goals we needed to sneak through."

Rangers saw off Celtic in the other semi-final and suddenly Hearts knew Walter Smith would make his final stance as Rangers manager in the Celtic Park final. The Gorgie side were also still on the fringes of the title race. Every player suddenly had a cup final place in their sights although striker Hamilton almost shot himself in the foot.

He recalled: "I was panicking a bit before the final because I got myself suspended for two or three games and ended up losing my place. I had been the top scorer but I didn't get right back into the starting XI and I was left sweating for a wee bit. Fortunately, I got on the bench and I was also lucky enough to get on in the final. I have Jim Jefferies to thank for that although if I had missed the game then I knew I couldn't have blamed anyone but myself."

Jefferies decided to take his squad to England to get away from the media glare and finish his final pre-match preparations – although one Hearts player, Quitongo, – had their hotel staff up to high do with his wild antics.

Brown explained: "We knew that when it comes to cup finals that all the focus is on the Old Firm and we, as the so-called smaller team, would be secondary, so we decided to just get out of the way. We went down to Stratford and we had a great time away. We were in this really posh hotel and I remember we were sitting at the dinner table and suddenly we heard this cat.

"We thought surely there can't be a cat running about in a hotel like this? The staff and boys were looking everywhere for this cat, outside, behind curtains, under the tables. Then suddenly some of the boys burst into hysterics. Jose Quitongo had been the culprit. He had mastered this skill of a cat meowing and screeching and it had left the hotel staff in a right flap. I remember he also did it when we were away to take off on a flight during one pre-season. The pilot wouldn't let the plane take off until the whole plane had been checked to make sure there wasn't a cat on-board. Jose was absolutely mad."

For two other main players it was injury that left them sweating on their Celtic Park place. Dave McPherson had struggled for part of the season with injury while Locke had been left battling a knee problem. Locke said: "The manager gave me every chance to make the final. I think he knew what playing in that game meant to me. He even left me up in Edinburgh to work with the physio to get my right knee sorted while the rest of the boys headed off down to England for their pre-final camp.

"But, I knew by the Monday or Tuesday that I was never going to make it. I was heartbroken but to be fair to the manager and the boys they did everything to lift my spirits and to make sure I was involved, including going away with the team the night before the game. It was a nice touch and helped me get over the disappointment a wee bit."

Experienced defender McPherson did get the nod to start against his former side, even though it was his first appearance of that Scottish Cup campaign. He explained: "I had trouble with my ankle and my knee throughout the season so I actually didn't play in every game. I played in a lot of the league games but I didn't play in many cup games in the cup run until the final. It was a lot different preparing for a final with Hearts than Rangers.

"At Rangers it didn't matter who we played we were expected to win. At Hearts, the club and fans wanted to win. They expected you to go out and give your all and then basically see what happened on the day. It was the same in that final because everybody expected Rangers to win. They had just lost the league and it was the end of an era for Walter Smith and a lot of my former team-mates."

Flogel, despite his semi-final failings, was also surprised to be pitched in from the start. He explained: "I didn't expect to start in the final. Then when I saw my name in the starting 11 it was amazing. It was my first major cup final and I was determined I wasn't going to let myself, the manager or the fans down. I wanted to come away a winner."

The Hearts fans turned out in force in hope and expectation that after more than 40 years this could finally be their Scottish Cup year. McPherson admitted: "When we walked out on the pitch and saw the massive Hearts support I think that gave all the players a big lift. There was white and maroon everywhere and the fans got right behind us from the moment we walked out of the tunnel.

"I think that got us going because we knew the importance of not letting Rangers settle. We got our tactics spot on. I remember watching the game back and Ian Ferguson gave the ball away so many times. He was normally decent in possession but we just put all their boys under so much pressure and didn't give them time to get into their stride."

The Hearts players also knew the pressure was all on Rangers, as they had just blown the chance to make history by losing the title and their dream of making it ten in a row. Cameron claimed: "We put in a decent fight and we knew over the course of the season we showed we could match both sides of the Old Firm. That gave us a lot of belief going into the final. People said we would have to be at our best and Rangers would have to have an off-day but I was really confident that if we played well then we were going to win the cup regardless of what they did."

Jefferies had gone to extreme lengths to tell his players of the importance of making a positive start. He got what he asked for, from an unlikely source. Stand-in skipper Fulton showed an unlikely burst of pace to ghost into the Rangers box before he was brought down for a second-minute penalty.

Fulton admitted: "To have a real chance against Rangers or Celtic you really need to score first. That was why we were determined to start well. I thought we did that and we got our rewards when I got between two Rangers players and ended up getting clipped in the box. Some people thought I dived but I never. I never had a reputation for anything like that in my playing days. I was definitely caught. I still have a photograph of it in the house and there is absolutely no air between me and the defender. A lot of Rangers fan still give me stick but, believe me, it was a definite penalty."

Cameron was charged with the responsibility of sending Hearts on their way. He explained: "I think the penalty was actually my first touch of the ball. As soon as I spotted the ball I went away into a world of my own. I just focused on the kick. I knew I was up against Andy Goram and I was also more than aware that he would have done his homework on my penalty-taking. So I decided, with that in mind, that I would put my kick in the opposite corner.

"I ran up and as soon as I hit the ball I knew it was in because Goram had flown off in the opposite direction, where I usually put my penalties. When I saw the ball hit the net and all the Hearts fans celebrating it was just such a great moment. It was like a surge of electricity had gone through me, just to have scored in a cup final."

Hearts pushed on and seven minutes after the break they knew they had one hand on the cup when Adam netted their second. Adam recalled: "I remember I spoke to Billy Brown the week before the final and I told him I felt we were going to do it. We made the perfect start going ahead through the penalty and then I grabbed the second. I watched the ball bounce up and I knew Lorenzo Amoruso wasn't going to get there.

"I sneaked in on his blindside, took the ball off him and I remember opting to take my shot early to deceive the keeper. Andy Goram got a hand on it but couldn't keep it out. It was an amazing moment to see the ball go in. Then for 20 seconds it was something special and I really felt this connection and buzz with the fans. It wasn't my most spectacular goal but it was my most important."

That goal should have calmed the nerves of the Gorgie boys but in the end it signalled a late charge from Rangers – who were desperate that theywouldn't go down without a fight. Nine minutes before time Ally McCoist did pull one back to put the game back into the melting pot.

Keeper Rousset joked: "After Rangers scored I thought 'oh f***!' I shouted to the bench how long to go? When they said more than ten minutes I thought we were in trouble here. Rangers really put us under pressure as they tried for an equaliser. McCoist went down on the edge of our box and I genuinely thought Willie Young (referee) was going to give a penalty against Davie Weir.

"Fortunately Willie gave a free kick. Then I remember Willie added on five minutes of injury time. I was swearing and shouting at him just to blow the whistle. I firmly believe that God was a Jambo that day, rather than a blue nose because it could well have been a penalty."

A relieved Cameron reckons that if Rangers had equalised then they would also have walked away with the cup. The midfielder said: "When the final whistle went it was such a relief. I was delighted to have won the cup but equally as pleased that we had got over the line. After Rangers had scored their goal we were hanging on for grim life. I, personally, was just about out on my knees because I, like the rest of the boys, had given absolutely everything. I honestly think that if Rangers had equalised and taken the game into extra-time then we would have had absolutely no chance. We had gone but thankfully we managed to walk away with winner's medals as our reward."

McPherson knew Hearts were running on fumes in those final minutes and it was their fans who got them to the end. "Our 18-yard box became a fortress after they scored," he acknowledged. "It was a real backs-to-the-wall job. Rangers put us under all sorts of pressure. Having played for Rangers I knew their mentality. They were never going to lie down. They were always going to fight until the very last whistle. We were really struggling but once again the Hearts fans got right behind us and there is no doubt their support and backing helped get us over the line."

For the injured Locke, it had been a nightmare having to watch from the stands, while an SFA jobsworth also tried to deny him his moment of glory with his team-mates. He recalled: "I am not the greatest spectator anyway but the final was even worse because I am a massive Hearts fan and I knew what winning the cup meant to everyone connected with the club. I had been at cup finals as a fan and as a player and I was still waiting for us to win one.

"Me and a few of the other boys, like Allan McManus, Lee Makel and Neil Pointon, all went down to the dressing room with a few minutes to go. We were confident because we were 2-0 up. Then when we got down to the dressing room Rangers scored and we were all standing there biting our nails. Thankfully we held on and what a feeling when the whistle went and we knew Hearts had finally done it.

"The only dampener was that an SFA suit tried to stop us getting on to the pitch to celebrate with the boys. He said we could have sparked a riot but thankfully Jim Jefferies came into the tunnel to do an interview and he and Chris Robinson demanded we got on the pitch. Chris said the team wouldn't be going up to collect the trophy if we didn't get out. In the end, we pushed past him and what a celebration."

Fulton decided before the game that he wanted skipper Locke to come up and lift the cup with him. Fulton explained: "I had been captain for the majority of the season but I knew if Gary had been fit then he would have been wearing the armband. So, for me, it was a no-brainer. He was a massive Hearts fans and I knew what it meant to him. I actually look at the trophy presentation now and I was probably lucky that Gary allowed me to get one hand on the cup. He almost ran off with it himself."

A deeply touched Locke admitted it was a dream come true for him as a lifelong Jambo – in a season where rivals Hibs ended up getting relegated. He said: "It was a great touch from the boys to let me go up and pick up the trophy. Stevie Fulton was the captain but he let me lift the cup with him. What a moment. It is something that I will never forget –

being a Hearts fans. Just to have lifted the cup after all those years. It was massive for everyone to finally get that monkey off our back, that Hearts could win trophies.

"I knew what it meant to the fans but even I didn't know how many people would hit the streets that weekend. There was something like 250,000 people and it really was a great occasion. I still get goose pimples now when I think about it. The fact Hibs also got relegated that season made it the perfect season for every Hearts fan."

Fulton had played for Celtic and at the highest level but also reckons lifting the cup with Hearts was the highlight of his career. "It was the best thing that ever happened to me in my playing days," the midfielder proudly claimed. "It was my first real success as a player. I had been involved in Scottish Cup final wins with Celtic but this was the first game where I had actually played. To win the cup was great but to lift it as captain was amazing.

"When the final whistle went it was just a feeling of sheer relief, especially after we had lost our previous two cup finals to Rangers. There was also a bit of pressure on us because we had done really well in the league and the last thing we wanted was to finish the season empty-handed. I was probably more happy for my team-mates and the fans than I was for myself. I could see what it meant to them all."

Goalkeeper Rousset was handed the man of the match award for his heroics – although it didn't help him when it came to the post-match drug test. The Frenchman said: "I was given the man of the match champagne and I literally just grabbed it and ran off to celebrate with the team. Then I was selected for the drug testing.

"I was sitting there drinking my champagne and I really felt for the Rangers defender Lorenzo Amoruso. You could see the disappointment in his face. I had been in that situation a couple of times and I knew how bad he must have felt to lose a cup final.

"When I eventually got back upstairs somebody had stolen my shirt. I ended up jumping back on the team bus with my suit and tie on but no shirt. It was just a brilliant occasion to have been part. Even now when I go back to Edinburgh the Hearts fans still talk about it. Ironically, I know where my two loser's medals are but I am not entirely sure where my winner's medal is – although I know it is in the house somewhere."

Fulton was also drug-tested although he joked that they were lucky the entire jubilant team weren't tested by the time they got back to

Edinburgh. He said: "I was the last one on the bus because it took me so long to provide a urine sample. By the time I got on the bus I was struggling so you can imagine the shape of some of my team-mates. There was one point where we came into Edinburgh and the manager had told me and Gary to sit down the front with the cup.

"I turned around and all our team-mates had disappeared. The skylight in the roof had been hauled down and they were all on the top of this moving coach. The open-top bus parade wasn't due to happen until the next day! Needless to say I didn't need a second invitation and I sneaked up on to the roof to leave Gary on the bus holding the cup himself."

Jefferies was more concerned that one of his new heroes was going to end up in accident and emergency. He admitted: "Coming back on the bus was something else. We were greeted by a couple of police cars to take us into Edinburgh and even they were draped out in Hearts scarves and flags. We passed the local fire station and all the firemen were out with their scarves celebrating.

"The cup win showed what it meant to so many people. Then when we got to Edinburgh I have never see so many people out on the streets. It was so busy that we would have been lucky if we had been going at five miles per hour. It is just as well because the bulk of my first-team were up on the roof."

Former Rangers star Dave McPherson was delighted to have finally got the chance to take a bow on an open-top bus parade. McPherson said: "The whole weekend back in Edinburgh was amazing. There were so many people out in the streets and the open-top bus was something that was really special. I had never savoured that when I had been at Rangers. There were estimates of 200,000 people out in the streets. You just don't get that in Glasgow.

"I had been through the good times and bad times at Hearts so that moment was even sweeter for me. A lot of people also questioned my decision to leave Rangers for Hearts, but that day and that win will live with me forever and went some way to justifying my decision."

Hearts boss Jim Jefferies also saw first hand what his team heroics meant to the Hearts support. Jefferies explained: "We stayed at a hotel in Edinburgh. We all had a few drinks too many and I woke up quite early on the Sunday morning. I needed a wee pick-me-up so the girl at the front reception told me Boots the Chemist along the road was open. So, still wearing my Hearts tracksuit, me and a few of the family started walking along the road.

"We saw this Hearts fan walking along the road. His head was down and his scarf was just about hitting the pavement. He certainly looked like he had a decent Saturday night and an even better Sunday morning. I asked him if he had had a good day? He didn't even look up. He just said: 'God bless that Jim Jefferies, that is all I have to say'. He just kept walking and then about five yards up the road he turned and looked at me. He just said 'no, it can't be'. I think he thought he was still drunk."

Frenchman Stephane Adam knows his cup final goal has assured him legendary status among the Tynecastle faithful. He said: "After so long without winning the Scottish Cup and to be part of the Hearts team to finally win it again was great. It still makes me feel enormously proud and happy. It was also good to help give something back to a club who had made me feel really welcome from day one. Even when I go back to Edinburgh today it is the same. It makes me feel great, especially as a foreign player, that I have written my name into the history books of the greatest club in Scotland."

Jefferies returned to manage Hearts for a second time but he is in no doubt the team he had that season was right up there. "There is no question that was the best Hearts team I have ever had," Jefferies beamed. "There may have been better players individually but as a team that was the best group I have worked with. There were also a lot of talented players in that squad and that was shown by the fact so many of them went on to play at the very highest level.

"I am proud to say I managed them and to have played my part in Hearts winning the cup. I had been a player and I knew how all the Hearts fans longed to see the team lift the cup again. I am really proud of everyone who was connected with the club back then because we made so many dreams come true. It is certainly a time I will never forget."

HEARTS' SCOTTISH CUP RUN 1997-98

* Third round (24th January 1998 at Tynecastle)
Hearts 2 (Flogel, Weir) Clydebank 0
* Fourth round (14th February 1998 at Tynecastle)
Hearts 3 (Quitongo 2, Cameron) Albion Rovers 0
* Quarter-final (7th March 1998 at Tynecastle)
Hearts 4 (Ritchie, Flogel, Fulton, Hamilton) Ayr 1 (Ferguson)
* Semi-final (4th April 1998 at Ibrox Stadium)

Sir Alex Ferguson and his Aberdeen team celebrate clinching the 1979-80 title at Easter Road.

Aberdeen captain Willie Miller kisses the European Cup Winners' Cup in front of Neil Simpson and John McMaster.

Sir Alex Ferguson celebrates with European Cup Winners' Cup goal heroes Eric Black and John Hewitt during their open-top bus parade in Aberdeen.

Aberdeen's European Cup Winners' Cup-winning squad make their triumphant return to the Granite City.

Aberdeen's all-conquering squad make it a European double as they celebrate their Super Cup victory over Hamburg.

Aberdeen's Eric Black and captain Willie Miller hold the 1983-84 league trophy up in front of their championship-winning squad.

Captain Courageous Willie Miller scores the Aberdeen goal against Celtic that clinches the 1984-85 title.

The Dandy Dons celebrate their final title success under Sir Alex Ferguson in 1984-85.

Left above: Aberdeen's Sir Alex Ferguson celebrates his only League Cup win with his goalscorers, Billy Stark and Eric Black, from the 1985 win over Hibs. *Right above*: Aberdeen midfielder Billy Stark dives to net against Hearts in the 1986 Scottish Cup final.

Pittodrie legend Alex McLeish celebrates with the 1986 Scottish Cup.

The Aberdeen side celebrate their 1986 Scottish Cup win over Hearts.

The Aberdeen team celebrate their 1989-90 Skol Cup win.

Penalty hero Brian Irvine joins Theo Snelders, Alex McLeish, David Robertson and Robert Connor in keeping out Celtic in the 1989-90 Scottish Cup final.

Coca-Cola Cup goal heroes Duncan Shearer and Billy Dodds celebrate with Aberdeen captain Stewart McKimmie.

Aberdeen's Coca-Cola Cup-winning squad lap it up after their win over Dundee.

Adam Rooney slots home his penalty shoot-out winner to clinch the 2014 League Cup for Aberdeen.

Captain Russell Anderson lifts the League Cup with his Aberdeen side.

Injured Jonny Hayes, Ryan Jack, Andrew Considine and Niall McGinn celebrate the cup win with a young fan.

Aberdeen manager Derek McInnes takes his Celtic Park salute.

The 1982-83 Dundee United title-winning team lift manager Jim McLean aloft.

Dundee United star Ralph Milne leads the celebrations after their Dens Park victory.

Craig Brewster scores the 1994 Scottish Cup winner for Dundee United.

Ivan Golac's Dundee United team that toppled treble-chasing Rangers to lift the 1994 Scottish Cup.

Dundee United skipper Andy Webster and injured club captain Lee Wilkie lift the 2010 Scottish Cup.

David Goodwillie scores in the final against Ross County.

Craig Conway scores to help United seal the 2010 Scottish Cup.

Dundee United manager Peter Houston lifts the Scottish Cup.

The Dundee United team celebrate their 2010 win.

Ian Ferguson scores the only goal to sink Dundee United and fire St Mirren to Scottish Cup glory.

Saints boss Alex Smith, Paul Lambert and Kenny McDowall celebrate their Hampden win over Dundee United.

The St Mirren team that lifted the 1987 Scottish Cup.

John McGinn goes to celebrate with Esmael Goncalves after his equaliser.

Steven Thompson fires St Mirren ahead.

Conor Newton slams home the glory goal.

David van Zanten lifts aloft the League Cup, as Marc McAusland and Lee Mair look on.

The St Mirren team lift the 2013 League Cup.

Motherwell captain Tom Boyd and Colin O'Neill show off the 1991 Scottish Cup.

Cup final goal heroes Stevie Kirk and Phil O'Donnell help their Motherwell team-mates Craig Paterson and Jim Griffin challenge in the Dundee United box.

The Motherwell team who saw off Dundee United in the 1991 'Family Final'.

Raith Rovers stars Davie Sinclair, Gordon Dalziel, Stevie Crawford and Scott Thomson show off the Coca-Cola Cup after their shock win over Celtic.

Raith Rovers defender David Narey beats Celtic's Andy Walker to the ball.

Falkirk 1 Hearts 3 (Adam 2, McCann)
* Scottish Cup final (16th May 1998 at Celtic Park)
Hearts 2 (Cameron PEN, Adam) Rangers 1 (McCoist)

HEARTS' SCOTTISH CUP-WINNING TEAM

Gilles Rousset, Dave McPherson, Gary Naysmith, Davie Weir, Stefano Salvatori, Paul Ritchie, Neil McCann, Stevie Fulton, Stephane Adam (Jim Hamilton), Colin Cameron, Thomas Flogel. Manager: Jim Jefferies.

18

• LIVINGSTON •
THE LIONS BECOME THE PRIDE
OF HAMPDEN

BORN out of the ashes of Ferranti Thistle and Meadowbank Thistle, the switch along the M8 to the new town of Livingston was met with much controversy back in 1995. Yet, despite some initial resistance, Livi became a major asset to the Scottish Football League.

They quickly rocketed up the divisions, thanks to the generous financial backing of John McGuinness, Willie Haughey and Dominic Keane, peaking in the 2001-02 season when they finished third in the Scottish Premier League and qualified for Europe.

However, their crowning glory wasn't to arrive until later, although the early signs didn't look too promising after the Livi hierarchy's controversial decision to bring in Brazilian Marcio Maximo Barcellos as head coach, pushing the vastly experienced Davie Hay to the side. Marcio's claim to fame had been his discovery of the Brazilian legend Ronaldo – although it is fair to say that as a boss he was hardly a phenomenon at the Almondvale Stadium.

First-team coach Allan Preston admitted: "His philosophy was just, to put it politely, strange. Half the time I just stood there scratching my head. There is the film *Mike Bassett England Manager*, where he actually trains his team without footballs and Marcio was exactly the same. It is ironic they have the same initials. I had trained under a top manager like Jim McLean and he would have been absolutely appalled by Marcio's methods."

Hay acknowledged that if it hadn't been for his close working relationship with Keane then he would have walked. He explained: "I was no longer taking the day to day training and I wasn't happy but Dominic insisted that I stayed on. We were meant to be working together but Marcio didn't grasp that. I stood back and nothing against the guy but right away I could see his appointment was a mistake."

French defender Emmanuel Dorado had arrived the previous season but had hardly kicked a ball because of injury and had hoped to make his mark under Marcio. Dorado said: "I arrived for the pre-season 100 per cent and I was determined to make an impact. I owed Livingston because they had kept faith in me when I had been injured. David Hay had also phoned me every couple of weeks to see how I was getting on.

"So when I arrived back Barcellos had come in but he basically told me from the off that he didn't know who I was and I wasn't in his plans. It was amazing because he hadn't even seen me kick a ball. It was clear from the start he was never going to last. He failed to adapt to Scotland. He thought he was still training players on the Copacabana beach and that was his biggest problem. His appointment was a disastrous one for the club."

Marcio's methods might have been different but he did take his side to Hampden, albeit, in the second round of the CIS Cup to take on lowly Queen's Park. Preston said: "I remember I said to the lads we are starting at Hampden so let's finish our campaign here. I don't know if many guys actually believed me but I was being deadly serious."

Livi eased past Queen's thanks to a Lee Makel spot kick double and another from Quino in a 3-1 win. "That was actually my best season for goals," Englishman Makel recalled. "I netted quite a few in that cup run. I had started the season well and my confidence was up so I kicked off on penalty duty and scored a couple in our win over Queen's Park, which was good because it is always nice to score at Hampden, no matter who you are playing. The only disappointment was that I never got a hat-trick and the match ball because I had another chance with a shot that cracked back off the bar late on."

Next up came another away tie as Livingston were drawn against SPL rivals Dundee United. The Tannadice clash remained very much on a knife edge until captain Stuart Lovell took centre stage even though he was robbed of his big moment of glory. The match was eventually decided by, what went down as, an own goal by United keeper Paul Gallacher.

Lovell explained: "It went down as an OG but I am still adamant it was my goal. The ball was cut back and it fell to me about 15 yards from goal. I shaped and hit it well with a decent side-footer that beat Gallacher but came back off the bar, hit him and dropped behind the line. I was telling all the boys it was my goal and they were all saying we will see. Then right enough I picked up the papers the next day and it was there in black and white as an own goal. It is fair to say I was far from happy."

The club also grabbed the headlines again when Marcio called time on his disastrous reign at Livi and Hay was put back in charge. His first task in the Co-operative Insurance Cup was to take on crisis club Aberdeen at Pittodrie. Skipper Lovell started to fancy his sides chances and put an each-way flutter on his team to make the final.

"We had a good record against Aberdeen and I remember I stuck £20 on us each way at 40-1 to win the cup," Lovell admitted. "The draw had already been made in advance and I knew if we could get past Aberdeen, who weren't great at that time, then we were only 90 minutes away from a return to Hampden. Thankfully Hibs did all the hard work by putting out the Old Firm along the way."

His bet moved a step closer to fruition as Livi edged out the Dons 3-2. Fernando Paquinelli and Derek Lilley got on the scoresheet before Makel, once again, hit the winner. Makel rated that as his goal of the season. He said: "I grabbed another goal with the winner against Aberdeen. I picked the ball up from distance and decided to let fly and it flew into the net. That was probably my best goal."

Suddenly, Livi were looking forward to a last-four place where they were drawn against Dundee, while Rangers took on Hibs. But there were rumblings of discontent that suggested all was not well financially at Almondvale.

"We were meant to be training outdoors but the weather was that bad we had to train inside," defender David McNamee recalled. "We were in the gym when the chairman, Dominic Keane, came in and told us there was nothing to worry about but our wages would be a few days late. A few of the boys joked that the club was in trouble. We didn't realise how close to the truth we actually were."

Livi's stunned players didn't know if they were going to have a job never mind be able to play in the Easter Road semi-final versus Dundee, as the club announced they were to go into administration. To their credit, the players managed to rise in the face of adversity with Lilley scoring a late penalty to ensure Livi's League Cup campaign was to start where it finished.

Preston said: "Before the semi-final we were hit with the bombshell news that all the money had gone and Livingston were teetering on the brink. We actually went into administration the day before that game. We didn't even know what team we were going to be able to pick. It was sad because the number of players we lost was devastating. But credit to the boys that were left, they went out and got the job done. We got our late winner through Derek Lilley. The way things were going it was more like a fairytale or a script from a Hollywood blockbuster."

The pressure on Lilley's shoulders as he went to take the kick was immense but he admitted he had to try and block that out. "It wasn't a great semi," the striker confessed. "I had taken most of our penalties that season and hadn't missed so I was quite confident. I knew it was late in the game and it was now or never. I knew where I was putting my penalty and I actually thought I had hit the ball quite sweetly but after I watched the video back I actually lost my foot and slipped after I had made contact.

"The keeper still went the wrong way and the ball went in the top right where I wanted it to go. I think when I saw the ball hit the net I realised the enormity of what we had achieved. I knew we weren't going to give it up."

Defender McNamee admitted he couldn't even watch the penalty because he knew how important it could be for the club. He joked: "The penalty was a wee bit dubious. Maybe the referee didn't fancy extra-time but we were more than happy to accept his decision for that foul on Pasquinelli. I couldn't even watch the penalty. I was just so nervous. I stood at the halfway line and looked the other way. If Dundee had broken then I wouldn't even have noticed."

The celebrations were somewhat muted with so much uncertainty surrounding the club. The administrators came in and asked players to take wage cuts. They also ripped up the deals of Quino and Juanjo Camacho, among others. Dorado felt for everyone including his friends and countrymen who were shown the door. "We were all close," Dorado admitted. "We all got on really well and it didn't matter what nationality you were. We all felt for our team-mates who lost their jobs. It was hard for guys like Quino and Camacho but they all knew they had to go. It wasn't a football decision. It was a financial one."

McNamee also recalled the chilling events of that day. He said: "We basically sat in the dressing room and one-by-one we had to go in and see Davie Hay to find out if we were going to be kept or not. Some boys came back in relieved and others left absolutely heartbroken. It was a horrible, horrible day. We also knew how important it was if we could go on and win the cup. We knew it could keep people from the kitman to the cleaning ladies in a job. What happened, probably, brought the rest of the lads more together and, to be fair, also quite a few more fans turned out and rallied behind us as well."

Manager Hay was left to hold the fort but admitted if it hadn't been for the generosity of David Fernandez then Pasquinelli could also have found himself on the dole queue. He explained: "It was like the confessional box as I took the players in one at a time. Telling Quino he had to go was the hardest one. He was a first-class player and a gentleman into the bargain and it was tough telling him.

"A lot of the boys also had to take a drop in their wages. I was also going to release Pasquinelli because I didn't have enough money so David Fernandez actually agreed to pay some of his wages so we could keep him until the end of that season. It was an unbelievable gesture and summed up the bond we had."

Eventually, after the dust had settled, eyes started to turn to Hampden with a cup final place against Bobby Williamson's Hibs, who had already seen off the Old Firm. Preston revealed how a stealth-like move enabled him to unearth the Easter Road side's Hampden starting XI.

Preston explained: "The week before we played Spartans in the Scottish Cup while Hibs played a closed-door friendly against Brechin City at Easter Road. I got wind of it from Dick Campbell and I knew it was a great chance for us because Bobby Williamson would be putting out his strongest team. Don't ask me how I got in. I managed to sneak in and I watched most of the game from behind a pillar. As expected Bobby put out ten of the 11 players who were to start at Hampden. Alan Reid was the only surprise but that game still gave us the basis of their team."

Preston may have struck it lucky but midfielder Makel wasn't having such a good run. Makel recalled: "I was driving in Edinburgh and I tried to take a short-cut through Leith and I ended up knocking down a tramp who walked out in front of my car. The poor man ended up with a broken leg. I was also concerned about my own health, being a former Hearts player down in Leith.

"My brother-in-law ended up giving me a hat and told me to put it on at the side of the road just in case I ended up getting stick. The police arrived and took statements and then told me it was a common occurrence, tramps walking out in front of cars, so they can get a free night in a hospital bed. I am sure the tramp didn't think he would end up breaking his leg. I felt really bad and it was hardly ideal preparations in the build-up to the cup final."

The club managed to scrape enough money together to take the players away for their pre-final preparations. Manager Hay even brought in a former top sprinter to help make sure his players could beat their rivals to the CIS Cup winning line. McNamee said: "The manager took in the former 100 metre runner George McNeill. He does a lot of motivational talks and he was brilliant at the hotel. He basically slaughtered all the players and then built them up again. It was great because it relaxed everybody."

Midfielder Burton O'Brien had made the move to Livi along with McNamee when they left English top-flight side Blackburn Rovers. They had also moved to Ewood in a joint deal after breaking through the ranks at St Mirren. Their careers at that stage had gone hand-in-hand and that hadn't gone unnoticed by McNeill, who set the pair up, in his speech.

O'Brien recalled: "George McNeill was great and managed to totally relax us with his script. It was pretty funny and every single one of us got it. David McNamee and I got it tight. I can't put what he said into print because it was too crude, but he alluded to the fact that we had been pretty close throughout our careers. It left the rest of the boys in hysterics."

The preparations looked to have gone well until Hay's plans were thrown into turmoil, as Makel had to deal with the shock death of his girlfriend's dad. He recalled that awful night. He said: "I got a phone call in the room from my then girlfriend, who is now my wife, to tell me her dad had suffered a heart-attack. I was still in the hotel room and then I got another call five minutes later to tell me he had passed away. I knew I needed to get back to my family.

"I explained things to the management team. Paul Hegarty was great because he drove me straight through to Edinburgh and back to the house. I told him I had to stay and he said not to worry about the game, just to go and do whatever I needed to do."

Room-mate and friend Lovell admitted the shocking events also left him shaken and unsure whether or not Makel would return for the final. He said: "We had been watching television and it was just after 10.30pm when Lee took a call. Right away I could see there was something wrong because he had turned chalk white. He came off the phone, put his trainers on and said he had to go.

"I asked him what was wrong and started to walk downstairs with him. He told me that his father-in-law had passed away. I was really close to Lee and we used to drive in together so I really felt for him. I was also a bit shaken up when he left. I ended up having a glass of wine at the bar."

Makel, however, with the blessing of his family decided to play. He said: "I ended up all night and didn't get a wink of sleep, obviously everybody was just too upset. Everybody told me I had to go to the game because that is what my father-in-law would have wanted. I wanted to play in the game but I didn't really want to leave them. I decided to play and I ended up getting a lift with my friend Brian McLauchlin, from the BBC, who was going through to cover the game."

There were more than a few team-mates who were shocked but, equally delighted, that their playmaker Makel had returned to bolster their cause. Captain Lovell said: "I certainly didn't expect to see Lee at Hampden, but he turned up at the team hotel in the morning. I thought he would have been in no state to play because he would have been up all night comforting his family but he was determined to play. I was delighted when I saw him at the hotel because it must have been really difficult for him to concentrate on football when something like that happens. Lee took to the pitch and wore a black armband as a mark of respect."

Hibs went into the game as firm favourites. Everybody including the Hibs staff and players were certain the cup would be heading back to Leith. The open-top bus parade had already been planned, as over-confidence seemed to seep through the Easter Road ranks – acting as extra motivation for the already fired-up Livi players.

Preston admitted: "I went to Hampden early with our kitman Danny Cunning, Billy Kirkwood and Paul Hegarty to get everything ready. Danny had brought a special Livingston cup final strip to swap with the Hibs kitman Jim McCafferty. So when we got there Jim was nowhere to be seen. His assistant, Tam McCourt, told us he had gone back to Easter Road because he had forgotten their winners' t-shirts.

"We then found out that Hibs had already agreed to do a deal with a television company to film their big day. The same company had also come on to us but we told them we weren't interested until we knew whether or not we had won the cup. It wasn't the same in our opponent's camp. There was even a proposed map of their open-top bus in the Edinburgh Evening News. Needless to say all these things were stuck up on the wall and used as motivation for our boys."

The circumstances of the way the club were plunged into administration upset chairman Dominic Keane, so much that he decided to stay away from Hampden. Manager Hay recognised what he had done for the club and decided to take the team to see him on the morning of the game.

McNamee said: "On the way to the game we actually stopped at Dominic Keane's house. It was sad because he wasn't going to the game because of what had happened. He came on and wished us all the best. It was a difficult moment because we all knew Dominic and felt what he was going through. But after that we headed to Hampden and I was confident we were going to win."

That inner belief seemed to swell within the Livi ranks and they took it into the game, which was just as well because Hibs had about three quarters of the stadium. But those fans in green and white were quickly silenced as Livi netted the first goal through semi-final hero Lilley.

"I never felt like I kicked a ball at all in the first-half," he modestly admitted. "It was the most nervous I have ever felt going into a game. It was my first cup final but there was also so much going on. I actually felt tired before a ball was kicked and it was just down to nerves. It was a relief to go in at half-time 0-0. It was then we woke up and started to play. We got the opening goal. The ball was switched to Burton and he cut it back in. I was at the centre spot and I managed to move their defender, Colin Murdock, and fire it past the keeper."

Hibs barely had time to recover when within minutes Livingston had doubled their advantage from a less than likely source – left-back Jamie McAllister. "We were defending a Hibs corner when the ball was cleared," McAllister explained. "David Fernandez picked the ball up. I sprinted out from our six yard box and as I broke forward David released the perfect pass for me to beat the offside trap, as Gary Caldwell tried to appeal that I had run offside.

"I knew I had timed my run to perfection and then from 20 yards I managed to place the ball past the keeper. It was a massive moment for me, what a feeling to score in a cup final, in front of a packed Hampden, with all your family and friends watching."

That goal knocked the stuffing out of Hibs and they were never going to recover. The CIS Cup was going back up the M8 – but only halfway along. A clearly emotional Makel admitted the final whistle, at last, gave him something to smile about.

He said: "I have to say the game was a bit of a blur. I can't remember much about it at all. All I remember was the final whistle. I just slumped to the ground and just sat there. I was just completely drained after everything that had gone on. I eventually got up and joined the celebrations and it turned out to be an emotional day. From a football point of view, it was great, to help Livingston to a major cup success.

"It is special to say I was part of that team and it was great to say we achieved something with that team because there is no doubt my spells at Hearts and Livingston were the real highlights of my career in Scotland."

Lovell did the honour as he led his team up the Hampden stairs to lift the CIS Cup. He admitted it was a surreal moment, lifting a trophy against his former side, as the national stadium was all but empty apart from a small section of Livi fans and a few Hibs supporters who had stayed behind to give him pelters.

Lovell admitted: "It was bizarre because when I walked up to pick up the cup the stadium was nearly empty. It was almost eerie because most of the crowd had been Hibs fans. At the time I didn't really appreciate how much of a landmark occasion it was. I now ask myself when are Livingston going to win another major trophy? Probably, not in my lifetime. It was great to win the trophy but my only disappointment was that it was Hibs we beat.

"I had some great times at Easter Road and some of the guys we had played against had been my team-mates. I have actually watched the DVD back and a Hibs fan threw a scarf in front of me. I thought it was a joke but when I watched it back he was clearly fuming at me."

Hero McAllister reckons that victory was thoroughly deserved because Livi had a quality team who could hold their own, on any given day, against anybody in Scotland. McAllister insisted: "It was an unbelievable achievement, especially after everything that the club had gone through. It was a great time and we also had a great side and a top management team. I think the fact we won something means that Livingston team will never be forgotten."

Dorado knows his side helped to put Livingston on the Scottish footballing map. "Looking back I played in two cup finals," he explained. "My first was as a youngster with PSG when I was starting out and the second was at Livi when I was coming to the end of my career. What we did at Livi was amazing. Livingston is a little town and we helped this young club to lift one of the major trophies in Scotland. It was a fantastic achievement and one I won't forget. I still have the shirt from the game that all the boys signed that day. It still gives me enormous pride when I take the shirt out and look at it and think what we did at Livingston."

O'Brien saw it all in his time at Almondvale and believes that cup win was right up there with the day he helped Richard Gough's side to remain in the SPL as they relegated their final day opponents Dundee – at the end of a real nail-biter – a few years later.

O'Brien admitted: "To win any cup at Livingston is unbelievable. It was an amazing feeling. I still remember walking up the steps to get my medal. I looked around and the stadium was just about empty as the majority of Hibs fans had disappeared. It was a great day and I am just proud to say I was part of that Livingston side. For me, it is up there on a par with the season we managed to stay up on the final day. That was a few seasons later but I will never forget either of those seasons."

After the team had done their lap of honour and all the fans had gone home, boss Davie Hay allowed his backroom staff, Preston, Billy Kirkwood, Hegarty, Roy Baines and Cunning, to take the cup on their own private victory parade. Preston said: "Davie Hay was great and after everybody had left Hampden he told the coaching staff to go out and take it round Hampden on a second lap of honour."

Hay has achieved so much in the game but was proud of that Livi's achievement. He said: "I had been at clubs where success was expected. Every success should be cherished. It was certainly great for Livingston because it might never happen to them again."

Livingston hit the road for home, via the local Hampden off licence, for their own open-top bus parade. Many of the players feared their heroics had gone unnoticed until they got nearer Almondvale Stadium and it was then the fans and locals came out in force to salute their team.

McNamee explained: "We actually went into Haddow's outside Hampden to get our carryout and to fill up the cup. It was strange with everything that had happened that we were sitting popping champagne. It was a bittersweet moment. I was delighted to have won my first major trophy but I also felt for all the people who had lost their jobs.

"It was funny when we got back to Livingston and headed out on the open-top bus. When we left there were about five people out on the streets but by the time we got back to the ground the place was absolutely packed."

The scenes at Almondvale that night and into the early hours of the next morning descended into utter chaos with an infamous scene from Mike Basset Football Manager being played out by Hay, while another member of the coaching staff decided to sleep with the cup. "The celebrations were just crazy," Preston conceded. "I ended up sleeping with the trophy in my office. There was even one point when Davie Hay was up on his desk doing the Mike Bassett dance. He had promised to do it if we had won the cup but thankfully he never stripped down to his underpants."

Captain Lovell not only had a CIS Cup winner's medal but also walked away with a pocket-load of cash after his side's shock heroics. He admitted: "I ended up going to the bookmakers and walking away with £1200. It wasn't a bad end considering we weren't getting any win bonuses at that time."

For everyone connected with Livingston the 2003-04 season was one that was against all odds.

LIVINGSTON'S CIS LEAGUE CUP RUN 2003-04
* Second round (23rd September 2003 at Hampden)
    Queen's Park 1 (Clark) Livingston 3 (Makel 2, Quino)
* Third round (28th October 2003 at Tannadice)
    Dundee United 0 Livingston 1 (Gallacher OG)
* Quarter-final (2nd December 2003 at Pittodrie)
    Aberdeen 2 (Tosh 2) Livingston 3 (Lilley, Pasquinelli, Makel)
* Semi-final (3rd February 2004 at Easter Road)
    Dundee 0 Livingston 1 (Lilley)
* League Cup final (14th March 2004 at Hampden)
    Livingston 2 (Lilley, McAllister) Hibs 0

LIVINGSTON'S CIS CUP-WINNING TEAM:
Roddy McKenzie, David McNamee (Scott McLaughlin), Jamie
McAllister, Oscar Rubio, Marvin Andrews, Emmanuel Dorado,
Lee Makel, Burton O'Brien (John-Paul McGovern), Stuart Lovell,
David Fernandez (Fernando Pasquinelli), Derek Lilley.
Manager: Davie Hay.

19

• HEARTS •
BELIEVE! THE ROMANOV REVOLUTION

A BRIGHT new hope was given to Hearts when Lithuanian-based banker Vladimir Romanov pulled the club back from the brink in 2004. He agreed to buy the majority shareholding of Chris Robinson and immediately got the Gorgie faithful on side by vowing to keep them in their Tynecastle home. Plans, by the previous board, had been put in place to sell the ground to a housing developer in a bid to cut the club's spiralling debt.

Romanov had looked into buying a number of Scottish clubs, including Dundee United and Dunfermline, before he made his move for Hearts. The Russian-born Romanov came in with big plans for the maroon and white side of Edinburgh. He vowed to win the league, topple the Old Firm and bring Champions League football to Scotland's capital.

Manager Craig Levein wasn't quite so convinced and decided to leave for the challenge of English football with Championship side Leicester City. He was replaced by his former Tynecastle playing team-mate John Robertson, who was only given the job on a temporary basis. Romanov clearly had his eye on a more high-profile appointment and he delivered precisely that when he lured the former Scotland international and Ipswich Town boss George Burley back across the border in June 2005.

Levein had already left an impressive foundation from which to build, with the likes of Scotland caps Craig Gordon, Robbie Neilson, captain Steven Pressley, Andy Webster and Paul Hartley all signed up on long-term contracts.

Romanov also wasn't shy in splashing the cash to add more than a bit of continental flair to that Scottish core – although it remains uncertain whether Burley or Romanov was actually identifying the players.

The likes of Czech stars Rudi Skacel, Michal Pospisil and Roman Bednar signed, along with Julien Brellier, Ibrahim Tall, Champions League winner Edgauras Jankauskas and Takis Fyssas, who helped Greece win Euro 2004.

Bednar said: "When I first went to Hearts it was the best time ever. It was all so new, I did not speak any English, but it was not important because we understood each other on the pitch. There were 11, 12, 13 fantastic players and we just fitted well together. I got a knee injury after seven games, but I was still made to feel very much part of things."

Everything looked good on the pitch as well. Burley's new-look team made a blistering start to their SPL campaign. They went on an unbeaten ten-match run which saw them hit the top of the table. It was clear, however, that all was not well behind the scenes. Constant stories of Romanov's meddling in everything from transfers to tactics and team selection were never far from the back pages. Things finally came to a head on 22nd October when Burley quit as Hearts manager.

Czech striker Bednar, like the rest of Scottish football, was left stunned by Burley's departure. He recalled: "After nine games we had seven wins and two draws and then they sacked George Burley as manager! I went to the pre-match meal before the game and I asked: 'Where is George?' The guys told me he had been sacked and I just couldn't believe it. I remember, I really wanted to cry, it was crazy because everything was going so well and just like that, it was finished."

A number of big-name managers were linked with the post, from Ottmar Hitzfeld to Kevin Keegan, but once against Romanov grabbed the headlines when he appointed the highly controversial Graham Rix, who had a far from impressive managerial CV.

Romanov continued to back the club financially and brought in the ill-fated Bosnian Mirsad Beslija – who arrived in a club record £850,000 deal – during the January transfer window. Hearts, under Rix, were unable to maintain the high standards they had set under Burley and Celtic pulled away from them in the league. Their best hope of success looked to be the

Scottish Cup. On their day, Hearts knew they were as good as anybody in the country.

The third round draw certainly could have been a lot kinder as they were paired against SPL Kilmarnock, although, at least, they were given home advantage. Skipper Pressley got the opener. 'Elvis' recalled: "Robbie Neilson took a long throw into the box and I got above my marker to head it into the far corner."

That set things up for Jamie McAllister to clinch the 2-1 win. McAllister said: "I didn't score that many goals for Hearts, but that was a big one because the Scottish Cup was a competition we believed we could win. We had done well in the league and the cup was only five or six games. We knew, if we played the way we could then we would have a right good chance."

Next up it was Aberdeen at Tynecastle and they were seen off with somewhat more ease in a 3-0 win. Goals from Pospisil, Calum Elliot and a Pressley penalty were enough to dunt the Dons. Pressley admitted: "I didn't have much variation when it came to penalties. When you look at the majority of them they were aimed to the same place – which was to the goalkeeper's right. That was my only penalty. I used to put them all there."

Just when things looked to be settling down Hearts imploded again. Rix confirmed to his players ahead of a match against Dundee United that he wasn't in control of team matters and Romanov was picking the team. The joke was that the owner used to fax the starting XI to Tynecastle on the morning of the game.

Rix and Hearts tried to blank things out, as best they could, although it was becoming increasingly difficult. The quarter-final, at least, brought lower league opposition, in the shape of Partick Thistle, to Tynecastle. However, the First Division side proved to be one of the toughest nuts to crack in that cup run.

"Our hardest game out with the final was our quarter-final clash at home to Partick Thistle," Pressley confirmed. "We really struggled that day. We were very fortunate to win. What I recall from that day was that Partick got in early and took control of the players' lounge. I thought it was quite a good move from them. It was a statement of content and it showed that they were coming without fear. It was a very bold psychological move and it worked because that day they played really well. Deividas Cesnauskis scored a world-class goal that day and it was that sort of quality that was needed to beat Partick Thistle."

Hearts weren't helped by the sending off of Roman Bednar, who had only appeared as a second-half substitute against the Jags. Bednar joked: "It was amazing. It was a crazy cup run! I came back from injury to play in the quarter-final against Partick. I came on after an hour. As soon as I came on a Thistle player took a fast free kick which hit me because I couldn't get out of the way and the referee gave me a yellow card.

"After ten minutes, I got the ball in the area, I pushed it too far in front of me and the keeper got there first. He got a little bit of a touch on me and I thought if I go down it must be a penalty. But instead he gave me another yellow card and I was sent off. It looks absolutely terrible on television but I was definitely touched."

Neilson also acknowledged his side had been lucky against Thistle. "I remember 'Elvis' said after the Partick Thistle game it doesn't matter how you play because the result is the most important thing," the full-back said. "That was certainly true in that game."

Cesnauskis and Jankauskas scored the goals. It was also a difficult time for the Lithuanians in their new surroundings. They also had to deal with the ongoing claims that Romanov was giving them preferential treatment. Certainly, the same faith didn't extend to Rix and he was sacked in the middle of March.

Bednar said: "The players were fantastic, we were very together, but after that season, it got more difficult because after George there was never really a gaffer. The chairman picked the team, there were lots of changes at the club and we lost what we had, which was sad because things were so good under George Burley."

Rix was temporarily replaced by director of football Jim Duffy before Lithuanian Valdas Ivanauskas was brought in as the new coach. He had previously been in charge of one of Romanov's other clubs, FBK Kaunas. It was another upheaval Tynecastle could have done without.

Defender Robbie Neilson said: "We had a great team at the time, in the league we were still up at the top end. We had a few upsets along the way with all the changes of manager but we believed in the quality of player we had. We believed it was our time and we had a great chance of winning something."

Skipper Pressley also reckons some of the Lithuanians were talented players and got a rougher ride than maybe they should have. "The Lithuanians were only there because of Mr Romanov but that is not to say they didn't have the ability to play," Pressley insisted. "They were all good players. Deividas Cesnauskis was a talented individual. All the Lithuanians could play. Jankauskas had won the European Cup with Porto and Saulius Mikoliunas was also a great talent but I just think he was mismanaged as a youngster. He should have been protected more but he was just thrown in. All the Lithuanians made significant contributions to Hearts that season."

It came down to the semi-finals. Both the Old Firm had fallen by the wayside. High-flying Gretna were racing away with the Second Division. They were drawn against Dundee while Hearts faced an-all Edinburgh derby against rivals Hibs.

It was a night where a former Hibee and a real Tynecastle stalwart came to the fore. Scotland cap Paul Hartley grabbed a glorious hat-trick before Jankauskas netted another to seal a memorable 4-0 win. Hartley admitted: "That will always be one of my best memories from my time at Hearts. It was one of those games I will never forget. I'm always reminded of that day. Scoring a hat-trick at Hampden against your biggest rivals is a memory that will never leave me."

Neilson believes Hartley's performance will forever guarantee him legendary status at Hearts. He said: "Paul Hartley had a great season for us and that was probably the highlight of his season, getting the hat-trick in a semi-final versus Hibs. That has put Paul into the folklore of Hearts' history and assured him he will be a Tynecastle legend and hero for the rest of his days. I think everyone believed that whoever came out on top of the derby was going to win the cup."

It might have been a night that Hartley will never forget but it is one that captain Pressley can hardly remember. The central defender admitted: "I only remember the first-half. I took a head knock at half-time and because of my previous concussion they had to take me off. I felt a little light-headed. I actually felt a bit emotional when they took me off."

Fellow defender Andy Webster was forced to keep Hearts' reshaped defence together, after Pressley left proceedings. "The Edinburgh derby was massive for us," Webster confirmed. "It was a great display that night, particularly from Paul Hartley. I ended up having to play with two or three different central defensive partners during that game. Fortunately, it was our attacking players who came to the fore. To beat our local rivals so convincingly made it a good night, that everybody enjoyed, especially knowing we had a Scottish Cup final to look forward to."

It also gave the Jambos bragging rights over their city rivals. Even the foreign arrivals knew the importance of being the top dog in Edinburgh. Ibrahim Tall said: "Beating Hibs was good. I have played in a few derbies all over the world but the Hearts v Hibs game has been the most passionate. The fans, on both sides, are amazing and it was even better that night in the semi-final of the Scottish Cup.

"The Hearts fans really had something to celebrate. I know it hurt the Hibs fans because I got a bit of stick from them in and around Edinburgh after the game, although as always it was good-natured."

Gretna had also seen off Dundee in the other semi-final, so a Scottish Second Division side, despite the millions spent by their owner Brooks Mileson, stood between Hearts and their second Scottish Cup in eight years.

Leader Pressley admitted: "There was a belief. I think that season we had players who started to believe that Hearts team could achieve something. In previous seasons we had gone to places like Parkhead and Ibrox in hope more than anything but that year we knew we had good players and believed we could win these sort of games, regardless of who played for them."

The team, despite all the upheavals, could still have something tangible for their efforts. The league ended up out of their reach, as Celtic finished 17 points clear of second-placed Hearts, who, at least, went into the Champions League qualifiers. Their cup final opponents, Gretna, clinched the Second Division title with relative ease and prepared for Hampden in a far different way to Romanov's men.

Neilson explained: "We went down to a hotel in Greenock for a couple of days before the final while I think Gretna ended up going to La Manga for a week in the sun. The final became a bit of an anti-climax because everybody just expected us to turn up and win. Maybe that reflected in the performance because we didn't play well.

"We went into the final having clinched second place in the league and that meant that the manager completely changed the team for that final game at Rangers before the final. We weren't at our best and it was the greatest day in Gretna's history. They put up a great fight."

Ivanauskas also had problems of his own as he tried to get Hearts in shape for one final push. Pressley admitted: "I felt the final was a step too far. I didn't train a lot in the run-up to the final and many of the players had played a lot of really intensive games. I genuinely believe it took too much out of us. We started aggressively and after an hour we looked dead on our feet and had to hold on. We had been through a lot that season and things finally caught up on us."

Ex-Sochaux defender Tall admitted he was boosted by the massive Hearts support, who outnumbered their rivals by three-to-one at Scotland's national stadium. Tall said: "When we got to the stadium the atmosphere was amazing. There were just so many Hearts fans in the stadium, it was unbelievable. We had so many fans compared to Gretna and it really fired the players up to win the cup for them."

Hearts opened the scoring through Rudi Skacel but there looked to be very little left in the tank and a spirited second-half comeback saw Gretna equalise through Ryan McGuffie. Czech star Skacel said: "It was an important goal and I thought it would be the winning goal. I was pleased to score and I had always hoped I was going to score in the final because I knew it was going to be my last game for Hearts. I had decided a couple of weeks before that I was going to be leaving the club.

"It was good to score but then the game became a lot more difficult than people first thought and that is all credit to Gretna. Even when Gretna equalised I was still confident we could win although the way they came back at us was a big surprise. Inside I always felt confident we would win the match and we wouldn't lose the chance to win the Scottish Cup."

Jankauskas admitted many of the Hearts team, including himself, were on their knees. He explained: "My leg was cramping and I couldn't move, but we had already made three substitutions and I couldn't leave my team with ten men. I have never had that feeling in my life before. It was the end of a long season and the game was very difficult. The pitch was hard and there were other players suffering from cramp as well."

The match went all the way to extra-time and the Tynecastle cause wasn't helped by Paul Hartley's red card. He blames referee Dougie McDonald's failure to award Hearts a penalty, after Alan Main had tripped Rudi Skacel, for putting him over the edge.

Hartley said: "I watched the incident again after I was sent off and it was a stonewall penalty. For McDonald not to give a penalty was wrong and I think it brought the red mist down. I got a yellow shortly after that and then Derek Townsley took a boot at me before I got my red. It was tough watching on TV, because I would have been first to take a penalty."

Hearts were the team who held their nerve from 12 yards. Pressley, Neilson, Skacel and Pospisil all netted while Gavin Skelton and Derek Townsley missed in the penalty shoot-out to hand Hearts the cup.

Neilson admitted: "If we hadn't won that game it would have gone down as one of the biggest upsets in Scottish Cup history. Thankfully we got the job done and six or seven years down the line nobody remembers how we won it. They just know Hearts lifted the trophy. It was just relief that we got over the line."

Skacel remained confident even in the lottery of a penalty shoot-out. "I was always felt the end would be good for us," the midfielder claimed. "I just focused on scoring my penalty and that is what I did. I also had a lot of confidence in our penalty takers and I believed the maroon side of Edinburgh would have something to celebrate."

Goalkeeper Craig Gordon had played a major part in the penalties and accepted his team got lucky. Gordon said: "That was one of the poorest performances we produced and I think the effects of a long, hard season took its toll. It was a big pitch and I think everyone was looking at Gretna running out of steam, but it was the other way round. We put a lot of effort into getting the Champions League spot and we fell over the line a bit at Hampden."

Captain Pressley also hailed keeper Gordon as the hero that day. "What was had over Gretna was experience and a world-class goalkeeper," he claimed. "Sometimes things are just meant to happen and that day it happened for us. It brought a huge relief and satisfaction. We had come through a tremendously taxing season, in terms of the off-the-field activities. It has been very turbulent and it had taken its toll. I had been at the club for eight years and I had never lifted silverware. That day I did and it was a very significant moment for me and the group. I knew what we had gone through, on and off the field, and I felt it was a very fitting end to what had been an extremely difficult season."

Hartley, despite his red card, was just delighted to have won his first piece of senior silverware. He admitted: "You must give Gretna credit. They were absolutely fantastic and we were lucky to win the cup. I had waited for this since I was a young lad playing with Barry Ferguson at Mill United Boys' Club, though. It was fantastic knowing I had finally won something."

Defender Andy Webster had to watch the games from the stands after he had been controversially dropped by Romanov. The owner claimed he couldn't be trusted and left him out after he refused to sign a new contract. That eventually led to him making the now famous Webster ruling – although he later returned to Tynecastle for a second spell.

Webster acknowledged: "We were fortunate to win the cup. I don't think anybody could have argued if Gretna had won the cup. Losing a cup final on penalties is certainly a horrible way to bow out. I really felt for the Gretna players. I think in the end we just found a way to grind out the result and to just get over the line.

"That was down to the character in the side. We had a lot of strong minded individuals and experienced players. Winning the cup was vitally important. We had done well in the league, finishing second, and I think it showed everybody we had a really good team. Winning something showed everybody we could be winners and I think that cup win laid the foundations for Hearts to go out and challenge again."

Skacel and Tall had won cups in other countries but they admitted that Hearts win eclipsed everything. Skacel said: "The celebrations were amazing and they are something I will remember for the rest of my life. Any trophy is great but it was even more special because of the support we had at Hampden. There was a great atmosphere. People were so happy and the celebrations went on for three or four days after. I won the Czech Cup with Slavia Prague and the celebrations were nothing like at Hearts. It was as if we had won the World Cup. It was the most incredible season for me and the club. The supporters also backed us every step of the way."

Defender Tall added: "I was part of the Sochaux squad that won the League Cup in France in 2004. I played in some of the matches but I wasn't involved in the final. With Hearts, I played the final and it really felt like I was part of things. I have two trophies in my career and the one I won with Hearts, obviously, means the most to me."

It was hardly any surprise that coach Valdas Ivanauskas got to keep his job after that win.

Ivanauskas admitted: "It was a great achievement for Hearts to win the Scottish Cup that season. I was extremely proud of what the players achieved. They delivered success in some very difficult circumstances. The players deserve all the credit because they went out and delivered on the field. We had a very good squad of players and some strong characters in that dressing room and that is why the club was so successful."

Delighted owner Romanov had been hands on all season but even he was prepared to step aside and let his players take centre stage at

Hampden. "Mr Romanov came down to congratulate us and to celebrate with the team," defender Neilson revealed. "He never really said much. He pretty much took a back seat. I think he was just pleased that the team had won something. That win and day probably sparked him a wee bit. It made his realise what could be done with some half-decent investment."

But in typical Hearts style the team couldn't go back to Tynecastle to celebrate and had to head to the home of Scottish rugby – Murrayfield – for their party. Neilson explained: "I remember we couldn't even go back to Tynecastle because there was a wedding that day. It was madness. One of the biggest days in the club's history and we weren't able to go back to Gorgie. It could only happen at Hearts."

Captain Pressley played for both sides of the Old Firm but he admitted the maroon and white celebrations in Edinburgh that weekend blew him away. He said: "It was a special day because my son was on the bus although he missed the Sunday celebrations because he was playing football himself. Coming back to Gorgie, the roads were lined with supporters and we went back to Murrayfield for the after-match celebration.

"We travelled along Gorgie Road and down to Tynecastle and it is something that will live with me forever. I had experience winning trophies with Rangers and Celtic but nothing compares to winning it at a provincial club like Hearts. The scenes were remarkable and then that is when it hits home when you see the euphoria winning a cup brings to a club like Hearts."

Hearts players and fans, alike, are never likely to forget that Scottish Cup triumph.

Neilson admitted: "We went to the City Chambers on the Sunday. The scenes, with all the Hearts fans, were unbelievable. It started at the City Chambers to The Mound and away down Gorgie and Dalry Roads all the way up to Tynecastle. When we got back to the ground they opened the stadium and it was packed as well. It is something I will remember forever."

Bednar was delighted to lift the cup but is in no doubt they could also have won the league as well if Romanov had kept faith in Burley. He said: "We ended up well behind Celtic that season, but still we were runners-up and we won the Scottish Cup but it was all thanks to George because even after he left, we held on to that spirit."

Other players are not so sure if Hearts had the squad to win both competitions. "I don't know," skipper Pressley admitted. "We had to deal with several changes of manager and with every change came a different style of football. I don't think it was ideal in terms of consistency. We had the players to win the league. When I went to Celtic I saw what you needed. It is also hugely demanding not just physically but also mentally. Could we have won it? I don't know. Celtic won it and you need to give them credit for winning the league. You need quality, know-how and the mental strength."

The bond between that team and the Hearts support is likely to live forever and was one of the reasons why cup final hero Skacel decided to return to Tynecastle for a second spell. Skacel admitted: "If somebody supports you it gives you confidence. The Hearts fans have always been great to me and that was one of the main reasons why I came back to Hearts. They have always got behind me and have backed me in all my time in Scotland."

HEARTS' SCOTTISH CUP RUN 2005-06
* Third round (7th January 2006 at Tynecastle)
     Hearts 2 (Pressley, McAllister) Kilmarnock 1 (Nish)
* Fourth round (4th February 2006 at Tynecastle)
     Hearts 3 (Pospisil, Elliot, Pressley PEN) Aberdeen 0
* Quarter-final (25th March 2006 at Tynecastle)
     Hearts 2 (Jankauskas, Cesnauskis) Partick 1 (Roberts)
* Semi-final (2nd April 2006 at Hampden)
     Hearts 4 (Hartley 3, 1 PEN, Jankauskas) Hibs 0
* Scottish Cup final (13th May 2006 at Hampden)
     Hearts 1 (Skacel) Gretna 1 (McGuffie) (AET, Hearts won
     4-2 on penalties)

HEARTS' SCOTTISH CUP-WINNING TEAM
Craig Gordon, Robbie Neilson, Steven Pressley, Ibrahim Tall,
Takis Fyssas, Deividas Cesnauskis (Saulius Mikoliunas), Bruno
Aguiar (Julien Brellier), Paul Hartley, Rudi Skacel, Roman
Bednar (Michal Pospisil),Edgauras Jankauskas.
Manager: Valdas Ivanauskas.

20

• HIBERNIAN •
THE FIVE STAR HIBEES LIFT
THE CIS CUP

THE 1996-97 campaign started earlier than most Hibs players would have liked when Easter Road boss Tony Mowbray decided to take up the SPL's InterToto Cup invitation. The Leith squad kicked off while most of their rivals were still lying on exotic beaches, sunning themselves. Mowbray was more interested in sunshine on Leith.

He knew more European experience would be vital to his young side. They comfortably disposed of Latvian minnows Dinaburg Daug before they bowed out on away goals to Danish side Odense. Their early European exit, however, left a hangover which lingered into the start of their league campaign.

It was a different story in the CIS Cup as they thumped Peterhead 4-0 at Easter Road. An Iain Good own goal and further strikes from Abdessallam Benjelloun and Scott Brown had them on easy street, before James McCluskey rounded things off with a penalty. The goals continued to rain in. The happy Hibees hit emerging Gretna for six, as they visited the capital. Rising star Steven Fletcher, Brown, Rob Jones, Benjelloun and a Dean Shiels brace blitzed the Borders side.

Shiels said: "I scored one from close range and my second was a curler. It was a really good result because Gretna had spent a fair bit of money and were starting to climb up the leagues. A lot of people thought it could be a sticky fixture for us but we put on a really good performance and it was a pretty convincing win. To score ten goals in two matches against lower league opposition certainly stood us in good stead."

The Hibs fans were then given the quarter-final tie they all craved – a home game against their city rivals Hearts. But the Easter Road preparations were left in turmoil when their highly-rated boss Mowbray and his assistant Mark Venus were headhunted by Championship giants West Bromwich Albion. That left the Hibs board searching for a new manager. They turned to Hibees favourite and former Scotland star John Collins. He had very little coaching experience but had played at the highest level with Everton, Fulham, Celtic and Monaco and he brought in the vastly experienced Tommy Craig as his number two.

Collins said: "I had connections with the club, as Hibs was where it all started for me as a player. I had watched them over the previous few years, with my friend Tony as manager, and enjoyed watching them. So when the job came up I knew it was a great job. There was also a good group of young players there and that was another reason for me taking the job."

Fletcher admitted that appointment allowed the Hibs youngsters to continue the progress they had made under Mowbray. The striker, who had previously been linked with Real Madrid after his heroics for Scotland in the Under-19 European Championships, said: "John Collins came in and introduced a new way of training. The boys took to it well and it was good. We just wanted to learn and go out and try to improve. We had a good young side at that point and everything just fell right for us that year. We knew we were never going to win the league but we still felt we could do something in the cup competitions. We also knew it could have been the last year we could be together so we felt we had to try and do something."

Collins opened up with a 2-2 draw with Kilmarnock in the SPL before he was thrown into a CIS Cup baptism of fire against Hearts. The pair had drawn 2-2 in Leith in their first SPL meeting before the new manager checked in. It also gave Hibs the chance to avenge their derby thrashing in the previous season's Scottish Cup semi-final – a competition Hearts went on to win.

Midfielder Guillaume Beuzellin, who had just recovered from a cruciate ligament injury, said: "We had lost the Scottish Cup semi-final 4-0 to Hearts. That was a bad night. I loved my time at Edinburgh and I quickly realised how important the derby was to the fans and everybody in the capital. We went into the match determined to win."

There was a major foreign contingent at Easter Road but it didn't take them long to realise the importance of gaining the upper hand in the capital clashes. "The derby atmosphere was always really good," defender Shelton Martis admitted. "It was also something at Tynecastle because the fans were so close to the pitch and would just shout and abuse you. I remember Mark de Vries (the ex-Hearts player) told me that he couldn't park his car in certain areas of Edinburgh because Hibs fans would vandalise it. I never came across anything like that but passions always ran high on derby day."

Hibs were also boosted by turmoil in Gorgie. Colourful Tynecastle owner Vladimir Romanov put cup-winning coach Valdas Ivanauskas on sick leave, leaving sporting director Eduard Malofeev in charge. That gave Hibs a massive pre-match lift. The feeling it could be Hibs' year was also boosted when Falkirk knocked Celtic out on penalties. The draw had suddenly opened up and the boys in green and white took full advantage, beating Hearts thanks to a goal from skipper Rob Jones.

Moroccan magician Merouane Zemmama admitted: "The derby is always big but that game was even more important. Hearts had just won the cup and we knew we had to win this game for the fans. The manager told us if we beat Hearts then we could go all the way to the final and to be fair all the players took that belief on board. We got the goal through Rob Jones and I thought we played really well that night and we could have won by even more goals.

"It didn't matter because the most important thing was that we had beaten our great rivals and we had booked our place in the semi-finals and the fans were absolutely delighted. There was a great atmosphere at the end of that game."

If Hibs needed any extra encouragement that this could be their year then they trooped off the Easter Road pitch and news filtered through that a Steven Milne double had left Rangers red-faced against St Johnstone. Now the cup really was there for the taking, with Falkirk, Kilmarnock and the Perth outfit joining them in the last four. Hibs drew St Johnstone with the semi-final to be played on the enemy soil of Tynecastle.

Before that Collins had more pressing matters, like trying to keep his top stars like Kevin Thomson and Brown who were being chased by big clubs on both side of the border. Collins had hoped to keep them both but had to admit defeat when Rangers came in for Thomson, although he was able to persuade his friend and midfield partner Brown to stay on until the end of the season.

Collins's cause also wasn't helped when he lost the injured New Zealand international Killen for a large chunk of the season. His squad was seriously depleted, although Guillaume Beuzilin did recover from serious injury. It was hardly ideal preparation for a semi-final – where they knew they would meet Kilmarnock, who had beaten Falkirk 24 hours earlier, in the final.

Hibs got the perfect start when Fletcher scored three minutes in and were able to see that lead out until half-time. Fletcher recalled: "I scored quite early on. Ivan Sproule had charged up the wing and crossed it for me. I managed to catch it with a side-foot volley to put it past the goalkeeper. I thought we might kick on but we struggled and St Johnstone came back into it."

Influential midfielder Michael Stewart struggled with a mystery virus and had to make way for Benjelloun. Stewart explained: "I started to feel empty in my legs when I was out for the warm-up and when I went back inside I threw up. I felt my legs were lifeless, totally weightless. There was no power, no energy or drive. We don't know what it is yet. The doctor had to do blood tests and things like that to see what exactly was wrong."

It wasn't a great night for Hibernian's Northern Irish contingent either. Shiels tore his thigh muscle and then Ivan Sproule was left frustrated as he was subbed early. Shiels explained: "I had to come off in that game because I took a corner and I tore my thigh muscle. I just felt like this ton weight had landed on my leg and I could hardly move. I tried to play on but I only ended up making the injury worse and I had to come off.

"I was already in the dugout when the manager substituted Ivan and he was furious. He came off and he actually punched the dugout in frustration. They caught it on television and that was the clip they kept playing over and over again. I had to try and calm him down and that was easier said than done."

Sproule, in his defence, admitted he was unhappy although delighted that Hibs went on to make the final. He said: "I had come off the bench and had set up Steven Fletcher for his goal. I thought I had done OK against St Johnstone but then I got taken off. I wasn't happy because as a player you want to play every minute of every game. In the end the team got through and even though I was disappointed I had come off early I was also delighted that we had made the semi-final."

Sproule's mood wasn't helped when St Johnstone struck 14 minutes from time, through Jason Scotland to level the tie, and take it into extra-time. That was where Hibs eventually came out on top thanks to an early strike from David Murphy and a last-minute goal from substitute Benjelloun.

French midfielder Beuzellin admitted: "The thing that was very strange that night was the match was at Tynecastle. It was a good atmosphere but normally you expect the ground to be full of Hearts fans but this time it was mostly Hibs fans. I felt we should have won it in normal time but fortunately we won the game in extra-time thanks to goals from Murphy and Benji."

Benjelloun had been signed by previous boss Mowbray but it was, arguably, under Collins that he played his best football at Easter Road. The talented but often frustrating Moroccan admitted: "I did feel partly Scottish when I was at Hibs. I used to joke that people could call me McBenji. I also had a special relationship with the gaffer. I remember he asked me to go to his room in our hotel about 10pm one Saturday night. He showed me a DVD of my goals and my good work that season. There was music, good Scottish music in the background, but I don't know what it was. John Collins had this knack of filling you with confidence."

Shiels, Killen and Zemmama then faced a frantic race to be fit for the final against Kilmarnock. There was to be a mix of joy and heartbreak for the trio. A disappointed Shiels explained: "Big Chris and I both travelled to the hotel in Glasgow with the team but we knew we weren't going to be fit enough to play. I was disappointed because I didn't think my injury was that bad but it ended up being a tear and I missed the final. I roomed with Chris and we both felt very low but we wanted to be there to give the team our support."

There was better news for Zemmama as he was declared fit and was to come off the bench at Hampden. The African admitted: "I was really worried I wasn't going to make the final. I had missed the semi-final with a hamstring problem and it took me a bit of time to get over it. I was desperate to play because although I had played in finals in Morocco this was my first cup final in Europe. The manager also told me if I was fit I would play so that gave me hope and fortunately I made it."

Manager Collins had other big decisions to make and he brought in Chris Hogg for his first start in the competition and left Martis, who had played in every round, on the bench. The former Darlington star, who at least got off the bench, admitted: "I was really disappointed because I had played every minute of the cup run up to the final and then suddenly I found myself on the bench. I have to admit I was going through a rocky patch but it was still a blow not to start that game. I thought I would get on for the last 20 minutes to half an hour because we were well ahead but I had to wait until the last five minutes to get on."

Former Scotland star Michael Stewart was also left heartbroken, not even being named on the bench. Sproule recalled: "I roomed when Michael when he was told he wasn't involved. You want all your pals to play and although I knew I was starting I was also disappointed for him. I knew I had to try and raise his spirits although at that time he probably didn't want to speak to anyone."

For others, like self-confessed Hibee Andy McNeill it was a dream come true. The youngster had been in the crowd when his heroes had been left red-faced in the same competition against Livi. He was determined it wasn't going to happen again.

McNeil said: "The last time Hibs were in a final I was in the crowd, so it was a complete role reversal for me. That Livingston game was a big disappointment for everybody, particularly me. I had flown up from Southampton in the morning after playing in a game and met my parents. I had to fly back down again afterwards and it was maybe a bit of a wasted journey. I might have been better staying in bed."

It just showed the strength and depth that Collins had at Easter Road that he could leave so many big names out. There was a real confidence that the CIS Cup was going to be heading for the capital.

Northern Irish cap Sproule explained: "I have never been so confident going into a cup final in all my life. It wasn't over-confidence, it was just that we were so focused on winning something as a group. I remember the morning going to the game. It was almost a monsoon. It was so wet but luckily for us it was all to rain goals. It was also rather ironic because the Hibs fans were left singing their anthem 'Sunshine on Leith'. It still gives me goosebumps when I think back to that moment."

The nerves were settled when captain Jones put them ahead and from then on Hibs never looked back – although keeper Andy McNeill also had to play his part to stop Kilmarnock from fighting back. Captain Jones said: "Andy's save really kept us in it because we were a bit nervy in the opening stages. We had played a lot better in games and lost that season, but it showed we were growing up as a team and told a lot about the character we had in the dressing room.

"We had some spells where we played really good football and spread the play well, but we also had spells where we gave it away easily. The emphatic way we got the victory was perhaps the biggest shock. Although it doesn't matter who puts the ball in the net, it was nice to get the opener and we drove on from there."

The Hibees never looked back and doubles from Benjelloun and Fletcher put the polish on an impressive performance, despite Gordon Greer's consolation for Killie. Benjelloun proudly recalled: "It had been a long time waiting for a cup to come Hibs, but we changed that. All the newspapers in Morocco talked about me and Hibs that year when we got to the final. There were loads of stories when we played in the CIS Cup final and it was the same in Scotland. Also the fact I scored a couple of goals in the final also helped me. It was a proud day for me and Hibs and also for Moroccan football. Playing in the final and lifting the cup was massive for me."

Strike partner Fletcher added: "We were always confident even going into the final that we could win, even though we didn't have the best of records against Kilmarnock. Also both teams knew they had a chance with both sides of the Old Firm out. As soon as big Rob scored we just relaxed and all the nervous tension seemed to disappear. The atmosphere at Hampden was just amazing with all the fans that were there.

"I was young and nervous but I probably felt a bit better because I had been having a half-decent season with Hibs. To get two goals in the cup final was just amazing. My first goal saw Benji play the ball to Scott Brown and I made a third man run. We used to do that all the time and I managed to stick it under the keeper from the edge of the box. I just went a bit mad when I scored.

"My second goal I will now admit that I shanked it. I told people at the time I meant to put it under the keeper but I didn't. I tried to chip him and the ball took a funny bounce and I ended up knocking it under him. Even I was surprised at the final result because normally when we played Kilmarnock it was a tight, tight game. I remember turning round to Steven Whittaker and laughing because I knew we had finally achieved something."

For teenager Fletcher, it was the start of a glittering career that would see him go on to star in the English Premier League. He admitted: "Going up to pick up the trophy just seemed to go by so quickly. Winning that first medal with Hibs and my first cap for Scotland are the two biggest things of my career so far. Playing in the Premier League is massive but to win a trophy is just amazing. I know I was lucky to get a medal so early in my career because so many good players never get the chance to lift a trophy."

Jones, Benji and Fletcher may have got the goals but it was another Easter Road protege, Lewis Stevenson, who claimed all the plaudits as he walked away with the man of the match award after his Hampden master class. Modest Stevenson, who had still been cleaning the boots of senior pros like Stewart and Murphy, said: "When it was announced I'd won it, I wasn't sure if I'd heard it right. I thought Benji had a good game with two goals and the likes of Rob Jones, Scott Brown and Guillaume Beuzellin played really well too. Everyone did."

That left the stage clear for Jones to go up and lift the CIS Cup as Hibs captain. It was some rise to fame for the big towering English defender, who had started off at Gateshead and had been initially working full-time with kids with learning disabilities.

A proud Jones admitted: "Lifting the CIS Cup as captain of Hibs was beyond my wildest dreams. First and foremost, being captain of a club such as Hibs was a massive honour for me and not something I expected to happen so soon, if at all. I had only been at the club for eight or nine months and you can't become a legend in that time. I still can't describe what it was like to walk up those stairs and lift that trophy and hear what it meant to the Hibs fans.

"Scott Brown and I lifted the cup together and that was a decision between the gaffer and me. Scotty has been an integral part of the team all season. He has been the driving force and the main influence, so we felt it was only just for him and me to lift the trophy together."

Boss John Collins admitted that win brought some light at the end of a long dark tunnel for his family. He painfully revealed: "I lost my father a few months ago and he was desperate for me to win the cup," explained Collins, with television viewers having witnessed his raw emotions at the final whistle. "I was thinking of my father at the end of the game and he was with me. It was a wonderful feeling to win the cup. My mum was there which was good."

Defender Hogg admitted that afternoon was a career highlight. Hogg said: "It was the best day of my life. When the fourth and fifth goals were going in, I looked round and all the boys had big smiles on their faces." Keeper McNeil, who had been part of the Scotland team who had got the final of the Under-19 European Championships, also reckons that win silenced a lot of the critics who questioned whether or not that Hibs team had the bottle to win things.

McNeil said: "I spoke to a lot of my friends who are Hibs fans and I'm a fan too, so I know what it meant to people. There had been a lot of near misses with this club. People talked about hoodoos, but this was an entirely different set of players from the last time we lost a cup final. It was good to win the cup and to get that hoodoo out of the way."

Collins admitted that afternoon justified his decision to enter into the cut-throat business of football management. He explained: "They are heroes in the city for winning the cup. Sixteen years is a long wait between wins and I'm happy for the fans. A generation haven't seen us win the cup, there were kids here and it's nice for them. It's a wonderful feeling and that's why I came into the game again – to win things. It's even more pleasurable winning as a boss. When you see young players with smiles on their faces enjoying the moment it's all worthwhile. As a player you focus on yourself and as a boss you worry about the whole group."

Zemmama revealed that Hibs' heroics also made headline news in Morocco. The playmaker said: "There is no doubt taking the cup back to Edinburgh that day was just brilliant. It has been the best day of all my time in Scotland and I have had a lot of times here. I was just so happy I could give these great fans something back. Also I knew my family were back watching the match on television back in Rabat."

Injured pair Dean Shiels and Chris Killen were both promised medals although they failed to materialise. "It was a blow not to play but it was great for the fans to see the team win the cup," Shiels admitted. "Hibs fans had been starved of success in recent seasons and it was great to see them all out enjoying their day. Edinburgh was just awash with green and white everywhere. I think the Hearts fans went into hiding that night.

"Chris and I were both told by John Collins we would get medals but that never happened. It would have been nice to get them but we also knew we hadn't played in the final."

Scott Brown, who was soon to leave for Celtic, admitted he was left flabbergasted by the number of Hibs fans who took to the capital streets to join the green and white celebrations.

Brown said: "It was the first time the club had won a trophy in 16 or 17 years. I remember the lot. After the game we went back to Easter Road and got an open-top bus around Princess Street, Leith Walk and back to the ground. The fans were frightening. They came out in their thousands. I think there were 50,000 there. For Hibs to pull out a support like that, to see us win the cup, meant a lot to us."

Sproule also admitted it was surreal going round Leith on an open-top bus and seeing so many people he knew crammed on to the streets. He admitted: "Going back to the Edinburgh was amazing, especially when we went on the bus back around Leith. I used to stay in a flat down Leith and it was so surreal going past that and seeing so many people I knew out in the streets. When we got back to the stadium it was packed as well.

"I also had all my family there and it was good to have them there to share in the moment. It was probably a bit overwhelming for them. But it was a night I will never forget."

There was also a tinge of sadness and regret in among the champagne and celebrations.

Fletcher said: "My mum keeps all my strips, medals and memorabilia. She keeps them all in order for me. I would have loved to have had my dad there to see my first professional game and even in the cup final but it wasn't to be. I still had all the rest of my family there and to see them at Hampden meant the world to me. They always let me know how proud they are of me and I am sure my dad would have been the same."

Sproule also lost his still-born daughter a few years later and he laid her to rest with his cup winner's medal. He emotionally recalled: "We lost my daughter and I just wanted her to have my medal. I got a lot of enjoyment from winning the cup but it meant more to me to let my daughter take it to heaven with her. I still have my memories. I will never forget her or our cup win."

HIBS' CIS SCOTTISH LEAGUE CUP RUN 2006-07
* Second round (22nd August 2006 at Easter Road)
    Hibs 4 (Good OG, Benjelloun, S. Brown, McCluskey) Peterhead 0
* Third round (19th September 2006 at Easter Road)
    Hibs 6 (Fletcher, S Brown, Jones, Shiels 2, Benjelloun) Gretna 0
* Quarter-final (8th November 2006 at Easter Road)
    Hibs 1 (Jones) Hearts 0
* Semi-final (31st January 2007 at Tynecastle)
    St Johnstone 1 (Scotland) Hibs 3 (Fletcher, Murphy,

Benjelloun)
* League Cup final (18th March 2007 at Hampden Park)
    Kilmarnock 1 (Greer) Hibs 5 (Jones, Benjelloun 2, Fletcher 2)

HIBS' CIS CUP-WINNING SQUAD
Andy McNeil, Chris Hogg, Rob Jones, David Murphy, Steven Whittaker, Lewis Stevenson, Guillaume Beuzellin, Steven Fletcher, Scott Brown, Abdessallam Benjelloun, Ivan Sproule (Merouane Zemmama).
Manager: John Collins.

21

• DUNDEE UNITED •
A SCOTTISH CUP TO CELEBRATE
THE CENTENARY

IT IS fair to say that more than a few Dundee United fans feared the worst when their boss, Craig Levein, was headhunted to become the new Scotland manager in December 2009. The highly-rated manager had turned the ailing Tannadice club's fortunes around, helping to transform them from SPL strugglers into one of the most combative sides outside of the Old Firm.

Levein's loyal assistant, Peter Houston, had also played his part so, perhaps, it was the logical thing for Dundee United chairman Steven Thompson to turn to ask him to hold the fort while the club took stock and considered who was going to replace Levein.

Things didn't exactly go to plan as United's season appeared to spectacularly come off the rails as an embarrassing 7-1 thrashing at Ibrox left Houston wondering what he had done in their final match of 2009. At that point he decided that being Dundee United manager wasn't for him.

Chairman Thompson recalled: "Peter had never been a manager in his own right. It was a big ask. It was quite a stressful time for us all. Peter came in after that Rangers result and told me he didn't want to be considered. It came at a time when a lot of our players were feeling sorry for themselves. I had a chat with Andy Webster a few days before and then he called a meeting in the dressing room. The players were all a bit lost and that was a bad result."

United captain Andy Webster, who has been on a season-long loan from Rangers, knew things weren't right and used his own personal experiences to get the team back on track. "The manager had left and a lot of things at the club were up in the air," Webster admitted. "It also didn't help that we weren't playing well either. I remember going back after one of the games and I really beat myself up because we had lost again. I rolled everything around my head as to why things were going wrong.

"I knew as one of the more experienced players and the captain that it was up to me to take the lead. I had also been in a similar position, although, I was a lot younger when Craig Levein left Hearts for Leicester City. I knew I had to pass on my experience so we got all the boys together. It was a good meeting because all the boys aired their views and thoughts and it allowed us to wipe the slate clean and to get back to focusing 100 per cent on what we had to do on the pitch."

It seemed to have the desired effect as results improved, while United had identified the man they wanted to become their next manager – Pat Fenlon, the highly-successful boss of Irish side Bohemians. He even visited Tannadice for a guided tour and spoke to Houston but that move eventually hit the rocks over compensation.

It left United back at square one. Houston continued to be a safe pair of hands, as the Scottish Cup sparked United's stuttering campaign into life. The first match was against First Division side Partick Thistle at Firhill, where United were given a helping hand by their Argentine striker Damian Casalinuovo. His opening goal was as blatant as his fellow countryman, Diego Maradona, when he scored with his hand against England in the 1986 World Cup, and just as controversial.

"It was not a nice moment," Casalinuovo, who was branded a cheat in the aftermath, admitted with more than a slight hint of remorse. "I saw every paper after that game and they all had headlines that I had cheated. I have to admit it isn't a goal I am proud of, of course, but these things happen. I was still relatively young and playing in a foreign country so to be called a cheat was hard to take."

United team-mate Sean Dillon was warming up at the side of the goal and even he was stunned that the officials allowed Casalinuovo's strike "I was dropped for the Partick Thistle game so I wasn't happy," Dillon admitted. "I ended up on the bench and was warming up at the side of the goal where Damian scored. I saw it clear as day that he had handled the ball. I just kept my eyes on the referee and the linesman but they were signalling for the goal. I couldn't believe it."

There was no such discrepancies with United's clincher. Young David Goodwillie stepped off the bench to score a virtuoso goal that was one of the best of the tournament. "I wasn't really getting a game at that time," Goodwillie explained. "I came on when we were 1-0 up. I then got on a ball over the top and I thought will I just take it into the corner and run down the clock or will I just go for it?

"I decided to gamble and as I started to run things just opened up and I ended up sticking the ball away. Looking back that is probably one of my most enjoyable goals. I took a lot of confidence from it and from then managed to keep myself in the team."

Manager Houston acknowledges that win was to be the catalyst for what was yet to come.

Houston said: "Craig left to be the Scotland manager. We drew with Kilmarnock and then lost heavily to Rangers and Aberdeen. The thing that was bugging me was that although I wanted the job that the best thing for the players was maybe to get a new manager in, but I was encouraged by guys like Walter Smith not to walk away, but to stay and give myself a chance.

"At that stage the chairman was talking to Pat Fenlon and it looked like it was going to go through. I was quite happy to keep working and show my commitment. I was still the assistant manager and I had a contract with the club. Then things changed with a good run of results that all started with Partick Thistle in the cup."

The next obstacle was to come in the shape of a local derby with a trip to St Johnstone. Derek McInnes had to put together a decent side in Perth which pushed United all the way – until Goodwillie, once again, came to the fore.

The on-form striker recalled: "The ball just fell to me and I smashed it in off the bar. It proved to be the only goal and I was just delighted because St Johnstone were a good team and with it being a local derby it was even more important to get through."

United might have been getting a head of steam up but the last place they would have wanted to go in the quarter-final was to Ibrox to take on SPL champions Rangers – especially with that 7-1 defeat still fresh in the memory.

A similar theme looked set to emerge. United scored through Andis Shala but two, controversy penalties from Kris Boyd and another goal from Nacho Novo looked to have all but killed them off.

Houston knew he had nothing to lose and went for broke. It was a gamble that more than paid off as a Steven Whittaker own goal and a collector's item from Mihael Kovacevic ensured a replay at Tannadice.

The manager admitted: "I always say that Rangers had that first game in the bag when they went 3-1 up. I think they downed tools a wee bit after they had gone ahead. If they had kept their foot to the floor they would have won the tie but we got one from a wicked deflection and Kovacevic, who I don't think had scored a goal before in his career, equalised to give us another crack at Tannadice."

Kovacevic revealed revenge was the real inspiration behind their spirited come back. The Swiss defender said: "We were angry about the 7-1 defeat and wanted to show we are better, but we showed great character to come back from 3-1 down. That was the real Dundee United."

The result also proved to be the perfect antidote for Goodwillie, who was floored by a mystery bug in the build-up. "I actually fell ill at the team hotel the night before the game and ended up getting sent home," the Scotland star revealed. "When Rangers scored to make it 3-1 I thought oh no. I thought we were out and it made me feel even worse. Then when we eventually pulled it back to 3-3 I was jumping up and down in the living room celebrating."

The United squad, however, knew the job was only half-done. They had to dig deep one more time and they did when midfielder David Robertson came up trumps with the only goal of the game in the dying embers of the Tannadice return.

A proud Houston admitted: "A lot of people still had Rangers down as favourites. It was a right ding-dong battle but if there is ever a time you want to score against them then it was when we did, in the last minute, when there is no comeback. David Robertson sneaked in there and got the break of the ball. Wherever it come off I wouldn't like to say. After we won that game I thought to myself we have a right chance here."

Robertson's goal also saw him win great acclaim within the Tannadice dressing room, even if it was tongue-in-cheek. Goodwillie explained: "He took a lot of his stick after his goal and the boys started to call him 'the treble buster' because at that time Rangers were still going for the domestic clean sweep."

Things were going well and the manager's jacket suddenly looked the perfect fit for Houston. "After we strung a few results together I thought the team are now responding to what I want them to do," the proud United caretaker acknowledged. "However I was never going to jump into the chairman's office and say I now want the job. He ended up coming to me and asked me if I would take it until the end of the season. We both wanted to see how it went and, fortunately for me, things took off. The players were magnificent."

After that result, United did get more than a slice of luck in the semi-final draw. They were paired with Raith Rovers while Celtic drew First Division side Ross County in the other Hampden clash.

They excitement of a trip to Hampden was saddened for United midfielder Prince Buaben after his dad passed away back in Ghana. Buaben emotionally recalled: "I spoke to my mum and she said that my dad had always wanted me to do my best and be a good person – to work hard at whatever I do. People asked why I didn't go to my dad's funeral, but I spoke to my mum and she told me I could stay and that it wasn't going to be a big deal because my dad would always be with me no matter what I do. She said that I should stay and finish my season then go back home and see the family."

Away from that, United's preparations couldn't have gone any better. They were also helped when Ross County, playing at Hampden 24 hours earlier, left Neil Lennon's Celtic red-faced and stunned as they produced one of the biggest shock results of recent times. United knew they could be on the brink of something special.

"We missed Celtic and got Raith Rovers and that was a huge break for us," Houston admitted. "That is not being disrespectful to Raith Rovers because they are a good team and John McGlynn is a big mate of mine and a top manager. The weekend of the semi-final we trained at Tannadice and the team headed to our hotel at Westerwood ahead of the game.

"I jumped in my car to watch Falkirk's game. Just before I left Ross County scored and I thought to myself Celtic will come back in the second-half. Then Ross County scored their second and then it dawned on me – what an opportunity to win a Scottish Cup. Once again, I reiterate, that wasn't being disrespectful to Raith Rovers or Ross County because if Dundee United couldn't win our next two games then we didn't deserve to win the Scottish Cup."

Chairman Thompson had problems of his own as he tried to scramble back from a family holiday to make the game. He explained: "I was stuck in Canada. The flights had been cancelled two days running and I had to fly back via Nova Scotia. I got into Edinburgh about 11.30am and ended going to the semi-final without a suit."

Star man Goodwillie had already scripted his big day and it went to plan as he finally broke Raith's dogged resilience. He explained: "I roomed with Danny Swanson before the game. We always have a wee laugh and joke before games asking each other if we are going to score and then we say how we are going to do it. It was a wee laugh, nothing more. I remember I wrote down that he would get a knock down and I would spin and run. He would then play it through for me to take it round the keeper and score. I am not joking! That is what I wrote and when it happened Danny and I couldn't stop laughing. It was just unbelievable, just so surreal."

It was then left to captain Webster to guarantee United their final appearance. The reliable defender recalled: "Raith actually started the game well and it took a good early save from Dusan Pernis to keep us level. David Goodwillie showed great composure to score his goal and that really was our stepping stone to the final. I then managed to get the second from a set piece. Craig Conway swung in a great ball and I managed to make a decent run to stick it away. I knew that at 2-0 we were in a great position and the final was now in sight."

United ended the SPL season on a high, sealing third spot, and suddenly all the focus turned to Hampden and Ross County. Houston had been up and down the A9 to Dingwall more times than he cared to remember but it proved invaluable. He admitted: "I felt a lot more nervous before the semi-final than I did before the final. I just got all my stuff done early the week of the final and told the players what I expected and just let them get on with it.

"I also got the chance to see Ross County umpteen times because they still had loads of outstanding fixtures at the end of that season, so I knew what their team was going to be. I was so relaxed but I had to name my team early because all the players were hyper. They were all kicking lumps out of each other in training because they were all desperate to play at Hampden."

Defender Dillon was looking forward to the biggest game of his career although half his family missed it – for differing reasons. The Irishman explained: "My dad was out with the United Nations on a peace mission in Chad while my sister was due roundabout the cup final so my she had to stay at home and my mum wanted to be there for her. My dad had got some of the newspapers cutting sent over and he slaughtered me for making a big thing out of the fact he was on the frontline and I was looking forward to a Scottish Cup final. There was so much going on because we had also found out just before the semi-final that Michelle, my wife, was pregnant so there was so much going on at that time."

There was a real buzz of confidence around the camp although nobody publicly, any way, was naive enough to write off Ross County. Webster, looking back, said: "After Ross County beat Celtic I always thought to myself that had been their cup final. I never said anything like that publicly. Also there was a bit of pressure on them because they had beaten Celtic and people then predicted they would beat us. I always felt confident we would win the game. I am not being big-headed when I say that I just felt that we had played well, we had good players and the confidence among the squad was there for everyone to see."

This time, Goodwillie wasn't so well prepared – and sent the United team coach off on an unwanted detour as they made for their cup final camp. "I had a nightmare before the game," he joked. "I forgot my shoes to go with my club suit. I had to get my mum to go to Stirling Services so I could get the bus to stop off there on the way down. Then the morning of the cup final I put my suit on and I realised I had forgotten my tie. I was all over the place although I made sure the two things I did have were my boots and shin pads."

The big day was an emotional one for Thompson, who had seen his late dad, Eddie, invest so much time and money into his beloved Dundee United. He explained: "I was on high do from the moment I got up. All the pressure was on us. We were the big favourites. I remember going to the lunch before the game. My father used to hate going to them but it was fine although I was delighted to get away for the pre-match interviews. We had 20,000-odd fans and it was brilliant."

Houston, also showed a nice touch, as he stepped aside to let club captain Lee Wilkie, who had seen his career cruelly cut short by injury, lead the team out at Hampden.

An emotional Wilkie said: "It was a big thing for me and as it wasn't planned it was a big surprise as well. Even just standing in the tunnel looking out and seeing all the United fans was a massive thing."

The tangerine faithful turned the majority of Hampden into a sea of orange and black – with many sporting cult t-shirts which read: "Put your hands up for Jon Daly". It was a tribute to the Irish striker's bizarre goal celebration.

"There was a YouTube sensation at the time," Daly revealed. "There was a song called 'Put Your Hands Up For Detroit'. I remember one of the guys, Paul Reid, at the club showed me it on the internet. Then I thought for a bit of crack I would do it if I scored a goal. I scored at Pittodrie and pushed my hands up into the air and things just took off from there. The fans really got into it and it was really humbling for me and all my family to see so many Dundee United fans at the Scottish Cup final wearing orange t-shirts with the slogan 'put your hands up for Jon Daly'."

Goodwillie, like in the semi-final, once again showed he has a sixth sense when it came to the big Hampden occasion as he netted the opener. He explained: "I saw Michael McGovern (the Ross County goalkeeper) come out and I knew there was a chance the ball would come back out to me. I just wanted to put myself in a position where I knew the ball would fall to me and it did.

"I took the ball on my chest and just lobbed it towards goal. To be fair I try in most days in training and very rarely does it come off. When I saw the ball hit the net it was just an unbelievable experience. I then ran off to celebrate and pulled up my jersey to dedicate the goal in memory of my Nana."

After that there was always ever going to be one winner and Craig Conway made sure of that as he netted a brace of his own to cap off a perfect day for the Terrors. Conway said: "To get the two goals was a dream come true. You always dream about scoring goals in a cup final at Hampden. We had a young group of players and it really was a brilliant achievement for everyone associated with United."

By that stage the game was done, the ribbons were tied and the big question left to be answered was who was going to lift the cup in United's centenary season? Captain Webster explained: "I said to the boys in the dressing room before the game that I wanted Lee Wilkie to come up and lift the cup with me if we won it. The boys all agreed. So when he was in the dressing room I told him he had to come up with me to lift the cup but he was a bit reluctant to say yes.

"Then after the game when we won it I said to Lee come on but he wasn't going to come up with me. In the end I told him 'if you aren't going up then I'm not going up either!' In the end he came up and it was great to see. He was the club captain and out of respect everyone agreed he should be here. I was delighted to win the cup especially in Dundee United's centenary season. It made our win even more important. It was also only the second time the club have lifted the Scottish Cup so it was a big thing."

A proud Wilkie added: "I didn't feel too comfortable but you are not going to knock back something like that. I think if I hadn't done it I would have regretted it."

Manager Houston was proud as punch, watching his team walk up the steps to lift the famous, old trophy. "It will be a day I will never forget," he insisted. "It never happened for me as a player and when I think how many good managers that Dundee United have had but they never got the chance to lift the Scottish Cup. It was also massive for the fans because it had been 17 years since Dundee United had last won the Scottish Cup. It made me very humble and proud. As I said, I never won the cup as a player so to win it as manager, after everything that had happened, made it even sweeter, given the circumstances."

It meant so much to so many players like Conway who had come from Ayr United and Senegalese international Morgaro Gomis, who had been plucked from Scotland's lower leagues. Gomis said: "Prince wasn't really playing football three years ago before the final, Danny played for Berwick, I was with Cowdenbeath and Craig was with Ayr. It proves what can be achieved if you work hard.

"I can barely remember my first game for Cowdenbeath. I am pretty sure it was a friendly against Dunfermline when I was on trial. I signed a one-year deal with them to see how things went and I was surprised when United came in for me after six months. I never thought signing for Cowdenbeath would lead to something like winning the Scottish Cup with Dundee United."

Former Hartlepool star Daly was also pleased to give the club something back, after they had backed him through two seasons of injury hell. The striker acknowledged: "It was great to be involved in that day. For me it will always be right up there as the proudest moment of my football career. It also meant so much as I had suffered a bad couple of injuries at the club. The club had showed faith in me and it was good to give everyone, including the fans, something back."

Cup final star Goodwillie admitted: "It has been the best day of my life so far. It was great celebrating at Hampden with all the boys and the fans. To the fans that team are legends and that day means so much to them. I didn't probably appreciate what we had done until I was sitting watching the Motherwell v Celtic Scottish Cup final the following year."

Also if Ross County hadn't seen enough of Dundee United they then had to watch as their cup final conquerors gatecrashed their post-cup final dinner. Defender Dillon explained: "The bus driver wouldn't stop at an off-license or supermarket to let us get drink. The only place he actually agreed to stop was our normal hotel which was the Westerwood at Cumbernauld. I remember Andy Webster, Jon Daly and myself all jumped off the bus with our medals still round our necks as we went into the hotel.

"We suddenly realised that Ross County had gone there for their post-match meal so we quickly took off our medals and stuck them in our pockets. It was funny because one of the Ross County directors was being interviewed and you actually seen us walking past him with our happy heads on. That was us making to the bar for our carry-out."

Jubilant manager Houston had two major headaches to deal with the following morning – although his cup win allowed him to pull a few strings ahead of United's civic reception.

Houston explained: "My family and Gary Kirk and his family all stayed at the Hilton Hotel in the city. My son-in-law, Jamie, couldn't make the game because he had a junior match. My daughter, Kelly, said to him I have left all my stuff hanging up for the Sunday for you to take to the hotel. Jamie forgot my daughter's stuff so she started giving him pelters. So we ended up getting up early, along with Gary's wife, to try and get something for her to wear.

"There were still people going home from the night before and there was a young teenage girl, who was going to work, she came across to me and started crying and said that winning the cup had made it the happiest day of her life. Then the next thing I knew my daughter starting crying as well.

"We then continued up to the shops but everybody kept telling us that they didn't open until 11am. Then somebody recognised me and they ended up opening the shop for daughter to get something to wear. It was nice and you don't forget moments like that."

Irishman Dillon also revealed how a wind-up on the open-top bus parade saw Noel Hunt grab centre stage – although he had left for Reading two years earlier!

"Quite a few of our old team--mates, like Nicky Weaver, Jim O'Brien, Noel Hunt and Danny Grainger all came out with us back in Dundee on the Saturday night," said Dillon. Everyone went home on the Sunday apart from Noel. He stayed on and he was even on the bus as we went on our open-top parade. Jim Spence was the PA at the City chambers so he was introducing all the players as they went out on the balcony. So we went and told Jim that Noel was desperate to come out and take a bow.

"We then went in and told Noel that Jim wanted him out there. He refused until we told him he had to do it so bold as brass he went out and took a bow and ended up getting interviewed for ten minutes. The rest of us got 20 seconds if we were lucky."

By the time the party had finished there was only one thing left to do – give Houston the job on a permanent basis. Thompson admitted: "Life has this way of making decisions for you. I don't know how I couldn't have given him the job."

The cup win and third spot left Houston holding the aces but there was no way he was going to turn the job down. Houston joked: "John Colquhoun, my agent, did well for me. I was in a strong position when John went into to speak to the chairman. He got me a lot more than I was asking for never mind thinking about. But it wasn't about the money it was about wanting the job. Why should I have walked away and given somebody else the chance to work at this club with such a great bunch of player?"

Thompson has admitted it will be a season he, his family, the club and the fans will never forget. He recalled: "I don't think I took everything in at the time. A lot of questions were asked about my dad. It had been 18 months since he had passed away. My dad never got to appreciate the plans he had laid down for the club or seen the team win a cup. I actually took the cup home with after the celebrations at Tannadice because I was actually one of the last out of the ground and we had to take it to a function the following day.

"Somebody said to me 'that cup cost your family £5.5m' but you don't look at it that way. You look at it as a success and what it means to all the fans and the city as a whole. We are a good family club and I was delighted for everybody connected with the club. I have to say the year the cup was at Tannadice it had a better social life than anybody I have ever known. It has been at every primary and secondary school, Ninewells Hospital and it just made so many people so, so happy. It put a smile on so many people's face and that is what it should be all about."

DUNDEE UNITED'S ACTIVE NATION SCOTTISH CUP RUN 2009-10

* Fourth round (9th January 2010 at Firhill)
    Partick Thistle 0 Dundee United 2 (Casalinuovo, Goodwillie)
* Fifth round (6th February 2010 at McDiarmid Park)
    St Johnstone 0 Dundee United 1 (Goodwillie)
* Sixth round (14th March 2010 at Ibrox)
    Rangers 3 (Boyd 2 PENS, Novo) Dundee United 3 (Shala, Whittaker OG, Kovacevic)
* Sixth round replay (24th March 2010 at Tannadice)
    Dundee United 1 (D Robertson) Rangers 0
* Semi-final (11th April 2010 at Hampden)
    Dundee United 2 (Goodwillie, Webster) Raith Rovers 0
* Scottish Cup final (15th May 2010 at Hampden)
    Dundee United 3 (Goodwillie, Conway 2) Ross County 0

DUNDEE UNITED'S SCOTTISH CUP-WINNING TEAM

Dusan Pernis, Mihael Kovacevic (Keith Watson), Andy Webster, Garry Kenneth, Sean Dillon, Danny Swanson (S. Robertson), Prince Buaben, Morgaro Gomis, Craig Conway, David Goodwillie (D. Robertson), Jon Daly.
Manager: Peter Houston.

• KILMARNOCK •
TRIUMPH AND TRAGEDY

WHEN Mixu Paatelainen left Kilmarnock to become national coach of Finland in March 2011 it left a big hole to fill at Rugby Park. The flying Finn rejuvenated the Killie faithful by producing some great attacking football. Paatelainen didn't even last a full year but his efforts still saw him rewarded with the Scottish Football Writers' manager of the year award.

It was left to his assistant, Kenny Shiels, to hold the fort and see out the season. The caretaker, who had managerial experience of his own in Northern Ireland, with the likes of Larne and Coleraine, struggled initially although the Ayrshire side still managed to finish in fifth spot in the Scottish Premier Division.

Over the summer Kilmarnock chairman Michael Johnston considered his managerial options as the likes of Mexican legend Hugo Sanchez and former Liverpool assistant Alex Miller all threw their names into the ring.

Johnston, however, decided to keep faith in the former Northern Irish youth coach. The one stipulation was that he needed to bring somebody with experience in alongside him and he duly did that as he appointed his fellow countryman, Jimmy Nicholl, as his number two. Nicholl had managed Raith Rovers, Cowdenbeath and Millwall and had also previously been assistant at Killie to Jimmy Calderwood

Johnston said: "There were applicants from England and further afield. Some of them were very attractive on paper but the world in which they have lived would have been vastly different from the one we have here. Kenny knew the players, gets on well with them and the backroom staff. I also knew he had the right type of style of play in mind. So there were no unknown factors with Kenny's appointment."

It took a bit of time for the new management team to find their feet as they made sweeping changes to their squad, as Shiels attempted to make it back-to-back seasons in the top six. The success of the previous campaign also helped Killie as they were given a bye in the opening round of the League Cup. That meant they didn't open up their campaign until they met First Division strugglers Queen of the South at Rugby Park.

The tie brought a return of an old familiar face as Doonhamers boss Gus MacPherson was part of the Kilmarnock team who lifted the 1997 Scottish Cup. Some of the Kilmarnock players had played alongside him at Rugby Park.

Garry Hay said: "Gus was an experienced player when I broke into the team and you always sensed he was destined to go into coaching or management. He was always very approachable and there to pass on his experience and to give you a push or shove in the right direction.

"We had a lot of good experienced players who would help the young boys at the club, but Gus was good for me being a fellow full-back. He is fondly remembered by the Kilmarnock support and rightly so because he was a good servant to the club and was part of the Scottish Cup-winning team."

It was a game where Killie showed there was very little room for sentiment as they brutally disposed of Queen of the South. Gary Harkins netted after 90 seconds and things got worse for the visitors when striker Kevan Smith was sent off. Killie then went for the jugular and came out 5-0 winners with Ben Hutchinson and a Paul Heffernan hat-trick sealing this one-sided affair.

Former Sheffield Wednesday star Heffernan recalled: "We went on to win quite comfortably and I managed to get a hat-trick which was good. My third was probably the pick of my goals. I managed to take a touch and then chip the goalkeeper as he came off his line. That was the third hat-trick of my career and it was my first one for four or five years so things couldn't have worked out any better."

The prize for that was another home tie in the quarter-final. This time it was Second Division side East Fife, although they couldn't be taken lightly as they had already taken the SPL scalps of Dunfermline and Aberdeen, who came calling.

Killie were pushed all the way by John Robertson's plucky part-timers, who had on-loan Hearts striker Robert Ogelby red-carded. It wasn't until late on that goals from Mohamadou Sissoko and Gary Harkins broke down their stuffy resistance and booked the Ayrshire men's semi-final place.

Manager Shiels admitted: "If you compared East Fife to Ayr United then East Fife were far more creative and inventive than Ayr United. It was a really tough game even after they had a player sent off."

Hampden was suddenly calling and the draw certainly opened up as First Division outfit Falkirk, who had shocked Rangers, went into the hat, along with favourites Celtic and local rivals Ayr United. The whole of Ayrshire was left celebrating and licking their lips in anticipation as Ayr and Killie were paired together. For some of the newcomers it was a bit of an eye-opener.

Irishman Heffernan explained: "I didn't know much about the Ayrshire derby but before the draw the likes of James Fowler and Garry Hay both said that was the game they wanted because it would be massive. It certainly turned out that way. We stayed at the Park Hotel the night before the match and when we came out I couldn't believe how many Kilmarnock fans were there. They were everywhere and they cheered us on to the bus, which was great. They were really willing us to win, I think we would have had to go into hiding if we had lost that game."

The scene was already set well for the Hampden showdown before boss Kenny Shiels lit the blue touchpaper by playing mind games with his Ayr counterpart Brian Reid. "I do try and get an edge wherever I can and I listen to the interviews of the other managers to see if there is anything I can pick up and use to my team's advantage," Shiels revealed. "I listened to Brian's interview before they played Hearts and he highlighted the fact that his side were part-time. I knew he would bring it up again before he played us and I was ready for him.

"I did a lot of press interviews saying that Ayr weren't part-time because they had two full-time players in from Blackpool. I also said I had also managed part-time and full-time clubs and so had Mixu Paatelainen and Jimmy Nicholl and they both agreed it that it is basically a full-time job, the only difference is you have to wait until the evenings to train your players.

"I knew my comments would hit a nerve. I have been a part-time manager myself and you try to play that card when you bigger teams but I felt I was able to take that edge away from him. It turned into a bit of a war of words and I was quite happy when I picked up the papers and I saw Brian had taken the bait.

"Things definitely worked in our favour because his team adopted the small-team mentality during the semi-final. They never came out and I think there was a bit of fear in their minds. I have never seen anything like it, they defended for 86 minutes and didn't come out until the last four minutes, when they could have scored."

For local lad and long-serving defender Garry Hay he knew that game had to be won at all costs. "The Ayr game was just the biggest banana skin ever," the left-back acknowledged. "We were the favourites for a third game in a row but Ayr had done really well putting St Mirren and Hearts out of the competition. It was also the first all-Ayrshire semi-final in a major cup competition. I have to say I really felt the pressure in that game more than I did in the final.

"The only other time I felt pressure like that was on the final day when we beat Falkirk to stay in the SPL. I think it was worse for me because I am a local boy, I am a fan and a lot of my family and friends are from Kilmarnock so I knew defeat just wasn't an option."

Shiels was in no doubt his mind games helped give Killie the edge although they had great difficulty turning their domination into something tangible against their stuffy rivals, who ensured the match would go all the way to extra-time.

Shiels admitted: "We attacked from the first minute and we really pounded them but we just couldn't score. I kept telling the players not to panic because it would come but then I started to think to myself is this going to be one of those days? We hit the post, the bar, had one cleared off the line and their goalkeeper made a string of top stops. We produced an emphatic performance and had 33 attempts at goal. I did feel that if they had managed to take it to penalties then it would have been a real freak result."

Kilmarnock's perseverance and patience was finally rewarded when Dean Shiels, the son of the manager, finally broke the deadlock when he hit his extra-time winner in the 109th minute. The Northern Irishman, who fought off a virus to become a Hampden hero, had only extended his Rugby Park deal in the January after he had initially moved from Doncaster Rovers on loan.

Shiels dedicated his goal to his father. He said: "This was payback for him because it was his influence that helped me become a professional footballer. He was the one who took me out in the rain when I was ten and things like that so I was delighted for him. I was also delighted for the supporters most of all because they deserved this – and, to be honest, the prospect of a final was one of the reasons I extended my stay at Kilmarnock."

It was also a big afternoon for Michael Nelson, who made his Killie debut at Hampden that afternoon. The big defender, who had arrived from Scunthorpe, admitted: "I had a few options and a lot to weigh up. I was obviously impressed with Kenny Shiels and he also mentioned the fact that Kilmarnock were in the League Cup semi-final, so it was a nice way to kick off my Kilmarnock career.

"We were never really under much pressure because Ayr sat in so it was a good game to ease me in, especially with it being at Hampden. Winning the game and not having too much to do was ideal. It was great knowing we would be going back to Hampden for the final."

Kenny Shiels made significant captures in the January window as Ben Gordon also returned from Chelsea and Belgian front-man Dieter Van Tornhout came in after a glowing recommendation from former Killie striker Mark Burchill.

Van Tornhout explained: "I played with Mark Burchill in Cyprus. We stayed in the same complex and we got to know each other really well. I moved on to another club but things didn't really work out for me and Mark asked if I would be interested in going to Scotland and then the Kilmarnock thing came up. Mark had contacts there because he had played at Kilmarnock. I signed just before the semi-final and I went to watch that game from the stand."

All the new boys and the rest of the squad suddenly had a cup final to look forward but standing in their way was a Celtic team, who had seen off a battling performance from Falkirk. Celtic were also on the verge of clinching the title and were also looking for a domestic clean sweep.

Kilmarnock's cause also wasn't helped when they lost one of their top stars through injury, as skipper Manuel Pascali broke his right leg in a freak training ground incident. The Italian admitted Hampden wasn't the first thing on his mind. He said: "The final was a very important match but my initial concern was over my future because I was out of contract at the end of the season," the former Parma player claimed.

"I thought I could be out for six or seven months and I would be left without a contract. I was training, the pitch wasn't the best and my foot twisted on the ground and immediately I heard a loud crack and I realised immediately it was something very bad. I eventually got my head round that and felt I had a wee chance of making the final but after a month I knew I had no chance because I still wasn't running. I had played in all the matches up to the final and it was disappointing knowing that I wasn't going to be involved but I also knew we had a top team and I was confident that we would still win the cup."

All the pressure was piled on Neil Lennon's Celtic as they ran away with the league, after Rangers had been plunged into administration, and they were tipped to go on and claim a domestic clean sweep.

Boss Shiels, once again, used that to his advantage as he tried to get inside the heads of the glory-seeking Celtic stars. He joked: "I wind people up at times when I shouldn't but you have to get an edge. I told all my players to mention Celtic and the treble as much as they could in any interviews they did in the build-up. I spoke about the treble and used the phrases 'travesty of justice if they didn't win it' and 'we don't deserve to be in the same league as them because they are so far ahead of us'. Yet in our dressing room I told the players we could do it and our slogan was 'believe to achieve'.

"We built up the confidence and worked on things that we felt could win us the game. I also spoke to quite a few supporters. They all said to me it was going to be tough and I think a lot of them had resigned themselves to the fact that the Ayr game had been our final. I spoke to the players about that and I also highlighted some of the comments the Celtic players had made about the treble going into the final. I firmly believed and so did my players."

Killie's task was big enough without Pascali but top scorer Paul Heffernan also left manager Kenny Shiels in a sweat in the lead-up to Hampden. Heffernan revealed: "I knew in the week of the cup final that I would have no chance of being fit unless I took an injection. I had nothing to lose because if I hadn't take it then I knew I wouldn't have been involved. I spoke to the manager and the physio and I persuaded them to take the risk. Thankfully I got the injection and it did the job and I was able to play. It was such a massive relief because it was a such a big game for me and Kilmarnock."

Shiels also relaxed his team by naming his starting 11 early on. Hay admitted: "The manager named his team quite early and I was pretty relaxed. I think naming the team helped settle the nerves and, as I said before, I felt more pressure going into the semi-final."

James Fowler admitted the build-up was intense. "Normally teams go away a few days before the final but the manager decided he wanted us to stay at home," the midfielder, who was in his testimonial season, revealed. "We did all our training and then we had to watch DVDs about the strengths and weakness from our team and also Celtic's. The manager left no stone unturned and I actually felt tired by the end of the week although he also managed to inspire the confidence and belief in us that we could win."

However, there was still plenty of time for some of Killie's top stars to leave their manager browned off on the morning of the cup final. "There were three or four of us who turned up with brown shoes," Heffernan revealed. "I think Dean Shiels, James Dayton and myself all turned up with brown shoes on. The gaffer wasn't happy when he saw us. I told him that you don't tell us what colour of trainers to wear with our tracksuits so what difference does it make if we wear different coloured shoes? He wasn't having it and neither was the captain James Fowler. He was tried to get us fined £50 each for the drinks kitty."

When the team got to Hampden they were backed by a big support although the most nervous of them was, probably, their captain Manuel Pascali, who sat among them. He said: "A lot of my family and friends said they wanted to come over for the Ayr game but I told them maybe they should wait because there could be a chance we could get to the final, so they decided to take the gamble.

"I think there were 25 of my friends who booked to come over and then I broke my leg, but by that time it was too late for them to cancel their travel arrangements. So I ended up sitting in the stands with my family and friends and it was like little Italy in my section of the stand. I must have been a nightmare to sit beside because I kicked every ball."

Manager Shiels also decided to buck the trend, rather than trying to stop Celtic he wanted his Kilmarnock players to go out and take them on. "I felt the best way to go and beat Celtic wasn't to go and frustrate them and kick lumps out of them," the Ulsterman revealed. "The best way was to get the ball and hold on to it and that was what we focused on."

The tactics and the importance of a good, solid start, however, were almost thrown out the window after an early blunder from Mohamadou Sissoko gifted Celtic's normally lethal striker Gary Hooper a golden opportunity.

Defender Michael Nelson admitted: "I don't think there would have been many people putting money on us to win. The build-up was all about Celtic and I think that suited us because it took all the pressure off us. I thought we started well and then Momo Sissoko put Gary Hooper in. I thought: 'oh no, here we go'. I was too far away to do anything about but thankfully Cammy Bell made a great save, although to be fair to him he made a number of top saves in the final."

After that Killie gave as good as they got and more than matched a Celtic team who struggled with the weight of expectation. With the match still goalless Shiels decided to go for it in the latter stages of the second-half when he sent on another striker in birthday boy Dieter Van Tornhout.

"We had more possession than them and that shows how well we played," Shiels proudly admitted. "Cammy Bell made a terrific early save and then next thing I heard he had made a dozen saves but Fraser Forster made as many saves as him. I said before the game that I was going to go for it in the last 20 minutes. We had created chances and Dean Shiels could have had three himself before we scored.

"Celtic are used to teams keeping it tight and the longer that goes then the opposition retreat further and further back. We did the opposite because just after 70 minutes I sent on an extra striker, taking Gary Harkins off and putting on Dieter. I told my players to go for it."

That switch proved to be a managerial master stroke as minutes later Van Tornhout grabbed his moment of glory. Van Tornhout beamed: "I was just happy to be on the bench because there were a few boys who weren't involved at all. Also the boys had got the team to the final so there was a chance I may have missed out so I was delighted to just be involved. I then came on midway through the second-half and we got our goal.

"We picked them off as they tried to hit us on the counter-attack. Paul Heffernan picked the ball up and then he found Ben Gordon who pushed it forward to Lee Johnston and he put in the perfect cross for me to head into the net. As soon as I saw the ball coming in I thought it is mine. It was an incredible feeling when I saw the ball hit the net. I also saw how happy the fans were and it was an amazing moment. It wasn't only me who scored the goal it was the whole team because without each other we would never have won the cup."

There were time for some late drama as Celtic tried to rescue their Hampden dream as Anthony Stokes went down looking for a penalty under a challenge from Michael Nelson. Referee Willie Collum ended up booking Stokes, leaving the experienced Killie defender to breathe a huge sigh of relief.

Nelson revealed: "A Celtic midfielder took the ball down and I saw Anthony Stokes drop in behind me. He was going to the side of the goal and narrowed his angle. I couldn't get to the ball and I saw Cammy had shut off the near post and I tried to put my foot out to close off the back post. He then took an extra touch and tried to go round Cammy at the near post and he went down.

"Whether there was contact or not was debatable but there certainly wasn't enough for him to go down. When the referee blew I thought he was coming over to give me a red cared. When he walked past me to speak to Stokes I was just so relieved. I think you can see from the replays that there was no real contact and justice was done."

Come the final whistle you could see what it meant to everyone in blue and white as they celebrated their first ever League Cup triumph. "When Dieter put the ball into the net I almost burst out crying," long-serving Hay admitted. "I just start welling up because I knew how big that goal could be. I had waited since 1997 for an afternoon like that, it meant so much to me. I looked up at the big digital clock and it said 84 minutes.

"I remember the boys were shouting 'don't sit back', but I was like stuff that we will be sitting back and we will get everybody behind the ball. It ended up being a long six minutes with another four minutes stoppage time after that. I spent the entire time asking Willie Collum how long was left? When the whistle went I just put my hand to my face and shed a few tears."

Van Tornhout was pleased to have finally broken his cup final duck at the third time of asking. "Everything just drained out of my body at the final whistle," Van Tornhout said. "We were very happy until we heard the news of Liam's dad. That was difficult. It took something away from our cup win but I still look back on that day with great pride. I played in cup finals in Belgium and Holland and lost them both when I was at Club Brugge and then Roda so it was good to finally win one. I know what it means to Kilmarnock fans. Every time I see any of them they come up and thank me, so that is good and I am so happy for them."

Stand-in skipper James Fowler also made sure that injured captain Manuel Pascali was going up to lift the Scottish Cup with him. Fowler admitted: "I spoke to the press in the pre-match interviews I told them that I wanted Mani to go up and lift the cup but at that point I hadn't decided whether I was going to go up with him or let him go up by himself.

"But after we won the cup I wanted to be part of it because I quickly realised what a big achievement it was. It was also my testimonial season so it was also special to win the cup in that year. It was just amazing and what a feeling to lift that cup and to look round to your family and the fans was amazing."

Pascali's biggest concern wasn't getting his hands on the trophy but getting up the steps on his crutches. He joked: "James had said to me during the week that if we win you will come up with my and Garry Hay to collect the cup. I told him that Garry and James deserved to go and pick up the cup more than me but he was adamant we were going up together, like Franco Baresi, Alessandro Costacurta and Paolo Maldini at the end at AC Milan.

"I couldn't wait to get up the steps after the game. I was still on crutches but I live in a flat so I had plenty of practice of trying to get up and down the stairs so I was ready for our big moment. I had five weeks of daily practice and I turned into the crutch-climbing world champion. I also got a medal which I really appreciated. I don't know how I got one, maybe I stole somebody else's but whoever it was they have no chance of getting it back."

Nelson was also pleased and reckoned it justified his decision to move north. He said: "Winning the cup was good for me. Winning the championship (in League 1) with Norwich was massive but lifting the cup with Kilmarnock was great as well. It would probably have meant a lot more to me if I had been there from the start of the run, but it was still amazing to play and beat Celtic at Hampden, so early in my Kilmarnock career."

That joy however quickly turned to despair when news filtered through that Liam Kelly's dad, Jack, had collapsed in the stand. Manager Kenny Shiels was seen walking around the pitch forlornly himself as his team celebrated their success.

He emotionally revealed: "It was great but that feeling didn't last too long because I was told about Liam's father. The jubilation only lasted a couple of minutes. I was aware of the situation when the team were going round the park celebrating, that was when it really hit me. It was such a weird situation. I didn't know what to do because I had gone from a feeling of such joy to grief in a matter of seconds. It was hard."

Captain James Fowler said: "Garry Hay told me to go and get the gaffer because he was himself on the pitch but when I went across he told me about Liam's dad. At that point we headed back in and the boys then found out what had happened. I remember the dressing room it was so quiet. Our thoughts had gone from our success to suddenly keeping our fingers crossed and hoping for the best for Liam's dad."

Hay was chosen for the drug test along with Paul Heffernan and Celtic's Charlie Mulgrew and Cha Du Ri. Hay said: "I had to get driven down to Kilmarnock by car because I was picked for the drug test. I got down in time for the open-top bus. It was strange because we had won the cup but we were all thinking about Liam and his family. It did put a dampener on things, although it was still important we paraded the cup for the fans.

"I didn't know what to expect in the town but I got word that John Finnie Street was absolutely jam-packed. Some of the boys were asking where John Finnie Street was and when we turned into it the scenes were amazing and some of the boys couldn't believe how many Kilmarnock fans were out to welcome us home."

Manager Shiels had also been told the heartbreaking news that Liam's dad had passed away although he kept it from his team so they could enjoy their open-top bus parade and celebrations with the fans.

Shiels said: "It was a great feeling for the players as they went on the open-top bus. The players deserved their moment of glory. I knew before they went on the bus that Liam's dad had passed away but I didn't tell the players until after the parade. I wanted them to enjoy the celebrations because there were thousands of fans out on the streets to greet them. I felt really proud of all my players although it was a bittersweet day, we had won the cup but we really felt for Liam and his family."

The Killie players paid their own tribute in their next match as they wore t-shirts and dedicated their league win over Motherwell to Jack Kelly. It was a sad end to what was one of the greatest days in Kilmarnock's history.

KILMARNOCK FC'S SCOTTISH LEAGUE CUP RUN 2011-12

* Fifth round (20th September 2011 at Rugby Park)
  Kilmarnock 5 (Hutchinson, Heffernan 3, Harkins) Queen of the South 0
* Quarter-final (25th October 2011 at Rugby Park)
  Kilmarnock 2 (Sissoko, Harkins) East Fife 0
* Semi-final (28th January 2012 at Hampden)
  Kilmarnock 1 (Shiels) Ayr 0 (AET)
* Scottish League Cup final (18th March 2012 at Hampden)
  Kilmarnock 1 (Van Tornhout) Celtic 0

KILMARNOCK'S SCOTTISH LEAGUE CUP-WINNING SQUAD

Cammy Bell, Gary Hay, James Fowler, Michael Nelson, Ben Gordon, Mohamadou Sissoko (Zdenek Kroca), Liam Kelly, Danny Buijs (Lee Johnson), Gary Harkins (Dieter Van Tornhout 73), Dean Shiels, Paul Heffernan.

Substitutes not used: Kyle Letheren, James Dayton.

Manager: Kenny Shiels.

23

• HEARTS •
THE CAPITAL KINGS

IT IS fair to say that most Hearts fans feared the worst as the 2011-12 season started to unfold. The Gorgie outfit, under the guidance of Jim Jefferies, who was in his second managerial spell at the club, looked to be on a solid footing. Yet that quickly changed as weeks into the new season owner Vladimir Romanov decided changes needed to be made and Jefferies and his assistant, Billy Brown, were dismissed. The club were still in the middle of their Europa League assault when former Sporting Lisbon coach Paulo Sergio was plucked from left-field to replace cup-winning legend Jefferies.

The Tynecastle club was having serious cash-flow issues as Vladimir Romanov decided he was no longer willing to continue funding and also put it up for sale. It was a reality check for everybody at Tynecastle knowing they had spent out with their means since the Lithuanian-based banker had walked through the door. It was also an instant eye-opener to Sergio who had come to Scotland looking to win the title and suddenly he had to quickly re-adjust those goals.

The alarm bells started to ring as bills were late in being paid, HMRC took them to court and the players' wages were late in being paid. It was clear something drastic had to be done and the Tynecastle board immediately set about cutting their crippling, wage bill by making their top earners available for transfer and setting out plans to go with a more youthful approach.

"I don't know how much a factor things had," Scotland international Andy Webster insisted. "Obviously, it had some bearing. Circumstances at times were difficult but as professionals we just had to concentrate on the football and let other people sort the things off the park. We had to remain focused on the games because that was the only thing we could influence."

Sergio's management skills were taxed to the full, on and off the park. He tried to keep the team in the European push while also keeping his disgruntled players together behind the scenes. The Tynecastle stars were left struggling as they had to wait months to get their wages. That led to them calling in the Professional Footballers Association (Scotland), who made an official complaint to the Scottish Premier League that led to them getting their wages. The situation also caused striker Ryan Stevenson to go on a one-man strike.

Ian Black also did a bit of painting on the side to supplement his lack of earnings. The midfielder said: "I wasn't close to being a painter and decorator, it was blown out of proportion a bit. One of my mates has his own company and I went to give him a hand one day. He saw me alright and it looked as if I was looking for a new trade. It might be something to look at after my career."

It had been feared there would be a Tynecastle fire sale when the January window opened. Eggert Jonsson was sold to Wolves and quickly followed by Stevenson who went to Ipswich Town while John Sutton was loaned to Australian side Central Coast Mariners. The one bit of incoming business Hearts did manage to do was to re-sign Rudi Skacel for the rest of the season.

Slovakian keeper Marian Kello was in the final five months of his contract and the club had looked to cash in on him when Austria Vienna came in with a last-minute offer. Kello upset the Tynecastle board by refusing the move and was then told he would never kick another ball for the club. That proved to be the case as he was paid up weeks before the end of his contract.

Kello claimed: "I was punished for not going to Vienna. They said, 'If you don't go, don't take this transfer, you might not play.' They had already told me they didn't want me for the following season."

Ironically, Kello had been left out of their opening Scottish Cup clash when they were drawn against Ayrshire junior outfit Auchinleck Talbot.

Jamie MacDonald was given the gloves as Sergio gave a number of the Tynecastle youngsters a run-out. Talbot more than gave Hearts a run for their money as they had goal, wrongly, chalked off before Gordon Smith scored a late winner for the home side.

"It was a strange cup run because we did things the hard way as well," MacDonald admitted. "Even the Auchinleck game we struggled over the line a bit and the next two games we had to go to replays."

Scottish Premier League rivals St Johnstone were the reward in the next round. David Templeton's goal was cancelled out by Cillian Sheridan's leveller that forced a McDiarmid Park replay. The Perth men went ahead through Murray Davidson before a controversial stoppage time penalty from Jamie Hamill forced extra-time, where skipper Marius Zaliukas managed to drag Hearts through.

Republic of Ireland international Stephen Elliott said: "There was a great sense among that squad and we got a feeling its might be our year, especially when we played St Johnstone away and it looked like we might be going out the cup. When you score with 15 seconds to go you start to think your name might be written in the stars."

That win allowed Hearts to find some cash to controversially sign former Celtic and Scotland striker Craig Beattie, who had been released by Swansea City. It upset both Kilmarnock and St Mirren who had made rivals offers and came as Hearts struggled to pay their existing players.

Bizarrely, it was St Mirren who came calling in the quarter-final. Beattie and Skacel got on the scoresheet but their strikes were cancelled out by goals from Graham Carey and a Marius Zaliukas own goal. Hearts were forced to go the distance at New St Mirren Park before extra-time goals from Jamie Hamill and Skacel saw Hearts through.

There was also the encouraging news that third place could be enough to guarantee Champions League football as Rangers were plunged into administration, although in the end that was a bridge too far as Stuart McCall's Motherwell streaked ahead.

Hearts were left to fight it out for the Europa League places although they looked a better bet via the SPL than the cup as they were drawn against favourites and Scottish champions Celtic, while their Edinburgh rivals, Hibs, met Aberdeen in the other Hampden semi-final. Nobody fancied Hearts' chances especially as Celtic were still hurting after their last appearance at the national stadium where Kilmarnock had left them red-faced in the League Cup final.

Yet, there was the added incentive for Hearts to make it an all-Edinburgh cup final as Hibs had gone out and beaten Aberdeen 2-1 in the semi-final 24 hours before. The Jambos rocked Neil Lennon's side when they took first-blood through Skacel. All appeared to be going to going to plan until Gary Hooper netted three minutes from time for the Hoops. The momentum seemed to have swung back in Celtic's favour until it was adjudged that Marius Zaliukas's shot had been handled inside the box by Joe Ledley.

Beattie kept his cool to net the last-minute penalty to sink his old team. Celtic had a similar penalty claim against Andy Webster but it wasn't given and that led to Celtic boss Neil Lennon losing the plot with referee Euan Norris after the final whistle.

Beattie said: "It was great because I felt I had made an impact in the cup run. I'd played a big part in it, in the quarter-finals and semi-final and so that helped me to get the fans on side. The Hearts fans were great to me."

Suddenly, Scottish football was looking forward to its first Edinburgh derby Scottish Cup final in 116 years. Cup fever gripped Edinburgh as it was dubbed 'the salt and sauce final'. Hearts and Hibs fans both agreed it was the biggest Edinburgh derby ever. But before thoughts could drift back to Hampden there was still work to be done by both in the league.

Hibs, under the management of Pat Fenlon and former Hearts number two Billy Brown, still had to secure their SPL status as they battled it out with Dunfermline to beat the drop while Hearts still hoped to seal European football ahead of the cup final. Hibs eventually did it by thrashing Dunfermline 4-0 at Easter Road while Hearts had to wait until the final league day as they lost to Celtic and Rangers beat St Johnstone to guarantee themselves fifth spot and European football.

That allowed the build-up for the Scottish Cup final to really kick in. Fenlon decided to take his side away from it all by heading to Dublin while Sergio decided to remain closer to base camp.

Jamie Hamill, who had scored some important on the way, snapped his cruciate in a freak training that saw him miss the cup final while midfielder Ian Black delayed a hernia operation to ensure he was fit for Hampden.

The former Inverness man recalled: "I took an the injection as I had done in previous weeks so I could play in the final. I would have played with a broken leg if I could have. It was such a massive game, nothing was going to keep me out of it."

The clamour for tickets was the biggest challenge for people on both sides. One of Craig Beattie's biggest fans vowed to go to extreme lengths to make sure he was at Hampden for the semi and then the final.

"It all started when I got stuck with two tickets for the semi and I thought I would have a carry-on on Twitter," Beattie explained. "I said I'd give the tickets to whoever made me laugh the most. There was a lot of stuff about Hibs but eventually I said to send a joke and this lad sent me a cracking one so I met up with him and gave him the two tickets.

"Then, straight after the game against Celtic, he said he would get my name tattooed on his backside if I got him two more for the final. I agreed as long as I got proof first. He came up the other day and told me he had booked in for Monday to get the tattoo and that I had better get him his tickets now.

"After that I had to tweet him asking if he really wanted my name on his backside for the rest of his life! He tweeted back saying it was his only chance of getting two tickets and he needed to do what he needed to do and I thought 'he's desperate!'. So I gave him the two tickets anyway and he's not getting it done, but he was serious about it."

Life-long Jambo and first-team coach Gary Locke also knew there would be no hiding for the loser and there was also a bit of added spice that his long-serving assistant Brown was in the opposition dugout once.

Locke said: "If you ask anyone not just people who work at Hearts but fans, and they would agree it was the biggest derby they have seen. It was actually a nightmare in the build-up because everybody wanted to talk about the cup final even though we still had a lot of important league games to play. I actually had two holidays, one for Turkey and another for Siberia if we had lost."

The mind games started before a ball was even kicked but Hearts boss Paulo Sergio refused to get involved – claiming the match wasn't any bigger than their opener against Auchinleck Talbot. Sergio said: "It was just as important to win the final as it was to beat Auchinleck. "If we didn't beat Auchinleck, we weren't going to be there to play Hibs."

Ryan McGowan also took his revenge on Andy Webster for all his moaning as he slaughtered one of the club's most elderly statesman by calling him 'Granddad' in the match day programme. "Rather being called Granddad what I think you would call it was being a responsible adult," Webster joked. "I normally give him a hard time on the pitch so that was probably him getting his own back on me."

Striker Craig Beattie overcame a tight hamstring and virus to take his place on the bench, while Sergio's starting 11 included several others who were out of contract including Stephen Elliott, Rudi Skacel, Suso Santana and Ian Black.

Pre-match claims that the pressure was all on Hearts were quickly blown away by Sergio's rampant side. Darren Barr picked the perfect time to net his first goal for Hearts – just months after he feared his future would be elsewhere. He volunteered to take a wage cut to go to Bristol Rovers on loan but that deal collapsed and he managed to get his chance at Tynecastle as a defensive midfielder.

"I think my brother and dad would have had money on me for first goalscorer," Barr, who had lost his previous cup final with Falkirk, admitted. "I was hearing 40-1 but I don't really know. I had been at Hearts a while and I hadn't really played and that was frustrating because I felt I could do a job. I am playing midfield just now and no matter where it was I was always confident I could play. It is maybe bittersweet but you do dream about scoring in a cup final."

Skacel, who scored in the 2006 Scottish Cup final win, netted a second when his shot took a nick off Hibs captain James McPake. Hearts looked to be on easy street until McPake pulled one back at the other end just before half-time. That gave Hibs hopes but that disappeared seconds after the restart when Pa Kujabi picked up his second yellow card for taking out Suso Santana. The Spaniard was caught outside the box but referee Craig Thomson pointed to the spot.

That decision infuriated the Hibs contingent but Suso reckons it made very little difference to the final proceedings. "It was a penalty," Suso insisted. "He touched me. It was inside, that's what the ref said. Hibs say it wasn't a penalty? OK, no penalty. We still win 4-1. Even without the penalty Hearts would still have won. For me though it was a penalty."

Danny Grainger, who had tasted Scottish Cup final disappointment with Gretna and Dundee United, took full responsibility as he slotted home from 12 yards. "I didn't feel any pressure," Grainger insisted. "I spoke to my dad about it the night before as it was going to be between me and Rudi for the penalties. The manager confirmed it was going to be me in the morning and I put it where I told my dad I would. I was glad to see Mark Brown dive the other way."

Experienced defender Andy Webster knew at that point the game was done and dusted and the Scottish Cup was heading for Gorgie. "I was always confident we would win the game," Webster claimed. "Over the course of the season we always had the better of Hibs although I accept this game was slightly different because it was a final and there was more pressure being put on from out with, but I always felt if we went about things the right way, which we did, then we would come out on top.

"I was surprised at just how convincing the final scoreline was. Early in the second-half the match was over because we knew we had won it and they had lost it. It was just a case of running the clock down and I thought we played well from start to finish. We started reasonably well. We got an early goal and then getting the second one we felt reasonably comfortable and continued to play our football. Hibs getting the goal before half-time made things a bit more jittery but five minutes into the second-half and the game was finished."

At that point hundreds of Hibs fans headed for the exit and then there was a mass exodus when Ryan McGowan headed in number four from close range, after Mark Brown had saved to deny Elliott. Skacel then arrowed in his second to complete the rout with the fifth.

Ian Black was among the candidates for the man of the match award, but that went to Skacel, and Black got a standing ovation as he was substituted in the final minutes of the game. A touched Black said: "I never planned to come off but it was nice of the gaffer to give me the chance to say my farewells. To get my standing ovation was amazing and something that will live with me forever. There is no doubt the cup final was the highlight of my career and bowing out with a winner's medal was the perfect way to bow out."

Hibernian's misery was completed when boss Pat Fenlon was sent to the stands for an abusive gesture as the Hearts fans goaded him with chants of 'there's only one Pat Fenlon'.

Goal hero Skacel was delighted when the final whistle and he helped prove Hearts were the pride of the capital. He said: "There's only one team in Edinburgh and it is fantastic to finish this way. It was a huge game and we showed everybody in Scotland that we are the best team in Edinburgh. It was one of my best afternoons in football. It was the perfect way to finish the season because winning the cup is all everybody will remember from the season. Hearts will always be in my heart."

Defender Grainger was even surprised at how comprehensive the final outcome had been. Grainger said: "It was a fantastic performance from all the boys and we showed how good we are. We always knew we were the better team and if we went about our own business we would be able to get the result we needed. We still didn't expect it to be as easy as it was."

Ex-Tenerife star Suso Santana had an indifferent season in the build-up to the final with his family returning home but he was in no doubt lifting the cup was the biggest moment of his career. "It was the best day of my career," the little winger beamed. "I'm really happy. For me it's fantastic, for my wife, for my family. It's brilliant. It means so much. For me it has been difficult without my family being here. Now to win the cup it makes me happy."

Former Sunderland star Stephen Elliott believes there wasn't much else that could have been asked from the Hearts players in the final. He knows it is a result that will live long in the memory of the Tynecastle faithful.

"At the start of the season the chances of a team out with the Old Firm winning the league are highly unlikely so then you look to the cups," he claimed. "To get to the final and then beat your local rivals so convincingly – I don't think there's a better way to end the season. When our fourth went in I think everyone realised it was all over for Hibs."

Keeper Jamie MacDonald was part of the squad when Hearts won the cup back and he then lost out in the final when he was on loan at Queen of the South so was delighted to finally get his first winner's medal.

"I was there with Queen of the South in 2008 and lost so to win it today against our local rivals is just unbelievable," he claimed. "I can't really put what I'm feeling into words. It was just a great day."

Owner Vladimir Romanov flew into Scotland for the game and even though he had already delivered the Scottish once before under his ownership. This time it was a case of when in Rome when the Russian turned up at Hampden wearing a kilt. Romanov was delighted his team had delivered again.

"Mr Romanov showed a lot of emotion and said what he had to say to us," Zaliukas explained. "Every player was up to the job and it was good for him that we won the cup."

Webster had missed out on Hearts win of 2006 but he reckons this one more than made up for it. "It was different to lifting the cup as captain of Dundee United," he explained. "There were different pressures in this match because it was an Edinburgh derby, with all the history surrounding the game. It was always going to be a massive occasion and spectacle and in the end a great achievement for that Hearts team. It will take a wee bit to sink in over the coming weeks and months. It has been a massive achievement for everybody at Hearts and it will live long in the memory."

Striker Craig Beattie had starred and scored for Scotland, won titles and three league medals with Celtic but he admitted his Hearts success was just as big. He said: "It's definitely my sweetest achievement. It's a great moment in my career. Even if we hadn't won I wouldn't have needed to vindicate my decision. They're a massive club with big potential. It's fantastic and a great day for the club, for the boys, the management and everybody involved. The boys were terrific – I don't think Hibs were great to be fair – but we didn't let them be any good."

Skipper Marius Zaliukas believes his team showed their true colours through a difficult season. "The celebrations were amazing," Zaliukas claimed. "It was a special day for everyone especially due to the circumstances of our season. That's why I think we deserved it. On the open-top bus, it was amazing. Just seeing all the fans follow us, it was so special – better than I thought it would be. This club is the third biggest in Scotland. The trouble we had earlier in the season, made us stronger as a team. Through all the bad stuff, we started to play better and showed real character."

Coach Paulo Sergio had played for and coached some of the top teams in Portugal and he admitted he was amazed by the scenes in Edinburgh city as thousands of fans crammed on to the streets of the capital. Sergio admitted: "It was a great reception, great crowd, great supporters. A fantastic experience being on the bus. I knew when I arrived that this was a big club. I didn't know it was this big – but I know now.

"I knew about the passion of Scottish football fans, that is one of the reasons that I came to this country. But to feel that on the pitch, to feel that today, it is amazing. For me, for us, it's fantastic. I want nothing just for me – I did my job and I never do anything alone, I have a great technical staff. And of course, for me, the players are the most important part of the relationship. I will always have this club in my heart – for the rest of my life."

Webster also paid tribute to the maroon and white faithful and said: "Seeing everybody out in the streets of Edinburgh and back at Tynecastle was amazing. That is when you realise that you have achieved something significant and what it means to everyone. From that point of view, it was a great feeling for everybody and nice to share it with the fans and also my family. My boys love football and it was nice for them to be there."

Ian Black admitted he had a lump in his throat and shed a few tears as he walked out of Tynecastle that final time. Black said: "It was an emotional time and it was hard to hold myself together. It was difficult to say my farewells. I have watched the game back on DVD a few times and it gets even better every time I watch it. It is a day I will never forget."

HEARTS' SCOTTISH CUP RUN 2011-12
* Fourth round (7th January 2012 at Tynecastle)
  Hearts 1 (Smith) Auchinleck Talbot 0
* Fifth round (5th February 2012 at Tynecastle)
  Hearts 1 (Templeton) St Johnstone 1 (Sheridan)
* Fifth round replay (14th February 2012 at McDiarmid Park)
  St Johnstone 1 (Davidson) Hearts 2 (Hamill PEN, Zaliukas) (AET)
* Quarter-final (10th March 2012 at Tynecastle)
  Hearts 2 (Beattie, Skacel) St Mirren 2 (Carey, Zaliukas OG)
* Quarter-final replay (21st March 2012 at New St Mirren Park)
  St Mirren 0 Hearts 2 (Hamill, Skacel)
* Semi-final (15th April 2012 at Hampden)
  Celtic 1 (Hooper) Hearts 2 (Skacel, Beattie)
* Scottish Cup final (19th May 2012 at Hampden)
  Hearts 5 (Barr, Skacel 2, Grainger, McGowan) Hibs 1 (McPake)

HEARTS' SCOTTISH CUP-WINNING SQUAD
Jamie MacDonald, Ryan McGowan, Andy Webster, Marius Zaliukas,Danny Grainger, Suso Santana (Craig Beattie) Darren Barr, Ian Black (Scott Robinson), Andrew Driver (Mehdi Taouil), Rudi Skacel, Stephen Elliott.
Substitutes not used: Marc Ridgers, Denis Prychynenko.
Manager: Paulo Sergio.

• St Mirren • The 2012/13 Scottish Communities League Cup – The Saints are coming!

THE League Cup wasn't exactly a competition that had brought much joy to St Mirren or their fans. The Buddies had lifted the Scottish Cup in 1926, 1959 and in 1987 but the League Cup had always eluded them. The closest they had come was two final appearances, where they lost 2-1 to Aberdeen in the 1955/56 season and then in 2010 when Gus MacPherson's side were mugged by nine-man Rangers.

Defender Lee Mair admitted that afternoon against Rangers was heartbreaking. "That was the third final I had ended up on the losing side," he explained. "I lost a Scottish Cup Final with Dundee United to Celtic. I lost another one to Rangers with Dundee and then again to Rangers in the League Cup Final but the League Cup was the worst one to take because we had played so well. Rangers had Kevin Thomson and Danny Wilson sent off and we looked to be on top but they got the winner. We were all devastated and it took a bit of time to get over."

St Mirren went on to part ways with Gus MacPherson not long after that cup final and replaced him with Cowdenbeath manager Danny Lennon in June 2010. The new man brought his own brand of attacking football to St Mirren Park. Lennon won plaudits for his new-look side and was able to strengthen further with the signings of former Scotland caps Gary Teale and Steven Thompson – the latter being a self-confessed St Mirren fan.

Lennon knew his team was on the verge of something special. He said: "I believe that it is always possible for a team to pull together a good run in the cup, by squeezing all you can out of the players and channelling all your resources into one-off games. The club hadn't tasted national cup success for more than a quarter of a century, but I am a positive person and the terrific staff I work with are of similar mind. We knew that winning a national cup would be a tough challenge, but certainly not an impossible one."

Lennon's opportunity came in the 2012/13 Scottish Communities League Cup. The second round draw offered St Mirren the chance of revenge when they were paired with Second Division Ayr United. The Honest Men had knocked them out in the quarter-final stage of the competition, courtesy of a Chris Smith goal, the previous season.

This time there was to be no such giant-killing. Saints swept Ayr away, 5-1, with goals from Lewis Guy, Thompson, Paul McGowan, Kenny McLean and Gary Teale.

"I remember we went there and we were really fired up because Ayr had put us out of the cup," McGowan claimed. "I think that showed in our performance. We played some great stuff and blew them away in the first half. I would say it was the best 45 minutes of football I had seen us play in my time at St Mirren. I also managed to get on the scoresheet when I dinked one over their keeper, which wrapped up a good night for St Mirren and myself."

Their reward was a third round tie at home to First Division Hamilton. It proved to be a tight affair until Lee Mair won it late on. The experienced defender recalled: "We were in the middle of a really busy schedule and the last thing we wanted was a replay, especially midweek at Hamilton. I just remember going up at the end to try and get a goal and I managed to get the winner at the death. I got a few headlines for it but I have to say I actually get more of a buzz from keeping clean sheets than scoring goals."

That win came at a cost as they lost influential playmaker McGowan for several months. The former Celtic player admitted: "I had been feeling my shoulder for a while. I pulled away from a Hamilton player and I just felt it go. I went to see the specialist and he told me that I needed an operation and I would be out for three months. That was a real blow."

Things might have been progressing well in the cup but they weren't exactly so rosy in the Scottish Premier League which had seen them lose their previous six games. That was in sharp contrast to their hosts who had been heavily tipped to become Scotland's second force. One of the Aberdeen first team, Josh Magennis, was certainly overconfident with his pre-match Twitter boast.

Goalkeeper Craig Samson confirmed: "I am not on any of the social networking sites but some of the boys had picked up on a tweet from Josh Magennis. He had tweeted, 'quarter-finals tonight and we are ready to make it to Hampden two years in a row'. That got a lot of the boys' backs up and a few of us said to ourselves, 'we will see'."

Sam Parkin put Saints ahead before it was cancelled out by a Scott Vernon strike. Kenny McLean fired the visitors ahead but Aberdeen forced extra time through a late equaliser from Magennis, of all people. Neither side could find another goal and the game went to penalties. It was left to the St Mirren players to show their mettle.

Lee Mair, playing against his old home-town team and former employers, said: "The manager said his piece then Craig Samson, Steven Thompson and I all tried to lift the lads further. We all said we had come this far and we are not going out now. We should have won in normal time but they equalised right at the end through Josh Magennis. But we showed great character and I knew when it went to penalties that we would win because we had practised the day before and the standard of our finishing was unbelievable."

Mair's confidence wasn't to be misplaced. Kenny McLean, Gary Teale, captain Jim Goodwin and David van Zanten all scored while Stephen Hughes missed for Aberdeen. Saints were on the verge of the semi-finals and all the pressure was heaped on Aberdeen teenager Cammy Smith to keep the shoot-out alive. Samson made sure he got inside the head of the youngster. The keeper explained: "When it went to penalties I was confident we would win. When the manager asked who wanted to take the penalties nearly everybody's hand went up but we were also aware that wasn't the case in the Aberdeen ranks. That was shown when young Cammy Smith stepped up because there were more experienced boys who clearly didn't fancy it. Paul Mathers [goalkeeping coach] and I stood before the kicks and tried to work out where their penalties would be put. We both had our say and for the first three penalties I went the wrong way for them all – although Stephen Hughes hit the bar.

"Paul had said to me that if any of the young boys take a penalty then I should have a word in their ear, tell them what it is all about and get in their head. I just said to him: 'Remember wee man there is a lot of pressure on you here because if you don't score you are out.' As a goalkeeper you need to try and gain an advantage. I saw him walking up from the halfway line and I knew where he was going to put his kick and I managed to save it."

The win made the long return trip to Paisley more bearable and allowed Danny Lennon's players to celebrate their place in the Hampden semi-finals and to have the last laugh on Magennis. Samson joked: "After the game, Kenny McLean went on Twitter and retweeted Josh's comments. It was a bit of banter between players, just to tell him he could forget about Hampden."

Camaraderie was a big thing in the St Mirren dressing room. David van Zanten, in his second spell, can vouch for that. His lack of goals almost left him looking like the club's very own diva. The Irishman explained: "I had come close to scoring in a couple of games and David MacDonald, who does one of the fans' websites, said he would give £100 to charity for every goal I scored. I decided that the money would go to the sick kids' hospital at Yorkhill. More and more people got involved and then the guys came back to me and asked if I would do a forfeit if I didn't score, so I agreed. The next thing I knew they had gone to Lee Mair for the forfeit and he had told them I should sing Madonna's 'Like a Virgin', dressed in a mankini, in front of everybody at New St Mirren Park. It was a worrying time because I don't score that many goals. When I did get one at Dundee United I was just so relieved. Maybe even more relieved than I was after the final."

The semi-final draw was no laughing matter for St Mirren either. The last four was made up by high-flying Inverness Caley Thistle, financially stricken Hearts and league champions Celtic. It was fair to say that luck wasn't exactly on St Mirren's side when they drew the Hoops. Neil Lennon's side had reached the knockout stages of the Champions League and had the upper hand over his St Mirren namesake. The Celtic manager's head-to-head record read: eight wins out of eight with 22 goals scored and none against.

St Mirren boss Danny Lennon confirmed: "Our previous record against Celtic in my time at the club was pretty poor. We hadn't even scored against them, but again, I firmly believed that we had learned things from all those games and that helped us come up with the winning formula for the semi-final. We had experimented in those league games and tried a few different formations and personnel. Some had failed while others brought about a certain amount of joy that needed a little further fine-tuning. We spent a lot of the build-up to the match fuelling the players with belief, we walked through our modified shape and tactics and that, with some new signings, combined well for us."

The Saints boss strengthened his side by bringing in striker Esmael Goncalves on loan from Portuguese side Rio Ave and young midfielder Conor Newton headed north from Newcastle United.

Newton admitted: "I have the same agent as Paul Dummett and he had spoken to Danny Lennon about me after Paul had returned to Newcastle from his loan spell at St Mirren. I went up there for a couple of weeks and thankfully I did enough for St Mirren to sign me."

Skipper Jim Goodwin recalled the Celtic game and how he and his team were determined not to be left red-faced again. The team headed to Hampden knowing the winners would face Hearts, who had seen off Inverness in a nerve-shredding penalty shoot-out.

"Nobody gave us a hope in hell against Celtic," the former Celtic player stated. "We hadn't got close to them in previous games and they were also going well in the Champions League and were the best team in the Scottish Premier League by a country mile. I think the difference that day was that we were a lot braver than we had been in the past against them. Previously, we had been more worried about them than playing to our strengths but that day at Hampden was different."

Some touching words from assistant manager Tommy Craig also inspired the team. Mair revealed: "I remember Tommy Craig's speech. He said: 'If you are happy to just be here there is no point in going out. Nobody remembers the losers so make sure everyone remembers this St Mirren team.'"

Danny Lennon threw both his new boys in and it proved to be a masterstroke. Goncalves put Saints ahead in the eighth minute although they were left stunned when Gary Hooper scored on the stroke of half-time. Steven Thompson admitted: "Esmael came in as this unknown quantity. Nobody knew much about him but he has so much power and pace and is so raw and all that combined made him such a handful."

The tide looked to have turned against the Buddies when Goodwin was adjudged to have handled Lassad Nouioui's shot inside the box. It became a straight shoot-out between keeper Craig Samson and Celtic's set-piece specialist Charlie Mulgrew.

"I spent the night before watching every single Celtic penalty from what seemed like the last ten years," Samson laughed. "I had seen Georgios Samaras, Anthony Stokes, Gary Hooper, Scott Brown, Kris Commons and even Joe Ledley hit them. I thought I had done my homework and then they got the penalty and Charlie Mulgrew picked up the ball. I had wasted my time the night before. I am good friends with Charlie so I tried to psyche him out like I did with Cammy Smith against Aberdeen. I said: 'Hit it as hard as you can up the middle Charlie-boy because I am not diving.' I then made up my mind in his run-up where I was going and luckily for me it came at a decent height and I managed to save it. After that the pendulum swung in our favour."

That proved to be the case, as St Mirren went up the pitch and won a penalty of their own. Mulgrew's misery was completed when he handled a Gary Teale cross. The responsibility fell to Paul McGowan against his old team. McGowan admitted: "We got the penalty and Lukasz Zaluska came out to me and said: 'Same place as always, wee man.' I then saw him dive and stuck the ball away. It was just such a great feeling."

Dreams of a Hampden return looked all but certain when Steven Thompson netted a glory third. Thompson proudly said: "I was on the ground just before the ball came in. I managed to get back up and find half a yard in the box and I was able to tuck the ball away when it came to me. It was an unbelievable moment and up to the final it was probably my most important goal."

Celtic piled on the pressure and Mulgrew netted a consolation with almost the last kick of the ball but it was too little too late. "I was raging because I made a mistake at Charlie's goal," Samson admitted frustratingly. "It was my fault but nobody remembers it because the final whistle went right after it. All the boys were celebrating and I ran to the goalkeeping coach [Paul Mathers] and said to him: 'I can't believe I have let that in.' He told me to forget it."

Debut goal hero Esmael Goncalves was delighted to have made such an immediate impact in black and white. Goncalves said: "To have my first game for St Mirren in a semi-final was exciting enough, but to then score, to win the game and make it through to the final just made it unbelievable."

Paul McGowan revealed how Celtic boss Neil Lennon, his former

Parkhead coach, took time out to congratulate him. "Neil was unhappy with his team but he still showed his class by coming up to me and wishing me all the best," the little playmaker revealed. "He told me I now had to go on and lift the trophy. I owe Neil a lot from my time at Celtic and to hear those words from him was special."

That famous odds-defying win brought a mix of emotions to the victors. Penalty hero Samson dedicated his Hampden heroics to his sick Aunt Marlene.

"My Auntie Margaret had passed away a couple of months earlier with cancer," Samson emotionally explained. "My Aunt Marlene was the one who had looked after her. Then to hear that she also had cancer was a bit of a bombshell to the family. I told her that if we win the semi-final we were winning it for her. I managed to save the penalty and it seemed to be written in the stars for her that day."

It was also an afternoon rookie Conor Newton will never forget. He proudly said: "That was my first full 90 minutes as a senior footballer. I remember going to Hampden and seeing all the fans and I felt really nervous. I had only played in front of a few hundred fans before and suddenly I was running out in front of 30,000 to 40,000 fans. I had a few butterflies and it remained that way until I got that first pass. I felt we did OK and thoroughly deserved our win. Things couldn't have gone much better."

Chairman Stewart Gilmour's consortium had saved the club from death's door back in 1998. The last thing on his mind at that stage was cup final appearances. He explained: "When Bryan McAusland, George Campbell and I got involved our main objective was to save St Mirren. One of the first games we were involved in was a trip to Stirling which we needed to win to stay in the First Division. Fortunately, we won that match. The club was still in a perilous situation and it was a case of trying to keep it afloat and then getting it back to a self-sustainable position."

Now he and the club had suddenly very different ambitions – ahead of their final Hampden trip.

Paul Dummett had been at St Mirren on loan from Newcastle but faced an anxious wait to see if Alan Pardew was going to allow him to return for the second half of the season and a possible final appearance against Hearts.

"When St Mirren beat Celtic in the semi-final I didn't even know if I was going to sign again," Dummett admitted. It was on and off but in the end I got back up. I would have been gutted to miss out but I would probably have come up to watch the final as a fan if I hadn't come back to St Mirren."

Two other experienced St Mirren stars faced anxious sweats of their own to be fit for Hampden. Skipper Jim Goodwin suffered a grade one tear in his calf in a league game against St Johnstone and Lee Mair feared he had torn a hamstring. Goodwin explained: "The physio (Gerry Docherty) said I would be out for 10 to 14 days and I knew the final was three or four weeks away. I was gutted to miss the league games but thankfully I managed to recover. I had a job to convince the manager that I was fit because he didn't want me to mess up all his plans and the build-up. I was just delighted to make it because it was the biggest game of my career."

Mair's problems were complicated by a misdiagnosis. Mair explained: "As soon as I was injured, I thought, 'oh no, I will miss the cup final'. I was diagnosed with a grade two tear which means you are out for six weeks and straight away I thought: 'That's me missed out.' But gradually it got better and better. Then I felt fine and ready to train. The club sent me to a specialist in Edinburgh, who did a lot of tests, and he said that I was doing fine and just to crack on with training."

Goodwin was able to use his time out to spread the word amongst the Paisley public ahead of the Hampden visit. Goodwin said: "I didn't realise until we started doing some community visits how much the final meant to everybody and the town. Everywhere we went, schools or community centres, we would always come back with loads of good luck cards, posters and banners. We put them all up in our dressing room at the training ground. It was great and unknown to us our kitman, Alan Gray (a.k.a Ali G) took all the stuff down to Hampden and put it up in our dressing room. It was a nice touch and gave us a bit of extra motivation to do it for the fans and everyone in the local area."

St Mirren warmed up well as they beat Hearts 2-0 in an SPL dress rehearsal for the final. That defeat saw the Gorgie outfit sack manager John McGlynn. He was replaced by first-team coach Gary Locke, who was put in temporary charge before he was officially confirmed just 24 hours before the final.

Cup final fever had already kicked in at St Mirren. Conor Newton explained: "I had between 30 and 40 people up for the game from the north-east of England. Paul Dummett had the same and we ended up taking three buses up between us. I organised the match tickets but after that I wasn't getting involved because I knew it would be a nightmare. The only thing I did was to keep my family in one row and put my friends in another – just in case things got a bit rowdy!"

There was also a late setback for St Mirren fans when Scottish Football League chiefs gave the tickets they had in reserve to their cup finals rivals, Hearts. They had initially planned to release the 3,500 West Stand tickets to the Buddies after they had sold their initial allocation but then they gave them to Hearts. That left a bad taste in the mouth. The St Mirren players were also left raging by the actions of some disrespectful Hearts fans. David van Zanten explained: "Everything blew up with Hearts getting the extra tickets that had been set aside for St Mirren. I actually went on one of the Hearts fans' websites and I couldn't believe what I was reading. Their comments were so disrespectful towards St Mirren. They said things like why should we get 20,000 fans, when we are just a diddy club? There was also another thread saying they had produced t-shirts which read: 'Relax, it's only the Buddies.' It left me fuming and I ended up copying the link on Twitter for the St Mirren fans to see and then I told the boys. It is fair to say that it only fired us up even more to go out and lift the cup."

Manager Danny Lennon decided to take his side away from all the distractions with a pre-final trip to St Andrews. It got his squad away from all the Hampden hype, allowing them to bond, train and chill out. The Buddies also added to their squad by signing Estonian international Sander Puri. Lennon wanted his side back in their normal routine, with their families, before the game.

No. 1 Craig Samson recalled: "I normally have a chip-shop night before a game and I treated myself to a sausage supper. It is a family tradition. It used to be on a Friday night but I normally have one the night before a game. We then kept things as normal as possible. We had eaten pre-match at the training ground before the games and so we also did that before the trip to the stadium."

Others had found it a lot harder to relax, with Steven Thompson, a boyhood Saint, dreaming about the final since the last four win over Celtic. Thompson explained: "In the lead-up to the final I felt a fair bit of anxiety because I knew there was an awful lot of pressure on me. I live in the local area, I know thousands of St Mirren fans and I knew what the final meant to them all. That was the biggest pressure. I struggled to sleep at times and the night before the final I had to take a sleeping tablet. I actually visualised scoring at the end in front of the St Mirren fans, although that was with a header, then running towards them. Visualisation is a big sporting tool I like to use. It allows your brain to store things away and hopefully makes things possible when you play."

The biggest headache that remained for Danny Lennon was to pick a team that could make Paisley proud. The players had to wait until the day of the game to see who was in or out.

"Football management is all about making tough decisions that are right for winning a particular game," Lennon acknowledged. "There is little room for sentimentality or you can end up compromising your chances of success. I have great respect for all the players at the club and those who missed out on starting the match, or even making the bench, were players who had made other excellent contributions throughout the season. I knew these players would be hurting.

"We named the starting XI at lunchtime at the training ground and named the bench at the team talk in the dressing room at Hampden 90 minutes before kick-off. The players all responded professionally and supported each other. They are all a credit to themselves and their families."

Lennon, after he named his team and went through his final tactics, signed off with a short video.

He said: "We took all the good luck messages that the kids had sent in and put them up on the walls of the Hampden dressing room to remind the players that we were playing for the fans and their families. We even showed a short video made by one of the fans inside the dressing room, just before the players went out on to the pitch, to give them that extra bit of motivation and focus."

Lennon finalised his team talk and then left captain Jim Goodwin to have the final say before the team took to the pitch.

"I told the boys not to have any regrets," the Irishman revealed. "Everyone who meant anything to us was up in the stands and it was up to us to make them all proud. I know we owed a lot to our families, wives and everybody who had helped us along the way."

The preparations were complete but many St Mirren players struggled to get out of the blocks. Hearts got on top and took a deserved lead when Ryan Stevenson fired a low shot beyond Craig Samson. Defender Paul Dummett knew he had to take his share of the blame. "I feared the worst because a lot of people thought I should have been tighter so I thought I was going to get the blame for it," he conceded. "I was just hoping we would get an equaliser."

Hearts continued to threaten and created a number of chances that should have put them out of sight. Manager Danny Lennon knew the dream was in danger of turning into a nightmare. "The manager dragged me over and was screaming at me," David van Zanten admitted. "He said we hadn't got started and we needed to get a hold of the ball. He wanted me to get the players geed up. He was right we were lucky only to be 1-0 down and we needed somebody to give us a spark and thankfully we got it."

Danny Lennon confirmed the occasion got to his players in those opening exchanges. He said: "We started poorly and for the first 30 minutes we were not ourselves. That was nerves and emotional exhaustion due to the hype and build-up of the game. Cup finals don't come around often for a club like St Mirren. We changed our shape after 30 minutes and that got us on the ball more and we started to play."

That switch awakened the Buddies from their slumber when, through their first serious attack, they levelled eight minutes before half-time. Winger Gary Teale was the creator as he got on the end of a great pass from Steven Thompson. Teale said: "When I ran through on goal I took a touch to the side and my first thought was to shoot, but then out of the corner of my eye I saw Esmael Goncalves. I could have gone for glory myself but I'm not a greedy player and I would rather give a team-mate an open goal. It paid off because Esmael stuck the ball away and got us back into the match."

Goncalves knew he would never get an easier chance. "I knew Gary was going to pass to me, the on-loan striker claimed. "I just got in position and waited for the pass. It was an easy chance but players have missed opportunities like that before. I just remained focused and made sure I put the ball into the net. The feeling was amazing. It was the biggest goal of my career and one that will live with me forever. To score in a cup final is something you always dream of. Fortunately for me that dream came true and because of that I will never forget my time at St Mirren."

The goal got Saints out of jail and allowed Danny Lennon to give his inspired half-time team talk that turned the game around. The manager admitted: "We told the players to stop playing the occasion and start playing the game. We knew we couldn't play as badly as we did in the first

Kilmarnock manager Bobby Williamson on the open-top bus flanked by defender Dylan Kerr and captain Ray Montgomerie.

Paul Wright lifts the Scottish Cup.

Kilmarnock's Paul Wright scores his Scottish Cup final winner against Falkirk.

Kilmarnock's squad with the 1997 Scottish Cup.

Kilmarnock's Dieter Van Tornhout celebrates his shock League Cup winning goal against Celtic.

Kilmarnock's Liam Kelly and James Fowler tackle Celtic's Georgios Samaras.

Kilmarnock manager Kenny Shiels with assistant Jimmy Nicholl after they find out about Liam Kelly's dad.

Crocked captain Manuel Pascali with the League Cup.

Killie show off the League Cup

The 1998 Hearts team celebrate their Scottish Cup win over Rangers.

Hearts captain Gary Locke lifts the Scottish Cup along with stand-in Stevie Fulton.

Captain Steven Pressley lifts the 2006 Scottish Cup.

The Hearts team celebrate their 2006 Scottish Cup penalty shoot-out win over Gretna.

Scottish Cup-winning Hearts boss Paulo Sergio is thrown into the air by his team after their 2012 victory over Hibs.

Hearts star Darren Barr celebrates scoring the opening goal of the 2012 final.

Tynecastle cult hero Rudi Skacel celebrates another Scottish Cup final goal.

The jubilant Hearts team celebrate their 2012 Scottish Cup hammering of Hibs.

Livingston's Jamie McAllister scores his CIS Cup final goal against Hibs.

Hampden heroes Jamie McAllister and Derek Lilley celebrate with Livingston manager Davie Hay.

The Livingston team celebrate their 2004 CIS Cup win over Hibs.

Steven Anderson heads St Johnstone in front.

Steven Anderson celebrates his opening goal for St Johnstone.

Steven MacLean does his own strip as he celebrates putting St Johnstone 2-0 up.

Manager Tommy Wright (centre) celebrates with his management team, Callum Davidson (right) and Alec Cleland (left).

Michael O'Halloran, James Dunne, Stevie May and Lee Croft get to grips with the Scottish Cup.

St Johnstone captain Dave Mackay lifts the Scottish Cup with his St Johnstone team-mates.

Marley Watkins puts Inverness ahead.

James Vincent nets his glory winner.

Hero James Vincent
shows his love as he
celebrates his goal.

Captain Graeme Shinnie lifts the Scottish Cup.

The Inverness team take to the pitch to celebrate.

Inverness team takes their Hampden bow.

Michael Gardyne puts Ross County ahead.

Alex Schalk scores his winner.

Jackson Irvine with his man of the match award.

Manager Jim McIntyre and assistant Billy Dodds celebrate on the Hampden pitch.

Skipper Andrew Davies lifts the League Cup with his team-mates.

Hibs striker Steven Fletcher scores in the 2007 League Cup final win over Kilmarnock.

Hibs goal heroes Abdessalam Benjelloun, Rob Jones and Steven Fletcher show off the League Cup.

Moroccan star Merouane Zemmama shows off a different type of hat-trick.

The triumphant 2007 Hibs team that lifted the League Cup.

Abdessalam Benjelloun celebrates with manager John Collins.

Hibs manager Alex Miller shows off the Skol and League Cup trophies.

Hibs midfielder Brian Hamilton watches on as goal hero Tommy McIntyre battles with Dunfermline's Scott Leitch.

Hibs captain Murdo McLeod flies in to back up team-mate Gareth Evans.

Hampden and Hibs star Keith Wright challenges with Dunfermline defender Davie Moyes.

Anthony Stokes puts Hibs ahead.

David Gray scores his dramatic late winner.

Captain David Gray lifts the Scottish Cup.

Manager Alan Stubbs is the man who finally delivers for Hibernian.

30 minutes again. I told the players if they wanted to become legends at this club, they had to go out there and win the game as no one would be handing it to them. The lads are great professionals and they responded in the right manner and indeed made themselves legends."

Dreams became reality for one particular St Mirren star 60 seconds after the restart. Steven Thompson, who had been at Hampden in 1987, put his side ahead after he had got on the end of a Paul Dummett cross. "I knew I had to try and get across Danny Wilson," the former Scotland international explained. "I knew if I could do that then I would have a right chance because it was on my left foot. I managed to get there and after that it was just about concentrating on getting a good connection. I hit the ball well and luckily it flew past Jamie MacDonald. It just brought this mix of relief, joy and pride all rolled into one. I tried to get to the fans before I got flattened by my team-mates. I then made a point of going round all the players and saying to them: 'We aren't losing this now.'"

The Buddies were the team on top and went from strength to strength. They netted a killer third through Conor Newton. Newton explained: "I won the ball in the midfield and I gave it to Esmael and then I just continued my run. I saw the ball come through to me and I just decided to hit it right away. I knew if I hit it early it would catch Jamie MacDonald off guard and that proved to be the case. I hit my shot cleanly and it flew just inside the post. I ran to celebrate behind the goal where Lee Mair smashed me in the celebrations. The next thing I remember I was under 15 bodies getting crushed. When I was walking back I was speaking with Paul Dummett and Steven Thompson just gave us a stare and said: 'It isn't f*****' over yet!' That pretty much ended the celebration and got us focused again."

Danny Lennon admitted that goal will live with him for the rest of his days. He said: "I just felt that it was going to be our day when Conor scored. I turned to watch the Saints fans celebrate and let that image of joy burn into my memory. The most important people in football are the fans and I wanted to enjoy their reaction."

St Mirren, suddenly, had one hand on the cup but, as most Buddies will testify, things are never that straightforward. Hearts fought back. Ryan Stevenson hit the bar, pulled a goal back, forced Craig Samson into a save and then hit the woodwork in the closing stages. The keeper said: "I looked at the clock and it said 85 minutes. I then had to save another of his shots and then Ryan Stevenson hit the post. I looked up at the scoreboard again and it said 87 minutes. I thought, 'Has it stopped? Should the whistle not have gone?'"

Jim Goodwin was concerned with what was happening on the pitch and feared it might also have an adverse effect off it. "Those final few minutes were a nightmare for the players and they must have been even worse for our families," Goodwin claimed. "My wife was seven months pregnant and I feared it might push her into labour early. I spoke to her after the game and she said she couldn't even bear to watch."

St Mirren managed to see the game out by the skin of their teeth. Referee Craig Thomson's final whistle brought scenes of joy to everyone in black and white. David van Zanten pretty much summed up the general feeling: "I was just delighted and relieved that we had won the cup for the fans. I knew there was so much expectation on us. Before the game I refused to think about anything apart from us winning the cup. I just couldn't deal with the thought of losing. I was concerned that if I started to have negative thoughts then we might lose and so I just tried to remain positive, so when we got there it was just great. I went straight to the stand to see my wife, Lyndsay, and my daughters, Megan and Grace, because I knew what the win meant to them. It was amazing and then I went and joined the celebrations with the rest of the lads."

The Hearts players were gutted but Craig Samson took the time to seek out his old foe Ryan Stevenson. Samson admitted: "I went and spoke to all the Hearts players. I had been at the Kilmarnock final the year before and I don't want to slag Celtic off because they are a great club but hardly any of their players clapped the Kilmarnock team up the steps. I knew how hurt the Hearts players were and shook their hands. I got to Ryan Stevenson and he was lying on the ground, absolutely crushed. I told him he didn't deserve to lose. I am friends with Ryan because we were together at Ayr United but we had also played against each other since we played in a boys' club final when we were both 14. Ryan was the stand-out player in that final but he just couldn't score against me. I said, 'At least you have scored past me in a final,' and Ryan turned and joked: 'It has only taken me 14 years, mate!'"

The result made for a perfect St Patrick's Day for Jim Goodwin, as he led his side up the Hampden steps to be presented with the League Cup by the President of Malawi, Dr Joyce Banda. He said: "I remember walking up the stairs and I saw my wife, two girls, my mother and father-in-law and all my family. It was unbelievable that I was able to lift the trophy for the first time in St Mirren's history. I was only the fourth cup-winning captain for St Mirren and it was such a massive thing. It is so difficult to put into words the feelings I had when I lifted the cup. There were so many differing emotions and I didn't know whether to laugh or cry. I also really appreciated getting my daughters, Ava and Millie, on to the park because we were told before the game they wouldn't be allowed. It meant the world to them. Moments like that will also last with them forever."

It took time for things to sink in for Conor Newton. "It was amazing to lift the trophy and to see all my family and friends there," the midfielder said. "It really hit me when we got to Paisley on the bus and then in the pubs. Every two or three steps people and supporters were stopping and hugging me and others were saying, 'You are now a St Mirren legend!' That is when I realised just how big my goal was."

Danny Lennon was delighted to have become the first St Mirren manager to deliver the League Cup.

"There have been some exceptional managers at this club in its 135-year history and this cup win doesn't make me any better or worse than any of them," he insisted proudly. "But, I am ambitious. I want to achieve things and to help others fulfil their potential along the way. Winning the Scottish League Cup is something that I will be proud of until the day I die. I am also delighted for the players and staff at the club, who all worked so incredibly hard to achieve that cup triumph for themselves too. It was beautiful to see them celebrate with their families straight after the final whistle. This is a club I have fallen in love with. It is a very well-run club, with some incredible professionals in all the key positions. A club like that deserves success and I am thrilled beyond words to play my part in having made that happen."

There was to be even more silverware for another St Mirren player as Paul McGowan walked away with the man of the match award. "I had just gone into the game determined that we would win," McGowan claimed. "We had done all the hard work by beating Celtic and I was determined I wasn't leaving Hampden without the trophy. We played well and the scenes at the final whistle were amazing. I got grabbed by the BBC and asked to do an interview because I had been named as man of the match. I was a bit surprised. I had done well but so had all the boys and I thought they might have gone for one of the goalscorers, so to get the man of the match award just topped off a great day."

Chairman Stewart Gilmour was just delighted to get through the match and for the trophy to be Paisley-bound. "I have to say the final whistle brought joy, relief and a real high," he said. "If I am being honest I didn't enjoy the game because there was so much pressure on us. I hardly had a bite to eat at the pre-match meal because I was so wound up. It was in complete contrast to the semi-final which I really enjoyed because there was no pressure or expectation on us to beat Celtic. Now we have won the cup and it is my proudest moment. I know it has given everyone at the club and in the Paisley area such a lift."

Local boy Steven Thompson was delighted to bring a trophy to St Mirren some 26 years since he stood on the Hampden terraces watching Alex Smith's famous side lift the Scottish Cup. Thompson said: "People have asked if it means more than my other medals and yes, it does. St Mirren don't win a lot of trophies but when you are at a club like Rangers you are spoiled that wee bit more. You win things every other year but St Mirren don't. It has been a quarter of a century since St Mirren last won a major trophy. I am almost glad that St Mirren don't win trophies all the time because it makes what we achieved that little bit more special."

Gary Teale had seen a lot in his career but that afternoon was probably the pinnacle for him. "I said before the final that I had never wanted to win something so badly in all my life," the popular winger revealed. "I've been involved in great Scotland games and I've had promotion to the English Premier League but winning the cup with St Mirren means the most to me because it is a club where success isn't really expected. Plus we beat Celtic in the semi-final and a lot of people thought we had peaked then. So to get to the final and win it for the first time in St Mirren's long history eclipses everything I have done in the game."

There was a lot of emotion among the celebrations with reserve keeper Grant Adam, brother of Scotland star Charlie, wearing a t-shirt with an emotional message in support of his mum and in remembrance of his dad, Charlie (senior), who had passed away at the end of the previous year.

Paisley turned into party central but there was an unwelcome delay at the national stadium before the St Mirren team could join their adoring public, after Jim Goodwin and Conor Newton were selected for the drugs test. Newton said: "It was a nightmare because it took forever to provide a sample and I think I ended up making the bus 45 minutes late in leaving. I don't think I was too popular among the lads – as I was holding up the celebrations."

The open-top bus was ready and waiting to taking Paisley's returning heroes through the town and up to County Square. Thousands of locals turned out to pay their own tributes to their black-and-white champions.

Steven Thompson said: "I have some great photos of the fans in the street that I took from the open-top bus. I saw some familiar faces and it was just great to share that with the fans because it showed a real togetherness between the club and our supporters."

Captain Jim Goodwin echoed those sentiments. "It was amazing in Paisley," he added. "We witnessed grown men crying and that showed what the cup meant to them. The fans are the club, they are the most important people because they are the ones who keep St Mirren going. It was a public holiday on the Monday back in Dublin but you would have thought it was the same in Paisley. An awful lot of people must have phoned in sick because the pubs were all jumping. We were in one of the pubs for about five hours and they just had the game on a loop on the big screen. I think I watched the match about three times and it was even better knowing we were going to lift the cup."

Striker Steven Thompson is just as handy with a guitar as he is with a ball inside the six-yard box. He recorded a secret cup final song – which finally got an airing at the players' and family party at the Glynhill Hotel on the Sunday evening.

David van Zanten explained: "Thommo sent me his cup final song the month before. It was really good. I tried to convince him to release it as our cup final song but he wasn't having it. He said he wasn't letting anybody hear it but he played it at the Glynhill and then again for the fans in the pub on the Monday."

David van Zanten was also responsible for the early start to the Monday celebrations. Craig Samson admitted: "We were still dying from the Sunday night/Monday morning when I got a text from David van Zanten at 11.10am which read: 'I'm in the pub, hurry up boys. I'm in the Bull Inn.' I got there and it was just wall to wall with St Mirren fans. We can go into pubs with the fans and that is something special that Old Firm fans would never be able to do. It was great to celebrate with them."

Some of the supporters not only mixed with their heroes but also saw them pour their pints. "We went to this pub [the Bull Inn] in Paisley," said Paul McGowan. "When we arrived there was only two people in the pub and within about an hour it was absolutely mobbed with punters.

The bar owner must have been rubbing his hands with glee. They also had some extra help because at one point Grant Adam was behind the bar, pulling pints and serving the punters."

Danny Lennon acknowledged the importance of the cup win to the whole area – as the entire Paisley public were able to share St Mirren's success. Lennon proudly claimed: "All the scenes of celebration, where the players, staff, directors, fans and town joined together jubilantly as one, will live long in the memory. No one can take that away from us. We all did it together, as the fans were absolutely outstanding at the game. The whole community celebrated together for days after the final, which demonstrates the value that football has in the lives of people and the communities in which they live. Football, for me, is the beautiful game and this cup victory will live on as a beautiful memory in the life of Paisley, its people and its football team."

Once the partying eventually stopped it wasn't all a case of sweet dreams, especially for the family of one St Mirren player. Lee Mair, who, initially, slept with his medal by the bed, admitted: "I woke up at 4am one morning and the next thing I knew I was singing the Gary Teale song. My wife asked me what I was doing. She just shook her head and said to be quiet because some of us have work in the morning."

Steven Thompson hopes the 2013 Hampden heroes can help bring future generations of fans clicking through the St Mirren Park turnstiles. "The cup was won in a very difficult way," he beamed. "We had the extra round before the European teams came in and then we had to beat Aberdeen away and Celtic and Hearts at Hampden. It was a difficult path to the final and I think we deserve a lot of credit for what the team and club achieved. It is a time that will live with everyone for a long while. The good thing about that final is that there were so many families there and young kids and I just hope this success will help to bring future fans to St Mirren.

"I hope that will be the legacy from our League Cup win."

ST MIRREN'S SCOTTISH COMMUNITIES LEAGUE CUP RUN

*Second round (29 August 2012 at New St Mirren Park)
   St Mirren 5 (Guy, Thompson, McGowan, McLean PEN, Teale)
   Ayr United 1 (Moffat)
*Third round (25 September 2012 at New St Mirren Park)

St Mirren 1 (Mair) Hamilton 0

*Quarter-final (30 October 2012 at Pittodrie Stadium)
    Aberdeen 2 (Vernon, Magennis) St Mirren 2 (Parkin, McLean)
    2-2 AET (St Mirren won 4-2 on penalties)

*Semi-final (27 January 2013 at Hampden Stadium)
    St Mirren 3 (Goncalves, Thompson, Newton) Celtic 2 (Hooper,
    Mulgrew)

*Scottish Communities League Cup Final (17 March 2013 at
    Hampden Stadium)
    St Mirren 3 (Goncalves, Thompson, Newton) Hearts 2
    (Stevenson 2)

ST MIRREN'S LEAGUE CUP-WINNING SQUAD

Craig Samson, David van Zanten, Marc McAusland, Jim Goodwin,
Paul Dummett, Gary Teale, Conor Newton, Paul McGowan,
John McGinn (Graham Carey), Esmael Goncalves (Lee Mair),
Steven Thompson (Sam Parkin).
Substitutes not used: Grant Adam, Kenny McLean.
Manager: Danny Lennon.

25

• THE SHEEP ARE ON FIRE •
The inside story of Aberdeen's 2014 League Cup win

IT HAD been a long and frustrating 19 years for every Aberdeen fan, especially those who had savoured the glorious Eighties when Alex Ferguson, long before he had been knighted, had firmly established the Pittodrie outfit as a major force, not only in Scottish football but also on the European scene.

Since then, much to do with the changing financial landscape of Scottish football, the Dons have been left trying to play catch-up. Alex Smith, along with Jocky Scott, had led their Aberdeen side to Scottish and Skol Cup glory and came within a whisker of taking the title back to Pittodrie in the 1990/91 season, but apart from that and the Coca-Cola Cup glory of Roy Aitken's team in 1995 it had been pretty slim pickings for the best part of two decades for everyone connected with the Granite City's finest. It was fair to say success had been somewhat sparse, especially for a club of Aberdeen's proud standing.

There, if you pardon the pun, had been far too many false dawns. The likes of Alex Miller, Paul Hegarty, Ebbe Skovdahl, Steve Paterson, Jimmy Calderwood, Gothenburg great Mark McGhee and veteran Craig Brown had all tried and failed to deliver that evasive trophy the Red Army and the majority of the north-east craved.

Dane Ebbe Skovdahl had a far from spectacular record in the league but had been the last Aberdeen manager to take the club to a cup final. In fact he did it twice in the 1999/2000 campaign when the Dons lost the League Cup to Celtic and the Scottish Cup to Rangers.

After that Aberdeen's cup record became nothing short of embarrassing, losing to lower league sides like Queen's Park, Dunfermline Athletic, East Fife, Raith Rovers and Dundee.

However, probably the hardest to swallow was the 2008 Scottish Cup semi-final defeat to First Division side Queen of the South. The Dons, under the guidance of Jimmy Calderwood, had been odds-on favourites but the Doonhamers came out on top, 4-3, in a seven-goal thriller. That was a result and a day that took a long time for everyone connected with Aberdeen to get over.

Ironically, Calderwood's time at Aberdeen, between 2004 and 2009, had been one of the most successful periods in the club's recent history. He had led his team to a third place finish and put the club back on the European map in the 2007/08 season.

Calderwood left with his head held high in 2009, just days after he had guided Aberdeen back into Europe. He was replaced by Mark McGhee but this particular favourite Pittodrie son was unable to replicate the success he had enjoyed during his playing days under Ferguson and was quickly replaced by Craig Brown.

The former Scotland manager, the second consecutive boss headhunted from Motherwell, helped steady the ship and slowly got the club back on the straight and narrow.

There was a real opportunity for change in Scottish football at the start of the 2012/13 season, as Rangers were given the boot from Scotland's top flight. It was a chance for another club to become the country's second force and the Red Army certainly believed it could be their team. They came out in support of Brown, buying more than 10,000 season tickets, but were left disappointed when his side failed to make the top half.

Brown then made the announcement that he was to step down at the end of that season although he was to remain as a director, helping and advising the board on the majority of footballing matters, including helping to appoint his own successor.

Chairman Stewart Milne decided to move for Derek McInnes. He had built up a strong reputation as one of Scotland's top, young managerial talents. He had a decent playing career with Morton, Rangers, Millwall,

Toulouse, West Bromwich Albion, Dundee United and St Johnstone before he stepped into frontline management. He had got his big break at St Johnstone when Owen Coyle headed to English side Burnley.

The then Saints chairman Geoff Brown turned to his veteran midfielder and captain and gave him the opportunity to lead their club back into the Scottish Premier League. He did precisely that and transformed the Perth outfit into an established top-flight side, who could also boast a decent record in making the latter stages of the domestic cup competitions.

McInnes was linked with numerous jobs in England before Championship strugglers Bristol City came calling in 2011. He helped them pull off the great escape by keeping the Robins up, but a poor start to the following season saw him sacked from Ashton Gate in January 2013. McInnes's managerial stock took a bit of a hit, although people fully aware of the circumstances behind the scenes at Bristol City knew it had been an almost impossible task.

McInnes was keen to get back into the game and when Brown announced he was to leave his interest was confirmed with the Pittodrie hierarchy. That was all the encouragement Milne needed and it was quickly confirmed McInnes was to become the new Aberdeen manager and he was to be assisted by his loyal No. 2 Tony Docherty. The duo were to take over from Brown for the last five games after the split of the 2012/13 season.

The appointment, however, wasn't initially embraced by all sections of the Red Army. The main issue to a small minority of the Pittodrie faithful was the fact that McInnes had played for Rangers. He might have only been a squad player at Ibrox for the majority of his five years there, but no matter how it was sugar-coated that was never going to be easily swallowed by the more militant element of the Aberdeen support.

Chairman Stewart Milne acknowledged that when he confirmed McInnes's appointment. He said: "The feedback from the fans by and large was positive but we all know you never have 100% when an appointment is made.

"Derek knows the only way he will get the bulk behind him is through what he does on the pitch. Derek's past is not an issue.

"He spent a relatively short spell of his career at Ibrox and he has no ties whatsoever with the club.

"We took Derek on because of what he is capable of doing and nothing else.

"Football is all about opinions and Derek acknowledged there would be a reluctance within some supporters to support him initially.

"But he was confident he could turn them around by getting results."

McInnes set about it, head on, from his official unveiling. He immediately went on the front foot and tried to win over the doubters from the off.

McInnes passionately stated: "The demand of the support is part of the reason why I got the Aberdeen job. I want the same as them. They crave a team at the top end of the league which is constantly competing for silverware and getting into Europe.

"I want to reach every one of those targets and it is going to take a collective effort to do it.

It's not just about putting a manager in place, a good chairman, a great support or a fancy stadium – you need all of those things pulling together."

The new man was able to work behind the scenes while Brown continued with first-team matters up to the split. McInnes spent hours watching DVD footage of previous Aberdeen games as he got to know his new squad and what he needed. Aberdeen failed to make the top six and it meant McInnes would be eased in at the wrong end.

McInnes knew he had to strengthen his squad to deliver success but also had to get their 12th man on board – the Red Army. He admitted: "We went in and tried to get an honest team on the pitch and the support recognised that. They knew the players were totally committed, they were fit, full of energy and played the game the way any supporter would want their team to play.

"That gave them a level of appreciation and understanding that helped us create a bond between the players and fans.

"On the football side, there were things that I felt needed to be addressed. Once we had a way of working and the players recognised what was expected of them, we've gave them every opportunity to be successful because they are the most important part of it – and they've got to be made to feel important, so they can perform on a Saturday. I don't think we were doing that before."

The McInnes revolution made a solid although unspectacular start. The Dons finished the season unbeaten with four draws and a home win against Kilmarnock. McInnes knew his team was chronically short of firepower. That was something he had to address if he was going to be succsessful.

It was to be a summer of change, not only at Pittodrie but also in Scottish football again. The demise of Hearts and their fall into administration along with Rangers' continued rise up through the lower leagues meant Aberdeen had a real chance to make their mark in the inaugural season of the Scottish Premiership, brought about by the merger of the Scottish Premier and Scottish Football Leagues, under the guise of the Scottish Professional Football League. The Dons had one of the bigger wage budgets in the Premiership and Milne and the hierarchy were keen for the club to finally deliver. The biggest problem for McInnes was the bulk of his squad were under contract and so to get others in he had to be ruthless with those who were out of contract.

Out went veterans Gavin Rae and Stephen Hughes, cultured midfielder Rob Milsom, misfiring striker Rory Fallon, Isaac Osbourne, Mitch Megginson and reserve keeper Dan Twardzik. The only player McInnes gave a new contract to was versatile striker Josh Magennis, who was given a one-year extension.

McInnes moved to reshape his squad and made an immediate signal of intent when he persuaded Willo Flood to jump ship from Premiership rivals Dundee United. Flood confirmed: "I met Derek and he just gave me confidence as soon as I spoke to him. He brought that confidence to the whole club, not just the playing staff.

"People said I signed for Aberdeen Football Club but I signed for Derek McInnes first and foremost and then I signed for Aberdeen Football Club.

"When I first met Derek I just felt I could work with him and he could get the best out of me. I spoke to him on the phone and then when he came to see me I said to my missus, 'he will do something'. I had made my mind up.

"Craig Levein and Gordon Strachan were two managers who I had also got a feel for. Your instinct tells you they are the right ones for you. Thankfully for me it has worked out really well."

He was quickly followed into Pittodrie by Flood's friend and long-term team-mate Barry Robson. The former Scotland international may have been 34 but was still hungry to bring success to his local club, having been born and raised in nearby Inverurie. There was no doubt McInnes being at the helm was also a big factor in Robson's decision.

Robson added: "I knew how hungry the manager, players and club were and they would do anything to bring some glory back. I played with Derek at Rangers and Dundee United. I was a young kid when Derek was at Rangers. We were both more experienced at United where Tony Docherty was also the reserve team manager. Derek has done well in management and Tony is a top coach. Aberdeen did well in attracting them here as their management team. That was a big thing for me, knowing there were some very professional people at the top."

Flood and Robson were quickly joined by giant striker Calvin Zola from Burton Albion, freed Bolton winger Gregg Wylde, Lawrence Shankland from Queen's Park and experienced goalkeeper Nicky Weaver on a free from Sheffield Wednesday.

McInnes felt he still needed more defensive cover and added Michael Hector on loan from Reading. Arguably, however, his best piece of business was getting top scorer Niall McGinn to pen an extension, even though he still had a year left on his existing contract. The Northern Irish international had netted an impressive 21 goals the previous season.

All those moves gave the Aberdeen support real hope. They responded, once again, with more than 10,000 season tickets being sold and the average crowds started to really take off. McInnes's surgery didn't go unnoticed either, as the Dons were installed as second favourites to win the league behind Celtic. Not bad for a team who hadn't made the top six in their previous four campaigns.

McInnes, from day one, tried to play down those title expectations and lift some of the pressures off his new-look squad. "We hoped for a strong Aberdeen in the SPL but we couldn't sit there with any arrogance on the back of where we had been in the previous few years," McInnes insisted. "Just because I was a new manager and I'd made signings, it didn't mean everything was alright and everything in the garden was rosy. There was work to be done and we couldn't sit there and say we were going to do this or that because we hadn't proved ourselves. We still had it all to do. I was confident we could have a good season and progress from where we had been. But to be confident, you have to back things up on the pitch and we still had to prove ourselves."

McInnes kept his feet firmly on the ground and that also ebbed into his dressing room. They made a winning start with a 2-1 triumph over Kilmarnock, with Irish winger Jonny Haynes claiming the Premiership's first goal. He was delighted to make his own piece of history but immediately played down any possible title talk.

"They say the bookies never get it wrong," said Hayes. "I saw a thing in the newspapers saying Celtic were 1/50 to win the league. That says it all.

"They have a far bigger budget, squad and experienced players and I don't think anybody will come close to troubling Celtic if I am honest.

"That is the gulf in Scottish football and we will try to bridge it as much as we can but I don't think anybody in this league has a right to say we are going to challenge Celtic because every team is miles away, in terms of budget and players.

"There are a lot of good teams and the likes of Inverness and Motherwell play some positive football. There will be a lot of teams vying for second place again."

That was followed as Aberdeen went to Motherwell, who had finished the previous season in second spot, and won 3-1. The Dons then faced up to champions Celtic but Jamie Langfield's sending off cost them and further questions were raised as they also lost at Tynecastle to rock-bottom and administration-run Hearts.

The League Cup allowed Aberdeen the opportunity to get back to winning ways. There was an even bigger buzz about the competition after Rangers had crashed out to Forfar Athletic. The Dons kicked off in the third round. They were given a home draw against newly-promoted Championship side Alloa Athletic. It was seen as a potential banana skin. There was also a bit of nostalgia connected to the tie as Alloa were bossed by former Aberdeen captain Paul Hartley. He had gone on to manage the Wasps after leaving Pittodrie where he had called time on his top-flight career.

Part-time Alloa, under Hartley, had won back-to-back promotions and were adapting to life well in the Championship. They travelled north confident, knowing fine well that Aberdeen's recent cup record would hardly have struck fear into the hearts of lower league opposition, especially on their own Pittodrie turf.

Hartley had Alloa well-drilled and set up to absolute perfection. His defence and midfield were like two rugged mountains in front of their goal. Aberdeen chipped away but struggled. It also didn't help that Willo Flood and Jonny Hayes had to limp off injured. It took a superb reflex stop from Jamie Langfield, who tipped on to the bar from Jason Marr, to keep the tie goalless.

Aberdeen's superior fitness began to tell in the latter stages and in extra time but they couldn't find a way past Hartley's heroes or former Dons youth keeper Scott Bain. The game went the distance in every sense, including the penalty shoot-out. Alloa continued to match Aberdeen blow-by-blow. Niall McGinn, Nicky Low, Peter Pawlett, Ryan Jack and Scott Vernon all netted penalties to keep the Dons level before it went to sudden death. Jamie Langfield was the hero as he saved Michael Doyle's effort and that allowed Mark Reynolds to step up and slam home the winner, much to the relief of a big Pittodrie support.

Langfield was also pleased to have silenced the waiting critics. "It was good we were able to come away with a wee smile because I know what it is like to lose on penalties," Langfield claimed.

"People are always looking for us to falter."

Hero Langfield confirmed it was a case of practice makes perfect.

The long-serving keeper said: "We did enough penalties in training. The boys loved it and they had wee competitions against me all the time.

"If they scored five penalties past me then I'd buy their lunch and if I saved one out of the five then they had to buy my lunch. I was about £40 up on McGinn and Hayes. We normally went for a wee Italian and I would have a risotto or a wee calamari, it was good. I couldn't get the dearest thing on the menu because we would go for a set menu – the boys aren't that stupid."

That game was one of the early signs that McInnes hadn't only added quality but a real mental toughness that hadn't always been there in previous seasons.

A relieved McInnes admitted: "Alloa were used to enjoying the game, and we didn't let them do that. We didn't get a goal which was a concern and gave Alloa encouragement, but I had to praise my players for their mentality to see it through. The quality of penalties was fantastic for both sides, and their boy (Doyle) was really unlucky."

Captain Russell Anderson was also well aware that game and penalty shoot-out went some way to shaping Aberdeen's campaign.

"It was definitely a defining moment in that season," the experienced centre-half, in his second spell at the club, conceded. "Whether or not you call it luck I don't know but I remember our penalties were all top drawer, although there wasn't much between the two teams."

The Alloa win set Aberdeen off on another impressive unbeaten charge. A midweek visit to Falkirk in the third round of the League Cup was next up. It was another of those no-win situations. Gary Holt's young

Championship side were a decent outfit and on their day were capable of causing an upset, especially on their own artificial surface. There was also another Aberdeen connection to this tie with ex-Dons boss Alex Smith director of football with the Bairns.

McInnes did his homework in his own meticulous style. He took his team to Forfar Athletic to train on their plastic pitch and to get a feel for what was to face them before they stepped out in front of the BBC television cameras.

McInnes said: "The fact that the game was on television suggested that other people sensed an upset. But I was determined to get it out of our heads that win, lose or draw it would have nothing to do with the artificial pitch."

Aberdeen and the rest of the names in the League Cup were given a real boost when the Championship's bottom side, Morton, knocked out holders Celtic at Parkhead, thanks to a Dougie Imrie goal. Aberdeen were immediately installed as tournament favourites.

That added burden certainly didn't get to the Dons, who confidently strode past Falkirk. Pittodrie protégés Joe Shaughnessy and Cammy Smith got goals in the first half. Aberdeen's strikers, in particular Calvin Zola, had struggled for goals. The Congo-born striker was replaced by Scott Vernon 33 minutes into that game and it proved to be a masterstroke. The former Oldham Athletic forward had been top scorer in Mark McGhee's time at the club but the goals had dried up a bit until Craig Brown's final season. That Falkirk game was to be one of his finest games for Aberdeen as he capped off a five-star performance with a second-half hat-trick for the rampant Dons.

Vernon, who tweeted a picture of his hat-trick ball, confirmed: "I was determined to prove a point and it certainly worked out well that night."

The Aberdeen striker was also quick to praise the part the Pittodrie youngsters, like Shaughnessy, Smith and Nicky Low, had played in putting Falkirk in their place.

"The youngsters weren't born when Aberdeen enjoyed their golden era and some weren't born when we last won a cup so that shows you how long ago it was," Vernon joked.

"It was a shame a club of Aberdeen's stature has had to wait so long and we were keen to change that.

"This was my fourth season at the club and the young lads who played then were some of the best I had been involved with at Aberdeen.

"A lot of credit had to go to kids like Joe Shaughnessy, Nicky Low and Cammy Smith. They did really well for us. They stepped up to the plate and proved they were men."

Aberdeen were also battling it out for second spot with Inverness, who had come out of the blocks quickly, in the league. McInnes continued to give his players every chance and with the aid of some outside investment he was able to bring in sport scientist Graham Kirk from his former club, St Johnstone. He believed it would more than benefit his players over the longer term.

Kirk transformed the fitness programmes and eating patterns of the Aberdeen team. The Dons were getting physically stronger.

They were also about to be tested in the League Cup quarter-finals where they faced Motherwell, who had finished second in the league the previous season. The Dons had won there on league duty earlier in the season and Stuart McCall's Steelmen were out for revenge.

Derek McInnes's best-laid plans quickly went out the window when Joe Shaughnessy was given his marching orders in the 14th minute, for a late challenge on Zane Francis-Angol. It left his team up against it. They then got a touch of luck when a John Sutton effort was harshly ruled out for offside.

McInnes's tactical knowledge then came to the fore. He took off Calvin Zola and sent on Andrew Considine. Motherwell had Aberdeen camped on the edge of their 18-yard box but McInnes set up Considine alongside Mark Reynolds and captain Russell Anderson in a three-man defence with Jonny Hayes and Peter Pawlett employed as emergency wing-backs. It worked as Motherwell dominated but they couldn't crack the resolute Dons. Langfield only had one save to make thanks to his rock-solid back line.

Aberdeen then hit on the counter and scored when sub Considine climbed highest to head in Hayes's corner just seven minutes from time. Motherwell went for broke in the final minutes but Hayes sealed the famous win for Aberdeen in stoppage time. They were now in the semi-finals and a team everybody were beginning to sit up and really take notice about.

McInnes said: "At half-time we spoke about organisation, guts and character that we needed to win the game. We also needed a bit of belief and we showed determination to get there, especially playing so long with ten men. I thought Joe was unlucky because he made a challenge and I think he slipped as he made the tackle. By the letter of the law it was a red card and one he will have learned from."

Goal hero Considine was always confident that Aberdeen would advance, even in the face of adversity.

"I didn't see us losing any goals against Motherwell and I felt we would go on and win the game, even before Joe got sent off," he confidently claimed. "It was a great performance because we had to dig in – it was a tough second half with ten men. We took our chances and it was a tremendous result. I managed to score with a header but the most important thing was the result."

There was nobody more relieved that young Joe Shaughnessy, as his team-mates managed to dig him out of a hole, as he watched the majority of the match from the Main Stand at Fir Park. His lack of discipline was also to cost him – although not as much as it might have! Instead of a club fine he was offered the chance to take his team-mates for lunch or to buy the fish and chips at Auchterarder on the way back up to Aberdeen. "It cost me over £100 to buy the boys fish and chips which is too much, so I'll make sure it won't be happening again," Shaughnessy joked. "But it could have been a lot more costly for the club so I was delighted the lads got the result that took us into the semi-final of the cup."

Skipper Russell Anderson also knew that win at Fir Park was massive against a team who would also have fancied their chances of getting their name on the League Cup.

"We could have quite easily buckled against Motherwell," their reliable leader acknowledged. "But we showed a real resilience and it was a springboard for us to go all the way."

That gutsy win saw manager McInnes lead Aberdeen into the semi-finals at the first time of asking. The draw paired them with his old club, St Johnstone, while Hearts were to face Inverness in the other game. Aberdeen were able to put their cup ambitions temporarily to one side for a few months. They were able to concentrate on their Premiership campaign although their new-found success hadn't gone unnoticed by one of the club's most famous sons – Sir Alex Ferguson.

The newly-retired Manchester United boss confirmed: "There's been a big improvement at Aberdeen. Derek has got them scoring goals but the main thing is he has got them extremely hard to beat. I can see no reason why they can't win a cup. Derek was unlucky at Bristol City when he was in England. You can see his ability in the job he is doing at Aberdeen."

McInnes was flattered by the praise but, in his usual grounded style, refused to get carried away.

"It was nice to hear Sir Alex talking about Aberdeen in such a positive way," the boss admitted. "Normally when he's asked about Aberdeen it is about past glories but it was pleasing to see him talking positively about the future."

It was hardly a surprise that McInnes and his players weren't shouting from the rooftops. Their weekly press conferences turned into robotic affairs with his players programmed not to say anything controversial and to continually take things one step at a time. He didn't want his players to lose focus or to give the opposition any added incentives.

It was an approach that couldn't be questioned, as Aberdeen continued to do their talking on the pitch. They were pushed for second spot until the turn of the year by Dundee United and Motherwell, who had come up on the blind side. Aberdeen continued to pick up results and showed their superior fitness and will to win with a number of late goals. One of them came in a dramatic win at Tannadice in the New Year fixture, where Peter Pawlett had been the late hero.

The January transfer window then opened and allowed Derek McInnes to bolster his squad further. He lost impressive defender Michael Hector, who returned to Reading, but quickly replaced him with Swansea stalwart Alan Tate and then turned his attentions to another of his long-term targets – Adam Rooney. He had tried to sign him previously at St Johnstone and made it third time lucky when he fought off competition from Hibs and the player's former boss, Terry Butcher, to land him.

Irishman Rooney admitted: "I came close to working with Derek a couple of times in the past and it was something I always wanted to do. They did a good job at St Johnstone, down south and now things are going really well for them at Aberdeen. They have built up Aberdeen, told me how big a club it is and where they want to get to. It was something that really excited me."

McInnes was able to offer a financial package that nobody outside of Celtic and Rangers was able to pay, but, in fairness, the manager also played his part in balancing the books.

McInnes released veteran midfielder Chris Clark and sent several players out on loan, including Josh Magennis who joined St Mirren for the rest of the season. The Dons manager also showed his ruthless streak when he freed winger Gregg Wylde just months after he had signed him.

New boy Rooney made an immediate impact, scoring on his debut at Motherwell. The Dons had to come from behind twice to rescue a point that kept them in second spot ahead of their League Cup semi-final. Skipper Russell Anderson's controversial late goal against the Steelmen gave Aberdeen the perfect boost ahead of their final four show-down with St Johnstone.

Robson confirmed the never-say-die spirit was down to McInnes and his management team. He explained: "If you look at successful clubs through the years, they keep going to the very end and have this winning mentality. That's what the manager is trying to do here. You can see it in the players – we're never going to stop or let our heads go down. It's amazing how many points you can pick up that way. It comes from the manager and coaching staff through the week and on matchdays. If you're losing, you need to tell folk to keep it going. When you're at a big club, the fans expect it from you. It's a mentality thing but the manager can put it right through a club if everyone buys into it. I saw it at Celtic. If you're a goal down with five minutes to go, the punters are on to you, urging you to get that goal."

That draw in Lanarkshire did come at a cost as Ryan Jack was stretchered off with a hip injury that would see him miss the semi-final. That left McInnes with a bit of a selection headache. Joe Shaughnessy was also suspended after his Fir Park red card. McInnes moved into the transfer market again and brought in former Manchester City defender Shay Logan on loan from Brentford.

That was part of a manic semi-final build-up. There was a real buzz around the Granite City, so much so that their 12,000 ticket allocation, which was around 76 per cent of the Tynecastle capacity, was never going to satisfy the desperate demand. The Red Army were to be housed in the Wheatfield, Gorgie and Main Stands. The gold dust-like tickets didn't even make it onto general sale, as they were snapped up by season ticket holders and supporters' clubs. That left the authorities with a major problem as there wasn't the same demand for St Johnstone seats. Aberdeen supporters started buying up tickets for the St Johnstone sections. That led to both clubs issuing warnings not to buy tickets for the wrong side because if fans were caught then they would be ejected.

That didn't stop some of the more brazen Aberdeen supporters who defied orders and bought tickets. Some even went and tweeted photographs of their tickets on their Twitter social networking sites. That proved a costly mistake as St Johnstone were able to look at the number of their ticket and therefore cancel it without the holder even knowing – until they were turned away furiously at the turnstiles!

Aberdeen were always going to be heavily backed going into the game as cup fever swept across the north-east. The club also cashed in with their Redinburgh promotional campaign. There was a lot of hype but McInnes was determined it wasn't going to weigh on the shoulder of his players.

St Johnstone went into the game as underdogs and their manager Tommy Wright was keen to pile the pressure all on Aberdeen. That was dismissed as nothing but mind games as McInnes tried to keep things as normal as possible. So much so that they didn't do their pre-match press until the Thursday. McInnes calmly responded to Tommy Wright's claims, when he said: "It's stating the obvious that Aberdeen are the bigger club with a better history. Would I do the same in their position? Possibly, but pointing out the size of the club and the support is stating the obvious. St Johnstone have finished above Aberdeen for the last few years, they've been in Europe for the last two seasons. Just because you are a bigger club, have a bigger support and have a better history that doesn't make you favourites. We were favourites in some people's eyes but it was because we've done so well during that season."

St Johnstone suffered a damning blow of their own when their game with Dundee United was called off just before it. That meant St Johnstone No. 1 Alan Mannus was suspended for the semi-final, although he also suffered an injury in the run-in. Things started to fall into place for Aberdeen. The biggest obstacle was not St Johnstone but whether or not the Aberdeen players could handle the pressure of an expectant Red Army.

There was certainly an inner confidence within the Aberdeen squad. That was summed up by director and former boss Craig Brown outside the ground. Maybe he had his own crystal ball with him! When I asked him what the score would be, Brown replied: "We are in great form. We will win it no problem, it will be four or five nil."

Tommy Wright's ploy to pile all the pressure on Aberdeen certainly backfired as the Dons started like a house on fire, as St Johnstone failed to awake from their slumber. A poor kick-out from back-up keeper Steve Banks caught Frazer Wright unawares. Adam Rooney robbed him and squared for Jonny Hayes to slide home in only the second minute. St Johnstone responded by pinning Aberdeen to the ropes but it was the team in red who hit them with a real sucker punch. Lee Croft was robbed of possession by Hayes. The Irishman crossed, the St Johnstone defence failed to clear and Peter Pawlett skipped round a defender and coolly beat Banks for the second. Aberdeen suddenly had a convincing half-time lead, which was a little against the run of play. The Dons had one foot in the final but that didn't stop McInnes from telling his team they had to lift their game again. Pawlett was next to make the most of some Saints' slackness as he robbed Dave Mackay, burst forward and picked out Adam Rooney to net and maintain his goal-a-game start to his Aberdeen career. Even then McInnes wanted his team to remain focused and was quick to get on the back of keeper Jamie Langfield as he celebrated with the delighted Red Army behind his goal. Hayes capped their dream day with a long-range effort. Aberdeen fans knew they were now in the final.

A relieved McInnes said: "I hoped we could get to a cup final in our first season.

"We always felt we could be successful.

"We had put a squad together that summer we felt could improve the situation.

"The players had shown a great level of consistency this season in the league and the cup gave us that opportunity to be successful.

"We have had some tough matches in earlier rounds and St Johnstone was another tough nut to crack.

"Semi-finals are usually a lot tighter than that but we were clinical and we took our opportunities well."

Captain Russell Anderson had been part of Ebbe Skovdahl's previous final sides and he was delighted to be getting another chance so late in his career. Anderson said: "We had been crying out for a cup final and to be honest it has been too long for the size of Aberdeen –14 years is a long time for them to wait for another one."

The jubilant captain also praised Aberdeen's front players and believed Adam Rooney, Jonny Hayes, Peter Pawlett and Niall McGinn were the difference on the day.

Anderson insisted: "The front four were clinical, they were breathtaking at times. And the support, I've said it at every away game this season, it was incredible – I'm sure it'll be the same for the final."

McInnes was also relieved that Aberdeen had been so convincing because it showed everyone – including his own players – that they could deliver on the big stage.

The manager said: "If we had lost that semi-final, it would have been difficult to convince people.

"Not that we needed to convince people, we just needed to convince ourselves.

"Looking at the semi-final, I honestly expected them to handle it, although we were too motivated against St Johnstone – and some of the more experienced players were the ones charging about all over the place. You would rather have that than see them letting the game pass them by. But there were times when the players were too up for the performance."

McInnes, once again, moved to try and remove the burden of the club's previous successes and proud history.

"Judge us on our future, not the club's past," he passionately asked in the wake of the semi-final celebration. We can't affect what has happened in the past, whether it's talking about history that's been good or whether it's been disappointments of late. This is our team, this group of boys' first chance of a final together. They have done it at the first attempt and they deserve great credit for that, regardless of what's happened previously at Aberdeen."

Aberdeen's celebrations were well-deserved. McInnes and his jubilant players returned to the Dakota Hotel at Queensferry to party. All the team apart from goalkeeper Jamie Langfield, who spent the night with his family in Edinburgh to celebrate his daughter's birthday, partied into the early hours.

The hangover had hardly cleared when Aberdeen discovered they would be facing Inverness Caledonian Thistle in the final. The Highlanders had made their own history by beating Hearts on penalties to famously celebrate their first appearance in a senior final. Caley Thistle had seen off Dundee, Dundee United and the Jambos along the way. There was also an Aberdeen connection there as well. Aberdeen's very own Coca-Cola Cup hero and former assistant manager Duncan Shearer was part of the Inverness coaching staff.

The Scottish Professional Football League's biggest problem was finding a venue for the final with Hampden out of commission for that summer's Commonwealth Games. It was a straight choice between Celtic Park and Ibrox. It was the larger venue of Parkhead that got the nod much to the disgust of Rangers manager Ally McCoist.

It was good news for Aberdeen as it meant an increased capacity, with Parkhead holding just over 60,000. Aberdeen were initially allocated 30,000 tickets while Inverness were also given a much smaller share. It caused controversy as SPFL chiefs announced that they were splitting the Caley Thistle support into two sections across the Main and Lisbon Lions stands. Inverness chairman Kenny Cameron, not surprisingly, complained and forced the SPFL into a long, overdue rethink before common sense prevailed.

They agreed to keep the Aberdeen allocation intact but moved some of their seats, housing Inverness's fans in the bottom tier of the Lisbon Lions stand.

Such was the demand that the 30,000 seats quickly disappeared and the club had to go back to the SPFL to ask them for more. A further 10,000 tickets were released. They were just as frantically snapped up, especially when the ballot was opened up to fans who had a previous record of buying match tickets. The final dregs of the 40,000 went before their last game before the final when they entertained Dumbarton at home in the quarter-finals of the Scottish Cup. Arriving fans were met with disappointment as the SOLD OUT signs went up in and around the Pittodrie ticket office.

Once again, there was to be no public sale.

Frontman Adam Rooney confirmed: "I don't think anybody expected us to sell that many tickets. I remember when the first allocation came out and as a squad we thought we might get 25,000 or 30,000. But it went up to 40,000 and there were people asking for more. I think we could have sold over 50,000 with the way it is around the city. Every second person in the city seemed to be looking for spare tickets. It was incredible."

Those fans who couldn't lay their hands on tickets could still roar on their team from afar. Most pubs in Aberdeen would be jam-packed while the Belmont Cinema was to show the game live on one of their big screens.

Expectations also heightened as the Dons beat Celtic at Pittodrie with Jonny Hayes scoring the first goal that stopped Hoops' keeper Fraser Forster from breaking the European shut-out record in their 2-1 win. Adam Rooney netted the winner to send champions Celtic spinning to their first league defeat in ten months.

Final fever was gripping the Granite City and McInnes decided he needed to take his team away from it all. They headed for the Old Course at St Andrews. The move helped bond the team and get some of the players into the swing of things with the Aberdeen team's very own Ryder Cup.

"There were eight or nine of us in the winning team," defender Mark Reynolds recalled. "There was also a trophy because the boys at Aberdeen all love a bit of competition. I was more interested in the bragging rights than the trophy just to keep some of the boys on their toes. Big Calvin (Zola) was seemingly the first player from the Congo to play on the Duke's Course. He was breaking all different types of records as I think it was the first time he had ever held a golf club in his life as well. Nicky Low was another alleged novice. I asked him how he did and he said: 'I did okay, most of the holes I holed out in the number I was supposed to or at worst I was one over.'"

Dons No.2 Docherty knew the importance of getting the team together as one.

Docherty said: "The bond between the players is the strongest I have seen at any football club. We did a lot of things to strengthen that side of things. The golf at St Andrews before the League Cup Final and we also had them away clay pigeon shooting, as well as other things that have helped the boys to mix away from the pressures of playing. Strong team spirit doesn't come on its own. You need to work at it and it is something Derek and I have done at every club we have been at. If the bond in the dressing room is strong then you reap the benefits on a Saturday and you will work that bit harder if you know the guy next to you is also your mate."

The Pittodrie dressing room is certainly not one for your shrinking violets or those who want to keep a low profile. Young defender Joe Shaughnessy can vouch for that after a secret date went viral as his team-mates took to social media to try and smoke him out.

"I didn't tell anyone," the Irishman laughed. "I think it was Nicky Low that told all the boys. We went out for a quiet Italian and I thought nobody will find me here. I had a look at Twitter later and everything had got out of hand. It also made some of the national newspapers with some of the boys having tweeted pictures with the message: 'Where is Joe?' It was funny. There was always something going on in that dressing room."

Inverness held their pre-match press activities first and once again it was Aberdeen's rivals who blinked first. They went with the age old ploy, with their manager John Hughes again insisting that it was Aberdeen's cup to lose. McInnes and his team just laughed it off. It was now like water off a duck's back and over the course of the season that claim was beginning to sound a bit like a broken record!

Aberdeen boss Derek McInnes was pleased he and all his players had done all they could to prepare. He was also confident in his players, young and old, that they would deliver. That was something his team had consistently done over the course of that season.

McInnes admitted: "If you have experience of cup finals and big games, as these boys have, it's important to draw on that. There was a confidence that comes from the likes of Barry Robson, Russell Anderson and Willo Flood. That can only be good for the youngsters. But just because you're a youngster doesn't mean you have an excuse for not being ready."

The team headed north on the Wednesday but McInnes went even further north as he headed to the Caledonian Stadium to take one final look at their cup final opponents. He didn't see much although that was possibly a sign of things to come as Caley Thistle shut up shop in a goalless draw with Hibs.

The players were given the Thursday off to spend with their families before the final preparations were fine-tuned. Aberdeen were left sweating over the fitness of Peter Pawlett and Niall McGinn with groin problems.

Just when Aberdeen fans thought things couldn't get any better their club tabled their trump card – just two days before the final. They announced that McInnes and his loyal assistant, Tony Docherty, had penned extensions. They had initially signed deals until 2015 but extended that agreement to 2017. It was a major coup from Aberdeen chairman Stewart Milne, knowing fine well his manager would be attracting a lot of admiring glances from elsewhere.

Milne announced, "It's fantastic that Derek and Tony are committing themselves for the long haul and I'm sure our supporters will be as pleased as everyone at the club is. We were convinced from day one that they didn't see the task at the club as being anything other than a long-term project and having our management team on long-term contracts, in addition to an important nucleus of the playing squad on similar deals, bodes extremely well for the future. Derek and Tony have had a major impact on the club since taking over the reins. We are all delighted with the progress to date, but as Derek keeps reminding us, we are very much at the start of a journey, so hopefully Sunday will be another major step along the way. However, success to him will not be viewed on the back of one good season, but on being able to sustain the club at the top end of the league, competing at the final stages for trophies, playing in Europe, on a sustained basis, and that is also what everyone associated with the club desires."

McInnes was also more than happy to extend his stay. He said: "We both really enjoy working at the club but we are only some way towards what we would like to achieve here. It's great that the board also believes we are doing a decent job and the additional contract allows us time to really plan for the future in terms of developing the squad."

It, however, wasn't all to be good news as 48 hours before the game Peter Pawlett was cruelly ruled out of the Celtic Park clash. Pawlett had returned to full training and had looked odds-on to start against Inverness having got back to full fitness. Pawlett looked to be fit and well until tragedy struck when he went to take a shot and he felt his groin again at the end of the training session.

Pawlett knew right away his cup final dream was over. It was as much a blow to Aberdeen and to manager McInnes as it was to the player himself. The Dons had lost a major part of their arsenal while Pawlett had to resign himself to watching Aberdeen's biggest game in recent years from the stand.

"Peter was a sore one," McInnes admitted with more than a hint of disappointment. "He was devastated that he missed out. He played a huge part in getting us to the League Cup Final."

The loss of Pawlett was cushioned a little by the fact that Niall McGinn was passed fit and well.

McInnes has always been single-minded and ruthless as a manager. He had never been scared to make the big decisions for the benefit of his football club. Picking a team that was going to break an embarrassing 19-year trophy-less run was never going to faze him.

There were many questions. Shay Logan or Joe Shaughnessy at right-back? Captain Russell Anderson alongside Mark Reynolds or on-loan Swansea defender Alan Tate? The rest of his team picked itself, as it had for most of the season. Jamie Langfield between the sticks, Reynolds and Andrew Considine on the left-hand side of the defence, Willo Flood, Barry Robson and Ryan Jack in the middle of the park with Niall McGinn and Jonny Hayes providing the width for Adam Rooney up front.

The manager's other main headache was probably his Plan B and his substitutes' bench, especially as the substitutes were cut from seven in the league to five in the cup. Would he go for Scott Vernon or Calvin Zola or both? McInnes knew what needed to be done even if it was going to cause heartbreak and disappointment for players who had played their part over the course of the season.

McInnes was also well aware from his own bitter experience with Rangers how hard it can hit a player being left out of a cup final team. He was dropped for the 1998 League Cup Final win when Rangers beat St Johnstone.

McInnes explained: "The League Cup Final was the one instance where I felt really hard done by under Walter Smith. I had played in every game in the run-up to the final and had scored in the 6-1 win over Dunfermline. I was confident that I would at least be on the bench for the final. But when the gaffer named the team I wasn't in it or even on the bench. I was left gutted and couldn't fully understand why I wasn't involved. I felt really hard done by. I just didn't see it coming and I just felt I had been denied my first real piece of silverware where I had really played a part in the team's success. I went to see Walter the next day and he gave me a medal and told me to keep it because I had earned it. He then explained his reasons. It is only now as a manager that you have to make decisions, which aren't easy to make, but they have to be made for the sake of the team. I still have a joke with Walter about it but even today it still hurts and still doesn't sit right with me."

The boss decided to put his faith in Jamie Langfield, Shay Logan, Russell Anderson, Mark Reynolds, Andrew Considine, Willo Flood, Ryan Jack, Barry Robson, Niall McGinn, Jonny Hayes and Adam Rooney. Experienced back-up Nicky Weaver provided cover for Langfield while Alan Tate sat alongside him with teenager Cammy Smith, Nicky Low and Scott Vernon. That meant cup final disappointment for Calvin Zola and Joe Shaughnessy. They would be forced to become part of the Red Army – along with the injured Peter Pawlett.

The Dons were also charting for success off the pitch thanks to the passionate Aberdeen support. Pawlett might have lost his battle to be fit, breaking down in the build-up, but he was set to be a hit off the park.

The midfielder's new-found form had seen him become a cult hero amongst the Aberdeen fans. So much so that they doctored a classic Eighties track to pay their own tribute to him, alongside the also newly introduced 'Sheep are on fire'. Little did synthpop favourites Human League know that the Scottish Premiership would spark their own unlikely chart revival more than 30 years on!

Their iconic track 'Don't You Want Me' was a massive hit on both sides of the Atlantic. It was the UK's 1981 Christmas Number One while it topped the US Billboard Charts seven months later.

The timeless chorus which chants: "Don't you want me baby? Don't you want me? Oh!" was masterfully doctored by the Aberdeen fans to "Peter Pawlett baby, Peter Pawlett ooooh." The song quickly became a terracing favourite at Pittodrie and amongst the travelling support.

So much so that the Aberdeen fans started their own campaign, via the social networks, to get the Human League's original 'Don't You Want Me' to the top of the charts. Facebook and Twitter may well have been 21st-century inventions but they were used to champion one of the most iconic tunes of the 1980s. Ironically, the height of the Human League's success with their biggest single came some ten years before Pawlett was even born.

The band, formed in Sheffield, was left stunned by the response as Aberdeen fans downloaded and bought the singles in their thousands. The group even took to their own official Facebook page to thank the Red Army and to wish them all the best for the cup final.

They posted: "Amazing stuff you Aberdeen FC fans, simply amazing. Best of luck with your campaign and here's hoping the club appreciate your creativity and support as much as we do."

The revival was expected to cause a ripple of sales but instead it produced a flood, especially as the song was played over the Celtic Park tannoy before and after the League Cup Final.

Aberdeen's players, like Jamie Langfield, Nicky Low and Clark Robertson, also got in on the act, tweeting pictures of Peter Pawlett in the Pittodrie dressing room, holding a piece of paper saying: "Get me to No. 1."

There was also some national coverage with *Soccer AM* co-presenter Helen Chamberlain singing "Peter Pawlett baby" at the end of their Scottish football round-up while Radio 2 DJ Steve Wright played the Human League and finished off with the alternative Peter Pawlett version. The team and fans were very much on song.

The Red Army, who were lucky enough to make it to Celtic Park, were determined not only to be heard but also to be seen. Some of their supporters got together to start a display fund for the final. They raised around £6,000 from donations, as Jamie Langfield handed over a pair of gloves while Jonny Hayes and Niall McGinn both donated signed shirts to the cause. It was almost like a military operation as the organisers headed to Glasgow on the Saturday to start the preparations. There was even a hotel room donated for the organisers so they didn't have to come back up the road before the game.

There were also a lot of exiled Dons who made their way back home from as far afield as Australia and America to see their team. There were also some higher profile fans who were making their own sacrifices to head for Celtic Park. Professional golfer and former Open champion Paul Lawrie decided to put the Dons before his own career ambitions. Vital Ryder Cup points, for the 2014 event at Gleneagles, were up for grabs. Lifelong Don Lawrie was sitting 68th in the rankings and desperately needed the points from the Moroccan Open but the lure of seeing the Dons grabbing glory was far too important. Lawrie said: "Obviously it's not great to be pulling out of a golf event in Ryder Cup year if your football team is in a cup final – but they haven't been in many!"

The scene was set. Sunday, 16 March was the day of reckoning. The talking was over and it was time for heroes to step forward. Aberdeen manager Derek McInnes, flanked by two of his sons, Harry and Charlie, smartly and reassuringly led his team out along with counterpart, John Hughes, and his Inverness opponents for the 68th Scottish League Cup Final. McInnes had done all he could and now it was up to his players. It was their time!

The managers and players walked past the League Cup – knowing that come the final kick one of their teams was going to be celebrating with it firmly in their grasp. The other was going to be left nursing a feeling of serious heartbreak and a case of what could have been. Superstitious Aberdeen captain Russell Anderson said: "I never touched the cup in the build-up because I always said that the first time we should touch it is when we had earned it."

They walked out to a stadium primarily decked out in red and white. The pre-match card display, worked wonders in the West and North stands. The North Stand read 'AFC' and the '1903' in red and white and their initial yellow and black colours were prominently displayed in the West. It was more like Pittodrie than Celtic Park!

Anderson proudly admitted: "The hairs on the back of my neck stood up when you heard them chanting our names and we could see the size of our support. Initially, I think there were 25,000 expected to buy tickets so when you're selling 40,000 and they're asking for more because the club can't meet the demand it shows you what it means to the support. The final was for them as much as anyone, them and the staff behind the scenes as well."

The Aberdeen support's move to add a bit of colour to proceedings did cause one or two headaches to the match official Steven McLean. The toilet rolls, streamers and red and white balloons that were thrown on to the pitch left the stewards with some unexpected work as they tried to clear the Celtic Park pitch. It proved an almost impossible task and although the bulk of debris was removed by the ground staff, there were still a few stray balloons lying that saw Inverness's players booed when they burst them. Inverness boss John Hughes was keen not to incur the same wrath and diplomatically removed the balloons and threw them back into the Aberdeen section behind his technical area.

The opening stages proved to be a stuffy affair. Proceedings or Aberdeen weren't helped by Jonny Hayes's injury just seven seconds in. He came out on to the Aberdeen right and bravely went up for a challenge that Inverness defender Josh Meekings always looked destined to win. The Irishman landed heavily on his right arm. Hayes went off for some intense treatment with Derek McInnes screaming up the line to physio John Sharp to see if Hayes was fit enough to continue. Hayes did resume but it proved to be short-lived. He tried to run past full-back David Raven and then fell to the turf clutching his shoulder. He and everyone else in the stadium knew his cup final was well and truly over.

The loss of Hayes, on top of Pawlett, looked as if Aberdeen might lose a lot of their natural energy and pace from their team. Hayes's loss turned out to be Cammy Smith's gain. The 18-year-old midfielder was given the nod to come on and follow in the footsteps of another Pittodrie hero in the shape of Eoin Jess. He had played at the same age when Aberdeen had delivered the 1990 Skol Cup under Alex Smith.

Manager McInnes admitted: "It wasn't a great game but there are reasons for that.

"We weren't at our attacking best but we lost Peter Pawlett's dynamism because of an injury and then Jonny Hayes was injured with virtually the first kick of the ball."

There wasn't much in the first 45 minutes although Aberdeen did look the more threatening. They came inches away from taking first blood in the 24th minute. Substitute Smith was heavily involved in the build-up. He rose above James Vincent to force a header towards goal forcing Inverness keeper Dean Brill to punch clear. The ball fell to Russell Anderson 12 yards from goal. He hooked in a right-foot shot that came off Brill's right post and rolled along the line before Richie Foran booted clear. The Aberdeen players desperately claimed for a goal but referee Steven McLean was right to ignore their appeals.

Anderson joked: "My kids were impressed with my shot in the first half which hit the post – I surprised them as much as I surprised myself. I think it made me a cool dad for a day – if I'm lucky!"

The other main talking point of a rather nervy first half came via a 35th-minute penalty claim, when Adam Rooney got in front of Josh Meekings and went down under his challenge although the ball was already rolling out of play. Man in black McLean signalled for a goal kick rather than a penalty despite Rooney's furious protests.

There were a few half chances but you would have struggled to get a cigarette paper between the teams as they went in level at the interval. The second period continued in a similar theme. Aberdeen keeper Jamie Langfield was finally forced into his first save when he had to gather Greg Tansey's free kick.

The match turned into a chess match where there was very little movement. There were long lulls in the play and it was left to the Aberdeen fans to try and lift their team.

McInnes insisted: "At no point did I think that we would be anything other than inspired by the fans and although we were not at our attacking best I don't think anyone shirked their responsibility and that's why I love working with this group of players."

Aberdeen continued to edge matters but McInnes felt they needed a bit more. He sent on Nicky Low for the unfortunate Smith in the 69th minute. Low provided more steel in the middle of the park and allowed the likes of Barry Robson, Willo Flood and Ryan Jack to share more of the attacking responsibilities.

The game came alive in the final ten minutes of the regulation 90. Left-back Andrew Considine broke forward and charged into the box but he lost his footing and slipped as he went to pull the trigger and the chance went begging.

Barry Robson was next to let fly from distance. Inverness defender Danny Devine tried to clear it but redirected it back towards his own goal and his keeper Dean Brill had to get down sharply to keep the ball out.

There was another big penalty claim four minutes from time when Andrew Considine appeared to pull back Richie Foran as he tried to get on the end of Graeme Shinnie's corner. Foran was furious at the time and even after the match his frustration hadn't subsided. He told the referee he wanted a telephone apology the following day.

There was still to be one final chance for the Dons. Greg Tansey's attempted clearance ran through to the normally deadly Niall McGinn. He cut inside Josh Meekings, who lunged to try and make a second block. As he did the ball bobbled up and McGinn fired over the bar from just inside the box.

It was clear the match was going to go the distance – unless there was a mistake or a moment of magic. Jamie Langfield had to make a save to keep out Aaron Doran while Adam Rooney headed a Barry Robson cross wide.

McInnes admitted the game was very much on a knife-edge at that point. He confirmed: "I thought we controlled spells of the game and at no time in extra time did I think we would lose, but neither was I sure we'd win."

The half-time whistle went with the Aberdeen physios keen to give their players a bit more energy, handing out glucose drinks and jelly babies.

Aberdeen boss McInnes was still keen to go for the win and sent on Scott Vernon for defender Andrew Considine – although he might also have had an eye on penalties.

"The gaffer put Scott on to chase and get a goal," Considine joked. "There was also more chance of him scoring a penalty than me!"

Vernon got some last-minute pointers from McInnes.

"The manager was giving me little instructions of where he wanted me to be and where to press," he revealed. "He never said anything about the penalties. Maybe that was in his mind or he wanted to try and nick a goal in the last five minutes, pushing me up with Adam Rooney."

Derek McInnes was already making plans for the shoot-out before the final whistle. He and assistant Tony Docherty were already deep in discussion clutching a piece of paper contemplating their five penalty kick takers on the touchline as the majority of Celtic Park sat anxiously biting their nails.

Docherty claimed: "We knew our five takers and the order they were going to be taken during extra time. We had practised penalties all week. You can't simulate the pressure or being in front of a crowd but you can work on other things. Like walking from the halfway line and taking the ball off the referee, etc. We did all we could."

Aberdeen still had a couple of late chances with Nicky Low putting a free kick over the bar. The final opening fell to Scott Vernon who headed wide before referee Steven McLean blew the whistle to signal for penalties.

McInnes had left no stone unturned in Aberdeen's preparations.

"The penalty shoot-out is not a lottery," the manager insisted. "I reminded our players of how good the standard had been against Alloa earlier in the cup and also that they had been practising them all week.

"I told them to be confident, pick their spot and go bring the cup back."

It had already been decided in advance that the penalties would be taken at the goal in front of the Lisbon Lions Stand that housed the Inverness support. Caley Thistle had won the toss and decided to go first. They were confident having seen off Hearts in similar circumstances in the semi-finals.

Their top scorer Billy Mckay stepped up first but Jamie Langfield outwitted him and dived to his right to save his penalty. It was suddenly advantage Aberdeen.

McInnes knew at that point that the cup was Aberdeen's to lose.

"It's ironic that it was a great save from Jamie to get us going," the boss admitted.

"I can only judge him here in my time at the club and he's now showing composure brought about by a level of experience.

"His save gave us the momentum and got the crowd going for the shoot-out."

Assistant Tony Docherty was just as hopeful. He said: "We would have preferred to go first but when Jamie saved the penalty it swung the momentum our way. So I think that stood us in good stead."

Barry Robson kept his cool and made the most of his 35 years to put Aberdeen ahead. Greg Tansey was next up for Inverness. He has a reputation for his long-range shooting but he failed to keep his nerve from 12 yards and fired wildly over the crossbar.

Langfield had also done his background work on Inverness's spot kickers ahead of the game.

"People say penalties are lucky but we do our homework on players now," Langfield confessed. "Inverness had a shoot-out in the semi-final so I'm not saying I knew where Billy Mckay was going to go with his kick but I went the right way and I'm glad I got my hand on it and kept it out. And then Greg Tansey put it over the bar which was unfortunate for him."

Nicky Low turned the screw by sending Dean Brill the wrong way.

Nervous captain Russell Anderson wasn't as confident. He admitted: "When we were 2-0 up in the penalties you really didn't want to think ahead because you've seen penalty shoot-outs before when the advantage hasn't worked out. I was just hoping the players taking them could see it through."

Inverness sub Nick Ross netted before Scott Vernon maintained Aberdeen's advantage, making it 3-1. The striker was always confident from 12 yards.

Vernon joked: "I was chucked in at the deep end for the penalties. I put myself forward to take one and it worked."

Aaron Doran kept his nerve to keep Inverness in the competition. It was all left at the right foot of Adam Rooney. He knew if he scored Aberdeen's trophy drought would finally be over. The Irishman, who had netted six goals in just eight Aberdeen appearances, stepped forward. He spotted the ball, kept his head down and opted for a long run-up. He stepped forward and with a confident right-foot strike he sent Dean Brill the wrong way as he fired his shot high and straight under the crossbar.

He made it look all so easy although Rooney had been concerned Inverness back-up keeper and former Aberdeen player Ryan Esson might give Dean Brill the inside track on his penalties.

Rooney explained: "I have hit a lot in my career and I don't think I have missed as many as I have against Ryan Esson so with him on the bench I knew he would be telling Dean Brill where I would be going, so I decided to go down the middle. There was a lot of pressure but I was delighted to score the winning penalty. We practised penalties that week in training. The manager has been on to us to make sure we all had a penalty in mind that we would hit."

Keeper Langfield couldn't watch. He collapsed to the ground in a flood of tears when he saw the Red Army rise to celebrate.

"I didn't watch any of the penalties," the Aberdeen No. 1 insisted. "That's just something I do. But by all accounts the boys took them well so I was delighted about that. The boys weren't going to miss the way they were taking their penalties."

It meant even more to Langfield as just a couple of years earlier there was a real fear that a seizure threatened not only his professional career but also his life. He battled bravely back when other lesser characters would have thrown in the towel never mind bounced back and picked up the biggest prize of their career. Langfield and his defence had more than played their part in the League Cup win – going all the way without losing a goal which was a tremendous feat in itself.

An emotional Langfield said: "I was down on my knees as the emotion just came through. I've had a massive two and a half years since my illness and this is what I dreamed of getting back to. I wanted a level of consistency playing but to go on to win a cup was just something else. That was for my wife and my two kids who have put up with me the last couple of years. They've really helped me through. So I just got all emotional as I knew how they would be feeling. I knew they would probably be crying and I just got caught up in the moment."

There were few people who could begrudge Langfield his moment of glory.

"I'd gone from nearly dying two and a half years ago to winning a cup with a team at Parkhead with a team I love and I had wanted to be part of," he emotionally claimed. "For me, that's an incredible thing. I was 34 and these things don't normally come round. It was great to do it. I was so thrilled and don't think I'll get over it."

The Aberdeen players had stood side-by-side, arm-in-arm on the halfway line throughout the penalty shoot-out. But that broke as Rooney's penalty hit the net and the elated Aberdeen players charged to savour the moment with their penalty king and rejoicing fans.

Substituted Andrew Considine admitted: "Probably the one image that sticks out is just Adam scoring the penalty and seeing the place erupt, everyone sprinting over to celebrate. It was incredible."

Goal hero Rooney's glory was also couched by the disappointment that surrounded his former club and team-mates.

He admitted: "It wasn't nice to run and celebrate in front of them but, at the same time, it was an unbelievable achievement for Aberdeen to win their first trophy in many years. It was a great occasion. I spoke to a couple of them in the dressing room after the game. I'm still really good friends with Richie Foran and Ryan Esson. There is a lot of good staff at Inverness. A few I hadn't seen for a couple of years. A lot of good people are involved with that club and I really enjoyed my time there. I think it really helped me progress in my career and it is a great achievement for them to get to a final. It was slightly easier saying that when we had gone on and won it."

Delighted Derek McInnes blew a kiss to his family in the Main Stand before he went to shake hands with John Hughes before the celebrations really kicked in. He took a bow with the team and did the customary on-pitch interviews for which he had officials frantically searching about for an official AFC tie!

The one minor consolation for Inverness was that the man of the match award had been awarded to their midfielder Ross Draper but the main prize was heading for Pittodrie. The stage was set for Russell Anderson to go up and collect the cup but before he did he paid tribute to his Aberdeen team-mates who had held their nerve to deliver in the shoot-out.

Anderson admitted: "The players taking the kicks were incredible and Jamie played his part." The win was met with the same jubilation in the stands amongst the club's fans and staff. I went up and got the cup although I had to wait to get my medal. I got it later on because one of the staff had picked it up for me. The cup, however, was more than enough. I just wish I could have bottled up the feeling I had when I lifted the cup. It was without doubt the sweetest moment of my career. I, like everyone else at the club, had waited a long time for that. It's been a long time coming."

When asked if that was manager Derek McInnes's crowning moment as manager, he passionately replied: "Yes, because I've got so many good staff behind me at this club. I've got a good board, a brilliant chairman and our fans have had a lot to endure over the years and not a lot of pleasure in the cup.

"The fans have been with us through thick and thin and it was brilliant to deliver this trophy for them."

It was Stewart Milne's first trophy as chairman and he let emotions get the better of him, when, on national radio, he said: "19 years, 120 minutes then f**kin' penalties." Milne later said: "I had my head in my hands (at the penalties) when they scored and my own head was up in the air when we scored. It is a bit ironic we got through the first round (Alloa) with six perfect penalties at Pittodrie. Derek McInnes has got great confidence in the players. They worked hard and practised their penalties during the week and I was pretty confident our boys would score – I was certainly praying they would score."

Mark Reynolds was just delighted the cup final had ended the way he had hoped. "It was amazing," he admitted. "It was my first cup final and to win it was amazing. To lift the cup with this Aberdeen team is something

I will never forget. It has been the biggest game of my career and was one of the reasons why I signed for this club because I believed we could have success here. You walk around Pittodrie and there are pictures all over the walls of the famous teams of the past and now to have our team up there alongside some of those famous names and teams is amazing."

The Dons and their fans partied all night with the main A90 road nose-to-tail with supporters making their way back north, although their journey back to Perth would have been far easier than that of their heartbroken Inverness rivals. The Aberdeen team had a party to attend back at the Marcliffe at Pitfodels Hotel that delighted chairman Stewart Milne had put on for all the club's employees. The team managed to get there before a lot of the staff after their coach driver had gone via the Forth Road Bridge to break the back of most of the traffic. It was a time to be cherished.

Assistant boss Tony Docherty admitted: "It was better than anything I could have ever imagined. From the celebrations on the pitch to the bus journey and getting back to Aberdeen, everything was totally amazing. We were on the bus back to Aberdeen longer than we had anticipated, but it was great because it allowed all the players and staff to really celebrate what we had achieved in winning the League Cup. Everybody was involved, even the players who had missed out because it is very much a team affair at Aberdeen. It was a massive celebration and we had a right good old sing song all the way up the road. 'Peter Pawlett baby' was up there along with the Jonny Hayes song. It was a great experience to see the boys celebrate because they worked so hard to win this cup. Jim Leighton said that bus journey back was probably his best experience in football. Coming from somebody of Jim's stature and what he has achieved in the game, that says a lot."

The win and celebration also helped to numb some of the personal pain, especially of Jonny Hayes who was still in agony after his dislocated shoulder.

"It was quite sore and I had to be careful," he admitted with more than a wry smile.

"I had the doctor and the physios Dave Wylie and John Sharp man-marking me after the game, trying to make sure I didn't over-celebrate."

Peter Pawlett may have missed the game but manager Derek McInnes acknowledged the part he played in the run and gave him a medal.

"It was a huge disappointment not to play but it was a great day for the club," Pawlett confessed. "I would love to live that moment again myself where I help Aberdeen to win a trophy. I did get a medal, the manager told me he would get me one. I have actually put it away. I know I played a big part in helping the team get to the final but I want one where I have played in the final and I feel I have contributed to the triumph. That would mean a lot more to me."

There were quite a few hangovers to be had but after 19 years who could blame anyone connected with Aberdeen Football Club.

There were more celebrations to come as the returning heroes were awarded a civic reception and took the League Cup on a long overdue cup parade down Union Street, where more than 70,000 Aberdeen fans took to the streets in a sea of red and white.

Hometown boy Ryan Jack admitted: "It was some feeling walking out there in front of so many fans. It had the hairs on the back of the neck standing up.

"After lifting the cup that was another amazing experience. It is nothing like I have every experienced before. To come down Union Street with the lads on the bus was amazing and just some feeling.

"I was still quite young and to get the chance to savour something like this was absolutely brilliant. My family and friends were there and a few of my friends were also out on the streets so it is good for them. A few of my pals are Aberdeen fans and it means a lot to them as well."

It was the same for another north-east loon. Inverurie's Barry Robson insisted: "It just shows you the size and stature of the football club. Those people have waited a very long time for this and you can see what it means to them. We're happy for them.

"I remember watching the great teams in the past doing this – the great players like Willie Miller, Alex McLeish and Gordon Strachan. It's such a great feeling to be doing it as well as part of this great club. It means a lot to me personally, especially at my age and at this stage of my career."

Full-back Shay Logan had only been at Aberdeen a matter of months. He had been at Manchester City but reckons those celebrations topped everything he had ever done in the game.

"My time at Aberdeen is certainly up there with some of the best times in my career," the Mancunian insisted.

When we won the cup, I had never experienced anything like that. That is definitely my high in football.

I played in the Premiership and everyone wants to do that but to win that cup and have the success and going down Union Street on the bus was what dreams are made of."

It was a special affair for the players, management and chairman as they took the cup out on to the balcony to take a bow in front of their adoring public.

One-handed Jonny Hayes jokingly tweeted: "What a day!! Almost s**t myself when I nearly dropped the cup from that balcony!"

Jamie Langfield had witnessed the good and bad times and knew that first trophy was worth the wait.

Langfield admitted: "I probably thought even on the day of the final that I wasn't ever going to win anything at Aberdeen. There was so much expectation at the club and the amount of fans at Celtic Park and then in Aberdeen shows why there is so much expectation."

Aberdeen were League Cup champions and their fans also helped bring further chart success to the Human League. That weekend confirmed that 'Don't You Want Me', with the help of a certain Peter Pawlett, had been the top-selling single in Scotland that week – as well as breaking back into the UK Top 40.

That led to the delighted band releasing another statement. Which read: "For us to be waking up this morning to find 'Don't You Want Me' at number 5 on the iTunes singles chart was absolutely amazing and has to rank as one of the biggest surprises of our career to date, which after over 35 years in the music business is really saying something. We are slightly stunned but at the same time very honoured that the fans of Aberdeen FC have chosen our song as their anthem to Peter Pawlett and their achievement in getting it so high in the charts in the space of just one day is a real testament to both their dedication to their club and to this player in particular. Speaking as a band who have always enjoyed a deeply loyal and enthusiastic fan base of our own we know just how important the fans really are and what a difference they can make."

The Dons had finally ended their silverware drought but hero Considine knows that a DVD of the cup final was never going to be as much a best-seller despite the result.

Considine, who followed in the footsteps of his dad, Doug, to deliver success for Aberdeen, admitted: "I have never actually watched the final again. Let's be honest, it wasn't the greatest game! I have seen Adam's penalty and the celebrations. Everything else is still registered in my head.

You can show people as many DVDs as you want but I remember it all. On the pitch after the game, on the bus going up the road to Aberdeen, spending time with my family that night, it was something special."

Proud chairman Stewart Milne was in no doubt that this was the start rather than the climax of success for the dandy Dons.

"I've dreamed of this for Aberdeen and know I'm very privileged to be in this position," the chairman beamed.

"Winning trophies breathes a new energy into a football club and we have to make sure we harness that energy as best we can.

"There is nobody more conscious than me that we have underachieved in the last 19 years.

"But we have to put that behind us now and look towards a great future for the club.

"We have a lot of people committed to driving this club forward."

Ambitious Derek McInnes was also determined the League Cup was going to be a taste of things to come.

"Winning the trophy at Celtic Park was a day that few of us will forget and it was certainly one of the greatest moments in my career when Russell (Anderson) lifted the trophy," he insisted. "Winning a first trophy is always so important for any team because it gives you confidence that you can do it, but the difference between good teams and those who become a little bit more is that with winning one trophy it becomes an appetite and a hunger to go on and win more in the future."

The team certainly finished the 2013/14 campaign strongly, making the semi-finals of the Scottish Cup and finishing third in the Premiership – although they could have finished best of the rest had it not been for a late controversial goal by Motherwell on the final day at Pittodrie.

Yet, looking back it was still a season to remember for Aberdeen. They had won a trophy, booked their return to Europe and that success had seen Derek McInnes rewarded with a double of his own, the Professional Footballers' Association and the Scottish Football Writers' Association's manager of the year awards. Not bad for his first full season in charge!

ABERDEEN'S LEAGUE CUP-WINNING RUN

SECOND ROUND (27 August 2013 at Pittodrie)

ABERDEEN 0 ALLOA 0 (0-0 after extra time – ABERDEEN win 6-5 on penalties)

THIRD ROUND (25 September 2013 at Falkirk Stadium)

FALKIRK 0 ABERDEEN 5

QUARTER-FINAL (30 October 2013 at Fir Park)

MOTHERWELL 0 ABERDEEN 2

SEMI-FINAL (1 February 2014 at Tynecastle)

ABERDEEN 4 ST JOHNSTONE 0

LEAGUE CUP FINAL (16 March 2014 at Celtic Park)

ABERDEEN 0 INVERNESS 0 (after extra time, Aberdeen win 4-2 on penalties)

ABERDEEN'S LEAGUE CUP-WINNING SQUAD

Jamie Langfield, Shay Logan, Mark Reynolds, Russell Anderson, Andrew Considine, Ryan Jack, Willo Flood, Barry Robson, Niall McGinn, Jonny Hayes, Cammy Smith, Nicky Low, Adam Rooney, Joe Shaughnessy, Clark Robertson, Craig Storrie, Michael Hector, Alan Tate, Josh Magennis, Gregg Wylde, Nicky Weaver and Calvin Zola.

Manager: Derek McInnes.

26

• St JOHNSTONE •
History That Was 130 Years In The Making!

IF PATIENCE is a virtue then it is something every long-suffering St Johnstone fan could have claimed to have had in abundance. The Perth side have a proud and esteemed history. They, like most other provincial clubs, have had their ups and downs, relegations and promotions, but the one thing that had always frustratingly, eluded them was one of Scottish football's major cups.

They had won the current Championship, in its previous guises of the First and Second Divisions, on seven previous separate occasions, starting back in 1923/24 up to 2008/09 when Derek McInnes led the club back into Scotland's top flight. You could also throw in a Challenge Cup triumph the season before that but there was always one thing missing from the McDiarmid Park or Muirton Park roll of honour. The big one! The one major trophy that would allow Saints to finally step out of the shadows of their Tayside rivals Dundee and Dundee United and give them the last laugh on the rival fans who had mercilessly goaded them over that lack of success for decades.

There may even have been a distinct possibility that Saints fans feared they might never see their team or their heroes deliver them their Holy Grail, especially when you consider the likes of Third Lanark, Renton, St

Bernard's and Vale of Leven have all been and gone but are assured their names remain engrained in the history books as Scottish Cup winners.

It is hard to believe that Saints have put together so many top teams and produced so many top players throughout their first 130 years. Their golden generation was very much seen in the late 1960s and early 70s when the legendary Willie Ormond was in charge.

Saints were an established top-flight side until they were relegated from the newly-formed Premier League in 1975 and from there the club hit the skids. It took the intervention of local businessman Geoff Brown back in 1986, when the club was at its lowest ebb, to breathe new life into a club that had started to look like a lost cause.

Chairman Steve Brown, who has taken over the club from his dad, Geoff, admitted: "My dad bought the club and a couple of weeks later a few of my pals said to me: 'What is your father thinking about buying St Johnstone? They are a lost cause.' I didn't even know he had done it and I was totally taken aback. He was born and bred in Perth and I just don't think he wanted to see the club go to the wall and at that time I don't think he would have envisaged the team lifting the Scottish Cup. I know he only took over the club to safeguard it for the sake of Perth."

Construction magnate Brown came in, sorted the finances and set up the club to live within its means. Saints began to rise thanks to those solid foundations. They won promotion back to the top flight under Alex Totten and then bounced back again under Paul Sturrock. Sandy Clark then took them on and led Saints to third spot and a League Cup Final, followed by glory European ties against the like of Monaco and Vaasa.

It was always going to be hard to maintain those hefty heights and Clark stepped down before the team faced the heartache of relegation. There were several painful seasons in the First Division before St Johnstone finally re-established themselves as a top Premiership outfit.

Owen Coyle laid the foundations before Derek McInnes stepped in to lead them back into the top flight before he was eventually headhunted for a thankless spell in charge of struggling then-Championship outfit Bristol City. His good work at McDiarmid Park was then taken over by colourful Northern Irishman Steve Lomas, who led the team back into Europe after a top three finish. Lomas was assisted by his fellow countryman Tommy Wright.

The pair had played together with Northern Ireland and had strengthened that bond when Wright, who had managed Limavady

United, Ballymena United and Lisburn Distillery, helped the former West Ham United and Manchester City midfielder Lomas with some inside information when it came to his television summarising of the Northern Irish league.

Lomas turned to Wright when he was given his first management job by Saints. It came as no surprise when Lomas was also headhunted. The one thing that did raise a few eyebrows was Lomas's next destination – Millwall – the bitter rivals of his ex-team West Ham United. Lomas was also well aware of Wright's contribution to his team and tried to persuade him to join him at the New Den.

Wright had serious reservations and decided against the move and threw his hat in the ring to take over the top job at McDiarmid.

Wright recalled: "Steve decided to go to Millwall but I didn't think it was the right move for him. If I didn't think it was the right move for him then it definitely wasn't the right move for me. It left me in limbo because I didn't know if I was still going to have a job at St Johnstone. The chairman then said to me: 'What are we going to do now?' and I said: 'Well, I want to apply for it and I think you should give me the job.' The chairman knew me and didn't even interview me. He thought about things for a couple of days and then gave me the job. Steve (Lomas) and the chairman had a few run-ins and a lot of the time I was a buffer in between them. I think he had been impressed with the way I had handled things and worked with the players."

Wright took up that post in June 2013. He had the complete respect of the Saints dressing room and he only went on to cement that when he named club legend Callum Davidson as his No. 2. The ex-Scottish international defender had decided to hang up his boots after a second spell at McDiarmid Park and was given his first step on to the coaching ladder, with talented youth coach Alec Cleland making up the new-look management team.

Mannus said: "It was good to see Tommy stepping up because it was the same team we had worked with before apart from Steve Lomas. I liked Steve and he did well for us but it was good that there was a bit of continuity because Tommy had been his No. 2. The only thing for me was that Tommy was an ex-goalkeeper. So when he told me to do something I couldn't really argue with him, especially when it came to goalkeeping."

Wright had very little left in the bank to strengthen his squad although he was able to bring in Gary McDonald on a free transfer from Oldham Athletic, lifelong Saints fans David Wotherspoon from Hibs, back-up keeper Steve Banks from Dundee United and Brian Easton and Rory Fallon after their releases, from Dundee and Aberdeen respectively.

Shaggy-haired striker Stevie May had spent most of the previous season on loan with Hamilton Accies in the Championship. He had netted an impressive 26 goals and that came on the back of a similar spell with Alloa Athletic. He was given his big chance by Wright.

Wright was given very little time to find his feet as their Europa League campaign kicked off before the domestic campaign had started. Saints were keen to extend their adventure beyond the opening round they got against Turkish side Eskisehirspor the previous season. Their cause wasn't helped as they went into the second qualifying round unseeded. The draw was far from kind as they were paired with Norwegian giants Rosenborg, who had regularly graced the Champions League group and knockout stages during the 2000s.

Experienced defender Frazer Wright was the hero as his 19th-minute goal was enough to beat Rosenborg away and a 1-1 draw at McDiarmid Park handed the Saints take a famous scalp. That paired them with unfancied Minsk. Saints won away thanks to a Steve McLean goal but lost by the same margin in Perth and were left crushed when the time-wasting Belarusians went through on penalties.

St Johnstone keeper Alan Mannus admitted: "The Rosenborg games really kicked us off. They got us going and rather than playing friendlies in and around the United Kingdom we were playing competitive European football against top teams. We took a fair bit of confidence from beating Rosenborg and we really kicked on and it ended up being one of the most successful seasons in St Johnstone's history."

The team bounced back from their Europa League exit and continued to build on the domestic success they had, establishing themselves as a top-six outfit. They continued to progress in the League Cup and the end of November saw them open up their Scottish Cup campaign at home to Livingston.

Wright had found himself short of defensive options and Sanel Jahic, a Bosnian international, came in from Turkish side Karabukspor. His Saints career was short and sweet although he did grab his only goal for them away to Livingston. Stevie May sent them on their way with a first half goal and Jahic clinched the 2-0 win after the break.

Captain Dave Mackay said: "We started off against my old team and I don't think we were in much trouble, especially after we went ahead."

Manager Tommy Wright saw the tie as more of a challenge.

Wright claimed: "Looking back, the Livingston match was probably our poorest performance of our run but we managed to get the job done."

That put them into the fifth round which brought a trip to Angus to take on Forfar Athletic at Station Park on 2 December. It had potential banana skin written all over it.

Wright, however, had boosted his squad, bringing in Tim Clancy from Hibs, Michael O'Halloran from Bolton and Scott Brown from Bradford City, James Dunne on loan from Stevenage and veteran Scotland cap Chris Iwelumo in from Scunthorpe.

Forfar's colourful veteran boss Dick Campbell is never shy to fire up his players and the Loons had also been going well in League One and there was the added complication of Forfar's artificial surface.

There were to be no such concerns as Saints eased through. Lee Croft and Frazer Wright sent them on their way with first half goals before Michael O'Halloran and new loan signing James Dunne completed the 4-0 win.

Goal hero Frazer Wright recalled: "I remember the early tie we had at Forfar. It was on their plastic pitch and the bizarre thing was it also seemed like we were playing with a plastic ball that night. It was flying all over the place and seemed a lot lighter than our usual match balls. I got one of the goals and what I remember was we put on a very professional performance and deserved to progress."

Dunne said: "I hadn't been playing at Stevenage so I had seen it as a good opportunity to go out and get games at a good level. My first game for St Johnstone was at Forfar. I came on after 20 minutes and managed to get the final goal of the game so it was a decent debut."

Fellow goal hero Lee Croft added: "I scored and set up a couple of goals although that was the first time I had played a top-team game on Astroturf for years."

The rest of the competition was given a timely boost as Aberdeen sprung a surprise by knocking out holders Celtic at the same stage. Saints were drawn against Championship side Raith Rovers at Starks Park. Boss Tommy Wright knew it was a sticky tie as Raith had shocked Hibs in the previous round.

Wright warned: "We were in the quarter-final and we were away to

Raith. We began to think this could be a great opportunity for us. We had emphasised the point they had already beaten Hibs and I think that helped us focus the players so they would get the job done rather than thinking they already had one foot in the semi-final."

The tie also saw Saints come up against an old familiar face in Kevin Moon, who had left McDiarmid Park that summer for a move to Kirkcaldy.

Lee Croft said: "I remember I had a good bit of banter with Kevin Moon in the build-up. He was telling us there was a good chance of an upset but I kept telling him no chance."

Luckily for Croft and Saints it proved to be the case, albeit after a minor scare. A Gary McDonald goal gave the visitors the lead in testing, windy conditions before Raith equalised thanks to a long-range screamer from Joe Cardle in front of Sky's television cameras.

Mannus admitted: "I kept a clean sheet against Livingston and then Stevie Banks kept a clean sheet against Forfar before we finally lost a goal at Raith Rovers. The boy hit it from some distance to beat me in pretty windy conditions and it went in off the post."

The first-half performance left manager Tommy Wright far from pleased and he read the riot act to his team in the away dressing room at half-time.

Striker Steven MacLean, who had just come back from several months out injured, revealed: "My first game in the competition was against Raith Rovers. They gave us a good game and were, probably, the better side but we went ahead through Gary McDonald but they equalised through Joe Cardle and what a goal it was. We went in level at half-time and the gaffer absolutely roasted us. It turned out to be the best thing that happened to us. We came out and we were exceptional."

Wright's blast had the desired effect as a moment of magic from the enigmatic Nigel Hasselbaink put Saints ahead. Long-serving midfielder Chris Millar admitted the Dutchman, a cousin of Jimmy Floyd Hasselbaink, saved the team and himself just in time.

Millar explained: "I was on the bench against Raith and I remember Nigel Hasselbaink was away to get the hook because he wasn't playing well. The gaffer was going mental at him and then told one of the striking subs to go and get warmed up because he was going on for him. Nigel then picked the ball up, played a one-two and stuck the ball into the net."

Captain Dave Mackay also hadn't been shy in letting Hasselbaink know he hadn't been up to scratch prior to that.

"Nigel scored a great goal," Mackay confessed. "I remember winding him up by saying the manager did well to put you on at half-time. I had been winding him up because he had been having a nightmare but then he produced a bit of magic, which he is always capable of doing."

The game was then sealed by a Steve Anderson goal which could hardly have been described as textbook.

Anderson recalled: "I remember Lee Croft took a corner and he shanked it. I just ran to the front post and swung a leg at it. I got lucky and it flew in."

That saw St Johnstone join Dundee United, Rangers and Aberdeen make up the semi-final draw. Saints were paired with Aberdeen and that would have been enough to send a shiver down the spine of most St Johnstone fans. The Dons had been transformed into Scotland's second force by former St Johnstone boss Derek McInnes. They had been Celtic's main challengers and rather clinically disposed of the Perth side 4-0 in the semi-finals at Tynecastle on their way to lifting the 2014 League Cup. The afternoon was a hard lesson for every Saints player and especially Stevie May who had been mercilessly taunted by the gloating Aberdeen fans who had chanted: "Who the f*** is Stevie May!"

"When the draw came out there were a few moans and groans that it was Aberdeen," Wright admitted. "They had done us over in the League Cup. A lot of people disagreed with me but looking back at that game they had been superb on the counter-attack. We had opportunities in that game ourselves but we never took them. There was also something about Aberdeen because we felt we were due to beat them."

Wright is the first to admit he is superstitious and one of the team's lucky mascots during that campaign was Steven MacLean's son.

He confirmed: "My son, Luke, would come in and train with the team occasionally when he had a day off school and he trained with the team in Perth before we headed off to finish our preparations at Celtic's training ground at Lennoxtown."

The move to train at Celtic's headquarters the day before the game didn't prove lucky for everyone.

Former Manchester City winger Lee Croft painfully recalled: "We went to Lennoxtown and I pulled my hamstring. I had felt it earlier in the week but I thought it would be okay. I had got a lot of work done on it. I was due to start in the game and we had a small-sided game and it just felt as if I had been shot in the leg. I was in denial and even when we got back to the hotel I was trying to declare myself fit but it took five or six weeks to get it right."

Stevie May's preparations were far from ideal either – although not as bad as that of Clancy – as he bunked with Nigel Hasselbaink at their Crutherland House base at East Kilbride.

May joked: "I was rooming with Nigel and it was a nightmare. I have never heard anyone snore as loud or as much in all my life. I am normally a good sleeper but Nigel sounded like a lawnmower. I tried to get to sleep but he was just so loud. I even went into the bathroom and tried to sleep in the bath with my covers and towels over my ears but I could still hear him. In the end I had to go down to Paddy Cregg's door and I slept on his floor."

It took St Johnstone just as long to awake from their own semi-final slumber at Ibrox, as Aberdeen went in ahead, thanks to Niall McGinn's 15th-minute goal.

Manager Wright said: "Aberdeen had the upper hand. We were 1-0 down and they had a good chance to go 2-0 up before Stevie May had a chance but they went into half-time ahead. They changed their shape and that allowed us to change our shape and that helped us get more control of the ball. The main theme of my half-time team talk was this team has come so far we can't let it slip now. 'You need to go out and give every last effort.'"

The players quickly put to bed any claims that their team always froze when they got to the semi-finals.

Stevie MacLean said: "Everyone talks about the final but I played better in the semi-final than I actually did in the final. Aberdeen went 1-0 up and their players and crowd all thought they were going to turn us over like they did in the League Cup. The gaffer tweaked the team and played Stevie May in off the left. We had a chat at half-time and everyone goes on about how I said a few things in the dressing room. I did but I probably say things every week. I just talked about how these opportunities don't come around often and come the end of May we didn't want to be on the beach when we could have been in a cup final. St Johnstone were notorious for getting beat in semi-finals and I basically said come on let's not be known as bottle merchants all our lives."

It worked as Alan Mannus denied Adam Rooney before Stevie May took centre stage, as he did for most of that glory campaign.

May recalled: "I remember when they scored thinking to myself, not again! Just because they had given us a going over in the League Cup. I got moved out to the left-hand side for a bit of the game. James Dunne was on the edge of the box and put it in. I remember I took it over my shoulder and fired low and hard past Jamie Langfield. After we scored it looked like two different teams as we were on top and they looked like they were beat. I scored the winner. It came from a diagonal. I managed to get up and win the first ball and got it to Stevie MacLean who held it up and he laid it back for me to toe poke into the net. I had never scored a toe poke before but that was the only way I was getting my shot away. That feeling I had when it hit the net was probably the best I have ever had. I knew how much it meant to our fans."

It sparked wild celebrations and even more when St Johnstone saw the game out. May was also delighted to have the last laugh on the same Red Army who had a go at him back in the League Cup semis.

May recalled: "The League Cup semi was a very bad day. We got beat and I got a bit of stick. I was used to it as a goalscorer but it did motivate me for the Scottish Cup semi-final to beat Aberdeen. To beat them and to score the goals meant everything turned out perfectly."

Delighted Stevie Anderson was relieved to finally bury their semi-final blues.

The defender confirmed: "It was about time we had won a semi-final. I had been beaten that many times that it was getting ridiculous. I was beginning to get frustrated and I was thinking will I ever get over the line. So when we got there it was just a major relief."

Keeper Alan Mannus had been one of the heroes and he knew they had stunned Aberdeen.

"We love being up against it, defending and doing what we have to do to get a result," the Irishman insisted. "People would class it as a typical St Johnstone performance, where we just dig out results. I remember after the game the faces on the Aberdeen players, they couldn't believe we had beaten them. They were pretty devastated while we were all jumping for joy."

MacLean admitted the League Cup semi-final had been a major motivation.

MacLean claimed: "When we got the equaliser we knew and felt there was only going to be one winner. To beat Aberdeen was unbelievable. It was also bittersweet because they had hammered us in the semi-final and thought they would just turn up and hammer us again. People will say we were out for revenge but it was more professional pride with us going out to show that a hammering like that wasn't going to happen again. The gaffer also got in on the act and told us their fans hadn't sold out because they were keeping their money for the final and had booked their buses and hotels. It was all mind games but there is no doubt it gave us a little more motivation."

It was a big one for Steven Anderson against a management team, Derek McInnes and Tony Docherty, that had been a major influence on his St Johnstone career.

Anderson said: "You always want to get one over your old manager. Del is a great manager but I was desperate to beat him and Doc. We always wanted to rectify the League Cup semi-final defeat. Del and Doc aren't great losers but I suppose nobody is but Doc text me the next day to congratulate me and telling us to go on and win the cup. I used to clean Del's boots at Dundee United while Doc was my youth coach so I always had a good rapport with them and that continued when they came to St Johnstone. They were both great for me in my career."

It was also an even bigger day for another Saints star, Chris Millar. It helped him bring joy to thousands of St Johnstone fans but one very close to his hearts.

Millar said: "It was unbelievable. We deserved to win the game and it was great for me because our family had been going through a wee bit of a hard time. My dad, Ian, suffered from depression and that was a bad year for him. So it meant a lot to me knowing he was there and he had a great day watching the semi-final. I went up to see him at the hospitality, gave him a big hug and told him that was for him. It made him feel special."

Delighted manager Wright knew the enormity of what his squad had achieved.

"We beat, arguably, one of the best teams in the country," Wright said. "Aberdeen had won the League Cup and ended up finishing second in the league. People say you need the luck of the draw and you could argue we got that in the early rounds but we proved what a good team we were beating a team of Aberdeen's undoubted quality and calibre."

It meant a Tayside derby final as Dundee United had dumped Rangers on their own patch to book their slot 24 hours earlier.

St Johnstone went on before that to clinch another top six finish but both cup finalists had missed out on European football via the league and knew to qualify for the Europa League they had to lift the Scottish Cup.

Saints took the foot off the gas as they started to look towards the final as they lost their final league game 2-0 away to Inverness. That defeat left a few players sweating on their cup final places due to poor displays and injury.

Keeper Alan Mannus said: "I got a dead leg against Inverness and I couldn't really train. I didn't actually train the week of the final until the Thursday, when I started to do stuff again. Then on the Friday was when I first trained properly, in terms of diving and going full out. There was no danger of me missing the game although I just had to be patient for the muscles and leg to heal."

The spotlight was now on St Johnstone and it was a whole new ball game for some.

James Dunne said: "It was something new for me with all the media coverage we got. I was used to speaking to the local newspaper at most of my clubs but up in Scotland we had all the national papers interviewing people and even asking guys to do a daily cup final diary."

Tommy Wright knew the importance of getting his boys away from it all and he organised a getaway at the Dunkeld Hilton where his squad stayed at the start of cup final week. They took in the great outdoors and generally got to let off steam.

The Sunday night they were allowed to have a few beers as Wright headed down to Glasgow with his assistant, Callum Davidson, and chairman Steve Brown to watch young Stevie May pick up the Scottish Football Writers' Association's young player of the year award at their annual dinner in Glasgow.

MacLean said: "The gaffer told us we could have a couple of pints back at the hotel. Ten or 12 pints later Alec Cleland came down and told us we needed to go to our beds. We told him we weren't going and then he told us if we didn't get to our beds he was going to tell the gaffer. He threatened to get us all binned for the final and that was enough to get us all to our beds. It certainly relaxed us and got the Inverness game out of the system."

May was delighted to have been the toast of the football writers that same night.

"It was a good night," May admitted. "I was nervous about doing the speech but it was a good night to win such an award. The season had gone as well as I could have hoped. I scored a lot of goals but I couldn't have done it without my St Johnstone team-mates. They deserved the trophy as much as me."

That certainly blew away the cobwebs as the Saints players continued their build-up with some clay pigeon shooting and cycling that saw Wright come in for some hefty stick via the cup final diaries of Stevie MacLean, Lee Croft and Chris Millar, which appeared in various national newspapers.

MacLean in the *Daily Express* likened his boss to Bradley Wiggins as he only got halfway up a hill with his bike after a heavy breakfast.

MacLean got an earful from Wright. He admitted: "The gaffer phoned me after he read it in the paper. He came on and said: 'You didn't need to exaggerate it – I did get halfway up the hill and I never had a fry-up. I just had toast and beans!'"

Wright also claimed that story had been more than embellished and one of his own staff had come off far worse than him on the biking front.

The manager said: "They are always quick to tell stories about other people. I have asthma and Alec Cleland and Callum Davidson are a lot fitter than me. Anyway, who starts a bike ride up a hill? If you listen to the boys now I only got 30 yards up the hill even though I had gone about half a mile when my asthma really kicked in and I felt my chest. I turned back and went along the river instead, where it was a lot flatter. My players took a bit of journalistic licence with that one. Alec Cleland, though, was lucky he wasn't seriously hurt coming down the other side of the big hill. All in all it was a good break and just what we needed."

Stevie Anderson had more pressing matters and was given special permission to come away from their cup final hideaway.

Anderson said: "I had to come down because my wife, Sarah, had a scan for our first child, Fraya. I went down and then had to come back up. Going away and the way we did it, I had to say it left me feeling pretty relaxed throughout the build-up."

Wright gave his players some time off before they returned although it turned out to be a nightmare for defender Tim Clancy, as he ruptured his Achilles in training.

Clancy explained: "We had just finished a forwards versus defenders session and were about to go into a game. I flicked a ball up, took it on my chest and then took a step back and it just felt like somebody had kicked me from behind. I just fell to the ground and I was in real pain. I remember I asked Dave Mackay did somebody hit me with a ball? He said 'No' and that was when I knew my Achilles had gone."

Wright confirmed that Clancy would definitely have been on the bench had it not been for the injury.

"It was really disappointing because Tim had done really well for us since he arrived and was an important member of the squad," the manager acknowledged. "It is so disappointing for anybody to miss out on a cup final but in those circumstances, so late in the day, was devastating."

Clancy certainly didn't have the luck of the Irish as it was the second Scottish Cup Final in a row he missed. He had to watch Hibs lose to Celtic the previous season because of a groin problem.

Clancy: "I was devastated about missing the cup final, especially as it had happened two seasons in a row. I was actually more concerned about my long-term future when it happened. I was out of contract and I knew I was knackered although I had to put it into perspective. There were people being killed and dying all over the world – so my injury wasn't world-ending!"

The defender missed the game along with injured duo Tam Scobbie and midfielder Murray Davidson.

Wright addressed the press at Scone Palace – ironically the home of the Stone of Destiny – where he confirmed Clancy would miss out.

It was there he played his ace card, as he claimed Dundee United would take to the field without their star youngsters Ryan Gauld and John Souttar.

Wright explained: "I had told one of the local journalists up and I was getting bored with the press because I was doing that much and I was saying the same things all the time. So I decided to throw a spanner in the works and I set up a local journalist to ask me the question about Souttar and Gauld. In a way it was mind games but it was more a case of me just being bored but I knew by saying what I did that I might get under Dundee United's skin a little bit. I have since heard they delayed naming their team until the last minute as where I had named my team, apart from the subs, on the Friday night."

During that very press conference Steven MacLean called me during Wright's interview to do his cup final diary but luckily I had left my phone on vibrate.

A totally unaware MacLean said: "It is a pity it didn't ring because the gaffer is the biggest nightmare for that. He is always on the wind-up. If he knows they have a family meal or a night out then he tries to phone them just to annoy us."

The kind-hearted St Johnstone players also had other people in their thoughts in the build-up. They held a joint collection for St Johnstone stalwart Jocky Peebles as he battled bravely against illness and long-serving football administrator Paul Smith.

McLean revealed: "We had a wee collection just to say a wee thank you to Jocky, who hadn't been well and for Paul Smith, who had been at the club for years and does absolutely everything for us. Jocky is a legendary name at St Johnstone. When I first arrived he was like Mr St Johnstone. He did all the rubs and had been at the club over 27 years. These are the sorts of guys, as well as the kitman Tommy Campbell, who make any club."

Manager Tommy Wright and star man Stevie May were also in demand. Top scorer May saw fans sell t-shirts with his name and number on the back, May 17, which was also the date of the cup final. The striker also had more bizarre requests. He helped promote a specially commissioned Famous Grouse whisky that was launched to commemorate St Johnstone's cup final appearance.

May said: "We got a bottle of Famous Grouse which said May 17th – to celebrate St Johnstone getting to the final. We did a bit of promotional work for that and I still have a signed bottle. I also have a bottle of Old Perth whisky as well. The fans also wore the May 17 t-shirts. It was strange it fell on that day but it was kind of cool to see the fans latch on to that and make such a big thing. It was crazy."

The club put the finishing touches to their Scottish Cup Final preparations. More than 15,000 fans travelled from as far afield as Australia, America, North Korea and Canada to witness history in the making.

The players also had their own fan clubs to sort tickets for.

Some of Stevie MacLean's supporters had travelled halfway around the world to see him. He said: "My sister and her husband came back from Australia for the final. It was good because it was a surprise to most of the family. I needed to get something like 80 tickets because I had a bus coming up from Peebles."

Alan Mannus confirmed: "My then fiancée, now my wife Leeann, were across along with my mum and dad, Margaret and Davie."

James Dunne admitted: "My mum and dad were on holiday. My dad was trying to cancel it but my mum was having none of it. My cousins, my sister and some of my friends were up to support me, so that was good to have people close to me there."

Manager Tommy Wright was also keen to keep the routine as close to the semi-final as he could.

That included getting one of his player's sons off school for the day before he finished off their preparations at Celtic's Lennoxtown again.

Stevie MacLean explained: "The gaffer is superstitious and so he asked Luke to come back and train with us again before the final because it had worked in the semi-final. His mum had to write a letter to his school to get him off. We then went to Lennoxtown again the following day. There was work being done there and the pitch we were using wasn't even marked. We normally did set plays but the gaffer said we don't need to work on them. We know what works against Dundee United. 'We will get Ando round the back and he will score a header!' We also had a great record against United and so we went into the game confident."

Wright also demanded the same room at their pre-match base at East Kilbride's Crutherland House that he had used in the semi-final.

Assistant boss Callum Davidson also experienced first-hand the extent of Wright's superstitions.

Davidson revealed: "The gaffer did say our name was on the cup. But I never believed him because you have to work hard to get whatever you can in football and life. The manager is also unbelievably superstitious. Even when he turns his car stereo up it has to be on an even number and he does so many other things. He is unbelievable but he has been a massive help to my coaching career, along with Alec Cleland."

There were also more unusual routines amongst some of his players, in particular Stevie MacLean and Chris Millar.

MacLean joked: "I think the manager just put me in with the wee man to calm him down because he is absolutely hyper. I also had to shave his back before both games. He first asked me before the semi-final. I just looked at him because I thought he was joking but he was being deadly serious. I then said wee man if it makes you play well then I will do it! He gave me his electric shaver but it was a lawnmower I needed. He has the hairiest back ever – I don't know how his wife puts up with it."

Saints boss Tommy Wright also tried to calm nerves by naming his starting XI at the team hotel and then he named his substitutes on the morning of the game. It saw young Scott Brown left out and a frustrated Lee Croft left on the bench.

Croft recalled: "I missed a lot of football but I managed to get back for the final few weeks. During that time Michael O'Halloran had come in and done really well. The manager said it was a toss-up between me and him but he went for Michael because he had been doing well. The manager named the team the night before the game. I went to see him that night and I might have asked him why wasn't I playing? I felt better after I came out because he had told me that I still needed to be ready because I could still be involved off the bench."

An emotional Millar also had MacLean to thank for getting him back on track the morning of the game.

Millar said: "I got a text through from my mum and dad, my wife, brothers and all my family. I just had tears because they were all wishing me well and saying how proud they were of me. It was a massive deal for me because I was in a cup final and I wanted to win something. I have won the Third to First Division but to win a national trophy was something I always wanted to do. Macca told me not to peak too early. His words reassured me."

Other players also took some last-minute advice off more experienced heads.

Steven Anderson admitted: "I am an early riser and I got up early for breakfast and left Cup-tie (Dave Mackay) sleeping. I went down and there were a few coaches there, including Alec Cleland. He spoke to me and he said to me: 'Savour this day because they don't come around too often.' He was right because some boys don't even get the chance to play in a final."

Tommy Wright was glad when he finally stepped on the bus for destination: Celtic Park.

He claimed: "I was relieved to actually get on the bus to head to Glasgow because there was that much going on with the media commitments and I was organising everything from suits to shoes and what we were going to do after the game."

There was to be one more pre-planned stop before they finally reached their east end of Glasgow destination.

"I am more than a little superstitious," Wright insisted. "In the build-up to the semi-final we should have counted everyone on the bus before we left. We got 100 yards down the driveway, when somebody said Colin Levy, the fitness coach, wasn't on. There was a debate whether we should go back but I said drive on, as he should have been on the bus! We then saw him in the mirror and so we stopped half-a-mile away and made him run down to the bus. So for the final we did the same thing. It was a bit of fun and allowed us to relax and to take the players' minds off things."

The manager had done his homework and having won three out of four meetings against Dundee United he knew how to get one over his rivals.

"If you had let that Dundee United team dominate then they would have caused you loads of problems," Wright insisted. "Our boys had enough about them to stop them being as free-flowing as they would have liked over the course of the season against us."

He had done his homework and his pre-match speech was all about putting the finishing touches to his plans.

Wright admitted: "My team talk was that an opportunity like this might never come round again. It might not happen to any of us – including myself – again in my life – so we had to make the most of this opportunity. I touched on their families and to go out and make them proud. Whatever happened I knew the boys had done the club proud getting to the final. They had done the club proud and made history. I just wanted them to take the next step and become legends because I knew that would happen if they could become the first team in the club's history to lift a major trophy. St Johnstone are a great club and had been run the correct way for years and so deserved a long overdue bit of glory."

For former Celtic youngster Chris Millar it was a big day in a place he knew all too well.

"The final at Celtic Park was a big thing for me," the midfielder insisted. "I had played at Celtic all the way up to reserves and I felt with the final my career had gone full circle and now I was in a final at Celtic Park. It completed the whole jigsaw for me. We went out and the gaffer gave his team talk and kept it as normal as possible. I was thinking about my family, my friends and the fans and just trying to do the best I can for them. I didn't realise at the time what that day meant to so many people."

Alan Mannus was certainly one of the Saints squad who was no stranger to cup finals.

A successful Mannus said: "I played for four Irish Cups with Linfield and we won them all. I had also played in the FAI Cup with Shamrock Rovers but we lost on penalties. I thought those experiences stood me in good stead for the Scottish Cup Final."

Captain Dave Mackay also had a Scottish Cup Final appearance under his belt but he had come out on the losing side as Rangers beat Dundee back in 2007.

The gutsy defender admitted: "I remember people saying enjoy it because you might not play in another. At that time, I was like sure, I will play in plenty, if I don't win I will be back in a couple of years but it took me so long to get to another final."

That was part of Mackay's final words before he led his team into battle.

"The referee, Craig Thomson, asked myself and the Dundee United captain, Sean Dillon, into his room for a little talk before the game," Mackay confirmed. "Asking how we were and what he expected. It was a nice touch because I think Craig had sent me off in a couple of our previous games so it was good to go in and say it was all forgotten – even if it wasn't! We then went back into the dressing room and the manager said a bit and then myself and some of the experienced boys would say some things to get the boys going. We knew the importance of becoming the first St Johnstone team to win the cup – don't let it pass you by!"

The big occasion meant the first half was a nervy affair. The home nerves were nearly shredded when Dundee United striker Ryan Dow hit the woodwork.

Keeper Mannus admitted: "They had an opportunity when I think it was Dow went across me. I was at full stretch but it hit the post and came back out. I expected it to hit me but it never and rolled behind me before it was cleared. I just remember turning and seeing Dow with his head in his hands."

It looked like the teams would go in level at the interval until a trademark header from Steven Anderson broke the deadlock after United keeper Rado Czierniak had come out for a cross and got nowhere near it.

He explained: "I normally make back post runs at corners. The keeper came and made a mistake and I was able to capitalise on it. I was in a state of shock when I saw the ball drop into the net. I didn't really score that many goals although I managed to chip in with a few at the end of that season. I had also scored a similar goal against United in the league. The gaffer also did his homework and it paid off. It is great to go down as the first goalscorer in the final that St Johnstone won but it also gave us the ideal platform to build from in the game."

Anderson certainly marked his testimonial year in some style and also left a few of his family, friends and fellow St Johnstone supporters in ecstasy and in the money. He also made it a day to remember as he gave his mum the perfect 50th birthday present.

The defender said: "A couple of people had actually put me on for first goalscorer. My father-in-law also put a bet on me to score at any time so at least there were a few people who were left quids in. I think some of my pals even got 40 or 50 to 1 so they will be buying the drinks forever more. There was also somebody who tweeted me that they had stuck £20 on St Johnstone to win 2-0 and me to score first. They said they got more than £3,000 but I am still waiting for my cut!"

Manager Tommy Wright knew the timing of Anderson's strike couldn't have been better.

"My team talk was simple," the manager confirmed. "I got the boys calmed down and I told them to just keep doing what they were doing. Get the ball down and keep moving it and make sure you finish the job off."

James Dunne picked up an early second half booking and it made it a long 41 minutes to see out.

Dunne said: "I got a booking for a late challenge on Ryan Dow. I had to be in control in the second half. I did handball it although it was accidental but my heart was in my mouth for a second and I was just thinking: 'Please, don't send me off.' The referee gave me the benefit of the doubt thankfully even though I had shouted at him a few times during the game."

United's star turn Nadir Ciftci was always likely to offer the biggest threat and the St Johnstone defence knew they had to do all they could to keep him in check.

Frazer Wright joked: "I was in his ear most of the game winding him up. I had played against him a few times before and I was well aware that when he gets worked up he loses his focus and doesn't play as well. I was also well aware he was one of Dundee United's best players and when he plays they really tick. I actually started it against him a few weeks before in the last league game. The gaffer also told me that if I could wind him up then just to go for it. I also knew I had to get some advantage because he was always going to do me for pace. He caught me in the face and he also caught Ando at the end as well. We knew then he and United were gone."

Fellow centre-half Steven Anderson knew that he had the fiery Turkish international when he lashed out at him late on.

"United had talented players but they were soft," Anderson stated. "Ciftci was one of the best strikers in the league and you had to get in his ear to put him off his game otherwise he was a match-winner. You knew if you could get into him and he kicked out at me late on but that is what you needed to do against him."

Ciftci had a quiet afternoon but still caused a few nervous flutters when he curled a free kick off the woodwork.

A relieved Mannus admitted: "Ciftci had a free kick. I was at full stretch but this time it came off the bar. I saw it coming back towards me and I was thinking don't hit me and then go in. I didn't and I was able to grab it and avert the danger. I had a feeling at that point that we can actually do this."

Saints made a change and Lee Croft came on for Michael O'Halloran.

Croft said: "I kept making sure that I was in the gaffer's sight when I went to warm up. I then got on and he just said get on the ball and make sure we see it through. One of the things I remember was Andrew Robertson charging into the box and I slid in and I thought I need to get there or it will be a penalty. Luckily enough I won the ball, it hit him and we got a goal kick."

Stevie May managed to put the ball in but did it illegally with his hand but Saints weren't to be denied a second.

MacLean was the man who came to the fore six minutes from the end. MacLean admitted: "The gaffer told us that Gavin Gunning steps out a bit more than Sean Dillon and that left their defensive line a bit disjointed. Stevie May tried to slot it in and it came off a defender and broke to me. I am not the quickest and it was a 50/50 and I had decided to go through everything. The ball broke perfectly and I just slid it in. Everything was a blur. I ran into the corner with my boy and most of my family. I took off my top and I ended up getting a booking – it was the best booking ever."

Tommy Wright knew there and then the game was over.

"The second goal was even more joyful as we knew that was the winner," he claimed. "I didn't think they were going to score two against us and that proved to be the case. Callum tried to jump on top of me and I just ran towards our fans. I lost all sense of proportion of what I was doing. It was just a reaction of sheer delight and emotion."

Alan Mannus also knew there was no chance of his defence letting that lead slip.

Mannus confessed: "They put us under a bit more pressure in the second half but I thought we were pretty comfortable. We had a wee bit of good fortune with the free kick but I felt we saw the game out well and ended up being deserved winners. The defenders and boys in front of them put in a real shift and in all fairness I didn't really have a lot to do."

Wright was so engrossed in the game and after sending on Gary McDonald for David Wotherspoon late on his one regret was not making use of his final replacement.

"I only put two subs on," he revealed. "I could have put somebody else on but it wasn't until after it that somebody mentioned but everybody who was there had contributed and they all deserved a medal."

The final whistle from referee Craig Thomson brought wild celebrations.

Alan Mannus revealed: "Brian Easton was close to me when the whistle went. We ran over and jumped on each other, which looking back now was quite funny. But we all knew what it meant to the club and it is hard to put those feeling into words."

Chris Millar celebrated with the St Johnstone old guard.

He said: "When the final whistle went it was like wow. What a feeling! There was a picture taken with Dave Mackay, Steven MacLean and Frazer Wright all hugging. We were all the older boys and it was good to have that moment with all the older boys. I then went and got my girls, Sophia and Ellie, and got them on to the pitch with me. The girls still talk about that day even though they thought the noise was a bit loud and scary for them."

May's dream season was capped off in style. The long-haired star recalled: "I just remember celebrating, not really knowing what to do. I went about hugging everyone and I couldn't wait to get my hands on the trophy and the celebratory champagne. It had been a great season personally and collectively and I wanted to celebrate it because achievements like that don't come around too often."

Chris Millar gave a young fan a present he would never forget during St Johnstone's lap of honour.

"I gave my strip away to a fan as I was walking round," Millar said. "I saw a wee boy. I went across and spoke to him and then I thought it would be a nice gesture to give him my top. His dad tried to give it back but I said it would mean more to him because I will still have my medal and my memories. His dad worked down south but was a bit of a St Johnstone fan and tried to come up for quite a few games. He actually sent me a letter saying thank you and what a gesture it was to give him my strip. I actually see him at games now and then. The only thing was I needed to get a tracksuit top for the trophy presentation!"

Overjoyed captain Dave Mackay also found time to go round and commiserate with the dejected Dundee United players.

Mackay said: "The boys were jumping about mad while others were just standing taking it all in. I made a point of going round the Dundee United boys because I knew what they were going through and I told them well done and to keep their heads up because their chance would come again. It was to show a bit of respect to them before I went to see my family."

Alan Mannus had more winners' medals than most but knew this was one to cherish. "I have been lucky enough to win leagues and cups with my previous clubs," the Northern Irish cap admitted. "You can't say one more than any other because they all have reasons why they are important to you.

"This was very unexpected. Nobody would have given us a hope of winning the cup. It started off by beating Rosenborg in the Europa League so it ended up being a brilliant season for us."

The reliable keeper added: "It was great to just get to the final in the first place but to go on and win it was just brilliant. Winning the Scottish Cup is up there with anything I have done or achieved in my career. We had over 15,000 fans and we all saw what winning the cup meant to our them. I was just delighted I was part of the squad that made them so happy."

Lee Croft had played at the very top of the English game but knew the cup triumph would take some topping.

Croft claimed: "It was right up there. I have played for some big clubs and in the English Premier League and Championship but I have never actually won anything. To be involved in a team that wins a cup final is right up there, especially as St Johnstone had never won anything major in their history so that day will always be right up there for me."

It was left for St Johnstone to get their medals and for their skipper to get his hands on this long overdue trophy. Mackay also wore a pro-cam to give supporters a bird's eye view of the trophy presentation.

Mackay claimed: "I was coming down and somebody told me I had to put this on. I didn't know what it was and I just put it on. I have heard some fans say it was great to see the view of me lifting the cup but if I had to do it again I wouldn't have done it again because it didn't look great in the photos although it did let the fans see it. It would also have been better if we had been facing the St Johnstone fans rather than the United support. It was just an overwhelming feeling being the last man to get his medal and then you get the cup. It is something you always dream of. There was no doubt it was the best moment of my career."

The celebrations allowed the players to celebrate with family and friends.

Goal hero Steven MacLean said: "I saw my family and I get really emotional anyway. I have never seen my old man, Gus, cry in my life but even he was in tears after the game. It is great because it is amazing to see what it does to people who mean so much to you. I also saw my sister and the kids and missus and it was hard trying to keep myself together although you can see what it means to them. I was so happy."

Tommy Wright's initial thoughts went to the people who had supported him and the team. He admitted: "I was extremely proud for my team, the staff and myself but I took as much satisfaction, if not more, for the chairman, Geoff Brown and a lot of people who work so hard behind the scenes for the club."

The reality of the achievement still hadn't sunk in by the time the partying Saints squad had returned to their dressing room.

MacLean claimed: "It was actually a bit surreal after all the celebrations and we returned to the dressing room with the cup. We just said down a looked at each other as if to say what are we going to do now? We've just won a cup – how did that happen? So few of us had experienced anything like it in our careers and we just sat there, then a few of us kicked off and it was just absolute madness in the dressing room."

Chris Millar and David Wotherspoon had to delay their celebrations – although Wotherspoon almost missed them altogether.

Millar explained: "David Wotherspoon and myself were both picked for the drugs test. We were all given beer and I drank a few quickly to try and give my sample. I managed to do it and disappear but I felt for Wotherspoon because he couldn't provide his sample and missed most of the celebrations in the dressing room."

That gave Tommy Wright the chance to temporarily steal the Scottish Cup and take it to parts of Hampden it had, probably, never been before.

"I walked down the side of the pitch and up to one of the lounges," revealed Wright. "It was then I was thinking I am really taking the Scottish Cup up with me to show people – that, probably, hasn't been done before. That was when I realised what an achievement it was. I went in and my brother and uncles were across and we got photographs taken and almost everybody wanted their picture taken with the cup."

Anderson missed his mum but knew she would never forget his, her's and St Johnstone's big day.

Anderson said: "I never got to see my mum because she was up in the corporate seats but I did phone her from the bus on the way back to Perth. With it being her 50th she loved it, especially as we had won and I had managed to score. She said it was the best present I could have given her. I also saw my wife, Sarah, and her family and they were all really emotional as well."

It was the same for Chris Millar as it gave his dad something else to boost his spirits.

Millar emotionally said: "It was great for everybody, especially my dad, Ian. He had taken me everywhere since I was a teenager. He had been through it all and it had been a difficult year but winning the cup gave him a lift. It allowed me to give something back for all the time he had spent running after me and my football since I was a boy."

The bus journey back to Perth was a joyful one for Wright's cup final heroes. They had hit the right notes on the pitch although one of their stars wasn't quite on key on the way back – as Chris Millar entertained them with covers of Deacon Blue's "Dignity" and Journey's, ironically named, "Don't Stop Believing."

Steven Anderson said: "The boys were all throwing champagne around in the dressing room, but it was all a bit of a come down when we got back inside after we had celebrated with our fans, friends and family. The gaffer got soaked with his suit on so that was funny. But when we got back on the bus back to Perth it was just chaos. Wee Midge started singing on the bus. He had the mic and I think we let him keep it because he needed all the practice he could get. He was meant to be singing Journey's 'Don't Stop Believing' but it sounded nothing like it. He completely killed the song but he gave all the boys a good laugh although he still fancies himself as a bit of a singer."

The team and staff returned to McDiarmid Park where the chairman put on a party for his players to enjoy with their nearest and dearest.

MacLean admitted: "The club had a night out arranged for us back at the stadium for all the staff and our families. We all mixed and it was a special night because we were all together with the people who have been right beside us throughout our careers. There were a few of us who were worse for wear although the likes of Chris Millar and Michael O'Halloran were walking about without any shirts on and nothing but their winner's medals."

Tommy Wright capped off his dream day by heading home to watch a television rerun.

Wright confirmed: "I got home at 2.30am to 3pm. I had a cup of green tea and watched most of the game back. The tea was to sober me up. I was almost in a bubble on the day and I just wanted to see the celebrations and how the fans and players celebrated."

The party went on into the early hours and continued into the Sunday where the celebratory open-top bus parade allowed St Johnstone's players to take a well-earned bow.

Millar, despite his heavy night, was there early. He said: "I was still the first one at the ground that next morning. I walked in and Roddy Grant was there. He shouted 'Midge!' and got me into his office and he cracked open a bottle of champagne. It just continued from there so you could imagine the shape I was in at the end of the day."

Other St Johnstone players were under the influence and almost missed the bus parade. Steven MacLean hadn't got to bed back in Peebles until 5am and then was back up at the crack of dawn.

MacLean explained: "My mate owns one of the local pubs and I phoned him. He put on bacon rolls and champagne for us the next morning. My dad drove a minibus up because he doesn't drink. We picked up Tam Scobbie on the way to Perth and we ended up being an hour late. Paul Smith at the club called to ask me where I was. I told him I was close but I was still a bit away because we had been drinking. It was mental."

The bus eventually got away and there were early fears it could be something of an anti-climax.

Captain Dave Mackay said: "As players we were thinking what is this all about. We thought there would be about 2,000 people but when we got into the centre there was about 25,000 people there. It was unbelievable for a town that has a population of only 40,000. It is often said it is not a footballing town but that day showed what it meant to the people of Perth, whether they were football fans or not."

Anderson had tasted it before but to a lesser extent. He explained: "I had done it before when we won the First Division. It was well organised and there were so many people out compared to the first time. This was the first time the club had won a trophy and that was the big thing. There was also a band following the bus around but winning a major trophy was just massive for everyone."

Seeing the streets decked out in blue and white is something that will live with centre-half Frazer Wright forever.

Wright said: "I didn't know Perth had that many people and we had that many fans. Seeing so many people out in the streets to see our cup parade is something that will be my one outstanding memory from our Scottish Cup win."

Tommy Wright was just glad health and safety didn't curtail the celebrations.

Wright admitted: "There were more people on the bus than should have been. We went up the High Street and I was amazed at the number of people who were there. We just couldn't move because there were so many people there. It was good to mix in with the fans and to listen to their stories of the days."

Chairman Steve Brown added: "The bus took the team to the St George's Hotel where the celebrations really kicked off and the players and staff went round Perth to mix with the supporters."

The journey continued to the centre where some of the players and manager took to the stage to thank the fans. The event was compered by celebrity fan Stuart Cosgrove who, much to the delight of his fellow Saints fans, took the mickey out of Steve Lomas for leaving and Liam Craig and Rowan Vine for defecting to a perceived bigger club, in Hibernian.

An overwhelmed Steven MacLean said: "It was mad. We went round a few areas and I thought this is okay but then we turned up in the city centre it was just like bang – everybody was suddenly there! It was like where has everybody come from. It was like the 15,000 fans who had been at the game plus more had suddenly congregated in Perth city centre. Stuart Cosgrove was compering in the city centre. He hammered Steve Lomas and Rowan Vine and Liam Craig for going to Hibs. It was all good-hearted and banter. He wanted me and Ando to speak but I didn't really want to do it."

For some of the St Johnstone players it proved to be a hard day's night.

Chris Millar said: "I went out in the town in Perth. I must have had my medal on for two or three days. I don't think I got changed for three days. I had my club suit on all that time. I remember letting the fans put it on and then get their photo taken with it. They couldn't believe it but I felt it was just as important for them. I didn't see it as a big thing but it was massive for the fans to see and hold the medal."

Lee Croft explained: "It was a great feeling because not many people get to win a major cup final. Perth was just mad. The pubs and clubs were packed with St Johnstone fans. They kept buying us drinks and everywhere we went it was a massive party. One of the boys said he felt like one of the Beatles the way we were treated."

James Dunne also knew it would be a loan spell he was never going to forget.

Dunne said: "It was a good day for the club and me personally as I have never been involved in such a game like that personally. The changing room with the boys and then in and around Perth was just mental. It was good to show our appreciation to the fans for all the support they gave us."

Alan Mannus was happy to give the Saints something back for all the support they had given him.

"I never expected to be treated the way I have from the St Johnstone fans," he stated. "They were unbelievable to me from the start. You can't always give your thanks to them but to be part of the squad who won the cup I hope it says thank you to them for the support they have given me. It has left me a bit overwhelmed. It is the best way to show your appreciation back to the fans."

The joke was that manager Tommy Wright will never have to buy a drink in the Fair City again.

Steven MacLean joked: "The gaffer kept kidding on he was going up to buy a round but every time he went to the bar he was getting it for nothing. I am not sure if he will have to put his hand in his pocket in Perth again. He probably deserves it and he will end up as a freeman of Perth."

The joy was shown as I interviewed MacLean and Steven Anderson in The Sandeman pub. A delighted Saints fan interrupted to tell the goal heroes that his partner was due to give birth in five weeks and he was going to call his new baby boy Steven after them.

The night ended with Stevens Anderson and MacLean making a birthday stop-off at the Cherrybank pub before they headed for the club's player of the year awards.

Anderson admitted: "Stevie May won all the awards. I managed to lift the clubman of the year – that was all he left! I think I only got it out of sympathy because I had been at the club so long. Frazer Wright got goal of the season for his strike against Rosenborg although I think it was down to the size of the occasion. It was a big goal for the club."

Stevie May could not celebrate in style as he was on Scotland duty the next day.

He said: "I went away with the Scotland under-21s on the Monday so I had to curtail my celebrations after the Saturday night. I had to take it a bit easier and it allowed me to take everything in. There were people all over Perth. Its sums up Perth and the club."

Chairman Steve Brown knows that season is unlikely to be bettered.

Brown said: "It is funny because the manager had been telling me for months that our name was on the cup. I spoke to Tommy a few times and he was convinced we were going to win the cup. I just took it one game at a time because I didn't want to get carried away. I have been a supporter and I know how frustrating it had been. I followed the club in the early Eighties, when we weren't too clever, it was common to get knocked out early of every cup. To then see the Scottish Cup lifted was just unbelievable. I don't think St Johnstone have ever had a better season."

Callum Davidson thought he had seen it all and done it all at McDiarmid Park until that cup win.

He proudly said: "What an achievement it was and to have been part of it was very special. I achieved quite a lot in football. I played for Scotland and some top clubs in England but winning the Scottish Cup was the highlight for me. It will probably forever be the highlight for me because I don't think I will get to another club where they will have waited 130 years for their first major trophy. It means so much to me helping St Johnstone to lift the Scottish Cup. I owe the club so much because I started my playing career and then finished it here before Tommy gave me the chance to go into management."

Former chairman Geoff Brown was just as delighted and even more so as rival chairman Stewart Milne supplied the champagne.

Brown admitted: "Stewart Milne was one of the first people who text me to say congratulations. Aberdeen had won the League Cup earlier in the season. I had helped them get their manager Derek McInnes to Pittodrie because obviously I had worked with him at St Johnstone. So when they won the cup I sent Stewart a text saying: 'Asking when are you going to pay Derek's agent?' The following day a case of champagne arrived at my office with a note which read: 'Enjoy the champagne, you are certainly not getting paid!' So after we won the cup I was able to text him back and say well at least I know where to find the champagne to celebrate our Scottish Cup win."

Steven MacLean believes that 129th Scottish Cup was for all the unsung heroes at St Johnstone.

He said: "It was great for everybody at the club from Jocky Peebles to Tommy Campbell. People like that had been at the club for so long and given so much to St Johnstone so it was good to see people like that with the cup. Geoff Brown was another. What he has done for the club and that first major trophy was as much down to him as anyone. He ran the club the right way and never overspent like others and so us winning the Scottish Cup justified his decision."

Not that the party could go on forever and on the Monday manager Tommy Wright had to tell several of his squad they were being released.

Wright admitted: "I was back in on the Monday and unfortunately again football never stands still. I had to have meetings with players to tell them I wasn't keeping them. Telling Paddy Cregg he was released after his cup final was one of the worst moments of my management career. That is the highs and lows of football."

Personal tragedy for James Dunne also saw him decide not to make his move to Scotland a permanent one.

Dunne heartbreakingly said: "We had just lost a baby a few weeks after the final. It was a real blow to us and at that time my wife needed to be around family and it just wasn't right to move up to Scotland at that point. It was a hard decision to make but I had to do what was best for my family but at least I left St Johnstone with very fond memories and probably the highlight of my career."

Tommy Wright was rewarded with a new contract as he prepared for another crack at European football.

It wasn't until well into the summer that the significance of their achievements finally started to dawn on the St Johnstone players.

Steven Anderson, who also penned an extension, said: "It was a blur. After the celebrations I went to Portugal with my wife and I remember sitting there thinking we will be back in a few weeks for the Europa League, never mind trying to celebrate the Scottish Cup."

That St Johnstone team is now guaranteed legendary status at the club and the memories and their achievements will live on forever. It is a day every person connected with Saints will never forget.

Frazer Wright said: "My medal is now in a box in a cupboard in the house. I did have it out in the living room but the kids used to play with it all the time. The ribbon was started to get a bit worn so I decided it was time to put it away before it got damaged."

Alan Mannus passed his one for safe keeping. He explained: "Everything we get, me and my brothers win, we take back to my mum and dad's. Along with the other medals I have been lucky enough to get."

Chris Millar's medal is now proudly on display in his house. He admitted: "My wife, Danielle, made a wee presentation frame for me with articles I did and the programme in the middle with my medal hanging down in the middle."

Steven Anderson after some peer pressure has given his medal a public airing.

He said: "For the first couple of years my medal was in my wife's jewellery box. A few of my mates said is that all it means to you? Sarah has now done well for me and put it in a frame with my cup final shirt and now it is up on the wall. For me, the medal wasn't a big thing. It was more about the memories and also the history of being in the first St Johnstone team to win a major trophy."

Those sentiments were echoed by local hero Stevie May, who won a big-money move to Sheffield Wednesday on the back of that season. He confessed: "I would love to do it all again – it was so good. The club and city had waited over 100 years to win a trophy and seeing the joy it brought people was totally amazing."

The only downside was that the celebrations had only started to subside and the hangover kicked in when the Saints had to go marching in again a few weeks later on their Europa League return.

ST JOHNSTONE'S SCOTTISH CUP-WINNING TEAM 2013/14

Fourth round (30 November 2013 at McDiarmid Park)
St Johnstone 2 Livingston 0 (May, Jahic)

Fifth round (8 February 2014 at Station Park)
Forfar Athletic 0 St Johnstone 4 (Croft, Wright, O'Halloran, Dunne)

Quarter-final (8 March 2014 at Stark's Park)
Raith Rovers 1 (Cardle) St Johnstone 3 (McDonald, Hasselbaink, Anderson)

Semi-final (13 April 2014 at Ibrox)
Aberdeen 1 (McGinn) St Johnstone 2 (May 2)

Final (17 May 2014 at Celtic Park)
St Johnstone 2 (Anderson, MacLean) Dundee United 0

ST JOHNSTONE'S SCOTTISH CUP-WINNING TEAM
Alan Mannus, Dave Mackay, Brian Easton, David Wotherspoon (Gary McDonald), Frazer Wright, Steven Anderson, Chris Millar, Richard Dunne, Stevie May, Steven MacLean, Michael O'Halloran (Lee Croft).
Manager: Tommy Wright.

27

• INVERNESS – A HIGHLAND RISING •
The 2015 Scottish Cup Winners

THERE is no question Inverness Caledonian Thistle have been one of Scottish football's recent success stories. From coming into the senior ranks back in 1994 – when the merger of Inverness Caledonian and Thistle was so bitterly opposed – they have risen through the leagues and have been a major addition to the senior game.

Steve 'Pele' Paterson started to put Inverness on the map in the early years and topped things off with their famous Scottish Cup victory over Celtic that effectively cost John Barnes his job in 2000. Inverness followed that up by beating the Hoops again in 2003.

It was John Robertson who led them into the top flight for the first time and he was followed by Craig Brewster, twice, and club legend Charlie Christie who all had spells as manager. Christie walked away as the team struggled and they were relegated before Terry Butcher took them up at the first time of asking.

The former England captain laid the foundations from which John Hughes was able to build when he stepped into the Caledonian Stadium manager's position at the end of 2013. 'Yogi' led them to a fifth place finish and a League Cup Final appearance which ended in penalty shoot-out heartbreak against Aberdeen.

Midfielder Ross Draper admitted: "I have always been frustrated by that Aberdeen final because I saw it as a wasted opportunity. We didn't play well on the day. We sat in and played for a draw to some extent although we still wanted to win the game. We were too defensive and gave Aberdeen too much respect at the time when they were a good side but they weren't flying. It was definitely a case of one that got away."

Team-mate James Vincent admitted that defeat was just like any other game.

Vincent said: "I remember the League Cup preparations and we just turned up at Celtic Park on the day with our tracksuits on. For the Scottish Cup Final we had four or five days away in a hotel. It was Inverness's first Scottish Cup Final and the city got right behind it. There wasn't the same buzz at the previous League Cup Final."

What the team had achieved certainly gave hope going into the 2014/15 season. They lost in the second round of the League Cup but in the Premiership they were pushing for the top six. That gave them confidence going into their Scottish Cup assault.

Inverness opened with a fourth round tie away to St Mirren. The Buddies were struggling at the wrong end of the Scottish Premiership table and went into the match under pressure, having failed to win in their previous five matches.

A small band of travelling Caley Thistle fans failed to swell the crowd much as there were less than 2,000 at St Mirren Park.

It was a match that saw John Hughes and his players travel south and very much fancying their chances.

The struggling Saints, however, caused a shock when Marc McAusland turned in a cross to give his side a 17th-minute lead. It was their first goal in over 300 minutes under coach Tommy Craig. Inverness suddenly had it all to do but managed to draw level in the 63rd minute.

St Mirren failed to clear a corner. Ross Draper hit the post with a shot before Josh Meekings netted through a ruck of players.

Hero Meekings said: "That first match at St Mirren was a real struggle to be fair. I always liked playing down there because it is a nice little stadium but that day we had to battle. I scored the equaliser and it turned out to be a big goal in the end. There was a bit of a melee and the ball fell to me. I just put my foot through it and I connected well and I drilled it low into the bottom corner. It wasn't a great goal but in terms of the cup run it got us a replay so it was an important one."

Inverness finished on top and despite having 65 per cent possession they failed to conjure up a winner and they had to go again in a

Highland replay.

The victors by that time knew the prize was an away trip to Partick Thistle in the fifth round.

John Hughes' men made no mistakes second time around. They went out and duly smashed sorry St Mirren.

Garry Warren set them on their way with his 20th-minute opener. Warren said: "We battered them in the replay. I only remember that one because I scored and I don't get that many. It came from a corner and I got across the front post and I headed it in at the near post. That was the first goal and from them on it was total domination. We passed St Mirren off the park. It was 4-0 but it could easily have been eight or nine. That performance gave us a lot of belief going into the latter rounds."

Jim Goodwin got caught on the ball by Inverness's Marley Watkins and the St Mirren midfielder then fouled him inside the box for a penalty. Greg Tansey sent ex-Inverness keeper Mark Ridgers the wrong way from the spot for the second.

Tansey admitted: "I put it to my left and fortunately the keeper went the wrong way."

Prolific striker Billy Mckay hit the bar and St Mirren defender Sean Kelly failed to clear, allowing Danny Williams to add to the scoring.

Captain Graeme Shinnie finished off the rout with a solo fourth in stoppage time.

"We were so comfortable in that game," Shinnie claimed. "We were 3-0 up with a few minutes left. I ended up at centre-forward and I can't even remember why. Somebody played a pass and I was suddenly through on goal one-on-one with the keeper. I managed to slot it in and I didn't really celebrate too much as the game was already over."

That booked a trip to Firhill which was scheduled for 7 February. That meant that John Hughes had to perilously try and come through the January transfer market stronger. That wasn't to be the case. English outfit Wigan Athletic left it late before they came in with a £150,000 bid to land striker Billy Mckay.

The Northern Irish international, brought to the club by former boss Terry Butcher, was top scorer when he left the club with ten goals.

Former Crystal Palace striker Ibra Sekajja came in while John Hughes also decided to gamble on Nigerian international Edward Ofere and Estonian cap Tarmo Kink. Both were free agents who came in after the close of the window.

Edward Ofere explained how his move came about. He said: "My agent called and asked if I would be interested in moving to Scotland. I knew it was similar to the English league and it was something I felt suited my game. So I went up and trained and got the contract offer from Inverness and that is how it all started."

Hughes also had an ace up his sleeve. He moved Marley Watkins into a more central attacking role. He had come up from non-league Hereford but it was in this particular season he really sparkled.

Watkins rose to the occasion in Maryhill against the locals. He picked up a slack ball and ran on to slot the ball home to give Inverness a welcome 16th-minute lead.

Watkins said: "I shrugged off a couple of defenders and scored."

Caley Thistle took a foothold in the match and doubled their lead 11 minutes later.

Stephen O'Donnell lost possession and Greg Tansey beat a couple of players before he fired home.

"That is one of my favourite goals from all my time at Inverness," Tansey insisted. "I picked it up just inside their half. I turned and passed a player, went past two of their defenders and then stuck it in the bottom corner with my right foot. We knew it was going to be a tough game but that put us in a decent position."

Inverness looked to have one foot in the quarter-finals before Lyle Taylor pulled a goal back to make it a nervy finish. That goal also proved costly for Gary Warren.

He was booked for protesting the goal. A red-faced Warren said: "They scored their goal. I gave the linesman an earful and the referee ended up booking me for it. That proved to be very stupid and frustrating in the long run."

Inverness gave back-up keeper Ryan Esson a rare run out and he played his part, making a late save from Daniel Seabourne to squeeze Caley Thistle through.

The quarter-final draw was made by then World Championship darts winner Gary Anderson. His draw put Inverness on the oche in a tie against lower league opposition, in the shape of Championship Raith Rovers.

John Hughes knew at that stage it was a great opportunity to reach the last four – providing they played to their potential.

This time they not only had to get past Rovers but also had to beat the weather. A Highland opening left the Caledonian Stadium waterlogged and unplayable on Saturday, 7 March. It meant a quick turnaround with the game quickly rescheduled for the follow Tuesday.

Gary Warren was missing and that opened the way for a new home hero. It proved to be a hard-fought encounter and it was left to Danny Devine, who had arrived from Wrexham, to grab the glory, after he got his head on a Greg Tansey corner.

The Irish defender explained: "I think that it was the first game I played in the cup. I remember I got my goal, which turned out to be the winner. It came from a corner and it was a case of me being a big centre-half, getting up and trying to make my presence felt. Luckily I got on the end of it and it went in. It was a potential banana skin and I was just delighted to help us through. I never thought for one moment where it would end up leading to."

Caley Thistle had chances to put more daylight between the teams but missed chances while Danny Williams hit the bar.

Inverness midfielder Ross Draper reckons that Raith deserved credit for pushing them all the way.

He said: "Raith was probably our hardest of those early games, even though most people expected us to win. We eventually broke them down and got the result we needed. Looking back I think we actually played well in all those games up to that point."

It was also a match where former Malmo striker Edward Ofere was given his chance to lead the line. He was full of praise for manager John Hughes and how he wanted his teams to play.

Ofere explained: "John Hughes was one of a kind but he gave me a lot of confidence to go and play. He'd tell the players what they wanted to hear and he inspired them. He is a great coach and I learned a lot from him."

Inverness continued to look a decent bet for the top six while in the Scottish Cup they looked to be a 'Real Gone Kid' when Deacon Blue lead singer Ricky Ross paired them against the winners of the last eight replay between Celtic and his own team, Dundee United.

That left Hibernian and Falkirk on the other side of the draw and meaning one Championship side would be heading back to Hampden for the final.

It was to be no real surprise that the Highlanders were to play treble-chasing Celtic who saw off Dundee United 4-0 at the second time of asking.

It brought a mixed reaction from the Inverness dressing room.

"We just wanted to avoid Celtic," defender David Raven claimed. "I remember when we were drawn against Celtic everybody was laughing and joking and the boys were saying we are all done for now. That was just the lads though and we all believed. I remember as the game came closer and I had this proper feeling that we were going to win."

For others though it was an opportunity to grasp rather than to run from. Gary Warren fell into that boat. He had come up the hard way and made the switch from Newport County to the Highlands and didn't care about reputations.

Warren insisted: "The semi-final for me personally I wasn't too bothered. At the semi-final stage anyone can beat anybody else. I would always back our squad because look at the players we had in that squad and you only have to look at the players in that squad who managed to get big moves from leaving Inverness. We had a competitive squad and that brought out the best in us. So when we drew Celtic I didn't have much fear. They were the biggest team left in the hat but I was quietly confident. They were a good side but they weren't as dominant as the Celtic teams of old."

If there were any doubts amongst the Caley Thistle players then it was shown as they went to negotiate their win bonus.

"We could have a win and appearance bonus or just a higher win bonus on its own," James Vincent explained. "When we went into the Celtic game the boys decided to take the appearance and the bonus instead of the straight bonus."

Inverness boss John Hughes knew if his players were to have any chance against his old team then they would need to be at the top of their game. Their cause wasn't helped by injury.

First-choice keeper Dean Brill suffered a dislocated kneecap in a league encounter against Celtic that was to rule him out for the season and almost ten months. Their backline options were further limited by a problem for Danny Devine.

He explained: "I missed that game through injury. I did the ligaments in my knee in training. It was a grade one tear but it meant I had to watch the game from the stands."

The media glare grew over the Highlands the closer Sunday, 19 April came. A lot of the spotlight fell on young academy graduate Ryan Christie. The classy playmaker was son of the Inverness legend and ex-manager Charlie Christie, who had famously sunk Celtic for the first time in their history.

Christie junior confirmed: "I did a little bit of press before the game because my dad, Charlie, had been part of the Inverness team who had famously beaten Celtic under John Barnes."

Falkirk stunned Hibs in the first semi-final so both teams went in knowing who the winners would face.

Inverness were already well-drilled and John Hughes had hatched a game plan.

David Raven confirmed: "The preparation we did for the Celtic game was spot on. I have to take my hat off to John Hughes on that one. The preparations we did were absolutely spot on and he instilled us with a real confidence. He set us up with a game plan. He actually said we are going to get after them and press them and if we do it will go one of two ways. We will either win or get beat by five. Nobody does it against them because team are scared of doing it and he realised we had the legs in the team to go and do the job he wanted. We had Marley up front who did the damage. He was told to go and ruffle the feathers of van Dijk and Denayer and the way he played that day was unbelievable."

Hughes stuck with the same team that had held Celtic 1-1 with Ryan Esson coming in between the sticks for the injured Dean Brill. He also showed bravery by going with two strikers, pairing Marley Watkins with Edward Ofere.

Captain Graeme Shinnie led the battle cry. He explained the basis of his passionate team talk. Shinnie said: "I just said to go out and play without fear. It was a massive occasion and some of the boys had come up from down south and maybe didn't really know what the Scottish Cup meant. The pressure was also more on Celtic than us. We were the underdogs and we loved being in that position and we used it going into the game."

Marley Watkins was in impressive form and being out of contract at the end of the season knew this was the ideal way to showcase his talent.

Watkins admitted: "I had come up from the English non-leagues and moving to the Scottish Premier League was a chance for me to move up the leagues. Playing in big games against Celtic was a massive thing. I was out of contract at the end of that season so I saw the semi-final as a real chance to go out and help the team but also to go out and show what I could do against two top central defenders in Virgil van Dijk and Jason

Denayer, who both left Celtic to go and play in the English Premier League."

Celtic were keen to get the job done and started like a house on fire. Nir Bitton scorched the bar with a long-range shot while Ryan Esson had to save well from on-form Leigh Griffiths.

Things got even worse when Celtic took a deserved 18th-minute lead. Gary Warren let James Forrest in behind before he fouled him. It proved to be a costly foul for Warren and Inverness. The Englishman picked up a booking that was his second of the competition and would see him suspended for the final – if Inverness got there.

"I knew as soon as I did it I was getting booked and I would be out of the final," Warren conceded. "I had missed the League Cup Final through suspension and I knew what was at stake. The thing is when you are playing in these type of games you can't hold back. I knew as soon as James Forrest skipped round me that I was out the final. He is a quick lad and I tried to manoeuvre myself round him and it was a last-ditch tackle. I knew if he got past me he would have a clear sight of goal so I knew I had to make the foul and take one for the team. I knew I had to keep my head because I had let the boys down in the League Cup semi by losing my head. I had to keep my calm and get on with it and to help the boys finish the job. It was like Paul Scholes and Roy Keane when they knew they would miss the Champions League Final."

Warren's misery was heaped upon when Virgil van Dijk stepped up to curl the free kick off the post to give Celtic the lead.

Edward Ofere missed a chance as Celtic continued to dominate without finding a second. Ryan Esson saved from Stefan Johansen again and Leigh Griffiths flashed another across the goal.

Then came the moment of controversy that this game will always be remembered for.

Leigh Griffiths got free at the back post and headed towards goal. It was going in until it hit the hand of Josh Meeking. Referee Steven McLean and his officials somehow missed the glaring offence and waved play on. Meekings escaped a red card and Celtic were denied the chance to make it 2-0 from the penalty spot, which led to some angry reactions from the green and white camp.

Meekings admitted: "I remember at the time I thought I am going to walk here. Things happened so quickly. The ball did hit my hand but what I would say is that I wasn't even looking at the ball. I just tried to get my body in between Leigh and the goal as he tried to head it. I put my head down and my hand has gone up the way. I don't know if I did it for balance but it was just my natural reaction and it hit my arm. The officials missed it and it caused great controversy and Celtic got upset with it. Leigh Griffiths asked me during the game if it had hit my hand and I told him it did but I didn't mean it. If you look back and see that save, if anybody pulls it off and means it then they should be a world-class goalkeeper!"

Fellow defender David Raven came out in defence of Steven McLean because he had a similar view.

Raven explained: "I was right beside the referee. I had a similar view to him and when everybody was shouting handball I said no chance, there is no chance it was a penalty! From where I was I didn't think it was a penalty and the referee must have had a similar view. I have seen it back, obviously, and I remember thinking: Oh, no god! That was a stonewall penalty and it was blatant but at the time I didn't think it was. We actually saw the referee at a coaching course after it and we spoke about it. He said I heard the shouts for handball but I didn't see it and I never heard anything in my earpiece from any of the other four officials. I couldn't give what I haven't seen! I completely understood where he was coming from."

Ryan Christie, who went on to join Celtic, admitted that decision was raw at Celtic Park even a year later. He said: "It is funny, when I first went to Celtic a few of the boys brought the penalty up and they were still bitter about it. They still go on about the handball and it was still a very open scar for the Celtic boys who were involved in the game."

The midfielder also thinks it is wrong that talking point has gone on to overshadow what ended up being a very special performance.

Christie added: "It frustrated me that people say Inverness only won because Celtic never got that penalty for the chance to go 2-0 up. There was still a lot of football to be played after that. We played very well after that and thoroughly deserved our win."

Inverness had got off the hook and were able to get themselves together and ready to go again at the interval.

Christie explained: "We went in 1-0 down at half-time but we were all still very confident, which was strange considering it was Celtic. We started the second half very well and the red card pretty much turned the game on its head."

The second big decision to go Inverness's way came just before the hour. Inverness hit on the break, from a disappointing Celtic corner. Marley Watkins beat Adam Matthews to a through ball and was pulled down by goalkeeper Craig Gordon. He was sent off by referee Steven McLean, much to the disgust of the Celtic camp.

Watkins reckons the ordering off was never in doubt.

Watkins said: "I saw the goalkeeper coming out and I tried to knock it past him and put it into the net. I knocked it past him and he just took me out. I knew right away it was a penalty and I fully expected the red card that followed."

Scottish international winger James Forrest was sacrificed for sub keeper Lukasz Zaluska. The Pole delayed taking his place between the sticks, trying to pile the pressure on penalty taker Greg Tansey.

Tansey recalled: "I had a bit of a wait. It was the longest four minutes of my life, if I am being honest. The Celtic keepers were obviously just delaying to try and put me off. A few of their players were also in my ear trying to put me off. Van Dijk was at me, basically, saying: 'You'd better not f*** up, don't sh** yourself now!' Stuff like that. I just tried to zone them all out although I could still hear them. They must have seen my penalty from the St Mirren game because their keeper went that way and pretty early. Thankfully, I saw him early and I changed my mind and was able to roll it into the other corner. That was a big moment because if I hadn't scored that it could have been tricky for us because Celtic are still a top side, even with ten men."

John Hughes couldn't even watch. He stared at the crowd and only started to celebrate when he heard the Inverness fans go wild.

Neither side wanted to make a mistake and it was no surprise to see the contest go all the way to extra time.

Inverness still had the man's advantage and it finally paid off six minutes in.

Graeme Shinnie threw in a cross. Marley Watkins knocked it down and Edward Ofere got on the end of it to fire through Jason Denayer's legs and score.

Ofere beamed: "It was a great moment for me. I scored in extra time. I would say we were struggling a little bit so when we scored it gave us another boost and something else to aim to hold on to. We thought we were going to do it until they equalised again. At that point I was thinking that it was going to go to penalties and then anything can happen. I was glad we didn't have to worry about that."

It got Inverness dreaming of another famous Scottish Cup win over Celtic but the Hoops had other ideas. They equalised two minutes before the halfway point through a free kick from sub John Guidetti.

Confidence was still there within the Inverness ranks.

Charlie Christie claimed: "I thought we were playing well and looked pretty confident in extra time. I was always really confident we would win it."

Inverness had chances and it looked like things could come back and bite them when Nick Ross missed with the goal gaping.

David Raven claimed: "I was thinking we can't lose this. I had already visualised the win in my head. In fact, at the start of the season I had visualised us in a cup final with Celtic, ironically this was in a semi-final. I just remember thinking we just need to win this. I was astonished we weren't winning."

There was more heart in the mouth stuff for another Inverness star in Ross Draper. He would also miss the final with another booking and he took out Scott Brown but team-mate Nick Ross took the brunt and was cautioned for an earlier foul.

A relieved Draper admitted: "Scott Brown has gone through and Nick Ross has gone through the back of him and I have caught him at the front. Thankfully the referee booked Nick for the first foul. Maybe I did get a little bit of luck and I was just relieved that a bit of common sense prevailed."

Any hope of holding on for penalties certainly wasn't in John Hughes's thinking. That was shown as Inverness scored three minutes from time and it was set up and finished by his two full-backs.

Graeme Shinnie admitted: "It looked like it was going to penalties but David Raven stepped up at the end to score. It all happened so quickly. We were a man up and that gave us the opportunity to get both full-backs forward. John Hughes always wanted us to push forward. I played a one-two with Nick Ross and drove into the box. I found myself in a half-shot half-cross area and I wasn't too sure what to do. I thought if I had shot the keeper might have palmed it out but I dragged it right across the box into David's path. He did so well to score it and gave me one of the biggest feelings I have had in football."

Unlikely lad David Raven was the hero although it was just as well his teammates were there to celebrate with him.

"I wasn't surprised when I scored," Raven confidently said. "I said that after the game because I had visualised that a lot in my head as well. I was running on empty a little bit. I started to feel cramps in my groin and the last thing I remember was Shinnie crossing the ball to me. I felt a good connection and that was all I was trying to do at the back post. I remember the ball hitting the net and the emotion of it all. I was on such a high and it is something I have never experienced again in my professional football career. I think it was because it was Celtic, the way the game had gone and everything that was connected with it. It just felt like my moment. The funny thing is that I didn't have anybody at the game because my wife, Hannah, was at home watching our youngster, Iris, and my mum had just had a knee operation and my dad was away on holiday. I remember the next day there were headlines of the loneliest man at Hampden. My wife felt really bad but I told her not to worry about it."

It meant a lot to every one of the Inverness team.

Tansey said: "David Raven's goal was just pandemonium. I haven't been involved in celebrations like that when we scored or after the game that I did that day. No matter what I do in football I think they will be amongst my fondest memories. I think our performance got overlooked that day."

There were still several minutes and stoppage time left and it was a case of trying to get the job done.

Raven said: "I remember the last few minutes just welling up with emotion and I was just thinking I need to keep myself together."

The brave Highlanders got there and the final whistle saw John Hughes jump on to one of the Hampden gates to celebrate Inverness getting to their first ever Scottish Cup Final.

Ross Draper is in no doubt his team deserved their glory. Draper said: "We were brilliant on the day and we took our chances. It was one of those games where we knew it was going to be our day. There was so much hype before and after the game that really could have been our final. Without being disrespectful, the final was probably smaller because it was between two so-called smaller clubs. Falkirk had also beaten Hibs in the other semi-final and most people would have been hoping for a Celtic v Hibs final and so things became a bit of an anti-climax outwith Inverness and Falkirk."

Ryan Christie knew Inverness had pulled off a classic underdog triumph – much in character with the rise of Caley Thistle.

Christie claimed: "It was a tremendous feeling, even with the way the fans were set out. Celtic had their usual half and we only had this tiny little corner to the left of the dugout. It was great to go and celebrate with our fans. I went to see my mum and dad and my girlfriend. With me being from Inverness, it is that small that I probably knew half the people in the crowd. It was only a couple of hours after that it began to sink in that we had made history and were in our first Scottish Cup Final."

They knew they were in a final and out-of-character they were now the favourites rather than the underdogs against Falkirk.

Goalscorer Edward Ofere believes the win over Celtic was the main event.

"The semi-final really was our final," he insisted. "After we beat Celtic it really boosted our confidence. That was the game that won us the cup in my opinion. I know we still had to play Falkirk but I was always confident with the squad and players we had that we would beat them in the final."

The joy was mixed with disappointment and personal pain for Warren as the reality hit home he was going to miss his second final as an Inverness player.

Warren said: "I was over the moon for everybody at the club and especially the players because to get to that first Scottish Cup Final was a bit of history for the club. It is something I can look back on forever knowing I was part of that team. I didn't play in the final but I definitely helped the team along the way. On the other hand I was gutted because I was missing another final. I am also at an age where I know that might never happen again. All those things go through your mind. Emotions run high but that is part and parcel of football."

Warren did however get a medal from their League Cup Final defeat courtesy of his manager.

"John Hughes actually gave me his runners-up medal from the League Cup because he had missed it through suspension," Warren confirmed. "I didn't want to go up and get a medal. I said to him: 'I don't deserve to get one!' He told me to: 'F*** off' and to take his. It was a big gesture from him."

The cup final dream also quickly turned into a nightmare for one of John Hughes's Hampden heroes. Josh Meekings took abuse on-line for his handball as hurting Celtic fans failed to get over the fact their treble dream had been killed stone dead.

"I got called a cheat and got a lot of abuse from Celtic fans on Twitter," the former Ipswich trainee explained. "I knew it was always going to happen because they weren't happy because we had denied them a perceived treble and I am one of the players who helped to ruin it. There were some quite nasty bits of abuse but I understand how some fans can get frustrated and angered by things that can happen on the football pitch."

Meekings, temporarily, took himself off Twitter but his situation was to get even worse. His cup final place had been put in doubt by the Scottish Football Association's compliance officer, Tony McGlennan. The big defender was offered an automatic one-match suspension which if he accepted would see him suspended for the Hampden showcase.

Meekings frustratingly recalled the chain of events. He said: "I was training and the gaffer pulled me to one side and said: 'I can't believe what I have just been told but I just had a call to say the compliance officer has summoned you to a tribunal over your handball in the Celtic game. He has stated that you have meant it and you should have been sent off.' I couldn't believe it because I had never seen or heard of anything like that in football before. I was absolutely gutted. Yes, I handballed it but I never did it on purpose. I am an honest player and I didn't go out to deliberately cheat Celtic. It was an experience and it wasn't nice. I missed the League Cup Final after I got sent off and I managed to appeal and get that down to a yellow so I managed to play. Now I suddenly had a tribunal to face and it was as if I never made a final the easy way. I have to say the support I got from Inverness and even other clubs was unbelievable."

Inverness, John Hughes and Meekings were all united that this was an injustice they would fight all the way. It meant Meekings' cup final hopes would be decided by an independent tribunal who were sitting on behalf of the Scottish Football Association.

That legal fight may have been something of an expense for Inverness but at least they were able to save on transport costs as the tribunal was set for the same day as Ryan Christie to go to Glasgow to do press for the Scottish Football Writers' Award he was about to pick up.

Christie explained: "He had to go down to Hampden for his case and I was down in Glasgow the same day doing press because I had been named as the Scottish Football Writers' Association's young player of the year. I was getting texts asking what was going on because we had travelled down together. There was Josh, his lawyer and myself in the car on the way down the road. We were always confident Josh would get off because you saw by the television replays he didn't mean it. Josh got dropped at Hampden and I went to do the press and I thought it would be finished by the time I had returned but Josh's case was still going on."

It had been a successful trip for Christie and now Inverness were hoping Meekings' trip would prove just as fruitful.

Meekings explained: "I went into the tribunal and the compliance officer, Tony McGlennan, put forward his case and why he felt he had to act and put the case forward. He gave his evidence and I didn't even have to say a word. We were then asked to leave the room. The panel discussed it and then brought me back in and said: 'Josh, you are clear to play in the final. We have dismissed the case because we know taking action could open a real can of worms in football going forward.' I was just so relieved and the first thing I did was to ring up my dad, Steve, to tell him I was free to play and then I spoke to my mum, Fiona, my family and then I started to get a lot of goodwill messages. I think the support I had within football was one of the reasons why it was dismissed. I understand Celtic's anger and pain but that is football, sometimes you get the luck and sometimes you don't."

It turned out to be a happy ride home with both Meekings and Christie, while their Inverness team were also in the fast lane. They had already finished in a club record third place in the Scottish Premiership, behind Celtic and Aberdeen. It also meant they were guaranteed their maiden voyage into European football, via the Europa League, regardless of the result of the Scottish Cup Final. Lifting the trophy, though, would give them the advantage of kicking off their European campaign in a later round.

There was a double celebration to kick off their cup final proceedings. Christie was presented with his SFWA young player of the year award while John Hughes picked up the manager's prize. Christie was told to keep talk about the cup final to a minimum by his manager, who decided to employ a very different tactic.

Christie recalled: "A week before the final I went down to the Scottish Football Writers' Association's dinner to pick up my award. That was great because I had never expected to win anything like that. Personally, it rounded off a great first season for me in the top flight. I had to do a speech and people kept telling me not to mention the cup final. I did well to keep it under wraps but then John Hughes had won the manager of the year award. He went straight up and said I hope Peter Houston is not greedy because he has already won the Scottish Cup before."

There was a real buzz and expectation in the Highland capital.

More than 14,000 Inverness fans were going to be heading down the A9, hoping to see their team's crowning moment.

It was a special occasion for a lot of the English boys that Terry Butcher and Steve Marsella had plucked from down south. Draper confirmed: "The FA Cup is good but it is so hard for the smaller clubs to have a good run and even to get to a final. It is more achievable in Scotland, as we proved. It was a big day. My dad, Graham, hired a bus full of family members. He drove that from Wolverhampton although people had also come up from Brighton to get the bus. I had a lot of mates up for the game and it was a big, big occasion."

James Vincent was similar.

Vincent said: "My mum, Sandra, dad, Charlie and my brother, Alex, and my mate, Dan Pilkington, all came up for the game."

Local hero Ryan Christie had never seen anything like it.

"I supported Inverness all the way through the leagues," he admitted. "There was a real buzz in the city when we made the final. It was the biggest feeling of togetherness throughout the community and towards the club. It was good to be part of and to experience. I did feel a bit of pressure but not from the fans but due to the fact we were playing Falkirk and we went into the game as favourites. That was a bit harder to get our heads round because we were normally the underdogs going into most games. It was such a big opportunity and if we had messed it up then I am sure we would have been totally gutted."

The Hampden-bound stars found themselves very much in demand as public property.

Watkins said: "It was a busy time because we had to do a lot of publicity things with the cup and to do signing sessions, etc."

There was to be heartbreak for David Raven as the semi-final hero failed in his fitness bid for the final.

Raven explained: "I took a whack in training and was left with a dead leg. I knew deep down I was going to miss the final. I went back to try and train but it completely ruptured and that was me done. It was hard but things sat a little easier for me because of what I had done in the semi-final. Now I just wanted the lads to go and win it."

Those who weren't going to play in the final weren't to be forgotten either.

James Vincent said: "We agreed that all the boys in the squad would get the same money, regardless of whether or not you were involved in the final. It was only fair because we were such a tight-knit squad and it was only fair the guys like David Raven and Gary Warren, who had put so much into the season were rewarded."

Manager John Hughes also wanted all his players to be involved in the big day.

Warren admitted: "The manager said I know you are not playing but you are still a big part of this team and for getting the boys over the line. Just do anything you can to help the boys or the team. He kind of gave me a back seat role in the build-up to the final. That meant a lot and showed I wasn't just forgotten about."

Hughes was also prepared to show some loyalty and to put Raven on the bench but the full-back was adamant he wasn't worth the risk.

Warren said: "The gaffer was ready to put Raven on the bench because of what he had done in the semi-final. He even gave him a late fitness test but Ravs wasn't fit. He was still going to put him on the bench but he couldn't move and was right not to go on the bench. It was just as well he did because imagine what would have happened if he had to be sent on after Carl was sent off! But that was another good gesture from the gaffer."

Boss Hughes took his team to the central belt to continue their preparations while a late team talk with his players convinced him to rejig his makeshift defence.

Carl Tremarco explained: "I had expected to be on the bench for the final but then David Raven got injured. Carl was going to play me at centre-half, Josh Meekings at right-back and Graeme Shinnie at left-back. We had a team meeting and we had never done that before. I normally played left-back and Shinnie would fill in at right-back and the gaffer changed it to that after Josh said he wanted to play centre-half. The gaffer asked us what we wanted to do but I wasn't bothered because I was just delighted to be playing."

Josh Meekings was happier to be back in more tried and trusted territory.

"I feel much more confident at centre-back," he claimed. "I don't feel awkward at full-back but I do feel you need a run of games in a certain position to be at your best and I have played most of my career at the heart of the defence. Shinnie went to right-back and it wasn't a problem because he is such a good player he can play anywhere and I played alongside Danny Devine, which wasn't a problem because we had a good relationship. We all knew what we were doing and it was up to us to go out and produce on the pitch."

It was some rise for Carl Tremarco and Ross Draper who had been team-mates at Macclesfield and were now looking forward to a major cup final.

Tremarco proudly said: "Four or five years earlier we were nearly on that M6 together playing for Macclesfield in England's League Two. We were now getting to a final and it showed how far we had come."

Ross Draper had certainly struck it rich having played part-time and worked as a debt collector. He said: "I was working with a mortgage company in their collection department. I then did a bit of training to join their debt collection department. It was a promotion but Gary Warren heard about it and told all the press I was a debt collector and I used to chap doors and then carry around my baseball bat. It is normally mentioned in most away programmes so in fairness Gary has done a great job on that one. I was playing football at Hednesford Town."

Draper and Tremarco were also big personalities within the Inverness camp and were never too far away from the behind-the-scenes chaos.

Draper explained: "The young boys always congregated in one room to play FIFA. The likes of Ryan, Danny, Aaron, Josh and Liam always used to have tournaments. We actually played in the tournament but as two of the older boys we aren't that good so we got knocked out. We were opposite them and went back to our room and tied the door handles so they couldn't get out."

Tremarco added his own version of events. He said: "Drapes and I got a phone wire and tied it to one of the lads' doors. We then tied it to the next door handle. We then knocked and when they tried to open the door they couldn't get out. We had form for that sort of thing. Our target was whoever was nearest to us."

Players weren't their only targets.

Tremarco claimed: "This wasn't on the cup run but we always like to get Jim Falconer (the club secretary). We got to reception and we went to get our keys. Jim's was on top of the pile. So I stuck it in my pocket and raced off to his room. I went inside and trashed it and ran back down and left the key back on the side of the reception. He picked it up and went to his room and little did we know we were opposite him. So me and Drapes were up at the spyhole watching him. He opened the door and shouted: For f***'s sake and raced down to reception to complain."

Things weren't to end there.

Tremarco added: "He was at the dinner table and he left his key card again while he went to get food. I grabbed it, raced up to his room again and trashed it again. We waited until he was going back to his room and we raced to ours to look out the keyhole again. He opened the door and went absolutely mental. I think we got off with it because Jim blamed Danny Devine. We never owned up until maybe now!"

First-team coach Scott Kellacher was also in line for some similar treatment but ended up with the last laugh.

A disappointed Tremarco said: "We did something similar to Scott Kellacher but it backfired on us because he ended up getting an upgrade!"

Josh Meekings also knows you have to keep your eyes and wits about you within that Inverness camp.

Meekings said: "I roomed with Graeme Shinnie at that time. I used to take my X-Box with me and we would sit out and chill and play that. Then we would have the likes of Drapes and Carl playing tricks on us. They are the jokers in the pack. I once had my car wrapped up in toilet roll and a bike lock left on the door handle of my car. One of the boys has done it as a prank and they haven't given me the key and it looks like I will need to try and get a bolt cutter or something to take it off. It is madness but at Inverness anything can happen. There is a really good team spirit and set of lads and that was a big part of our success."

There were other double acts, as well as Draper and Tremarco.

James Vincent and Marley Watkins also had to be watched.

"I had played against Marley the season before we came up to Inverness," midfielder Vincent admitted. "We ironically were both pushing for promotion when he was at Hereford and I was at Kidderminster, so it was a bit of a Midlands derby. We became good friends at Inverness and we still remain in touch now. I always roomed with Marley."

They would then get together to gang up on Irish midfielder Aaron Doran.

Vincent explained: "Marley and I would also wind Aaron up or I would be playing them off against each other. During that week we did the bucket challenge, where you fill it with water and leave it on the door and when you come in you get soaked. I think Aaron went about that whole time at the hotel with soaking socks. That is what happens when you get a lot of spare time and that is the type of thing that happens."

Inverness manager John Hughes wasn't finding things so easy going. He was facing absolute turmoil behind the scenes with his father-in-law Eddie told he was dying.

"My father-in-law was told he didn't have too long to live and that was in the lead up to the cup final,"Hughes painfully revealed.

"I was grateful and thankful I was in the hotel in Edinburgh and so I could take the kids to the hotel with me to get them out of the way.

"Just to win the cup, with him still living, was absolutely fantastic and it was a great achievement for the family."

"In life with every high there is a low and just the week after he passed away.

"That hit very, very hard but he would have been very proud of what Inverness achieved, that is for sure."

The Inverness room-mates were going through their final paces. Marley Watkins and James Vincent were playing the Scottish Cup Finals out in their heads.

Vincent joked: "Marley does get carried away with things and starts talking about what ifs. I knew from the team shape and meetings I would be on the bench but because of the injuries I hadn't expected to start. We were talking about things and, as I said, Marley runs away with things and said we were both going to score. I remember Aaron Doran was in our room at the time. He said, 'No chance I am going to be the one that scores to wind Marley up.'"

Watkins reckoned they were nailed on for cup final goals.

He said: "I roomed with Vinny and it proved to be a lucky room. We were chatting rubbish and one of us said: 'I think we are both going to score.'"

For David Raven and Gary Warren it was more a case of what could have been.

Warren said: "We were sitting down at the bar the night before the final and I remember saying I can't believe I am missing a second final. Dave also said he couldn't believe his luck either. He'd scored the winner in the semi-final and then pulled his calf. It really was cruel. But six pints later we were ready to rule the world."

The harsh reality kicked in for Gary Warren at the stadium when his ban kept him out of the dressing room.

Warren admitted, "I was sitting there with my wife thinking I have come so close to getting on the pitch and I missed it. I wasn't allowed on the pitch and I had to go and wish the boys all the best a couple of hours before the game because I wasn't allowed into the dressing room after a certain time."

That is why the defender would love to see the authorities change the rule so other don't have to face the same heartbreak as him.

"I think to give lads more of a chance then when you come to a semi-final then it would be better if all previous bookings were wiped," the defender claimed. "It would give more guys the chance not to miss out on what could be the biggest game of their career."

Most of the Inverness squad woke up to the biggest game of their careers.

There was none of Scotland's traditional bigger clubs but fears of a half-empty national stadium were somewhat misjudged as Inverness and Falkirk united to make it a spectacle of noise and colour in a so-called family final.

Ryan Christie admitted: "A lot of people had said Inverness and Falkirk would never fill out Hampden for the final but I think both clubs proved a lot of people wrong that day. I remember the first time we came out for the warm-up and seeing all the fans was amazing. I couldn't stop smiling and they definitely played their part."

It showed how far the Highlanders had come in such a short space of time.

"When we walked out and saw all the fans it was so surreal," Danny Devine claimed. "It is something I will always remember. Both sets of fans turned out in numbers, but especially Inverness being such a young club. I think the fans, in the end, helped to carry us over the line."

Skipper Graeme Shinnie sent his Inverness players out with a simple pre-match rallying call.

He said: "You have done nothing in a cup competition until you have lifted it and we knew that. We had a celebrated after the semi-final and from then on all the focus had been on the cup final. We went into the game as favourites and we knew we could win it. Getting to a cup final you would expect to play Celtic, Rangers or Aberdeen and so to play a team from a lower league was a bit unusual and for once we knew we were going to be the favourites."

Inverness had looked to start the cup final with a bang – but not in the way one of their players had expected.

"I was fine walking out but then they let off fireworks and they made the loudest noise ever," Carl Tremarco joked. "I was walking past and I just jumped. I don't think I was the only one. Whoever was behind me started laughing. That got us all laughing and relaxed."

The much-travelled full-back then set the tempo for his team in this 130th Scottish Cup Final.

Tremarco said: "I smashed Will Vaulks with a good early challenge. I think that got me going and a few of the lads as well. I remember somebody crossed the ball and I remember thinking if I had run another five yards then I would have had a tap-in but for some reason I stopped!"

Falkirk midfielder Will Vaulks tried his luck with a couple of good long-range efforts. Inverness had to be patient and it was Aaron Doran who forced Jamie MacDonald into his first save and then he kept out another Marley Watkins effort.

Ryan Christie confirmed: "We could sense early on it wasn't going to be a classic. Falkirk made it hard for us and we struggled to get the football we liked to play going. I was lucky enough to start the game but I struggled to get on the ball and to influence the game. I did play a part in the goal. Aaron Doran came in off the left and I managed to play Marley through. When we scored the fans were jumping but from the players it was more about belief. I hardly celebrated because of that relief. I just thought we are ahead now so let's see the game out."

Inverness took the lead seven minutes before the half-time whistle.

Watkins ran on to an Aaron Doran ball to beat Jamie MacDonald, go round and score.

Watkins recalled his moment of glory. He said: "I knew Aaron Doran had it in his locker to create because he is a quality player. We were on the break and I was just trying to check my run to get in behind them. I went looking for a pass but it never came so I changed my run and then Aaron produced a nice bit of skill and threaded it through. The keeper came out and made my decision for me. I took a touch and slotted it home with my left foot."

The Inverness star's celebration was one of sheer emotion and a chance to pay his respects to one of his friend's late dad.

Watkins admitted: "You can't explain the euphoria. It was that bit more special because my best mate Sam Lewis, who played rugby for Worcester Warriors, had lost his dad, Roy, a few weeks before that. I knew his dad and his family really well so I had a t-shirt ready as a tribute to his dad. It simply read: 'R.I.P. Roy Lewis.' Sam was going to come up to the final but after what had happened he didn't. I knew he would be watching on television and he would see it. When I spoke to Sam he thanked me and I got a few texts from his family saying the same thing and that it was a lovely gesture."

The Premiership side were able to hold that lead to the break where the message from manager John Hughes was: "More of the same".

Carl Tremarco said: "Yogi said at half-time don't change and keep going. I don't know what happened in the second half. We were a different team and we were horrendous. Falkirk upped their game but I felt shattered and after 65 minutes I was feeling cramp. I don't know if it was nervous energy but a few of the lads felt the same. I don't think I crossed the halfway line in the second half."

Falkirk manager Peter Houston, against his former Falkirk team-mate Hughes, had other ideas. He made a tactical change that made things a little more uncomfortable for Inverness.

A frustrated Draper confirmed: "We were comfortable in the first half and from there I expected us to kick on and kill the game but it just didn't happen. They changed to a 4-4-2 and we struggled against it, so credit must go to their manager and players."

Falkirk turned up the pressure as Will Vaulks continued to try his luck from distance while Inverness dropped deeper and deeper, having to defend several set pieces.

Hughes went to his bench to try and protect the slender lead.

Ryan Christie admitted: "I got taken off with about 20 minutes to go. I was replaced by the supersub, James Vincent, so I couldn't really be angry with the manager's decision. I wasn't that spectacular and I knew I could have few complaints."

James Vincent went on knowing the balance was beginning to swing towards the Championship side.

Vincent said: "The manager was always good to me and I always felt there was a good chance I would get on, especially as I could play in a few positions for him. Ryan is a lot more attacking and the manager took him off because we needed to get more of a grip on the midfield because Blair Alston and Will Vaulks were beginning to dictate the play for Falkirk. I think I touched the ball once and suddenly Carl got sent off and the gaffer told me I had to go to right-back. We were just up against it and Falkirk were throwing everything at us. We were under the cosh and they were really bombarding us. I was thinking this is going to penalties or they are going to win it."

Another Caley Thistle star was to be leaving the field minutes later but it was in much different circumstances.

Carl Tremarco miscontrolled the ball at the back. It rolled under his foot and he fouled Blair Alston. He was sent off by Willie Collum for denying a clear goalscoring opportunity.

Tremarco's dream had turned into the ultimate nightmare. He left the pitch in tears and with his shirt over his head.

Tremarco painfully recalled: "I was last man. We had been on the attack and the ball came back to me. I have controlled it with my chest and I have tried to take another touch to get it out of my feet and it has got stuck under my foot and behind me. Before I knew what I was going to do I was doing it. I instinctively went to pull him down and I was just hoping there was somebody behind me and I wasn't the last man. Willie Collum had the red out before I was even off my backside. My first thoughts were for the boys. I shouldn't have been playing and then I get my chance and I have messed things up for them. People say my sending off changed the game but it never. We were penned in even before I saw red."

Gary Warren, watching from the stands, knew what Tremarco was going through and went down to the dressing room to make sure he was okay. Warren said: "I had been sent off in similar circumstances and I knew how he was feeling. I felt I had to go and see him because I knew he shouldn't have been alone in a moment like that. I knew from experience he would be sitting blaming himself and thinking he had let everyone down. It feels like the end of the world and I just wanted to be there for him. He was in a bad place and I don't think anything I said helped him, especially after they had scored."

Danny Williams was sent on for Aaron Doran and two minutes later Falkirk were level. Peter Grant got his head on a Blair Alston cross to level.

Defender Danny Devine admitted: "I remember the goal they scored because it was my man (Grant) who got it. It was one of those moments where I just wanted the ground to open up and swallow me. We were down to ten men and I knew it would be a tough task even just trying to get it to penalties."

That compounded Carl Tremarco's misery back in the dressing room, fearing he had blown it for his team.

"I was just back in the dressing room when Falkirk equalised," Tremarco claimed. "There was a television in the dressing room. When I went back in I had my head in my shirt and I was crying my eyes out. Richie Foran took me down the tunnel but I can't remember what he said. He left me and I just started crying. Deano our doorman came in and put the television on and it showed the equaliser. I thought: 'Oh no, the gaffer is going to go off his nut at me here if we lose this.'"

It was a hammer blow and the Inverness camp feared it was slipping out of their hands.

Christie, sitting on the bench, said: "They equalised and I thought we had lost it. Falkirk were piling boys forward and I felt it would be an achievement to get to extra time. I just feared we had thrown it away."

The match was ebbing away from the Highlanders but they managed to dig in. Their players were dead on their feet and hanging in for extra time until they managed to dig deep for one final time.

Marley Watkins set off on a solo run but his weak shot was saved by Jamie MacDonald and that allowed James Vincent a simple right-foot tap-in.

Vincent proudly recalled: "The midfielders didn't go and I know why because they had put in a real shift and were running on empty. Marley broke and I think Falkirk switched off a bit. I started running out. Marley got past a couple of players and I was about five or ten yards behind. I thought I have a chance of getting here when he skips inside and the pass was on. I always tell him he should have squared it to me at that point but I am so glad he never. He went on and had a shot and I was in the right place at the right time to put the ball into the net with my right foot. I can't really put into words the noise and my feelings at the time. Even after the game it was a bit of a blur. I don't think I will realise how big it was until I am finished playing."

Watkins was relieved he hadn't blown things.

"I didn't catch my shot the best," he claimed. "Vinny always tells me I should have squared to him but it ended up with the best outcome again because the keeper parried it into an open goal. Thankfully Vinny dared and he who dares wins."

It brought mass celebrations.

Ryan Christie admitted: "The whole bench erupted and it was absolute madness. Marley and James did so well. It wasn't until I watched the highlights that I realised James had run the length of the pitch to get there."

Inverness still had four minutes and three minutes of stoppage time to see out.

Ross Draper admitted: "The goal came against the run of play because we were defending like mad. It really did come from nowhere. That feeling was brilliant and hard to explain. I hardly had enough energy to celebrate so I just grabbed Danny Devine."

Danny Devine added: "When Vinny scored I was standing next to big Ross Draper. I remember we looked at each other in shock before we grabbed each other and fell to the ground. There was still something like six minutes left but we had to get up and try and see the game out. It was backs against the wall for the last few minutes. When the whistle went I couldn't believe we had won it after going down to ten men and winning the game."

Marley Watkins was replaced by Nick Ross in stoppage time as John Hughes tried to run the clock down.

Watkins said: "I had been carrying an injury and so I didn't last. I came off the bench and I just remember sitting there for the final few minutes hoping we would see it through."

Josh Meekings was to have the final say of the final. He said: "When they scored I thought it can't end with us losing it. So when Vinny scored I was just so relieved. There were still a few minutes left and it was just a case of trying to hold on to what we had. I remember I had the last kick of the final. I hooked it up the line and then the whistle went. I didn't realise what we had achieved at that point. You know what you are trying to do and what is at stake but to actually go and do it was something else. It was totally unbelievable with everything I had gone through and I was delighted to help the team win their first Scottish Cup."

Willie Collum's final whistle saw manager John Hughes jump on to the fence again of the Main Stand and mass hysteria amongst the Inverness ranks transcended – on and off the park.

Skipper Graeme Shinnie knew his side had made history.

"The scenes at the final whistle were unbelievable," the Inverness full-back admitted. "The celebrations with the team were great."

It was a day where dreams became true for James Vincent.

"Marley and I were talking to Aaron after it," Vincent recalled. "Aaron had obviously set Marley up for his goal. He said we had that chat in the room and now all three of us were Scottish Cup winners. Marley quickly shot him down and told him but he never scored. We did! We all had a dream and it came true. It does sound like a cliché but it was true."

Final hero Vincent was adamant it had been very much a team affair.

"I got some of the headlines for my goal but it was all down to the squad," he claimed. "We all did brilliantly and we won the cup through all our efforts. The manager came up to me a good few times after we had won it and said he was delighted for me and then he shoved me away – as he does. The manager was always up for a laugh and a joke but he was emotional after the final. He even had a tear in his eye. So did John Docherty our kitman. It shows what our cup win means to so many people."

Carl Tremarco came flying out of the dressing room and it was going to take a brave man to stop him joining his celebrating team-mates on the hallowed Hampden turf.

"I saw Marley running and I was screaming at the television for him to run it into the corner," Tremarco explained. It was on his left and I was thinking don't shoot, you are never going to score with your left foot. As he shot I saw Vinny coming in and he stuck it in. If there had been a camera in the dressing room then it would have been worth a fortune to see my celebrations with Deano. I tried to get out but they wouldn't let me on because I had been sent off. I told the security if that final whistle goes you won't be stopping me. My granddad, Tony Tremarco, passed away at the start of the season and I was praying to him to help me out. I ran on to the pitch and the first person I got to was Marley and then I started running about like a lunatic and saying sorry to the lads."

Gary Warren wasn't to be held back either.

Warren said: "I wasn't allowed to go on to the pitch until 15 minutes after but I just ignored that and charged on. It was just so emotional. To finally see the team achieve something and to make history and I just raced on to the pitch, running about hugging everybody."

Carl Tremarco was relieved his team had won and he could look John Hughes in the eyes.

"I saw Yogi on the field," he recalled. "He gave me a big hug and called me the luckiest guy in Scotland today. I couldn't argue."

Tremarco also knew he was indebted to James Vincent.

Vincent recalled: "Danny Devine was the first person who grabbed me after I had scored. He was just buzzing because he felt he was at fault at the goal. He then grabbed me at the final whistle because he was so relieved. Carl Tremarco came on and said: 'I owe you a pint.' I told him: 'No, you don't, you owe me more than one!' The guys were buzzing and then I went to see the family."

Things didn't sink in right away for Ryan Christie and others. "It was strange," Christie said. None of the boys had been in that position before. There was a lot of emotion and happiness. It wasn't until I saw my girlfriend, my family and my friends that I started to well up. We milked every last minute on the pitch."

The lap of honour allowed the players to celebrate their crowning moment with the fans and their nearest and dearest.

Josh Meekings said: "My mum and dad were on one side of the stadium and my close friends and family and my uncles, etc. So after the game I ran to one side and then the other to give my shirt to my dad. We then went up to lift the trophy. I had to go and get a t-shirt which we had made for getting to the final to lift the trophy. It was a moment I will never forget. It has been the highlight of my footballing career."

It was left to Graeme Shinnie to walk up the famous steps to lift the trophy.

Shinnie said: "There is no better feeling than knowing you are going up to lift the trophy. It was my first time and I had the captain's armband and one that will be very hard to top. I hope I can replicate it but if I don't I will always have the memories from that day. It will live with me forever. It was amazing and having my daughter, Penelope, on the pitch. She was only four or five months and it was good to have her on the pitch and it is something she can also look back on when she is older."

It was also sheer emotion for Carl Tremarco.

He admitted: "I took my little boy, Seb, to lift the trophy. It was a magic relief that I didn't let anyone down because it was massive for the club to win the Scottish Cup for the first time. The fact we had one hand on it and stupid old me almost threw it away. So all I felt was relief."

Media duties were next as the team returned to the dressing room together. This was where Gary Warren was to emerge from the shadows.

"Stripping is one of my specialities," the suspended defender said. "I tend to take my clothes off wherever I am. I did it and led the boys through a few sing-songs like: 'Oh what a lovely day, For a trip in May, hear the Caley Thistle boys sing: We've won the Scottish Cup.' I then realised the Sky cameras were in the dressing room and I had to quickly get my clothes back on."

Marley Watkins missed most of the celebrations because he had been picked for a drugs test.

"I was in for the drugs test and that ruined my celebrations a bit," Watkins claimed. "I missed all the champagne and the initial celebrations in the dressing room. By the time I had produced my sample everybody was just about ready to get on the bus. That was a bit annoying but I more than made up for things on the bus."

Injured David Raven admitted it was a nightmare watching the final.

"I hated it," the defender claimed. "I was so nervous and I didn't enjoy one minute of that final. The final whistle was unbelievable. I remember Gary jumping on my back and Richie being there. We were on the pitch and the fans were singing my name and it was just a dream come true. I got pictures with the wife and the little one with the cup and it was great. John Hughes came in after it and said milk every moment because it might never happen again."

The team did precisely that on the way back up the road.

Devine said: "It didn't really sink in at the time. It was great lifting the cup, the lap of honour and then the celebrations. The bus journey up the road was some journey. We stopped off in a pub on the way up the road and had a celebration. We also stopped and had a wee dance on the A9. I think there was a video put out as well and it was a day I will never forget."

Carl Tremarco also, unwittingly, managed to turn the national airwaves blue.

He admitted: "The bus going home – wow! That was fun. It was total madness. I had never seen Yogi drink before but with a few beers down him he was a totally different animal. His tie was round his head and his shirt was off. He did an interview with me for BBC on the bus. I had a good few bottles and I didn't even realise it was live. The gaffer came over with the mic and said: 'Carl, what were your first thoughts when you got sent off?' As I said, I didn't know we were live. So I said: 'I f***in' sh** myself didn't I!' Yogi shouts: 'No, no we are live!'"

Manager John Hughes continued to lead the celebrations.

Josh Meekings recalled: "The gaffer had a few beers and then he shouted: 'Everybody off we are going to do the Kolo/Yaya Toure song.' So we got off the bus and were on the edge of the A9 – one of the worst roads in Scotland for accidents – doing the Kolo/Yaya Toure Song. It was absolute madness and carnage but it was fantastic."

The celebration became something of a hit on social media.

James Vincent admitted: "Somebody had said the manager hadn't had a drink for a good few years but he had a few that day. I remember on the bus the gaffer was swinging from the luggage racks and suddenly he caught Aaron with a two-footed lunge. It was madness! The gaffer kept singing Jamsie Jamsie, Jamsie Jamsie Jamsie Vincent and then the others would start singing. We also did the Kolo Kolo, Yaya Yaya Toure song. We were doing it in the pub and we even stopped the traffic as we crossed the road. We did it again going back up the A9. It all stemmed from our Christmas night out when we got a busker to do it and then it just became a bit of an anthem for us. Our Toure celebrations became something of a phenomenon on social media."

The Inverness directors had organised a celebration back at the Caledonian Stadium when the rather bleary-eyed squad made it back home. Things went late on into the night and the next day for the open-top bus parade.

Carl Tremarco ended up with an unlikely housemate that Sunday morning.

"We partied really hard that night," he admitted. "My wife had stayed in Glasgow. I woke up and I heard a noise in my kitchen. I went down and saw David Raven standing there at my kettle with my wife's pink dressing gown on. I asked him if he had had a good night."

The day was to get even better even as Inverness came to see the club's first trophy in their 21-year history.

James Vincent proudly admitted: "The people of Inverness absolutely smashed it for us with the parade and the celebrations. I had never been involved in anything like that before. Marley stayed at mine until the Monday. He is the worst drunk ever and we eventually had to nurse him back to fitness to get rid of him at 10pm on the Monday night."

He knows it helped put Inverness on the map.

Vincent added: "I think the cup win took Inverness to the next level. There had been a division in the past with Inverness Thistle and Inverness Caledonian and I think the victory helped to bring people together and behind us."

Ryan Christie had never witnessed scenes like it in his home city.

Christie claimed: "It was amazing, the whole city was out. I didn't expect that reception to be fair. I had a bit of a hangover but it is one of the best hangovers I have had. The bus parade was when it really hit home that we had made history and how proud we had made everyone. The streets around Inverness were packed and then we went to the Northern Meeting Park. When we walked out I thought there would be a couple of thousand people but there were 15 to 20,000 people there. I will never forget that day."

Gary Warren continued to feel like the man who always missed out on the main event.

He confirmed: "I went home because the next day my wife, Ami, and I were driving to London for an early flight. I missed the bus parade and looking back I was gutted to miss it but at the time I just felt I had to get away. Emotionally I was drained and I needed to get away and to relax. It was just hard and I needed to refocus after missing the final."

The bus parade went through the city and came to a climax in Bught Park where the players were all given a heroes' welcome.

Tremarco said: "We got to Bught Park and we didn't realise how many people would be there. Yogi introduced us all individually and I was just relieved he never said anything about my red card. There was then a band playing and it ended up with Rav up on the stage. They got all the boys up and Rav started singing the Oasis song 'Half a World Away'."

It was something new for Edward Ofere.

He claimed: "It was exceptional. Inverness was extraordinary that day."

That Inverness team had made history but they didn't have long to clear their heads. The price of success was their first European campaign and they had to be back 20 days later.

David Raven said: "We had the bus parade round Inverness which was special. It was a real highlight for me. We had been drinking all the night before and it was unbelievable. I think we were all run-ning on adrenaline come the end. It showed what it meant to the people of Inverness and I am glad they have had a little taste of it. The only downside was that we were back 20 days later for pre-season although there was the added incentive of our first European campaign, although I was still struggling with my calf when I came back."

The players will all have their memories and momentos from their history-making run.

Ryan Christie said: "I have my medal, programme and shirt framed. It is not up on the wall yet but hopefully it will be at some point."

Man of the moment James Vincent was the man who shone on the day.

He admitted: "I have a signed programme, my medal, top and a picture of me scoring. People say I should put it where people can see it but it is in the conservatory. It is something that sums up the day and all the memories for me. It was meant to be and we got the win."

Josh Meekings gave his top away as a thank you to his parents.

He explained: "My dad has my medal in the house and he has my top framed. They put in so much hard work for me as a kid when I was at Ipswich. They had to travel 50 minutes to an hour for most journeys every Tuesday, Thursday, Saturday and Sunday. That is something back for my parents. They have a picture of me giving my top to my dad. I have never seen him well up before but you can see it in his eyes. That shows how much it meant to him and for me winning the Scottish Cup is the best feeling I have ever had."

Marley Watkins's winner's medal also went to his dad.

Watkins said: "My old man, Conrad, has a cabinet with all my medals from my younger years all the way up. My medal is in there."

For Edward Ofere it proved to be a short and successful stay in Scotland.

He added: "I have only won two medals. I won a league with Malmo and then the cup with Inverness so it was a big thing for me. It was good because I was part of an Inverness team that made history by winning their first major trophy."

There was to be more frustration for the likes of David Raven and Gary Warren.

Raven explained: "No, I never got a medal. The lads who weren't in the squad, Dean Brill, Garry Warren and myself never got one either. We tried to get one and we offered to pay for medals but they wouldn't do it for us. They said they only cut so many and they only went to the manager and the stripped players. So there were players on the bench who picked up a medal who didn't even play one minute and I had played in every minute up to the final and never got one. It was just a total shambles and that really disappointed me because the Scottish Football Association were adamant we couldn't get more medals because the Scottish Cup is one of the oldest in the world. It was poor because boys grafted all their careers for moments like that and the SFA simply take it away from them."

Defender Gary Warren was left in the same boat.

"Not getting a medal hurt me more than anything," he insisted. "It is something you work hard for all your life to win something like that. I don't really have anything at all other than my memories and photographs I still have. Knowing I had given everything to the team when I played in the run is what gets me through. That gives me the greatest bit of pride."

There was a price for this Scottish Cup as several of the team left on freedom of contract. Graeme Shinnie had already agreed a pre-contract to join Aberdeen while Edward Ofere couldn't agree terms on an extension. Marley Watkins also left Inverness on freedom of contract earlier that summer for a return to England with Barnsley. He was delighted to sign off on such a high and also knocked back a move to rivals Aberdeen.

"That was my last game for Inverness and it was a good way to go out," Watkins said. "I knew I had a few options but it was always in my thoughts to return to England and to play at as high a level as I could. Aberdeen were also interested but I thought it would have been wrong to go to another Scottish club after everything that I had done and achieved at Inverness. It was an amazing experience and to win the Scottish Cup just capped my time in Scotland off."

INVERNESS'S SCOTTISH CUP-WINNING TEAM 2014/15

Fourth round (29 November 2014 at St Mirren Park)
St Mirren 1 (McAusland) Inverness 1 (Meekings)

Fourth round replay (2 December 2015 at Caledonian Stadium)
Inverness 4 (Warren, Tansey, Williams, Shinnie) St Mirren 0

Fifth round (7 February 2015 at Firhill)
Partick Thistle 1 (Taylor) Inverness 2 (Watkins, Tansey)

Quarter-final (10 March 2015 at Stark's Park)
Inverness 1 (Devine) Raith Rovers 0

Semi-final (19 April 2015 at Hampden)
Inverness 3 (Tansey, Ofere, Raven) Celtic 2 (Van Dijk, Guidetti)
after extra time.

Final (30 May 2015 at Hampden)
Inverness 2 (Watkins, Vincent) Falkirk 1 (Grant)

INVERNESS'S SCOTTISH CUP-WINNING TEAM
Ryan Esson, Graeme Shinnie, Danny Devine, Josh Meekings, Carl Tremarco, Greg Tansey, Ross Draper, Marley Watkins (Nick Ross), Aaron Doran (Danny Williams), Ryan Christie (James Vincent), Edward Ofere.
Manager: John Hughes.

• ROSS COUNTY •
A Massive Stag Party. The 2016 League Cup Winners

IT WAS 1994 when Scottish football decided it was time for change again. This time the plan was to extend the number of clubs across four leagues from a Scottish Premier Division down to a newly-created and named Third Division. This meant there was an avenue for two new clubs to swell the senior ranks.

Inverness – through a controversial amalgamation of the city's Thistle and Caledonian Football Clubs – were odds on to get one of the slots while the likes of Gala Fairydean, Elgin City and Ross County all battled to get the vote for the remaining position.

The vote controversially went to Ross County. Many felt it was a poor and wrong decision with Inverness also coming in from the Highland League and some of the teams from the East of Scotland and Lowland leagues challenged the call.

There were also the cynics who questioned what could a team from a town in Ross and Cromarty, with a population of less than 6,000 people, bring to Scottish football?

More than 20 years on and there is no question that County or 'the Staggies' have more than proved their worth. They, along with Inverness, have been one of Scottish football's recent success stories. They have risen through the leagues, thanks to the vision and financial backing of oil magnate Roy MacGregor, and continue to challenge at the very top of our national game.

They had managed to lift the Scottish Challenge Cup on two separate occasions but the one final piece of the jigsaw that was missing was a major trophy. They came close under Derek Adams, who led them into the top flight, but came up just short as they lost the 2010 Scottish Cup Final to Dundee United.

Jim McIntyre eventually succeeded Adams in 2014 when he was headhunted from Scottish Championship side Queen of the South, along with his assistant, Billy Dodds. McIntyre took over with County in a perilous position at the bottom end of the table. He struggled to get his team going, failing to win a game in nearly two months before they won eight out of nine to go into the split full of confidence and picked up enough points to secure their top 12 status.

Assistant manager Billy Dodds said: "We were fighting relegation when Jim and I came in. We had a good unbeaten run that took us to safety. That was a minor miracle in itself because we were cast adrift at the bottom. Nobody could see us at Christmas turning things around but the boys did it."

Confidence was high and County went into the new campaign on a wave of optimism. The League Cup saw them drawn at the end of August at home to Ayr United in the second round. The Scottish League One side travelled to the Highlands looking to create an upset.

Northern Irish international Liam Boyce's first half effort was enough to douse those hopes.

The former Shelbourne striker recalled: "My goal was a bit lucky. Somebody played a long ball to Jackson Irvine. He took it down and laid it off. I tried to shoot across the keeper and it was going wide but it hit a defender and went in at the near post."

Any hopes of an Ayr comeback were killed off by long-serving Michael Gardyne's second half strike.

Gardyne admitted: "Ayr were doing well. They came well organised with a four and a five and were hard to break down. The gaffer had a bit of a go at us at half-time. It worked because we came out and played a bit better. I don't think we were in any danger, especially after I got a second."

That brought another home tie to Victoria Park. This time it was

Championship hopefuls Falkirk. They hadn't been far away from promotion to the top flight and were a decent side. There were many who were even tipping the Bairns to get the better of County.

Boss McIntyre didn't seem to share those fears as he rested a number of key members from his squad.

Australian Jackson Irvine was given the armband in the absence of Andrew Davies.

Irvine admitted: "A lot of people were tipping Falkirk for an upset because they were flying in the Championship. There were a lot of statements coming out that the gap between the Championship and the mid-to-bottom end of the Scottish Premier League wasn't that big. Falkirk were certainly a lot better than they showed that night. It was a memorable game for us and for me because it was a great win. I also wore the captain's armband for the first time. I was only captain three or four times when Andrew Davies wasn't involved. It was one of those nights when everything we hit seemed to go in. We were very convincing and it was a great night for the club."

It was a match that did end up raising a few eyebrows as County went goal-crazy. It was a case of the Magnificent Seven in the 7-0 thrashing. It was goalless after 30 minutes until a ten-minute hat-trick from Liam Boyce quickly dismantled the Bairns.

Boyce proudly acknowledged: "We played really well. We were doing really well in the league and scoring a few goals but the manager wanted to mix things up and give a few of the boys a run out. I scored a first half hat-trick, I think I managed to get all my goals within a ten-minute spell. Two of my goals were headers at the back post and the other came from a corner. It fell to me and I managed to back-heel it and it went in via a few bodies. Everything hit that night seemed to end up in the net."

That was certainly the case as Raffaele De Vita made it 4-0 at half-time before goals after the break from Jonathan Franks, Brian Graham and Darren Holden completed this one-sided affair.

Boyce also managed to grab a momento from the night. "I have got the match ball and got it signed by all the players," he said. "It is even more special as it was in a run that saw us go on and win the cup. The funny thing is that I hadn't scored a competitive hat-trick until I had come to Scotland. I now have scored four or five so Scotland has proved lucky."

Manager Jim McIntyre knows his team had luck on their side that night.

"Falkirk went on and had an unbelievable season that year," the County boss insisted. "When you look at things it was a freak result. Everything we did worked and for Falkirk they would have had a lot to pick the bones out of."

County continued to look impressive in the league and were very much in the fight for a top six finish. McIntyre still felt they were short of firepower coming out of the August window, despite being able to bring influential midfielder Martin Woods back from Shrewsbury Town.

Woods said: "When I went down south I just felt it wasn't what I really wanted. There were a few teams who were interested but I knew what I would be getting at Ross County. I had been there the previous season and I knew all the boys and Jimmy McIntyre. We were all part of the team who had kept the team up that previous season and that had created a real bond between us. So I knew Ross County was where I wanted to come back to."

Jim McIntyre also decided to take a chance on the relatively unknown Dutch striker Alex Schalk, who had been recommended by former Rangers player Neil Murray. Schalk had ripped up his contract at Go-Ahead Eagles in his homeland and was still a free agent come October. He came in on trial and did enough to win a deal for the remainder of the season.

"I ripped my contract up before the close of the transfer window with Go-Ahead," Schalk explained. "They kept playing me on the left wing when I am a striker and it wasn't for me. I then heard Ross County were looking for a striker similar to my style. I was lucky because I knew a couple of Dutch players, including Marc Klok and he was really honest with me and that helped me make up my mind. I went there for a week on trial and things were really positive. I won a contract and eventually broke into the team and since then it has been an upward spiral for me."

One of Schalk's first matches was the Highland derby against Inverness in the quarter-finals of the League Cup. The Caledonian Stadium may only have been 24 miles away but it wasn't a happy hunting ground for County. County had also failed to win in their previous six derbies going into this midweek clash and thrown into the mix was the fact that their Highland neighbours had also lifted the Scottish Cup that summer.

If the omens weren't good then it also looked like luck was in short supply as well as first-choice goalkeeper Scott Fox missed out after suffering ankle ligament damage in the home derby defeat to Inverness back in October. Former Manchester United keeper Gary Woods was brought in to deputise.

County, however, looked to be in safe hands when they took the lead minutes before the half-time interval. The visitors had been the better team and more than merited their lead thanks to Jackson Irvine.

The former Celtic youngster said: "It was a ground we hadn't won at in a long time. It was set up with it being a derby day. It was very exciting and I was lucky enough to score the first goal. It was straight off the training ground. We managed to block some of the Inverness players off and that gave me a free header seven or eight yards out. Our tactics paid off because you don't get many chances like that in a game. I don't think our domination for the first 70 minutes was reflected in the scoreline. We did get a second goal just after half-time. We were playing brilliantly but we couldn't get that third goal to kill things off."

Gardyne, in his fourth spell at the club, once again was heavily involved as he grabbed the killer second.

Gardyne admitted: "I thought we were brilliant in that game and we should have been 2-0 up before I scored. Inverness tried to play it out from the back and we nicked it. Craig played a ball through, I controlled it and drove at Carl Tremarco and then curled it in the bottom corner. It is always nice to score against them. It was our first win at the Caledonian Stadium and first semi-final appearance in the League Cup."

Greg Tansey made it a nervier end than it should have been with a long-range goal but County managed to hold on and progress.

"I came on for the last few minutes," Schalk explained. "I didn't make much of an impact but I was just glad to get some time for my new club. There were big celebrations after the game but I have to say it was a quiet one for me. I just went home to bed and looked at that game as a start and something to build on."

County were in the last four along with Celtic, Hibs, and St Johnstone. Keeper Scott Fox was sent down for the official photo call and Hampden draw.

Fox said: "I went down to represent Ross County at the draw. Brian Easton from St Johnstone was there, along with John Collins from Celtic and James Keatings of Hibs. We came out the hat and it was Ross County v Celtic. It was the one we didn't want but we knew we had to beat them at some point. I don't think Celtic cared who they got. When we got Celtic the gaffer joked the next day: 'I'm not sending you to a draw again.' We always gave the boys jib if we got a poor draw and I knew I was going to get it. I told him: 'I don't want to go again!'"

Treble-chasing Celtic were the team everybody wanted to avoid although they weren't exactly firing on all cylinders under the guidance of their Norwegian boss Ronny Deila. McIntyre's situation wasn't helped when on-form striker Liam Boyce suffered an injury.

"I hurt my hand in a league match against Kilmarnock," he admitted. "I got my hand tangled in a challenge and ended up cracking a couple of bones in my hand. I was out for six weeks and it was really touch and go whether I was ready for the Celtic game."

McIntyre was able to make full use of the January transfer window to bring in David Goodwillie as cover on loan from Aberdeen, while an old familiar face also made the same journey for a second stint with County.

Defender Paul Quinn decided to quit the title-chasing Dons for family reasons and decided he wanted to return to his second home. His second homecoming was in the Hampden semi-final against his boy-hood heroes, Celtic.

Both teams knew that whoever came out on top would face Hibs, who had seen off Dundee United 24 hours earlier in the first semi-final.

McIntyre thought Quinn would add some solidity to his defence heading to the national stadium but with less than 60 seconds on the clock they were 1-0 behind to a Gary Mackay-Steven opener.

Jackson Irvine explained: "We went in there quietly confident because we were unlucky not to take something off them at their place. We went into the game and we lost the goal after 26 seconds. I remember looking up to the clock and I couldn't even believe it. I was thinking: 'Here we go. This could be five or six.' They created several chances and I remember thinking is there any chance we will be able to ride this out? It was the longest ten minutes of my career. It was three or four minutes of backs-to-the-wall football but we managed to get through it and turn the game around."

Irvine, the majority of his team-mates and their much-travelled fans were also left fearing the worst.

Gardyne said: "Leigh Griffiths squared it to Gary Mackay-Steven, who scored after 14 seconds. I remember thinking this is the worst possible start but we started playing and the game changed with the sending off."

County had to dig in and weather the storm which, to their credit, they did.

Efe Ambrose had almost been the Celtic hero, when he had an effort cleared off the line by Richard Foster, and then ended up being the villain.

Alex Schalk managed to get away from Mikael Lustig before he was caught inside the box by the Nigerian international defender Ambrose, leaving referee Craig Thomson no option but to show a red card and award a spot kick.

Schalk insisted: "The game changed when Efe Ambrose brought me down. There was a through ball into the box. I was first to react and I got there just before Ambrose and he brought me down. We got the penalty and he got a red card. It was 100 per cent a penalty and I wasn't sure if he would be sent off or not. That brought a massive change in the game and from that moment on we felt like it was our game to win."

It was left to Martin Woods to take responsibility from the spot. Celtic tried everything in their power to put him off with delaying tactics after Ambrose's red card but he managed to keep his nerve.

He recalled: "I just put the ball down. It seemed to take an eternity for me to be able to take the kick. I just kept myself focused and never looked at the goalkeeper. I just kept looking at the ball. I knew where I was going to put it. I put it low to the keeper's left and fortunately he went the other way."

Wood also managed to lose a few family and friends in the process with his leveller.

Woods added: "My dad, Charlie, and a lot of my friends are all Celtic fans. A lot of them drink in the Imperial Bar in Airdrie. So when I scored I ran in front of the Celtic supporters. I tried not to go over-the-top but I just had this huge smile on my face running up the line knowing I had scored at Hampden against Celtic."

The Highlanders knew that with the numerical advantage they had the edge and it was up to them to make full use of it.

"The sending off was pivotal," Paul Quinn acknowledged. "We grew into the game and got that bit of luck you need against a team like Celtic. To go 1-0 down against Celtic and the way we came back was remarkable. We still had to beat ten men, we still needed to create and to score the goals. It was a magical day and led to the fairy tale ending."

Celtic were just delighted to still be level going in at the interval while County knew they were the team in the ascendancy.

Boss Jim McIntyre also made a change, bringing off defensive midfielder Stuart Murdoch and sending on the more attacking threat of winger Jonathan Franks.

"The manager saw an opportunity to be a little bit more attacking against ten men," Jackson Irvine claimed. "It allowed us to get more involved in the game."

Paul Quinn smelt blood. He said: "When we came out at half-time we felt we could cause an upset. We quickly eradicated any negativity from the early part of the game. We said they would have been vulnerable going to 1-1 and down to ten men. The manager said if we could get the next goal it would put doubt in Celtic's minds and allow us to go on and win the game."

Just three minutes after the restart Quinn was the hero – and Celtic's slayer again.

Quinn claimed: "It is one we worked on. I'd go to the front post and try to interrupt their markers to try to get space for one of our players in behind. The ball was over-hit and Andrew could only head it back and so in that position I hang out in case anything drops back out. It left me with an easy tap-in. To see it work on that stage and to put us 2-1 up against the champions was surreal. Scoring was unbelievable because I had a good record against Celtic. I had done it for Motherwell and Aberdeen and was doing it on a bigger occasion with Ross County. I thought scoring for Aberdeen to put us top of the league was massive but that goal helped us put one foot in the final."

While there was one goal in it Celtic always had hope but that was killed just after the hour when Alex Schalk put them to the sword.

"My goal came on the counter attack," he beamed. "Martin Woods played me in and I took a shot with my left foot and it ended up in the top bin. My right is my strongest but it was a good finish on my left. The boys still give me stick for my celebration. I crossed my arms as if the game was over but I didn't realise we almost had half an hour to play."

Paul Quinn is in no doubt Schalk's strike was the one.

He claimed: "The third goal sticks out for me more than my own. It put a marker in our heads. 'This has gone in our favour and we are going to make the final now.'"

There, as always, was still to be some late drama when substitute Brian Graham, who had replaced Schalk, was adjudged to have handled inside the box.

That put 40-goal Leigh Griffiths eye-to-eye with Scott Fox, who came out on top as the penalty hero.

Scott Fox said: "Scott Thomson (the goalkeeping coach) told me Leigh Griffiths will go to your left and go early. I went there and thankfully it has just hit me and the ball cannoned away. It was a confidence boost for the whole team. We still had a two-goal cushion and we were looking to see it out. If they had scored then it would have been a lot harder to protect."

Hero Schalk admitted it was a nightmare seeing out the game on the sidelines.

"It is always more nervous when you watch games from the bench," the former Dutch under-21 cap claimed. You can have no influence on the pitch and watching the rest of the game killed me. The boys were fantastic and managed to see the game out."

County were also afforded the luxury of getting talisman Liam Boyce some game time as he took to the pitch with a wrist protector round his hand.

Boyce knows he was lucky. "I came off the bench but I wasn't 100 per cent," he confessed. "I was struggling with my balance and frightened in case I knocked my hand."

Jackson Irvine could even have added a fourth late on but even that couldn't dampen the perfect day for him against his former employers. County were going back to Hampden for their first League Cup Final.

A delighted Jackson Irvine said: "It was weird because we had achieved something huge in the club's history. It was our first time in the League Cup Final and only our second major cup final. We knew we had done something memorable. We all knew it was a massive occasion but we were also aware we still hadn't won anything."

For Irvine it had only been a few months earlier he had quit Celtic – although he had several loan spells away including his first stint at County.

Irvine said: "I had only left Celtic six months before, technically. I played with Callum McGregor and Kieran Tierney all the way through, along with some of the other boys. I was five-and-a-half years there and it was special doing it against my old team. Signing for Ross County permanently was one of the best things I could have done."

Another hero and former Celtic player Scott Fox also knows that was a day when it was shown the underdog really can bite.

"We got a bit of luck but on the whole we played some good football and we deserved it," Fox claimed. "It was a great day. Nobody believed we could do it but we believed in ourselves."

Hampden hero Paul Quinn admitted it was a big moment and one he felt he had owed County and their boss Jim McIntyre.

Quinn said: "That was the first time in my career where I felt I got caught up in the emotion of it all. We don't get to many semi-finals or cup finals. So to score was overwhelming. I had only been back at the club a few days but I had managed to repay some of the trust and belief the club had shown in taking me back. That was a big thing for me."

Fellow goalscorer Alex Schalk still thinks that has been his best performance in a County shirt although there was still more magic to come.

Schalk admitted: "The semi-final was an unforgettable game for me. It was one of the best games I have played for Ross County. To play against a big club like Celtic was massive for me at Hampden Park."

Martin Woods grabbed further glory when he was named as man of the match.

"I was doing an interview after I had got the award," he explained. "I remember the build-up to the game was about Anthony Stokes and Liam Henderson (both on loan from Celtic) being allowed to play against their parent club in the final. I felt we had been written off and everybody had just handed Celtic the game. So I had a pop at the people who had claimed that. They then went back to the studio and put it to Alan Stubbs. He wasn't happy and told them he was going to phone me because he knew me from Sunderland. I did text him but we had a laugh and joked about it."

Liam Boyce joked his team had spoiled a family celebration.

Boyce explained: "My brother, John, is a big Celtic fan and they were also across for my cousin's (Sean) stag party. I think I spoiled their day and the only good thing is that they had quite a bit to drink so I am not sure how much of the game they actually remember. Things couldn't have been that bad because they all came back across to watch me in the final."

Martin Woods also took his chances by returning to his dad's Celtic-minded pub, the Imperial Bar, in Airdrie.

The cultured midfielder said: "I went back and some of the Celtic fans in there gave me a bit of it and I was expecting that. My dad, Charlie, was there. It was probably bittersweet for him. He was disappointed Celtic were out but he was delighted for me for getting to a final. It was the same for my mum, Marie."

All eyes were now on the Hampden return on Sunday, 13 March.

Jim McIntyre wanted his team to keep their focus and to keep their place in the top six but minds were always going to wander. They also wanted to follow in Inverness's footsteps, who had lifted the Scottish Cup at the end of the previous season.

"The idea of both trophies being in the Highlands was quite an attractive proposition," Jackson Irvine claimed. "People will always underestimate what an achievement that was for two former Highland League clubs. We had all the hype and it was everywhere we went. It was hard for us because we were sitting comfortably in the top six without getting near the top three. Our eyes were on that final for five or six weeks and we all wanted to be involved."

Boss Jim McIntyre tried to keep things as normal as possible. He also got a useful insight into how County could do a number on their fellow cup finalists by their Highland rivals Inverness.

Assistant Billy Dodds explained: "A couple of weeks before the final we went to see Hibs play Inverness. I was working for the BBC and Jim McIntyre was there to scout on them. We saw Inverness go 3-5-2 against Hibs for a spell and it really worked. We hadn't played that formation all season and we knew it was a major gamble but we just felt it could work against Hibs. Jim and I both agreed it was the way to go because it cancelled out their midfield. They played a tight diamond in the midfield and they were all good footballers and we felt with that system we would nullify them.

"We kept Richard Foster at the back to start with to look like we were playing with a four at the back before we moved him forward. I think it was a gamble that paid off."

McIntyre's preparations were going to plan until one of his stalwarts suffered a serious injury.

Keeper Scott Fox painfully recalled: "We were playing Dundee United and I tried to make a block for their second goal but my knee had opened up a wee bit and then one of my players landed on top of me. I knew something was up but we had used up all our subs. I went for a scan and it showed I had suffered a grade two tear in my right knee although I didn't need surgery, so that gave me my chance."

The push for a cup final place, however, was to end in total devastation for Fox.

Fox explained: "Even if I had been on the bench it would have been great because I wanted to be involved in a final. It was gutting, really gutting. I knew the Monday before the final that I wasn't going to make it. The boys were great and looked after me. Gary Woods was gutted for me but I knew it had to be about him because we need him to win the cup."

Back-up keeper Woods knew he was going to get an unexpected opportunity.

"When I came up to Ross County the manager told me that I was coming up to fight for my place," Woods confirmed. "Scott got the gloves at the start of the season and did well. I was fortunate that Scott had been really unlucky and picked up a couple of injuries and that gave me my chance that season. I am delighted to have played in the final but I did feel for Scott because I know he was gutted to miss the game through injury."

Another of County's stars, striker Craig Curran, who had come up from the English non-leagues, also missed out with a head knock. He was forced to watch from the stands with more than 7,000 Staggies fans who had bought tickets for Hampden.

Members of the Irvine family were flying from the other side of the world to see the game. Jackson Irvine explained: "My mum, Danielle, and, dad, Steve, came over from Melbourne along with my sister, Maxi. My dad is Scottish so I also had some local family at the game along with a lot of my mates. Marcus Fraser and I have a lot of friends who are Celtic fans. They told us that the final was the most they celebrated a win that Celtic weren't involved in."

There was also a major Dutch contingent amongst the Scottish ranks.

Schalk said: "I had about 20 people who flew over from Holland for the final. My dad, Ad, and my brothers, Joost and Loek, were amongst my supporters. They all came across and stayed in Glasgow for a couple of days."

There was still time to swell the numbers even further in the build-up thanks to a baby boom in the cup final County squad.

Captain Andrew Davies and keeper Gary Woods both became dads the week before. That is one of the reasons why Jim McIntyre didn't take his team away from Dingwall.

Davies confirmed: "It was a mad week and one I didn't get much sleep in the build-up. To have our baby boy, Hugo, along with my other son, Jensen, and my wife, Lucy, before the final was amazing."

The only thing that was any different for the County team was the rousing send-off they got from the locals before they headed south.

Striker Alex Schalk admitted it was an emotional affair. He said: "We got a send-off from some fans before we left for Hampden. I remember seeing some of the older fans crying. We drove through the High Street and there were lots of people there. Seeing them all, that gave me goosebumps.

"It was about them and trying to get the cup back to the Highlands for them. People like these fans and our chairman Ray MacGregor."

It might have been a first League Cup Final and a step into the unknown but there was still pressure on the Highlanders. They had not only beaten Celtic but were favourites going in against a Championship side in Hibs, who albeit were gunning for a domestic treble of both cups and the second tier title.

No. 2 Billy Dodds acknowledged that. He said: "There was pressure on us because we were looking to win our first major cup. We also went in as slight favourites in a lot of people's eyes because we were the Scottish top-flight team. The pressure was on us. We had also got there the hard way beating a good Falkirk team, then the derby and Celtic at Hampden."

Defender Paul Quinn was confident his dressing room and the characters within it would deal with the occasion.

"We knew it was an even game," Quinn said. "We knew Hibs were in a false position in the league and knew the threat they posed. Yes, we were playing a team from a lower league but we were just preparing ourselves for any ups or downs on the day, basically for any eventuality. That stood us in good stead for going into the cup final. I had only played in two cup finals and won leagues and got to a play-off final down south but I think we handled the psychological side of things really well. It also helps we have a great group of lads and some huge characters in there."

There was still room for a headache or too and pre-cup finals sweats – although for all the wrong reasons as the County team holed up in their Cumbernauld base.

"I didn't train all week because I had the flu," worried centre-half Paul Quinn said. "I came in with sickness and diarrhoea. I trained on the Friday and felt dreadful. I was then up all night coughing and spluttering and Martin Woods was raging with me because he couldn't get to sleep. It turned into a disaster because before that everything had been going so well. It was a battle just to get on the pitch."

It gave Martin Woods an unwanted 30th birthday present when he eventually woke up on cup final day.

Woods joked: "He coughed all night and I think I ended up with about three hours' sleep. When I did wake up I felt as if I had a cold as well. I was thinking: 'Great Quinny, you have killed me.'"

While Quinn and Woods were burning up two of their team-mates were, ironically, watching *Man on Fire*.

"I roomed with Ian McShane," Michael Gardyne explained. "We always do. We normally go to bed about 1am and then get up for a leisurely breakfast. We normally just chill and get the tunes on, I love a bit of Whitney Houston and then we normally watch a movie. I think we watched *Man on Fire* with Denzel Washington."

The County management team were hoping Woods and Quinn would make it as Jim McIntyre looked to finalise his cup final team.

Assistant Billy Dodds said: "There were a couple of headaches. I have been there as a player. I was left out of the Rangers v Ayr United cup final although I knew I would be on the bench. Jonathan Franks was one we had been toiling with. He had done well in the weeks leading up to that and he just missed out. We also went to the 3-5-2 formation. We knew they could hurt us in the middle of the park but we felt we could get joy down the flanks."

Top scorer Liam Boyce still wasn't back to his prolific best, due to his hand problem, but his manager felt he was worth the risk.

"Liam had missed a lot of football with his hand," McIntyre conceded. "Taking him off pretty early was probably my biggest call. We took a chance on him and it clearly didn't work."

Jim McIntyre and Billy Dodds had done their homework and had left nothing to chance. They knew their team were in the big-time although their road to Hampden couldn't exactly have been called the fast lane.

Billy Dodds said: "We were actually ten or 15 minutes later than we had expected before we got to Hampden. We had spoken to the police. We stayed at the Westerwood at Cumbernauld and we usually left half an hour before we wanted to get to a ground in Glasgow. It was agreed we would leave at 1pm but the policeman didn't tell us we were being taken the tourist route. We would normally go in off the M73 but the outrider took us out over the Kingston Bridge, past Ibrox and in through Pollokshields to avoid the Hibs traffic. Even the outrider started to panic the longer it was taking. We were 45 minutes in and our secretary, Fiona MacBean, was on the phone asking where we were. By the time we got closer to Hampden there were six outriders trying to get us to the national stadium rushing us to Hampden with the blue lights on and racing down the wrong side of the road. Jim McIntyre and myself were just looking at each other thinking: 'What is going on here?'"

All their best-laid plans had to be re-adjusted, while their opponents had a far more relaxed approach.

Billy Dodds confirmed: "We eventually got there and most of our pre-match plans were in chaos. The Hibs players had been out on the pitch for a stroll and our boys got about 60 seconds out there before we had to rush them back in and I did a bit of video analysis and Jim did his team talk. I was late with the team lines and we had to shout at the boys to get ready. We had to rush everything and maybe that was a good thing because we didn't have time to worry or think about things!"

Jim had won and lost cup finals and knew this was an opportunity his team could let pass them by.

McIntyre, speaking about his rousing pre-match speech, said: "I told the boys not to have any regrets. I have been lucky enough to be involved in a few finals and the worst thing in the world is leaving as a loser or watching your rivals going up to lift the cup. When you get to your first final you are happy to be there. That was certainly the case for me when I was a youngster at Airdrie. I didn't want the players to have that mindset because there were a few in my squad that it was going to be their first final. We were conscious of that. We were there to win it and not just to make up the numbers, especially after beating Celtic in the semi-finals."

County's stars had stepped out and starred at Hampden in the semi-final against Celtic but this was something different again.

Liam Boyce had been involved in international football, in Germany and in cup finals back in his homeland of Northern Ireland but Hampden was something different.

He said: "I had played a few cup finals back in Northern Ireland and games at Windsor Park but that season was the first time I had played at Hampden. It was some experience."

The strain was showing more on other members of the Ross County squad in the build-up but it was nothing to do with nerves.

Martin Woods explained: "I went into the toilet before the game and Paul Quinn was in there being sick. I know Paul and having roomed with him I knew he was struggling. 'Coach' is certainly not the nervous type. He never has been. I was struggling as well with whatever he has passed on but both of us were determined to go out and do a job for the team, the club, our supporters and all our families and friends in the crowd."

Jim McIntyre went with Gary Woods in goal; a back three of Marcus Fraser, Andrew Davies and Paul Quinn; a midfield three of Ian McShane, Martin Woods and Jackson Irvine with Richard Foster and Michael Gardyne down either side and Liam Boyce and Alex Schalk leading the line.

McIntyre went with his secret masterplan of a 3-5-2 formation and it seemed to have the desired effect from the off.

Hibs had plenty more experience within their ranks when it came to League Cup glory, compared to Ross County.

Lewis Stevenson had won it previously with Hibs, while Kevin Thomson had lifted the cup at Rangers, John McGinn at St Mirren along with Anthony Stokes and Liam Henderson who had picked up winners medals at Celtic.

That was the one area where County were lacking. Paul Quinn had been a beaten finalist with Motherwell 11 years earlier while Michael Gardyne, despite various spells away, remained the only survivor from the County team that had lost the Scottish Cup Final to Dundee United in 2010, although Scott Boyd was named amongst the substitutes.

Even in his pre-match interview McIntyre refused to give too much away apart from the fact that the 11 he had picked could adopt a 4-4-2 or 3-5-2 formation.

"We caught a lot of people off-guard with the 3-5-2 because we had never really played in that formation before," Jackson Irvine believed. "Hibs played a diamond formation and that brought them a lot of success that season. We were able to counteract that formation."

It was an even affair with not much between the teams at all. It lived up to the pre-match claims of Hibs manager Alan Stubbs that: "It would be an open affair between two very evenly matched teams."

Hibs top scorer Jason Cummings had the first effort with a long-range effort from 20 yards that Gary Woods had to tip over. The English keeper also had to be brave and dive at the feet of David Gray to deny the opposition's skipper within the first 15 minutes.

County's first sight of goal came from a well-worked corner but Martin Woods couldn't keep his shot down.

Hibs, if anyone, were getting on top with Anthony Stokes forcing the busy Gary Woods into another brave block.

Then in the 25th minute came the turning point. Martin Woods managed to rob Liam Henderson in the County half. The former Doncaster Rovers midfielder pushed it on to Alex Schalk who managed to force himself away from John McGinn and tried to play in Michael Gardyne but the ball was behind him. Kevin Thomson picked up and then played a slack pass to Anthony Stokes, allowing Jackson Irvine to run forward.

Jackson Irvine recalled: "It was a counter-attack. They won the ball back but I cut out a square pass and managed to nip in and drive forward with the ball. It was all about picking the right pass and I managed to slip in Michael Gardyne."

It was left to County's soon-to-be record appearance-maker and goalscorer. He was played in and managed to ride a tackle and slot home easily home from eight yards in the 26th minute to spark mass celebrations amongst the dark blue and white Highland legions.

Michael Gardyne admitted: "We scored against the run of play. I made a run and never got the ball and I kind of went in the huff a little bit. The ball then fell to Jackson and he slotted me in. I was one-on-one and I was about to take it round the keeper but the boy Marvin Bartley has come in and made a great tackle. I was lucky. He kicked it off my left leg but it meant I still had control of the ball and I was able to knock it into the empty net. It was amazing. I put my arms out to look up at the sky. All sorts of things went through my mind. I had lost a Scottish Cup Final and to score in the League Cup Final was great. I scored at the Hibs end and that silenced them as well. What a feeling to have done that and to celebrate with all the boys."

It proved to be something of a temporary tonic for some of County's struggling stars.

"I didn't feel 100 per cent and even when I went to celebrate the first goal I felt drained," Woods confirmed. I knew it was a cup final and I just had to get through it. It was more a case of taking care of my man and doing my job rather than doing anything else."

Hibs came back fighting and a fine goal-saving tackle from Jackson Irvine on David Gray again just after the half-hour kept County ahead.

Jason Cummings then split the County defence and got through but Gary Woods again tipped wide.

County thought they had done enough to go into the interval with their lead intact. Hibs had other ideas just seconds short of the 45-minute mark. A Liam Henderson corner from the right was flicked on by the head of David Gray. Andrew Davies got there in front of Darren McGregor. Hibs defender Liam Fontaine then nicked it off Ian McShane and blasted the ball past Gary Woods and Richard Foster who was on the line.

Jim McIntyre had to get his players in and get them going again.

He said: "We were hoping that goal wouldn't see us capitulate. Normally, goals change games and can swing the momentum. We had to dig in because they had a few corners and defensive situations."

The manager geed us his team and told them to go out and start again.

Michael Gardyne revealed: "The manager was brilliant at the interval. He mainly spoke about belief. We had to believe in ourselves and to do more to win the game."

The medical staff also had their work cut out. They were left fighting a losing battle to try and get an off-colour Paul Quinn to end his cup final appearance prematurely.

Quinn said: "The doctor said to me at half-time you need to come off. I basically told him no chance – it is 1-1 in a cup final. The lads round me knew I was struggling and gave everything. They were running off in breaks in play to get me energy drinks and gels because they knew I had nothing left. The manager was even asking should he make his third sub. I was telling him I don't think I would have got through extra time but I wasn't willing to give it up. But I didn't want to let the team down either."

Anthony Stokes had a turn and shot that went just wide but apart from that the second period was pretty much null and void.

County boss Jim McIntyre turned to his bench, sending on Brian Graham for Liam Boyce.

Boyce knew it wasn't his finest hour. He admitted: "I got my hand support off just before the final. I was still a bit apprehensive about using my hand and putting it out. I was concerned it might break again and it did a couple of weeks later when I was away with Northern Ireland. I just wanted to get through it and to help the team. I don't think it was one of my best games."

Graham went on with simple instructions. He explained: "The gaffer told me to go on and ruffle up a few people and I felt I did that."

He more than did that, minutes later he was on the deck after Marvin Bartley, who was booked, caught him in the face as they tussled for the ball. It could have quite easily been a red card but the Hibs player got away with it.

There were concerns over Quinn long-term and Michael Gardyne who picked up a knock but it was Ian McShane who made way for Stuart Murdoch in the 78th minute.

That switch coincided with County's best spell of the second period.

Alex Schalk forced Mark Oxley into a flying save to keep out his free kick and then Brian Graham had the ball in the net but was rather harshly denied his moment of glory for a questionable foul on the Hibs keeper.

A frustrated Graham said: "I felt hard done by not getting the second goal. It wasn't a foul it was a goal but we never got it. I don't even think my first effort was offside. I was thinking was it about to be one of those days?"

It was a frustrating watch for the likes of Craig Curran and Scott Fox, who had to watch on nervously from the stands.

"I was in the stand with Craig," Scott Fox added. "We kicked every ball and it was a long 90 minutes. We had a few kids round about us and they had to listen to a few swear words."

McIntyre went for his final change. He knew his team had to win it in 90 minutes with so many of his stars having given their all and running on fumes. He was looking for one final push, sending on Jonathan Franks for the more defensive-minded Richard Foster five minutes from time.

It saw the former Middlesbrough winger Franks start down the left before he swapped with Michael Gardyne.

"The boys stuck at it and the subs made a real impact," Jim McIntyre stated. "I think we were brave because there were a few boys out on their feet. We didn't want to see it go into extra time and that is why we made positive substitutions with Franks, Murdoch and big Brian. Putting Franks on allowed us to switch with Gardyne to go with two wingers and we got the goal from that. Big Brian holds the ball up and gets it wide. The game was finely balanced and it really could have gone either way because Hibs put so much into it as well."

Tired bodies and minds saw players from both sides going down with cramp in the final minutes. Alex Schalk was one of them but he was able to dig deep and go one more time in the final 60 seconds.

Brian Graham won it ahead of David Gray and forced the ball on to Schalk. He played it to Gardyne on the left who raced away from Marvin Bartley and towards the Hibs box.

A fatigued Michael Gardyne admitted: "I started on the right. We made a sub and I moved on to the left. I got the ball. I looked up and I thought this park looks huge. I was knackered. I ran as far as I could then I threw a cross into the box and I remember Alex Schalk scoring."

His left-foot cross was cut out at the back post by Liam Fontaine but fell perfectly for Alex Schalk to score the easiest and biggest goal of his career.

The hero proudly recalled: "A lot of our boys were struggling with cramp a bit at the end so we couldn't have scored a winner at a better time. Midge had a 70-yard run and I raced to keep up with him on the counter. He did brilliantly to put the ball into the box. It was going to Brian Graham at the back post and a defender tried to intercept it and he hit the ball with the sole of his foot and it came to me at the near post. It fell into my path brilliantly and it was my easiest finish ever. I didn't have to do much."

The Dutchman ripped off his shirt and jumped into the front row of the Hampden Main Stand sporting nothing but a heart monitor on his top half. For every Ross County fan it might as well have been a superhero's vest. Schalk was yellow-carded for his celebrations but it was a small price to pay.

"As a striker you dream of things like that happening," Schalk added. "It was fantastic and that is the best feeling I have ever had."

The delight was there for everyone to see with Jim McIntyre punching the air before he was rugby-tackled in joy by loyal assistant Billy Dodds.

The County players knew then the job was done.

Paul Quinn confirmed: "When Alex scored I turned to Davo (Andrew Davies) and said we have done it."

Davies might have had one eye on the cup but in stoppage time he was caught by the flying elbow of Liam Fontaine and had to get treatment before he was able to return.

Referee Kevin Clancy indicated there would be four minutes of stoppage time plus the added minutes for Andrew Davies' knock.

It still turned out to be a nervy finale.

Billy Dodds joked: "I know it was a last-minute winner but in theory it wasn't. We had five minutes of additional time so we had another six minutes to see out. So we might have been rushed before the game but time certainly dragged at the end of it. What a relief because I didn't really fancy another 30 minutes. Both teams had players running on empty."

Hibs still had chances. David Gray's header was easily held by Gary

Woods. The former Manchester United graduate then had to make an even better stop six minutes into stoppage time by tipping Liam Fontaine's effort wide.

Gary Woods modestly acknowledged: "I made a couple of decent stops but the whole team in front of me was also amazing. They defended brilliantly to a man from the defenders right up to the strikers. It was a real team effort and I think that showed because Hibs played well and pushed us all the way but thankfully we got there in the end."

Hibs had one final push and even sent up keeper Mark Oxley for the do or die corner. Andrew Davies booted the ball clear and much to Michael Gardyne's frustration Kevin Clancy blew the final whistle.

Gardyne said: "The final whistle I remember well. They had a corner and their keeper went up for it. We won it and cleared it. I was up the pitch and I was behind Lewis Stevenson and John McGinn so I had a clear sight of goal and I thought I could score again but the referee blew the whistle. I realised we had won. I fell to my knees, hands over my face and I couldn't believe we had won the cup."

The County management team celebrated together on the touchline.

Assistant Billy Dodds explained: "When the final whistle went Jim, myself and all the staff were going crazy celebrating. It was remarkable what we had done. It was a fairy tale that Ross County had won that first national trophy. We were just relieved we had got over the line and got the job done. I know Jim and I looking back feel terrible about it now but we were celebrating and we didn't even notice Alan Stubbs and John Doolan were waiting to shake our hands. We did feel bad about that but emotions just took over."

McIntyre was equally as apologetic. He said: "I felt bad about Alan. He is a good big lad and we did our pro-licence together. He also sent me a text later on telling me to enjoy my night. That showed his class."

Jim McIntyre celebrated with his players and staff before he finally got round to the man who made it all happen.

McIntyre beamed: "It was a feeling of sheer relief. The chairman had given us so much backing since we had been at the club and how we had tried to upgrade the facilities to make the club better and to allow us to attract better players. He had been to Hampden before and although they hadn't won it that run had still been a fairy tale. So to get over the line this time and the first major trophy for Ross County was fantastic. He gave me a massive cuddle and in typical style he was more pleased for us as individuals than ourselves. It is typical of him. He is a ruthless businessman in his own right but he has helped create professional football at Ross County because he wanted to give boys in the Highlands the chance to fulfil their dreams."

That view was backed up by Billy Dodds.

"It was all for Roy," he claimed. "For the money he has put into the game and the club. He also backed us to get to that final. He deserves it. It was also a relief for him. He had put so much in but had got very little back for it. He is a supporter and every supporter wants success so to deliver the cup was great."

Dodds had seen and done everything in his own glittering playing career with Rangers, Scotland, Aberdeen, Dundee United, Partick Thistle, Chelsea and Dundee. That County win was as big as anything.

Dodds added: "Because of the size of Ross County this achievement is right up there for me. It was my first as a coach as well. Look at the scale of it. We are a small club and I hate saying that but we have top facilities now thanks to Roy's investment and now a top infrastructure is in place. It is still hard to achieve things with a small community-based club as Roy calls it. To go and win the League Cup was incredible. I have won every domestic honour but winning the League Cup was fairy tale stuff. You can't take that away from what that team achieved. Nobody expected that."

Jackson Irvine also got to pick up silverware of his own before he got his hands on his winner's medal.

A proud Irvine said: "That moment was unreal. It felt like it had never happened. It was ecstasy. You don't know what to do but it was incredible. It was one of the best days I had in my career. I was also lucky enough to win the man of the match award, across in front of my mum and dad which was good. We had a few minutes to let the madness in. Then you have the confetti and the flames and you just try to take it all in."

It was a moment for Ross County, Dingwall, the staff and players. It really was a family affair.

Paul Quinn admitted: "I found the energy to go and celebrate and then looking up to see my wife, Amy, mum, Linda, dad, Charles, my brother, Steven, and my sister, Jacqueline, that was something else. My mum and dad don't keep too well but I jumped the barrier after the game to find my mum. Just to show my appreciation. I knew she would be too sore to come down all the stairs. I gave her, my wife and my dad a cuddle. Those memories mean more to me than jumping about with the cup or with a medal."

Experienced midfielder Martin Woods got an unexpected smacker.

He revealed: "It was an unbelievable feeling. I saw a couple of my mates at the front of the stand. One of them jumped about five rows to give me a big kiss – which I was quick to wipe off. It was a great feeling to see that game out. When that whistle went it was one of the best feelings I have had in my career. I was just so sapped I hit the deck and burst into tears. We knew we had done something special and given our all to win the cup."

Liam Boyce knew the fans played their part.

"It was unreal how many fans were there," he acknowledged. "It was great to get the trophy and to come over to them to see your family, friends and supporters all so happy. It was a day we will all never forget, especially as it was the first major cup final Ross County had won. The team will go down in history and I know I am lucky to be involved. I won medals with Ireland but to come to Scotland and turn full-time professional and win a trophy so early on was massive."

Gary Woods had to wait that wee bit longer to see his nearest and dearest.

He said: "It has been a great week with the birth of my daughter and winning the cup. It had been a busy time. My partner and kids couldn't be there. I had family up and it was good to see them there supporting me but it will be good to get back and see them all. It is a special day and these are the kind you want to share with your families."

Jim McIntyre admitted there have been a lot of personal sacrifices to make Ross County the roaring success the club has now become.

"It was a reward for all the staff and all our families," McIntyre insisted. "A lot of the boys have their families in the central belt so there is also a lot of sacrifice there to try and bring success to the group. To get that win and to go on and seal sixth place was great."

Michael Gardyne was just relieved to be walking out of Hampden as a cup winner with Ross County.

He said: "I had been a loser in the Scottish Cup Final. I had been gutted and that win exorcised the ghost. We never turned up for that final against Dundee United but against Hibs we were brilliant. To win it in the last minute meant I was a winner with Ross County and I didn't have to think about that Scottish Cup Final again."

All the County players had experienced different things in their careers but it is clear that day at Hampden will never be forgotten.

Gary Woods said: "I won the league with Doncaster (England's League One in 2012/13) but that was different. That was over the course of a season but this was a cup competition with a one-off final which is amazing. It was great to go out and win the cup in front of all our fans. It is an amazing feeling, probably as good as I have felt in football. Just to go out on a day like that and to end up walking away with the cup just capped it all off."

It was left to captain Andrew Davies to lead his heroes up the steps for the greatest moment in Ross County's history. He had seen and done it all playing for Middlesbrough in the English Premier League, playing in European football and helping Bradford City to Wembley, by knocking out Chelsea, but he knew that moment was right up there.

Davies jubilantly held the trophy aloft. "I am captain and I am proud to have helped push the club forward," he claimed. "I have had some proud moments in my career. I've been at English Premier League and Championship clubs but that cup win was right up there. To be a part of that success was special."

The eyes of the nation were on the Staggies while goal hero Gardyne also decided to have a production of his own.

He said: "When we went and got the cup I took my phone. I have some great videos and pictures of the boys lifting the cup. Scott Boyd also brought my daughter, Harlow, on to the pitch and I got some pictures and photos with her. It was also her second birthday so that is a day she can always remember."

Jim McIntyre was left to take the cup down the stairs for its well-deserved lap of honour.

Heartbroken Alan Stubbs showed his class to go and congratulate his former team-mate.

"He wished me all the best for the rest of the season," Martin Woods revealed. "He was great at Sunderland. I was a Celtic fan and I used to go and watch him. I held him in high regard and the first thing he did was take us all out for dinner. He couldn't have been more helpful to the younger boys. He has always been a gentleman."

It was a team affair and everybody was involved before they returned to the unity of the County dressing room.

Schalk, who even made headlines back in Holland, said: "Champagne and beers were flying about in the dressing room. You have to do that when you win a cup. Those memories with those boys will live with me forever. The fans also still talk about my goal and that day. Who can blame, them it was a major win. It doesn't happen often and when they do they are special and magical. I feel lucky I was part of it. Ross County winning the League Cup was like Leicester City winning the English Premier League. It is something that will never be forgotten."

Martin Woods added: "I felt sorry for a couple of my mates who didn't play in the final. Craig Curran had a concussion and struggled to make it and Scott Fox missed out through injury. I tried to get them involved because they deserved to be part of it. I felt sorry for them but we got them going."

The likes of Fox and Craig Curran weren't about to be forgotten and the part they played in getting County to the final.

"The club ordered more medals for all the boys who played in games," Fox said. "That was nice because they didn't have to do it."

Jim McIntyre had told his players beforehand there would be no celebrations because of their midweek league clash with St Johnstone. The club had also planned a celebration the week later in Dingwall after the Highland derby league clash with Inverness.

Jackson Irvine reckons it was wrong to schedule games and to curtail the greatest moment of many of their careers.

The Socceroo stated: "It was strange because we had a game on the Wednesday and then the following Saturday. I think it was embarrassing that they scheduled fixtures after a cup final. The manager made sure we were professional and we were to an extent but you can't let a moment like that pass you by."

Birthday boy Martin Woods was relieved and delighted he was able to persuade McIntyre to change his mind.

Woods said: "We had a game against St Johnstone that midweek and the gaffer had told us we weren't getting out. I managed to persuade him and the boys got out on the town for a beer. I think we deserved it and the fact it was also my 30th birthday."

Some celebrations were a bigger affair than others.

An emotionally-drained Paul Quinn confessed: "My celebrations were limited because I was so flat. I have since made up for it. The plan was to go out with the boys but I ended up going back to my local with my family. I have to thank Liam Boyce for driving me all the way to Wishaw.

I had a quiet pint or two and it was probably the quietest celebration but I was delighted to have so many people close to me and around me."

When the team eventually made it bleary-eyed and on something of a high back up the A9 it was back to reality with a 1-1 draw with St Johnstone and then their big day of celebration was wrecked by a 3-0 defeat by Inverness.

Jackson Irvine admitted: "We missed two chances. I had missed one and it ended up as one of those days. Iain Vigurs absolutely clattered me and I was out for a month. I was on the bus tour and at the club party on crutches and wearing a moon boot. That night was more about the entire club and not just the players. It was great for everyone at the club."

The County players still took a well-deserved bow on their open-top bus parade and manager Jim McIntyre was determined that day's defeat wasn't going to spoil their achievements.

He said: "That was a real sore one for us that day because we got our pocket picked by Inverness on the counter-attack. It put a real dampener on us after the game and an hour later we had to board an open-top bus. We went out and celebrated with the fans and that was fantastic. I had done it with 45,000 at Kilmarnock and it was unbelievable but it was just as good a feeling with 10,000 in Dingwall. I pulled all the boys into my office as soon as we had got back because the club had gone to a lot of effort to organise a fantastic night. I told them all to forget about Inverness because what we had achieved was something special and I wanted them all to celebrate it. I didn't want any sad faces and I wanted us to go and enjoy it with our families, team-mates and people at the club."

Michael Gardyne had seen it all in his various spells in Dingwall. He knows more than anyone how far the club had come.

"We were in the Second Division when I went to County," he recalled. "We got relegated on the last game of the season. It is mental what was achieved in my four spells at Ross County, if you include my loan back from Dundee United. I am now nine years and counting at the club. To be top scorer and record appearance holder – I would never had thought that happened when I first went up there. Those are things I will also cherish."

Jackson Irvine was also quick to praise chairman and major backer Roy MacGregor for his part in the rise of this former Highland League outpost.

Irvine said: "It has been like a child to him. He has raised them from nothing and it wouldn't be anything near what it is now if it hadn't been for Roy MacGregor."

The achievements of that Ross County team will now go down in Scottish football folklore.

"I don't think anyone from the Highlands should forget what this team did and how we got our first trophy to the club," Martin Woods insisted. "I don't think Ross County got enough credit for that win and just how far the club has come since they came into the league."

Manager Jim McIntyre was pleased to go on and cap off their dream season by cementing their place in the top six – just.

"It was a fantastic period for us," he beamed. "We also made the top six. We had been in the top six from the second game of the season to the second last and then we fell out. To miss out on the top six would have put a real dampener on our season and the cup win. But your season's work is in the league and that was our bread and butter. To achieve both and get the accolade of the football writers was a fantastic personal award but it was for everyone at the club, not just me."

The team all have their medals and their memories.

Jim McIntyre said: "It is still in my drawer and I haven't looked at it since. That is maybe because I spend most of my time in Inverness and my mdeal is in my house in Dunblane. I am going to get that medal and some other league and cup winner's medals in together with a montage of photographs."

Some other medals have been more publicly paraded.

"My medal is at my mum and dad's," Quinn revealed. "A lot of people in the local area and my dad's friends wanted to see it. I will get it back and eventually put it in a safe so I know where it is."

Michael Gardyne's medal collection was given to his granddad for safekeeping.

He confirmed: "The replica medal I have framed with my shirt. The real medal my granddad has got. He has got them all since I was 18. I am hoping he will give me them all back when I finish playing."

Gardyne has also left some of his Dingwall housemates, Martin Woods and Ian McShane, waiting for their medals to be framed.

Woods joked: "I gave my medal, shirt and photographs to Michael Gardyne to get framed. I think they spent six months in the back of his car. He has told me it is now in for framing but we will see."

Jackson Irvine's has been taken out of the country for safe keeping.

"Mine is back in Australia," he claimed. "My mum and dad have a lot of my stuff but I think my granddad has my medal. It is good to give people something back because if I had it would just be in my house somewhere."

Alex Schalk, not surprisingly, was convinced to sign a new deal and to continue his Ross County love affair.

"I ended up with silverware and the winning goal in the cup final," he said unbelieving. "I remember going mental when I scored and I didn't know at that time what that goal meant. I was delighted for everyone connected with Ross County. I had taken a chance by walking out on a contract in Holland and Ross County had taken a chance on me so I felt it was the perfect way for me to repay their faith in them. Jim McIntyre and the team gave me my chance."

Jim McIntyre's dream season signed off with him being named the Scottish Football Writers' manager of the year.

We will let him have the last word from a dream season – even though it wasn't his best at Ross County.

McIntyre explained: "It is one of my biggest managerial achievements to date but I wouldn't say it was my biggest achievement at Ross County. I think keeping the team up the season before was bigger, without a shadow of a doubt. From where we were to what we did. We won ten out of 12 and those statistics were incredible and I don't think anyone will do that again. That gave us the momentum to go into that season where we went on to lift the cup."

ROSS COUNTY'S LEAGUE CUP-WINNING TEAM 2014/15

Second round (25 August 2015 at Victoria Park)
Ross County 2 (Boyce, Gardyne) Ayr United 0

Third round (22 September 2015 at Victoria Park)
Ross County 7 (Boyce 3, De Vita, Franks, Graham, Holden) Falkirk 0

Quarter-final (27 October at the Caledonian Stadium)
Inverness 1 (Tansey) Ross County 2 (Irvine, Gardyne)

Semi-final (31 January 2016 at Hampden)
Ross County 3 (Woods PEN, Quinn, Schalk) Celtic 1
(Mackay-Steven)
Final (13 March 2016 at Hampden)
Ross County 2 (Gardyne, Schalk) Hibernian 1 (Fontaine)

ROSS COUNTY'S LEAGUE CUP-WINNING TEAM

Gary Woods, Marcus Fraser, Paul Quinn, Andrew Davies,
Richard Foster (Jonathan Franks), Michael Gardyne, Jackson
Irvine, Martin Woods, Ian McShane (Stewart Murdoch), Liam
Boyce (Brian Graham), Alex Schalk.
Manager: Jim McIntyre.

29

• HIBS •
Perseverance to finally end 114 years of Scottish Cup heartbreak

THE Scottish Cup had looked to be a tournament that was going to give Hibernian Football Club a lot of joy, especially in their formative years. The Leith club lifted the famous old trophy just 12 years after their formation in 1875.

More than 15,000 fans flocked to the old Hampden to watch Hibs beat Dumbarton 2-1 in the 1886/87 season. They were back in the final nine years later, losing out to Hearts, but they didn't have to wait long to get their hands on the cup again. They did it in some style, seeing off Celtic on their own ground in the 1902 final. That, however, was to bring an abrupt end to the halcyon days and their glorious association with the Scottish Cup.

Instead of becoming a steady source of joy and celebration the cup became synonymous with more negative emotions like frustration, hurt and pain. It started as Hibs lost the 1913/14 and 1922/23 finals to Celtic. The next season saw them fall at the final hurdle again to Airdrie. It was a case of always the bridesmaid, as they were runners-up again in 1946/47 to Aberdeen, to Clyde in 1957/58 and were thumped by Celtic in the 1971/72 showcase. The curse of the competition continued to grip and was summed up in the 1978/79 season when they lost to Rangers after a second replay.

The Skol Cup was lifted in 1991 but the Scottish Cup remained a lot more elusive. So much so that every time the competition came around people continually spoke about the Hibs hoodoo, as many great Hibs teams and players had tried and failed to deliver.

The early 20th century didn't bring too much of a change of fortunes either. They were disposed of by Celtic in the 2001 final and then Irish manager Pat Fenlon suffered back-to-back final defeats. There was the crushing defeat to Hearts in the 2011/12 season and then Celtic made it a double whammy the following season.

Was the Scottish Cup every going to end up back in the trophy cabinet of Hibernian FC?

The 2015/16 season was Hibernian's second consecutive season in Scotland's second tier. The main goal, after missing out on promotion to Hearts, wasn't the Scottish Cup but trying to get back to the Premiership. Alan Stubbs, the former Celtic star and Everton youth coach, had built a young, exciting and attacking team, after he had picked up the pieces from Terry Butcher's indifferent stint at Easter Road.

Stubbs's prime objective was to get Hibs back into the top 12. That was also going to be a challenge with Rangers coming through the ranks and only one automatic promotion slot open with a second possible through the precarious play-offs.

Hibs opened the campaign brilliantly and after an early Challenge Cup exit, Stubbs got his team up and running. Their confidence was boosted by some big results in the League Cup. Lower league sides Montrose and Stranraer were disposed of before their first big challenge came from Aberdeen – who had stormed to the top of the Premiership with seven straight wins. Aberdeen were spectacularly floored 2-0 and then rivals Dundee United were also thumped 3-0 in Leith in the last eight.

That set up a semi-final with stuffy St Johnstone at Tynecastle but before that they were to kick off their Scottish Cup campaign away to fellow Championship side Raith Rovers in the fourth round.

Stubbs had made several signings in the January window including Norwegian international defender Niklas Gunnarsson, who came in on loan from Valerenga.

Gunnarsson made his first appearance on Saturday, 9 January at Starks Park, Kirkcaldy.

He recalled: "I remember it was a cold and windy day, a typical

Scottish day. It was a tough game but against a team we were expected to beat. In the cup anything can happen but we did our job well that day. That was my first game for Hibs in about nine weeks after the end of the Norwegian season. I was fit but I was short of match fitness and after about 50-odd minutes I was starting to tire and I had to tell the gaffer. I knew my race had been run in that game."

Hibs had won all three previous meetings so the odds were good for them going into this game.

Jason Cummings missed the game through illness and his striking slot went to new signing Chris Dagnall.

A save from Hibs keeper Mark Oxley denied Ross Callachan on the goal line while James Craigen lashed another shot well over as Rovers created the best first-half opportunities.

Paul Hanlon and James Keatings had efforts saved at the other end by Kevin Cuthbert.

Gunnarsson then made way for an inspired substitution for Hibs. Darren McGregor came on and managed to break the deadlock in the 61st minute when he took a pass from Lewis Stevenson and fired a low shot under Cuthbert.

Congolese striker Dominique Malonga then put the tie to bed with a glorious 25-yard effort three minutes later to put Hibs into the last 16.

Manager Alan Stubbs confirmed: "We knew we would be in for a difficult game. We had played each other that often both sides knew what each other were going to do. We controlled the match and went 1-0 up but it took a while until we got the second. After we got that it gave us a bit of breathing space. It was a tricky tie and I was just pleased we got through."

The signs that this could finally be Hibs' year were looking brighter – as the previous two Scottish Cup winners had disposed of Raith Rovers on their way to glory.

"I didn't know until a few weeks later that whoever had beaten Raith in previous seasons had gone on to lift the cup," Stubbs admitted. "We weren't aware of that fact until after we had knocked them out. Thankfully, it was a nice little omen that proved to be."

Momentum was there for Hibernian as they continued to push Rangers for the Championship title. They also booked their place in the League Cup Final by seeing off St Johnstone at Tynecastle. They were to face Ross County in the March final at Hampden.

Hibs were on track for a glory season and could have claimed a treble of their own.

Stubbs admitted: "I had said earlier in the season that we were the only team in Scotland going for a treble. People sniffed at my comments but it was a fact and if we had got a bit more luck then there was no reason why we couldn't have achieved all three. We were unlucky in the League Cup Final and we came so close in the play-offs."

Stubbs had also added some big-game experience to his squad and an Easter Road favourite into the bargain. The Hibs boss moved back into the transfer market again to hand Kevin Thomson his third stint at the club. He was a free agent after his deal at Dundee had been cancelled by mutual consent. Stubbs knew Thomson's time with Rangers and Middlesbrough could be vital to his young squad.

"It was ironic how I ended up at Hibs again," Thomson explained. "I had left Dundee and I thought I would be spending the rest of the season on the sofa, as I considered what I was going to be doing next. Alan Stubbs then gave me a call, asking me to come back to Hibs and it was a no-brainer. It is the club I support. I knew exactly what I was going into. I was told if I got into the team and did well I would stay there but I was more there for the boys and for passing on my experiences when the big games came around. I knew from the off where I stood under Alan. I was under no illusions."

The next part of the three-pronged attack brought even more anticipation when Hibs were paired with rivals Hearts in the Scottish Cup. The Jambos had pipped them to promotion the previous season and this was a chance for payback. Stubbs knew his squad was good enough but he had to reverse a trend that had seen the green and white side of the capital come off very much second-best.

Stubbs said: "My staff and I were aware that in previous seasons Hearts had a bit of the halo sign over Hibs. They always seemed to end up with the bragging rights from the derby. I think it was fair to say when the games came round it wasn't exactly one our boys really relished. Hearts players and fans were the opposite because they always felt they would win. They were also quick to mock the Hibs fans: 'Claiming they were going to beat the Hibs.' They had an air of confidence about them and I had to try and get my players to have the same belief. I sat our players down and told them that they were good enough to get a result and I tried to give them the confidence they needed. We knew as a staff they were good enough but we needed them to fully believe in themselves."

Hearts and their fans were keen to see their rivals put back in their place.

Sub Niklas Gunnarsson got it in the neck as he warmed up. He admitted: "Tynecastle is a traditional British stadium. It is really tight and compact with the stands on top of you. The Hearts fans were really up for it that day. It is fair they got right behind their team and gave us a lot of stick. I wasn't long in Scotland so thankfully I didn't understand too many of the accents at that time. It was maybe just as well because I knew what they were saying to me and the other Hibs players wasn't too complimentary."

John McGinn and Anthony Stokes had early chances before Alan Stubbs was forced to make a change.

Dylan McGeouch limped off after half an hour as Kevin Thomson came on for his third Hibs debut.

Any hope of the prodigal son returning for glory was quickly turned on its head by deadly Hearts. A long-range effort from Arnaud Djoum in the 32nd minute and another strike from Sam Nicholson a minute before half-time put the Jambos in total control.

Thomson said: "It was the second Hibs debut I had made against Hearts. In my second spell my first game was also against Hearts under Pat Fenlon. I thought we started that cup game really well at Tynecastle. We were on the front foot and we were really in the game and before we know it they had netted with a couple of great strikes and we went in at half-time 2-0 down. It was strange because if anything we had been the better team in that first half. I was hoping for my chance to show people I could still do it and show to some of the people why Hibs had taken me back. It wasn't exactly going to plan."

Manager Alan Stubbs wasn't overly concerned about the result because he knew it didn't reflect his team's performance.

Stubbs explained: "I emphasised to the players we were still very much in this game. They knew that as well because they had played well. That probably epitomised Hibs' previous performances against Hearts – played well but lost! We just told them how important the next goal was and we wanted them to be brave and to get on the ball."

Gunnarsson came on for David Gray in the 54th minute. He had a header saved by Neil Alexander before Anthony Stokes fired into the side netting.

Time was starting to tick against them but they got a goal back 12 minutes from time when Liam Henderson's dinked cross saw Jason Cummings score with a looping header.

Alexander then saved Darren McGregor's late header before Paul Hanlon followed up to scramble the ball into the net in stoppage time.

There was also still time for even more late drama, as Gunnarsson had to kick a Blazej Augustyn effort off the line at the death to ensure an Easter Road replay.

"The second half was one-way traffic," a delighted Stubbs claimed. "We were creating chances and we just needed one to drop and fortunately it did when Jason scored. I didn't actually realise how late on we got the first goal. We then got our equaliser and I know it was late on but if there had been another five or ten minutes I think we were the only team who looked like winning the game. We knew the home fans were on their team's back. They were very edgy because they knew we were on top and they didn't like it. I know we didn't win but I still think that result gave the players a massive confidence boost because I don't think they had battled back for a result like that, in those circumstances, at Tynecastle for a number of years."

Gunnarsson reckons cocky Hearts thought they had the game in the bag and switched off after half-time.

He admitted: "Hearts were the better team in the first half. They went 2-0 up and I don't know if they thought the game was won because they weren't the same team in the second period. It looked like they under-estimated us and thought they were through. We scored two goals and were the better team and that gave us great confidence going into the replay. I managed to clear one off the line in the final minutes but it was so easy to play in the game because Hearts just sat back and tried to defend. We had also beaten Aberdeen in the League Cup so we knew it would be no problem to beat Hearts."

Hearts remained bullish they would finish the job off but Stubbs could sense fear and knew they had their rivals where they wanted them.

"Going back to Easter Road we knew we had a real chance of progressing," Stubbs insisted. "I know Robbie Neilson said after the first game it wouldn't be a problem for his team to come to our place but I knew looking at him that he was very wary of it. He wasn't looking forward to the game because they had been outplayed at Tynecastle."

The replay was just nine days later on Tuesday, 16 February with Hibs now having home advantage and the majority of the 19,433 crowd. The numbers were boosted because of a television blackout due to the fact there were Champions League games on the same night.

Hibs were keen to make home advantage count and took just four minutes to take the lead. David Gray's cross was flicked high into the net by Jason Cummings on the half-volley.

Stubbs said: "We scored early which settled the nerves and then we had a few more chances, but didn't take them. I know it was 1-0 but we were still quite comfortable."

Hearts struggled with Hibs' slick attacking play and went for a more direct approach. Abiola Dauda and Juanma had the ball in the net for the visitors but both goals were chalked off.

Hearts' Blazej Augustyn was red carded after he picked up a second booking for hurling the ball away in frustration. Hero Cummings then turned to villain after he was also sent off after he got another booking for kicking the ball away.

His Hibs boss Stubbs insisted: "Jason was unlucky with his first booking and the second was for kicking the ball away when he had offered to go and get it."

Hibs were camped in at the end but were able to see it out.

"When things like that happen you have to respond and we did," Stubbs proudly added. It was one of those games where I knew the team would hold on. They were becoming more confident in themselves. They had big results from our League Cup run. We felt we had a Premiership team in the Championship and those early results proved we could go toe-to-toe."

The final whistle brought wild celebrations on and off the pitch.

Defender Darren McGregor said: "It was definitely No. 1 being a Hibs fan. To come away winning the derby and with 'Sunshine on Leith' playing at the end in a packed stadium was amazing. We rode our luck at times but we deserved our victory. It was a dream come true."

The club were keen to get their supporters back onside after the relegation and Stubbs believes that night helped lay the foundations.

Stubbs acknowledged: "We were trying to build bridges with everybody but more importantly between the players and the fans, especially after the club's relegation to the Championship. That connection seemed to have been lost. In our two years we tried to restore that connection between the team and the fans. The fans basically got their mojo back and started to back the progress we were making on and off the pitch. There was a feel-good factor and they could see the progress. The fans appreciated where they were but they could also see where we were going. Hibs have a history of teams playing football and we tried to do that on the pitch."

That put Hibs into the last eight and really fancying their chances after seeing off Scotland's third force.

The quarter-final made headlines for all the wrong reasons. Scottish Football Association president Alan McRae was forced to abandon the Hampden draw after one of the plastic capsules had separated and the name of Greenock Morton could be clearly seen inside the draw bowl. Hibs were still in the hat at that point after Dundee United had been paired with Celtic while the winners of the Dundee and Dumbarton replay were handed a home tie, but everything had to be scrapped and a re-draw was called in front of the live Sky Television cameras.

They red-faced officials did get it right at the second time of asking. Hibs were drawn at home to holders Inverness Caledonian Thistle, who were managed by former Hibs manager and player and fellow Leith native John Hughes. The fact that Hibs were at home was a major bonus.

Midfielder John McGinn confirmed: "We had not lost at Easter Road since I had been here and we had turned it into a bit of a fortress that season."

Hibs tried to use it to their advantage in that opening quarter-final tie with Caley Thistle.

Inverness's Welsh keeper Owain Fon Williams was the Highlanders' early hero as he denied Liam Fon-taine and James Keatings. He then tipped an Anthony Stokes effort on to the post before Keatings did score but was flagged for offside.

Luckless Dylan McGeouch limped off again to be replaced by Gunnarsson as Hibs switched to a 3-5-2 formation. It worked as a good move saw David Gray get wide to cross for Keatings to fire home in the 54th minute.

Gunnarsson had every confidence in his team. He explained: "Dylan picked up a groin injury and I came on early. We were the better team and Inverness only had one or two chances but managed to score. They were lucky to get a replay because we totally dominated in the second half."

The visitors sent on Andrea Mbuyi-Mutombo and Lewis Horner. The pair combined as Horner crossed to Jordan Roberts and he touched the ball on to Mbuyi-Mutombo to equalise 13 minutes from time. Hibs keeper Mark Oxley had to save late on to deny Danny Williams from stealing it for the visitors.

Stubbs claimed: "We took the lead in the game but we never looked comfortable at 1-0. Yogi made a couple of changes and they managed to get their equaliser late on."

It was a case of take-two on 16 March at the Caledonian Stadium.

Before then there was a small matter of a League Cup Final. It turned out to be a day to forget as they faced the heartbreak of a last-minute defeat to Ross County. There could well have been a hangover but Alan Stubbs knew the importance of bouncing back and trying to get back to Hampden. That was the only way they were going to exorcise that particular ghost. So they had to pick themselves up and get a reaction in the Highland capital.

The semi-final draw had also taken place for the Scottish Cup. Hibs and Inverness knew the winners of their rematch would take on Premiership strugglers Dundee United, as Celtic were paired with Rangers.

It was all to play for going into the replay and so it showed.

Carl Tremarco and Liam Hughes missed great early chances for Inverness. Anthony Stokes had gone seven games without a goal but ended that in the 36th minute when he fired home a low shot after the Inverness defence had failed to clear Lewis Stevenson's cross.

It took another five minutes before he netted his second. Liam Henderson set up Jason Cummings, who was denied before his strike partner slotted in the follow-up.

A proud Stubbs said: "People maybe thought our opportunity was lost not winning at home but we went to the Caledonian Stadium and we had a great start. We got ourselves two ahead thanks to a couple of goals from Anthony Stokes."

It was the perfect response from Stokes as critics had started to turn on him due to the fact he hadn't hit previous heights.

Stubbs admitted: "There was a bit of pressure building on Jason and Anthony. People were asking if they could play in a two or if they were two individual players. So it was good to see Anthony produce when it really mattered. It got a bit more apprehensive after Inverness scored but we had some unbelievable chances to win it. We had a few one-on-ones but never managed to score although we did see the win out."

There were to be a few headaches for Hibs as Inverness pulled a goal back through Iain Vigurs. The visitors were left holding on while keeper

Mark Oxley was booked in this match for time-wasting even though he was having problems with his contact lenses. That was to prove frustrating as it left him suspended for the semi-final. Oxley also took a head knock late on and had to be replaced by Finn Otso Virtanen two minutes from time for his debut.

A frustrated Stubbs stated: "I thought there was a bit of naivety from the officials because they didn't understand the situation with Mark's contact lenses. He had a problem and wasn't time-wasting and that booking meant he would miss the semi-finals."

Inverness's Josh Meekings missed a late chance to ensure Hibs went into the semi-final against United.

They were also planning for Hampden with a major headache. Oxley's suspension meant rooke Finn Otso Virtanen was their only fit, senior goalkeeper. Stubbs thought that was too much of a risk.

"I was speaking to George Craig (head of football operations) on the bus on the way home," he claimed. "I told him we needed a goalkeeper as soon as possible because we couldn't go into a semi-final with one goalkeeper, who was really inexperienced. Graeme Mathie (head of player identification and recruitment) was charged with seeing what was available and at that time of the year there weren't too many available."

The problem was that it was now mid-March and the transfer window had long since closed. They had to search for a free agent and that being the case they wouldn't have kicked a competitive ball for more than two months.

It was left to Mathie to come up with options and the most appealing was an Irishman named Conrad Logan. He had spent most of his career at Leicester City but most of that time had been out on loan. His CV could be described as journeyman-like at best. The keeper was a free agent but the reason for that was the fact he was just getting over long-term injury. He also wasn't exactly in prime condition or shape after playing for Rochdale a couple of years before.

Stubbs said: "Conrad had a difficult time with injury and was coming to the end of his rehab. He was out of condition but he still came in and his performances were very good. He is a really good communicator and I know being a former central defender how important it is to have a vocal goalkeeper behind you. We gave him a short-term contract until the end of the season and I didn't think it was a decision that was going to be as pivotal to our season."

Goalkeeping coach Alan Combe revealed how Logan worked hard to shed the pounds.

Combe admitted: "Conrad's experience shone through. He knew he had been out for so long with an Achilles injury. We managed his training and he worked hard himself. I think he lost nearly a stone in his time with us. It was an opportunity for him to go and shine and he did precisely that."

Logan's experience was a key factor in his capture and Stubbs knew it could be important. There was no bigger stage than their game with Hibs – the first of the weekend's Scottish Cup semi-finals at Hampden on 17 April 2016. It was back to an arena where the Easter Road side were looking for redemption in a bid to wipe out their League Cup heartache.

Stubbs insisted: "We were going back to Hampden and we wanted to put right what had happened last time we were there, when we lost to Ross County in the League Cup Final. Teams can freeze and not perform but I don't think that could be said on that day. I thought we played really well against Ross County but we made a couple of mistakes that really cost us. I told the players we would get back to Hampden that season and when we did we had to make sure we had learned from that experience."

The game brought Hibs together with another of their former managers Mixu Paatelainen. Dundee United might have been the top-flight outfit but the pressure was on them from all angles. They were stranded at the bottom of the Premiership and could hardly buy a win. That brought a new pressure for the men from Leith.

Stubbs said: "We played Dundee United and we went into the match as favourites this time. United were struggling for form in the Premiership. It wasn't a great game and we didn't hit the heights of previous rounds."

The game was far from a classic. Fraser Fyvie fired in the first shot with a long-range effort that dipped just over. United had the best chance of the first half. Billy Mckay pulled away from a defender with United's first chance but Logan came off his line to block with his left leg. Hibs went even closer. A combination of Darren McGregor and Fyvie robbed United's Mark Durnan. Fyvie then pushed on and crossed. The ball came off the body then hit Donaldson on the head and then came off his right arm. John Beaton wasted no time in pointing to the spot in the 29th minute. Top scorer Jason Cummings was charged with the job of adding to his impressive tally.

Cummings stepped up and confidently went for a Panenka-style penalty that went horribly wrong. He not only chipped Japanese keeper Eiji

Kawashima but also dinked his effort over the crossbar with his left foot. Kawashi was still in the middle of his goals and couldn't believe his luck as the ball sailed over his head. Cummings was just lucky manager Alan Stubbs missed his kick which turned out to be more tragic than magic.

Stubbs explained: "Jason got his penalty when the game was pretty even. He tried something, which Jason normally does and unfortunately got it horribly wrong. Believe it or not I didn't even see the penalty. I had been bursting for the toilet and so I had gone inside. As I came out I heard a roar and I ran out and Cummings had missed the penalty. One of the security guards told me we had won a penalty and by the time I had got back out Jason had missed it. I asked the bench and the basic theme of it was: 'You don't want to know but Jason has missed a penalty!' They didn't elaborate on it because the game was going on. Then somebody told me what had happened and I saw the penalty before I went in to speak to the players at half-time. I said to Jason: 'There is a time and a place for everything but that wasn't the time or the place to be trying something like that!' I was quite calm but inside I was thinking: 'What an earth were you thinking about, Jason?'"

There remained very little between the teams and it looked like Hibs' young gun had blown a major chance.

Strike partner Anthony Stokes fired a shot over but it was at the other end of the park a hero was emerging.

Conrad Logan confirmed that his nickname was 'the bear' and he started clawing things out. He justified Stubbs's decision in his first appearance since December 2014 when he was at Rochdale.

A long ball in behind Paul Hanlon let in Mckay again but Logan came off his line, spread himself and saved with his body.

Mckay put Anier through but his shot was too low and Logan got down to block again.

Even when United did find a way past him his defenders were there to bail him out, as Paul Hanlon showed when he headed Ryan Dow's effort off the line.

The teams couldn't be separated and they went at it for another 30 minutes.

He made further saves with the pick a low stop to keep out John Rankin's long-range shot that he got down to push away with his left hand and he had to make a handful of other stops. Jason Cummings had another shot saved before the game went into extra time.

A rather pensive Alan Stubbs admitted: "There wasn't a lot of action in the second period and it went into extra time and it was just a case of keeping the boys mentally strong. We wanted to get to the final and it was a case of them making sure we got there."

It went to the lottery of penalties. Hibs may have missed out in normal time but there was no shortage of takers when boss Stubbs went for his first five names. Right in the middle was sinner Jason Cummings who was looking for redemption.

Stubbs said: "Six or seven had their hands up looking to take penalties. Jason was one of them and I know he wouldn't say it, but he was nervous and I could see that."

It was just as important at the other end. Logan was given an insight into what the United penalty takers would do.

"We did our homework and Conrad and Alan Combe (goalkeeping coach) had all their previous penal-ties on the iPad," Stubbs added. "So he knew which side they were more likely to go for. Conrad had that information and it paid off."

United were up first. Blair Spittal went left of centre but Logan read it and pushed it away to give Hibs the advantage. John McGinn took full advantage as he put Hibs ahead by sticking it into the keeper's top right-hand corner.

United's Billy Mckay was next. He went to Logan's right but never put it in the corner and allowed the keeper to make the stop.

Long-serving Hibs defender Paul Hanlon took no prisoners with his effort. It was an old-fashioned run-up and he smashed it low into the keeper's bottom left-hand corner.

The Taysiders were sailing close to the wind but the trusty left foot of Paul Dixon sent Logan the wrong way, before Martin Boyle restored Hibs' advantage as he smashed it high into the roof of the net.

Ex-West Ham defender Guy Demel was next up and this was one penalty where Logan failed to listen to advice.

Alan Combe explained: "We had looked at their penalties. All the analysis was done but just before it Conrad told me he had a fantastic record with penalties. He was extremely confident. I did though tell him to stand up for the fourth penalty and he dived. I was a wee bit annoyed about that for their central defender (Demel) but he got away with it."

Jason Cummings was to take the fourth and the possible clincher. This time there was no fancy antics as he coolly placed the ball low into the right-hand corner of the net to ensure a Hampden return.

Cummings ran off to celebrate before he was joined by his team-mates who quickly went to flood Logan.

"He still showed great responsibility in volunteering to take the penalty," Stubbs insisted. "Believe it or not Jason was starting to grow up and it was a big moment for him to go on and score the winning penalty showed his character."

The headlines, however, were reserved for Conrad Logan – from nowhere to Hampden hero.

Logan admitted: "That was a pretty special day for me. To do it in a semi-final is fantastic.

'You hope to keep a clean sheet on your debut. That was pretty much perfect.

'But to do it in a cup game, and for it to end the way it did, it doesn't get much better than that.

'I only found out I was playing half an hour before the warm-up.

'But I was prepared for it. The other lads didn't know who was playing either – that's when the gaffer named the team. I was just delighted to get the nod as I've been out a long time.

'That was possibly the best day of my career apart from the final itself."

The dreams of finally ending the Scottish Cup hoodoo was given even greater hope when competition favourites, Celtic, were dumped out by Rangers on penalties the next day. It meant two Championship teams would go head-to-head with them both having a pretty even record over the course of the season.

The result was bittersweet for Anthony Stokes and Liam Henderson. Parent club Celtic may have lost the chance of a double but it also meant they could now play in the cup final. Hampden was a big thing but there was still plenty for Hibs to play for in the league. Cup final opponents Rangers had charged in front, under the stewardship of Mark Warburton, while Falkirk had also sneaked past on the blindside into second spot. Hibs followed up their cup final booking with a morale-boosting 3-2 home win over Rangers. That was backed up by a frustrating goalless draw at Morton while the regular season was capped off by home wins over Dumbarton and Queen of the South. Rangers walked away with the title and Hibs had to make do with the play-offs and had to go in at the first stage after they slipped behind Falkirk.

It meant Hibs faced a gruelling May where they would have to play six games if they wanted to lift the cup and return to the Premiership. Things didn't look too clever when they opened up the play-offs with a 1-0 defeat away to Raith Rovers before goals from John McGinn and Darren McGregor saw the Fifers off at Easter Road.

Next up was Falkirk, who had the added advantage of an extra week's rest. They travelled to Leith and got a morale-boosting 2-2 draw after a late goal from Bob McHugh after Liam Henderson and Darren McGregor had put them ahead, cancelling out Lee Miller's opener. It was a sore one for the Hibees as they should have had a stonewall penalty at 2-1 but it wasn't given.

It was a winner-takes-all affair at the Falkirk Stadium three days later. Blair Alston put the home side into a 14th-minute lead before a double from James Keatings put Hibs in the driving seat. Luke Leahy levelled nine minutes from time and then Hibs were left down and out after Bob McHugh's killer injury-time winner.

It was a cruel way for the team to have their main goal of the season snatched away from them.

A dejected Stubbs said: "When we went into the play-offs we were always confident we would get through. We were in good form. We were very good but we were on the end of a very poor refereeing decision at a vital time in the game. We were 2-1 up and Alan Muir, the referee, decided not to give a penalty for one of the most blatant handballs I have ever seen. We were playing well but we never got the decision and then lost a late goal. It was all to play for and they scored with the last kick of the game.

"It was cruel because that was our main aim and goal, to come up. When it didn't happen it was a real blow for everyone connected with the club. Everyone was devastated and we hadn't been able to achieve what we had set out to do."

It is fair to say Hibs had hit rock bottom.

Experienced Kevin Thomson said: "We saw the changing room and it was as low as a snake's belly and after that we had to go into a cup final week. I have been involved in quite a few cup final weeks and they are great. Everyone is on edge to try and see if they are in the team and normally it pushes the training up a couple of notches. I would say we went into that week and things were a bit flatter. It has also been a long, hard season but we had to get focused on the cup final. Nobody should need motivation for such games, especially one for the Hibees. We all knew how important it was to win the Scottish Cup for Hibs."

Hibs had missed out on promotion and lost the League Cup Final and now the doubters were questioning whether or not this team had the bottle. The new phrase 'Hibs-ed' it was also coined.

Stubbs said: "The team had been constantly questioned and there was this phrase going round, 'Hibsed it'. It basically made out as if we bottled it. I found it crazy, especially from people who didn't know the individuals in our group. How could they question somebody's character like that? I worked with them every day and knew them inside and out and the one thing that couldn't be questioned was their characters."

Stubbs had to earn his money to manage his men and to get them up for a massive cup final.

Stubbs admitted: "We gave the players a couple of days off to get over the disappointment. We came in and had a meeting. We spoke about the cup final and how we need to respond and bounce back. You have a lot of ups and downs as a footballer. It is a rollercoaster but we knew we had to go again for the Scottish Cup. I felt there was a real belief that we could win the game. Not just from the staff and me but the players as well. The more the week went on we could see they could get a result. We had also beaten Rangers 3-2 last time out in the league and so we knew we could beat them. The focus was all on how we were going to play and to exploit their weaknesses to our benefit, from set pieces to our shape and where we wanted to hurt them."

The boss then had to gauge his squad as to who was ready and up for the challenge of salvaging something from a season that had offered so much. Stubbs was left with some major selection headaches, starting between the sticks. Would it be Mark Oxley who had helped the team to the last four or the semi-final hero Conrad Logan who had blundered against Falkirk in the play-offs?

Goalkeeping coach Alan Combe confirmed: "Conrad made a mistake against Falkirk but he didn't let that affect him. We gauged it on the last week of training and how the two of them were looking. It was a hard one to take for Mark Oxley. He was a little bit down for a couple of days, as you would be, but to be fair he was massively professional."

There was also to be disappointment for Jason Keatings and Liam Henderson, who were left on the bench.

Alan Stubbs revealed: "It was a difficult one to leave Liam Henderson and Jason Keatings out. Keatings had been scoring goals and there were difficult decisions but we decided to go with Stokes and Cummings because of their previous results against Rangers."

Stokes in particular was keen to send out a message with manager Ronny Deila set to be leaving Celtic that summer, to be replaced by former Liverpool boss Brendan Rodgers.

Stubbs, speaking about the talented Irishman, said: "Stokes was a gamble when we brought him in but the thing that was never in doubt was his ability. He hadn't played a lot for Celtic and it would take him time to get up to speed but we felt because of his ability he could deal with it more in the Championship. I spoke to him a lot and he couldn't believe how hard it was in the Championship with teams looking to sit in."

Dylan McGeouch also didn't feel 100 per cent but was talked into playing by Kevin Thomson.

"Wee Dylan had come off in the Friday night game and he was struggling," the midfielder explained. "I told him he should play. I knew if he hadn't then Marvin Bartley would have started and I probably would have gone on to the bench. Dylan asked me if he should play on the day of the game and I told him the risk was well worth taking. He could have made the injury worse but I would have played with a broken leg for the Hibs in a cup final. I would only have given my shirt up if I wasn't able to walk!"

Others were disappointed not to start and had to make do with the bench.

Niklas Gunnarsson confirmed: "I was hoping to play. I felt I had done well and helped the team during the run. I had also scored the winner against Rangers in the league a few weeks before it. So I thought I had a chance of starting but the manager picked his team and I was on the bench. It was disappointing but you still have to be professional. I had to prepare to be ready if called upon and also more importantly to be a good team-mate in and around the squad."

Kevin Thomson wasn't even involved in the stripped squad but knew he would still have a part to play on such a big occasion.

Thomson said: "I would like to think I had an influence within the squad even when I wasn't playing. It never changed my mindset, I still wanted to play and felt I could have played, but I was always there for the boys. It would maybe have been a bit more difficult if it hadn't been a team I supported and everyone knows what Hibs means to me. Yes, players can get frustrated when they aren't playing but I think all my team-mates would back me up. I never changed from the guy who was playing to the guy who was on the bench or in the stands. I tried to be as a good a team-mate as I could and used my experience to pass on to the boys. If I gave one bit of advice and it helped then that was what it was all about."

Cup final fever was starting to kick in and erase some of the pending gloom. Stubbs was desperate to see his team come away as winners in front of his proud family.

Stubbs said: "My wife, Mandy, and family, Heather and Sam, were all there. When I was winning things as a player they were at a very young age. I left Bolton in 1996 and went to Celtic and Heather was only born then and Sam was born just two years later. I left Celtic in 2001 and the kids wouldn't have had any recollections of me with any trophies. They had come to watch me at Everton but that was more of a team trying to finish as high as we could and the best we achieved was Champions League qualification."

Hibs had also lost the 2012 and 2013 finals under Pat Fenlon and the Hibs fans were hoping this would finally be their time.

Niklas Gunnarsson explained: "Every time I went for a coffee or to a restaurant or even to a supermarket the fans would come up to me and tell me we needed to win the cup. It had been 114 years and they kept saying the same thing: 'We really need to win this game and if you do you will be a legend.' So every one of the players knew what was at stake."

Fans and families travelled far and wide to see the Hibs.

"I had my father and a couple of my friends Kristoffer Karlsen and Teddy Moen across from Norway," Gunnarsson revealed. "We were disappointed because we lost in the play-off to Falkirk but we had a meeting after that game and the manager told us we had to put that behind us and concentrate on the cup final. After that we had a good week training and we all went to Hampden extremely confident."

The build-up went to plan and Alan Stubbs produced a motivational masterclass by putting on a short video of the cup run to get his boys going.

Gunnarsson explained: "About three hours before the game Calvin Charlton, an analysist at Hibs, put together a video of our Scottish Cup run. It included all our goals and good play. I can't remember what the music to the video was but watching it all together was really motivating.

It gave us all a boost and got us going ahead of the cup final. We knew we had a big support coming and we had to produce for them after the disappointment of the League Cup Final and the play-offs."

All that was left was for Stubbs and his squad to deliver. It didn't take them long. Three minutes to be precise. John McGinn burst into the midfield and looked to have over-run things but showed good muscle and determination to turn away from James Tavernier and Andy Halliday. He played it out to Jason Cummings. He played it up the left to Anthony Stokes and he made full use of the space where Tavernier should have been and he cut in and curled a right-foot shot round Wes Foderingham which nestled into the bottom left-hand corner of his net. The irony was that Stokes did the business in front of the Rangers fans.

"Stokes started brilliantly," Hibs boss Stubbs claimed. "He attacked James Tavernier down his side and curls the ball in from a tight angle. If anything he catches the keeper by surprise by the fact he had hit the ball so early. Stokes hurt Rangers in an area where we wanted to attack from. We knew we could get joy down their right-hand side and their full-backs wanted to push on and we looked to pin them right back."

Both sides had attempts from distance until Rangers found a leveller in the 27th minute. Tavernier curled in a cross from the left and ex-Hibs star Kenny Miller rose highest to head in. It left Alan Stubbs frustrated.

He said: "It was a goal we could have prevented by stopping the cross and after that it was Kenny being Kenny and finding space for a really good header. The players responded again and we created a lot of chances up to half-time. I told them, in my view, we were the better team and we had to keep taking the game to them. We couldn't give them time on the ball and had to keep the pressure on them."

Stokes almost produced the perfect response with a right-foot shot from more than 20 yards out that beat Foderingham but came back off his right-hand post. Rangers then suffered a similar fate when Miller smashed a header off the Hibs bar.

Jason Cummings and Stokes had chances saved to ensure the sides went in level at the break. There continued to be nothing between the teams until Andy Halliday smashed a 20-yard shot into the top corner of Conrad Logan's net in the 65th minute.

Was the season really going to end in such heartbreak?

"We are a young but extremely talented side," Liam Henderson claimed. "I was thinking to myself on the bench, 'We can't have that much bad luck in one season.'"

Stubbs immediately sent on James Keatings for Cummings and with 29 minutes remaining Liam Henderson replaced defender Liam Fontaine.

"Halliday hit a strike to make it 2-1," Stubbs recalled. "I felt we were the team on top but that is what happens when you play teams of quality. We took Liam Fontaine off and went to a flat back four and pushed Liam Henderson on. He gave us more quality on the ball and I felt we were getting stronger."

Anthony Stokes was always confident Hibs would get back into it.

The Irishman said: "It is easy to say now that the two earlier setbacks were all building towards this.

"It didn't feel like that when we were 2-1 down with 15 minutes left. Even then I was thinking we would still get a chance. I have put one over the bar when I caught it too well.

"I just kept thinking we would get another chance and luckily it came."

That faith wasn't to be misguided, as Hibs levelled with ten minutes left. Henderson's corner was met at the front post by Stokes, who had got away from Tavernier, to head in.

"Henderson took the corner and Stokes was at the front post," Stubbs admitted. "It was something we had worked on all week. We knew Rangers were vulnerable there and it was a case of producing that bit of quality. Liam put in a great cross and all Stokes had to do was glance the ball into the net. You could see the confusion in the Rangers defence because everybody was looking at each other. They had played a zonal system and somebody hadn't picked up. We felt we at least deserved to be level. The equaliser gave us a real lift and the Rangers players looked like they were starting to flag."

Niklas Gunnarsson then got his chance as he replaced Paul Hanlon.

Gunnarsson said: "It was fantastic to come on and play on such a great stage with so many people watching. It was 2-2 and the game was in the balance and you could sense both sets of fans were nervous. I felt I managed to acquit myself well and we managed to win it at the death."

There wasn't another chance created until the fourth official put up the board to indicate four additional minutes. Anthony Stokes cut in from the left and fired in a shot that Wes Foderingham pushed behind in the 92nd minute.

Henderson took the corner from the left again. This time the delivery was deeper and was met by the head of captain David Gray, who powered his header into the net. He knew what it meant as he raced into the corner to celebrate.

Gray proudly beamed: "It's credit to everyone involved at the club that we stuck together and believed we could do it.

"We said all season that promotion was our aim and we failed to do that, so to manage to top the season off with the Scottish Cup was a real dream come true."

Alan Stubbs celebrated with the rest of the Hibs legions. He said: "The winning goal epitomises the team. David Gray won a tackle, even though he was shattered, that led to us getting the corner. Stokes forces the save that was going wide but the keeper had to save for the corner. What happens is what people, especially Hibs fans, will remember for a very long time. Liam puts the ball on the money again and David Gray loses his man and guides the ball towards goal. The rest, as they say, is history."

Henderson's set piece delivery was central to the win and he was just glad practice paid off.

"I practise corners and free kicks," the on-loan Celtic midfielder claimed. "At the end of the day the ball is only as good as the boy attacking it and all credit goes to Dave and Anthony for going in where it hurts."

Hibs still had a couple of fraught minutes to see out before referee Steven McLean sparked massive and wild celebrations from Hibs fans all over the world. Alan Stubbs embraced his assistant John Doolan.

"My feeling wasn't of relief but of profound pride at what the players had just produced," Stubbs joyfully said. "If one group of players deserved a change of luck in what they were doing then it was that group."

The joy of every Hibee was summed up by midfielder Kevin Thomson, who like them had watched from the Hampden stands.

He said: "It was hard to explain. It was a wee bit surreal. It felt unique and the whole aftermath was surreal. I had been a Hibs fan since I was a wee boy. My dad took me to the Skol Cup in 1992 and 24 years on I was part of the Hibs squad that had lifted the Scottish Cup. My boys were also at the game and I just wanted to see them when the whistle went. I knew how big it was. It was massive for me and it was every Hibs fans' dream to see the team lift the Scottish Cup."

Double goal hero Anthony Stokes was delighted to play his part in such a historic afternoon even though he was rather harsh on himself for not getting his hat-trick.

Stokes joked: "A hat-trick was probably a dream but I wasn't far off.

"It was a special day and I thought it was an entertaining game.

"We got a deserved win as overall we edged it on chances.

"People questioned the Hibs team about whether we had the mentality. I think we showed today that we do.

"I said when I joined that I came to win something.

"We were unlucky with the promotion and in the League Cup Final, but the Scottish Cup capped off the season."

Stokes was delighted to silence the critics – his own and those of Hibs! He defiantly claimed: "I take stick every year. Every week. Was it sweet for me? Of course, but I've always said that I never doubted my own ability.

"It's the old saying about form being temporary.

"It all worked out and you couldn't write the script for what happened."

Stokes also unselfishly laid all the credit at captain David Gray's door after his wonder winner.

"Dave popped up with the winner and it was fitting it was the captain," the frontman claimed.

"He has led by example even when it has been difficult for us all at times. I said coming into this game it would take a lot of the hurt away and it has.

"I keep saying that, even in the last spell I had at the club, it was: Will we do it this year? Will we do it this year?

"I'm just very thankful to be part of the squad which has managed to do it because it is almost history-making."

Midfielder John McGinn knows he and his team-mates, especially David Gray, will never be forgotten.

He said: "It's crazy to think that we'll be Hibs legends now. I've been told I'll never buy a drink in Edinburgh again – so I'll be going out every week!

"I'm just jealous that I'm not David Gray.

"At 2-1 down, I still believed we could win it. Ever since the Hearts game at Tynecastle earlier in the competition, we've known we could come back."

Lewis Stevenson came through the ranks at Hibs and was delighted to add the Scottish Cup to the League Cup he had already won as a Hibs player.

The full-back modestly said: "I'm not daft, there's been loads of players who are miles better than me who have been at Hibs.

"They've tried to get the Scottish Cup but haven't quite managed to do it.

"It was impossible to describe this feeling.

"Feelings like that don't come around very often."

Stevenson had lifted the League Cup with a thumping 5-1 over Kilmarnock in 2007. Alan Combe had been between the sticks for Killie but as a lifelong Hibee was delighted to have finally helped the club lift the Scottish Cup again.

Combe claimed: "It was a bit surreal to be honest. I will never forget standing on the podium because we weren't able to do that lap of honour. I had seen it before when Hibs beat my Killie team (in the League Cup Final). I didn't stand about for too long. I said congratulations to their players, waited for them to lift the cup and then I was back in the dressing room. It was nice to be part of a winning team and to hear the supporters sing 'Sunshine on Leith' was special. Just to be part of it was amazing."

It was a huge weight off the shoulders of the club. Chief executive Leeann Dempster acknowledged: "As soon as the Scottish Cup starts that is when the pressure was on. It was there for everyone and we could really feel it. The pressure was tangible. There was a nervous anticipation of the previous 114 years. It was a feeling of utter joy and relief after the (play-off) game at the Falkirk Stadium. There was also a sense of achievement with the club that others, for various reasons, hadn't been able to do. It then became a privilege to share the day with our supporters. There wasn't a day in my life that has been as good as that. It was unbelievable."

The on-pitch celebrations soon had to be curtailed as Hibs fans spilled on to the pitch to celebrate with their heroes. Things quickly turned ugly as Rangers supporters also came on to the pitch and trouble kicked off – with both sets of players having to be escorted off.

Niklas Gunnarsson recalled: "The feeling was great and then we thought Hibs fans had come on to the pitch. At that stage we were just trying to get back to the dressing room fully clothed because our supporters were trying to take our strips and boots off, anything they could get their hands on. Then we saw the Rangers fans come on and we knew then something could happen and the stewards started to escort us off the pitch. I have never seen or witnessed anything like it before in my life."

Liam Henderson also gave one of the pitch invaders a clip round the ear – but he got away with it because it was his little brother.

"I genuinely didn't know what had happened," Henderson said. "I went to my mum and dad and the rest was a blur. I managed to see my wee brother in the corner and I got a hug off him then I went to see my parents who have been a big part of my life. It was quite emotional."

Alan Stubbs was then taken away from his team and their celebrations as the police looked at a way of trying to restore calm. Unfortunately, that meant Hibs had to forgo the traditional Hampden lap of honour.

Stubbs admitted: "We were aware of it but the initial feeling was we, as a team, had achieved something monumental. The main thought when we got all the players off was the safety of all the fans because we knew something was going on, but we didn't know what. We knew fans had come on to the pitch and the players were ushered off the pitch. I was more or less taken away then with Leeann, the chairman and our head of security, Robbie McGregor. We met with the police and Scottish Football Association officials to decide what was going to happen in the aftermath. We found out the police had said no to a lap of honour, which was disappointing, but I can also understand it from their point of view. The thing for us was everything was back under control and the fans were back in the stands."

Calm was eventually restored but the ramifications of the aftermath was to rumble on for months with the Scottish Football Association setting up an independent inquiry and Police Scotland going into overdrive to bring the main offenders to justice.

The events, however, weren't going to rob Hibs of their big moment. They went out and after 114 years they finally got their hands on the Scottish Cup again.

An emotional Alan Stubbs said: "That was the first time my kids had seen me win anything. It brought a huge feeling of satisfaction but it was emotional as well. There were a few occasions, when the whistle went to a couple of hours after the game, where I had to compose myself and keep my emotions in check."

Niklas Gunnarsson may have been new to Scottish football but was still aware of what it meant to everyone at Hibernian Football Club.

Gunnarsson insisted: "It was good to get back out and to lift the cup was special. I have played for my country and had a good career but lifting that cup was probably right up there, especially knowing that Hibs had waited so long to win it again."

Kevin Thomson summed things up.

He said: "Winning that cup for Hibs has put those boys into stardom. They are going to be heroes for the rest of their lives. That is what comes of being successful at a club like the Hibees."

The party continued in the Hibs dressing room while Rangers failed to do any media commitments and quickly disappeared out of the national stadium. Kenny Miller, however, did find time to commend the Hibs players for the achievement.

Niklas Gunnarsson explained: "Kenny Miller came into our dressing room and congratulated us. That showed his class because he would have been hurting but he still found the time to tell us how well we had played. He didn't need to say anything and most other players in that position, after losing so late, would have wanted to just get out of the ground as quickly as possible."

Hibs then returned to Leith where the fans were waiting in their droves for a long overdue sight of the Scottish Cup and for the players, family and staff to have a celebratory meal.

"When we got back to the stadium the spirits were high with all the boys having been heavily involved in the celebrations on the bus," Stubbs admitted. "We were all looking forward to getting home to see our families and to enjoy our night. When we got back there was already a significant crowd outside the stadium. We had a night in the stadium before the boys ventured into town later in the night."

Nobody was going to deny the Hibs players their night of celebration although many were far worse for wear that following morning, ahead of the victory parade.

Stubbs said: "We had a sponsor's event before the bus tour and we had to meet at Easter Road at 11.30am. I am certain some of the boys had been out all night but to be fair to them they all turned up. Some were in very differing states. We then had the parade. We met the mayor, who did a speech and all the dignitaries were there. We then went back on the bus and I never envisaged what it was. The scenes, for me, were one of the proudest things I have probably witnessed in football. It was jaw-dropping and was crazy. It was mind-blowing. I have been involved in some fantastic things in football from celebrations and games but that blew me away."

It is claimed that there could have been more than 200,000 fans out to see the Scottish Cup homecoming.

Lee Dempster admitted: "The police estimated anything between 150,000 and 200,000 people easy. From the minute we left the City Chambers and up to the Playhouse I have never seen anything like it in my life. It will be a day we will all never forget."

Alan Stubbs had played in the English top flight, lifted cups on both sides of the border but reckons that day was his ultimate in football.

He beamed: "It was a day for all ages. You had the youngsters, teenagers, the middle-aged and then the elderly people there. A lot of those people had been waiting 60, 70 or 80 years to see us lift the cup. It was great to give people that. Words couldn't describe what we had done the day before and what it had done to people's lives. That is a monumental moment for something like that to happen. We potentially gave people one of the best days of their lives and that is a powerful thing. For me, it was right up there with everything I had done and achieved. Probably the best football moment for me. As a player, it is all individual goals but as a manager it is collective and what you have done as a team. This was a team achievement from the chairman to the fans – we gave them something we know they will never forget."

The green and white gathering was there for the new legends of Leith.

Kevin Thomson proudly said: "It was everything you would wish to be part of a top professional football club. We went from the City Chambers to Leith links and it is a journey I will never forget. It was just players and officials on the bus. The family were out on the streets but I never actually saw them and there were that many people on their phones I couldn't get through to them either. I got plenty of pictures from where they were and I must have passed them. It was a special day, me being a Hibs fan. I will be out on the streets to celebrate as a fan next time Hibs win a trophy. Hopefully, that will be sooner rather than later. So it was extra special."

Hibs knew they had achieved something special and were keen to make the most of it and they used it as a tool to get more people interested and involved in sport and football. It was rolled out under their 'Persevered Tour' and would see the Scottish Cup go on a tour of the local areas and communities.

Leeann Dempster said: "It came from Greg Mailer (head of marketing). He had worked at UEFA and they like to put their trophies on tour in the run-up to the finals. That was one of his roles at UEFA and so when we won it he had this idea to do it with the Scottish Cup. The energy surrounding the Scottish Cup win was really evident for the supporters. It was the biggest event we had had in a number of years and it just felt like the right thing was to take the cup out and let as many people get their hands on it, see it and get their photograph taken with it. It went from thinking let's put it around our supporters' clubs to thinking this could be a brilliant tool to try and reinvigorate the supporter base and also to try and get some new fans interested in football. It is Hibs-led but there is a whole raft of stuff that is to get people interested in our national sport again."

The motto was: "If at first you don't succeed then try again."

"We went round 114 primary schools," Leeann added. "That number is pretty relevant and important. We took players to the school visits and the kids would see the trophy at the assembly. We also had the narrative of perseverance and all about trying and never giving up. If you want to achieve keep trying to achieve your goal and we told them how we kept trying to win the Scottish Cup until eventually we did. We used Darren McGregor a lot because he was a local Leith boy and he knew a lot of the areas involved. We also took a photograph with all the kids and would then post it to the school. We are still in contact with the schools. After we got to 114 we went to just about 250 establishments in total and that doesn't include the personal visits, the more private visits to hospices, etc. We wanted people to get involved in community sport and football. It was available for people of all ages. We feel it has been really successful and on the tour alone we have seen 55,000 people."

Another Hibs player involved was fans' favourite John McGinn.

"I went to a couple of primary schools and it was nice," the midfielder claimed.

The kids just wanted me to dab in front of the cup and they were happy.

They were over the moon to have the cup at the school and it was brilliant to see their enthusiasm. Everyone who was involved in it put a lot of effort into it.

They covered a lot of miles and that's important, as important as what we do on the pitch. It's about getting people to come and watch the team, to win new supporters.

"It's really important the work people do off the pitch to help keep this club strong."

There is no doubt that those visits and brushes with the Scottish Cup will live with people forever.

Leeann Dempster said: "The thing that stands out for me was seeing all the children. Some of them were as young as four or five but to see them getting so excited seeing some of the Hibs players and hearing them sing some of the Hibs songs was amazing. It was a bit surreal."

The majority of players will have their medals and memories from that great day on 21 May 2016.

McGinn joked: "My medal is at my mum's – so I don't lose it."

Niklas Gunnarsson has it so he can take inspiration from it on a daily basis.

"I have the medal hanging up in my living room," he explained. "So I can see it every time I go into the room. I look at it and it brings back great memories. I will never forget."

As is so often the case with the Scottish Cup, there weren't enough medals to go round and there were squad members who were left empty-handed.

A disappointed Thomson confirmed: "No, I never got a medal. I did try and speak to the Scottish Football Association and Hibs to get more medals. There were some players who hardly kicked a ball who got medals and I never.

"It is a team game. I tried to get George Craig to try and he never got anywhere and I went to the SFA and I never got anywhere either – that was the disappointing thing. It would have been nice to have got a medal but astleast I still have all my memories of a day that will go down in Hibernian's Football Club history."

The last word goes to cup-winning boss Alan Stubbs. He looks back fondly on that season but reckons it is still tinged with regret.

Stubbs said: "If there had been a poll – Scottish Cup or Premiership football then I think it would have been very close. It might have been 60/40 one way or the other or even 50/50 but that shows how much it meant to the Hibs fans to see us winning the Scottish Cup. We set out with two goals and only achieved one and that was why it was disappointing because that group of players were worthy of achieving the two."

HIBERNIAN'S SCOTTISH CUP-WINNING TEAM 2015/16

Fourth round (9 January 2016 at Stark's Park)
Raith Rovers 0 Hibernian 2 (McGregor, Malonga)

Fifth round (7 February 2016 at Tynecastle)
Hearts 2 (Djoum, Nicholson) Hibs 2 (Cummings, Hanlon)

Fifth round replay (16 February 2016 at Easter Road)
Hibs 1 (Cummings) Hearts 0

Quarter-final (6 March 2016 at Easter Road)
Hibs 1 (Keatings) Inverness 1 (Mbuyi-Mutombo)

Quarter-final replay (16 March 2016 at Caledonian Stadium)
Inverness 1 (Vigurs) Hibs 2 (Stokes 2)

Semi-final (16 April 2016 at Hampden Park)
Hibs 0 Dundee United 0 (after extra time, Hibs win 4-2 on penalties)

Final (21 May 2016 at Hampden)
Rangers 2 (Miller, Halliday) Hibernian 3 (Stokes 2, Gray)

HIBERNIAN'S SCOTTISH CUP-WINNING TEAM
Conrad Logan, Darren McGregor, Paul Hanlon (Niklas Gunnarsson), Liam Fontaine (Liam Henderson), David Gray, Fraser Fyvie, Dylan McGeouch, John McGinn, Lewis Stevenson, Anthony Stokes, Jason Cummings (James Keatings).
Manager: Alan Stubbs.

• SCOTLAND'S TOP
FLIGHT LEAGUE CHAMPIONS •
(1890-2017)

* SCOTTISH LEAGUE WINNERS (1890-93)
1890-91 • Dumbarton and Rangers
1891-92 • Dumbarton
1892-93 • Celtic

* SCOTTISH LEAGUE FIRST DIVISION (1893-1975)
1893-94 • Celtic
1894-95 • Hearts
1895-96 • Celtic
1896-97 • Hearts
1897-98 • Celtic
1898-99 • Rangers
1899-1900 • Rangers
1900-01 • Rangers
1901-02 • Rangers
1902-03 • Hibernian
1903-04 • Third Lanark
1904-05 • Celtic
1905-06 • Celtic

1906-07 • Celtic
1907-08 • Celtic
1908-09 • Celtic
1909-10 • Celtic
1910-11 • Rangers
1911-12 • Rangers
1912-13 • Rangers
1913-14 • Celtic
1914-15 • Celtic
1915-16 • Celtic
1916-17 • Celtic
1917-18 • Rangers
1918-19 • Celtic
1919-20 • Rangers
1920-21 • Rangers
1921-22 • Celtic
1922-23 • Rangers
1923-24 • Rangers
1924-25 • Rangers
1925-26 • Celtic
1926-27 • Rangers
1927-28 • Rangers
1928-29 • Rangers
1929-30 • Rangers
1930-31 • Rangers
1931-32 • Motherwell
1932-33 • Rangers
1933-34 • Rangers
1934-35 • Rangers
1935-36 • Celtic
1936-37 • Rangers
1937-38 • Celtic
1938-39 • Rangers
1946-47 • Rangers
1947-48 • Hibs
1948-49 • Rangers
1949-50 • Rangers
1950-51 • Hibs

1951-52 • Hibs
1952-53 • Rangers
1953-54 • Celtic
1954-55 • Aberdeen
1955-56 • Rangers
1956-57 • Rangers
1957-58 • Hearts
1958-59 • Rangers
1959-60 • Hearts
1960-61 • Rangers
1961-62 • Dundee
1962-63 • Rangers
1963-64 • Rangers
1964-65 • Kilmarnock
1965-66 • Celtic
1966-67 • Celtic
1967-68 • Celtic
1968-69 • Celtic
1969-70 • Celtic
1970-71 • Celtic
1971-72 • Celtic
1972-73 • Celtic
1973-74 • Celtic
1974-75 • Rangers

* SCOTTISH PREMIER DIVISION (1976-1997)
1975-76 • Rangers
1976-77 • Celtic
1977-78 • Rangers
1978-79 • Celtic
1979-80 • Aberdeen
1980-81 • Celtic
1981-82 • Celtic
1982-83 • Dundee United
1983-84 • Aberdeen
1984-85 • Aberdeen
1985-86 • Celtic
1986-87 • Rangers

1987-88 • Celtic
1988-89 • Rangers
1989-90 • Rangers
1990-91 • Rangers
1991-92 • Rangers
1992-93 • Rangers
1993-94 • Rangers
1994-95 • Rangers
1995-96 • Rangers
1996-97 • Rangers

* SCOTTISH LEAGUE PREMIER LEAGUE (1998-PRESENT)
1997-98 • Celtic
1998-99 • Rangers
1999-2000 • Rangers
2000-01 • Celtic
2001-02 • Celtic
2002-03 • Rangers
2003-04 • Celtic
2004-05 • Rangers
2005-06 • Celtic
2006-07 • Celtic
2007-08 • Celtic
2008-09 • Rangers
2009-10 • Rangers
2010-11 • Rangers
2011-12 • Celtic
2012-13 • Celtic
2013-14 • Celtic
2014-15 • Celtic
2015-16 • Celtic
2016-17 • Celtic

• SCOTTISH CUP FINAL •
RESULTS AND WINNERS (1874-2017)

1873-74 • Queen's Park 2 Clydesdale 0

1874-75 • Queen's Park 3 Renton 0

1875-76 • Queen's Park 1 Third Lanark 1 (Queen's Park 2 Third Lanark 0 replay)

1876-77 • Vale of Leven 1 Rangers 1 (Vale of Leven 1 Rangers 1 first replay, Vale of Leven 3 Rangers 2 second replay)

1877-78 • Vale of Leven 1 Third Lanark 0

1878-79 • Vale of Leven 1 Rangers 1 (Vale of Leven won replay after walkover)

1879-80 • Queen's Park 3 Thornliebank 0

1880-81 • Queen's Park 2 Dumbarton 1 (Queen's Park 3 Dumbarton 1 replay after Dumbarton protested)

1881-82 • Queen's Park 2 Dumbarton 2 (Queen's Park 4 Dumbarton 1 replay)

1882-83 • Dumbarton 2 Vale of Leven 2 (Dumbarton 2 Vale of Leven 1 replay)

1883-84 • Queen's Park walkover Vale of Leven

1884-85 • Renton 0 Vale of Leven 0 (Renton 3 Vale of Leven 1 replay)

1885-86 • Queen's Park 3 Renton 1

1886-87 • Hibs 2 Dumbarton 1

1887-88 • Renton 6 Cambuslang 1

1888-89 • Third Lanark 3 Celtic 0 (Third Lanark 2 Celtic 1 replay)
1889-90 • Queen's Park 1 Vale of Leven 1 (Queen's Park 2 Vale of Leven
    1 replay)
1890-91 • Hearts 1 Dumbarton 0
1891-92 • Celtic 1 Queen's Park 0 (Celtic 5 Queen's Park 1 replay)
1892-93 • Queen's Park 0 Celtic 1 (Queen's Park 2 Celtic 1 replay)
1893-94 • Rangers 3 Celtic 1
1894-95 • St Bernard's 2 Renton 1
1895-96 • Hearts 3 Hibs 1
1896-97 • Rangers 5 Dumbarton 1
1897-98 • Rangers 2 Kilmarnock 0
1898-99 • Celtic 2 Rangers 0
1899-1900 • Celtic 4 Queen's Park 3
1900-01 • Hearts 4 Celtic 3
1901-02 • Hibs 1 Celtic 0
1902-03 • Rangers 1 Hearts 1 (Rangers 0 Hearts 0 replay, Rangers 2
    Hearts 0 second replay)
1903-04 • Celtic 3 Rangers 2
1904-05 • Third Lanark 0 Rangers 0 (Third Lanark 3 Rangers 1 replay)
1905-06 • Hearts 1 Third Lanark 0
1906-07 • Celtic 3 Hearts 0
1907-08 • Celtic 5 St Mirren 1
1909-10 • Dundee 2 Clyde 2 (Dundee 0 Clyde 0 replay, Dundee 2
    Clyde 1 second replay)
1910-11 • Celtic 0 Hamilton 0 (Celtic 2 Hamilton 0 replay)
1911-12 • Celtic 2 Clyde 0
1912-13 • Falkirk 2 Raith Rovers 0
1913-14 • Celtic 0 Hibs 0 (Celtic 4 Hibs 1 replay)
1919-20 • Kilmarnock 3 Albion Rovers 2
1920-21 • Partick Thistle 1 Rangers 0
1921-22 • Morton 1 Rangers 0
1922-23 • Celtic 1 Hibs 0
1923-24 • Airdrie 2 Hibs 0
1924-25 • Celtic 2 Dundee 1
1925-26 • St Mirren 2 Celtic 0
1926-27 • Celtic 3 East Fife 1
1927-28 • Rangers 4 Celtic 0
1928-29 • Kilmarnock 1 Rangers 0

1929-30 • Rangers 0 Partick Thistle 0 (Rangers 2 Partick Thistle 1 replay)
1930-31 • Celtic 2 Motherwell 2 (Celtic 4 Motherwell 2 replay)
1931-32 • Rangers 1 Kilmarnock 1 (Rangers 3 Kilmarnock 0 replay)
1932-33 • Celtic 1 Motherwell 0
1933-34 • Rangers 5 St Mirren 0
1934-35 • Rangers 2 Hamilton 1
1935-36 • Rangers 1 Third Lanark 0
1936-37 • Celtic 2 Aberdeen 1
1937-38 • East Fife 1 Kilmarnock 1 (East Fife 4 Kilmarnock 2 replay)
1938-39 • Clyde 4 Motherwell 0
1946-47 • Aberdeen 2 Hibs 1
1947-48 • Rangers 1 Morton 1 (Rangers 1 Morton 0 replay)
1948-49 • Rangers 4 Clyde 1
1949-50 • Rangers 3 East Fife 0
1950-51 • Celtic 1 Motherwell 0
1951-52 • Motherwell 4 Dundee 0
1952-53 • Rangers 1 Aberdeen 1 (Rangers 1 Aberdeen 0 replay)
1953-54 • Celtic 2 Aberdeen 1
1954-55 • Clyde 1 Celtic 1 (Clyde 1 Celtic 0 replay)
1955-56 • Hearts 3 Celtic 1
1956-57 • Falkirk 1 Kilmarnock 1 (Falkirk 2 Kilmarnock 1 replay)
1957-58 • Clyde 1 Hibs 0
1958-59 • St Mirren 3 Aberdeen 1
1959-60 • Rangers 2 Kilmarnock 0
1960-61 • Dunfermline 0 Celtic 0 (Dunfermline 2 Celtic 0 replay)
1961-62 • Rangers 2 St Mirren 0
1962-63 • Rangers 1 Celtic 1 (Rangers 3 Celtic 0 replay)
1963-64 • Rangers 3 Dundee 1
1964-65 • Celtic 3 Dunfermline 2
1965-66 • Rangers 0 Celtic 0 (Rangers 1 Celtic 0 replay)
1966-67 • Celtic 2 Aberdeen 0
1967-68 • Dunfermline 3 Hearts 1
1968-69 • Celtic 4 Rangers 0
1969-70 • Aberdeen 3 Celtic 1
1970-71 • Celtic 1 Rangers 1 (Celtic 2 Rangers 1 replay)
1971-72 • Celtic 6 Hibs 1
1972-73 • Rangers 3 Celtic 2
1973-74 • Celtic 3 Dundee United 0

1974-75 • Celtic 3 Airdrie 1
1975-76 • Rangers 3 Hearts 1
1976-77 • Celtic 1 Rangers 0
1977-78 • Rangers 2 Aberdeen 1
1978-79 • Rangers 0 Hibs 0 (Rangers 0 Hibs 0 replay, Rangers 3 Hibs 2
second replay)
1979-80 • Celtic 1 Rangers 0
1980-81 • Rangers 0 Dundee United 0 (Rangers 4 Dundee United 1
replay)
1981-82 • Aberdeen 4 Rangers 1
1982-83 • Aberdeen 1 Rangers 0
1983-84 • Aberdeen 2 Celtic 1
1984-85 • Celtic 2 Dundee United 1
1985-86 • Aberdeen 3 Hearts 0
1986-87 • St Mirren 1 Dundee United 0
1987-88 • Celtic 2 Dundee United 1
1988-89 • Celtic 1 Rangers 0
1989-90 • Aberdeen 0 Celtic 0 (Aberdeen won 9-8 on penalties)
1990-91 • Motherwell 4 Dundee United 3
1991-92 • Rangers 2 Airdrie 1
1992-93 • Rangers 2 Aberdeen 1
1993-94 • Dundee United 1 Rangers 0
1994-95 • Celtic 1 Airdrie 0
1995-96 • Rangers 5 Hearts 1
1996-97 • Kilmarnock 1 Falkirk 0
1997-98 • Hearts 2 Rangers 1
1998-99 • Rangers 1 Celtic 0
1999-2000 • Rangers 4 Aberdeen 0
2000-01 • Celtic 3 Hibs 0
2001-02 • Rangers 3 Celtic 2
2002-03 • Rangers 1 Dundee 0
2003-04 • Celtic 3 Dunfermline 1
2004-05 • Celtic 1 Dundee United 0
2005-06 • Hearts 1 Gretna 1 (Hearts won 4-2 on penalties)
2006-07 • Celtic 1 Dunfermline 0
2007-08 • Rangers 3 Queen of the South 2
2008-09 • Rangers 1 Falkirk 0
2009-10 • Dundee United 3 Ross County 0

2010-11 • Celtic 3 Motherwell 0
2011-12 • Hearts 5 Hibs 1
2012-13 • Celtic 3 Hibs 0
2013-14 • St Johnstone 2 Dundee 0
2014-15 • Inverness Caledonian Thistle 2 Falkirk 1
2015-16 • Hibs 3 Rangers 2
2016-17 • Celtic 2 Aberdeen 1

• SCOTTISH LEAGUE CUP FINAL •
RESULTS AND WINNERS (1947-2017)

1946-47 • Rangers 4 Aberdeen 0
1947-48 • East Fife 0 Falkirk 0 (East Fife 4 Falkirk 1 replay)
1948-49 • Rangers 2 Raith Rovers 0
1949-50 • East Fife 3 Dunfermline 0
1950-51 • Motherwell 3 Hibs 0
1951-52 • Dundee 3 Rangers 2
1952-53 • Dundee 2 Kilmarnock 0
1953-54 • East Fife 3 Partick Thistle 2
1954-55 • Hearts 4 Motherwell 2
1955-56 • Aberdeen 2 St Mirren 1
1956-57 • Celtic 0 Partick Thistle 0 (Celtic 3 Partick Thistle 0
              replay)
1957-58 • Celtic 7 Rangers 1
1958-59 • Hearts 5 Partick Thistle 1
1959-60 • Hearts 2 Third Lanark 1
1960-61 • Rangers 2 Kilmarnock 0
1961-62 • Rangers 1 Hearts 1 (Rangers 3 Hearts 1 replay)
1962-63 • Hearts 1 Kilmarnock 0
1963-64 • Rangers 5 Morton 0
1964-65 • Rangers 2 Celtic 1
1965-66 • Celtic 2 Rangers 1

1966-67 • Celtic 1 Rangers 0
1967-68 • Celtic 5 Dundee 3
1968-69 • Celtic 6 Hibs 2
1969-70 • Celtic 1 St Johnstone 0
1970-71 • Rangers 1 Celtic 0
1971-72 • Partick 4 Celtic 1
1972-73 • Hibs 2 Celtic 1
1973-74 • Dundee 1 Celtic 0
1974-75 • Celtic 6 Hibs 3
1975-76 • Rangers 1 Celtic 0
1976-77 • Aberdeen 2 Celtic 1
1977-78 • Rangers 2 Celtic 1
1978-79 • Rangers 2 Aberdeen 1
1979-80 • Dundee United 0 Aberdeen 0 (Dundee United 3
             Aberdeen 0 replay)
1980-81 • Dundee United 3 Dundee 0
1981-82 • Rangers 2 Dundee United 1
1982-83 • Celtic 2 Rangers 1
1983-84 • Rangers 3 Celtic 2
1984-85 • Rangers 1 Dundee United 0
1985-86 • Aberdeen 3 Hibs 0
1986-87 • Rangers 2 Celtic 1
1987-88 • Rangers 3 Aberdeen 3 (Rangers 3 Aberdeen 2 replay)
1988-89 • Rangers 3 Aberdeen 2
1989-90 • Aberdeen 2 Rangers 1
1990-91 • Rangers 2 Celtic 1
1991-92 • Hibs 2 Dunfermline 0
1992-93 • Rangers 2 Aberdeen 1
1993-94 • Rangers 2 Hibs 1
1994-95 • Raith Rovers 2 Celtic 2 (Raith won 6-5 on penalties)
1995-96 • Aberdeen 2 Dundee 0
1996-97 • Rangers 4 Hearts 3
1997-98 • Celtic 3 Dundee United 0
1998-99 • Rangers 2 St Johnstone 1
1999-2000 • Celtic 2 Aberdeen 0
2000-01 • Celtic 3 Kilmarnock 0
2001-02 • Rangers 4 Ayr United 0
2002-03 • Rangers 2 Celtic 1

2003-04 • Livingston 2 Hibs 0
2004-05 • Rangers 5 Motherwell 1
2005-06 • Celtic 3 Dunfermline 0
2006-07 • Hibs 5 Kilmarnock 1
2007-08 • Rangers 2 Dundee United 2 (Rangers won 3-2 on
      penalties)
2008-09 • Celtic 2 Rangers 0
2009-10 • Rangers 1 St Mirren 0
2010-11 • Rangers 2 Celtic 1
2011-12 • Celtic 0 Kilmarnock 1
2012-13 • St Mirren 3 Hearts 2
2013-14 • Aberdeen 0 Inverness Caledonian Thistle 0 (Aberdeen
      won 4-2 on penalties)
2014-15 • Celtic 2 Dundee United 0
2015-16 • Ross County 2 Hibs 1
2016-17 • Celtic 3 Aberdeen 0